W9-AXJ-038

Introduction
to Library Research
in Anthropology

Introduction
to Library Research
in Anthropology

SECOND EDITION

John M. Weeks

WestviewPress

A Division of HarperCollins*Publishers*

Westview Guides to Library Research

Copyright © 1998 by Westview Press, A Division of HarperCollins Publishers, Inc.

Published in 1998 in the United States of America by Westview Press, 5500 Central Avenue, Boulder, Colorado 80301-2877, and in the United Kingdom by Westview Press, 12 Hid's Copse Road, Cumnor Hill, Oxford OX2 9JJ

A CIP catalog record for this book is available from the Library of Congress.
ISBN 0-8133-9003-6

The paper used in this publication meets the requirements of the American National Standard for Permanence of Paper for Printed Library Materials Z39.48-1984.

10   9   8   7   6   5   4   3   2   1

Contents

Preface

This book is an introduction to library research in anthropology intended for the undergraduate student about to begin a research project. There has long been a need for a practical guide to library research in anthropology. This need has recently become more evident because of the strong pressures being exerted on the academic environment. The mass lecture section, with computerized instruction and examinations, has reduced contact and close interaction between student and teacher. There is also a growing realization that the complexity of anthropological problems increases the need for individual analysis and independent thought.

As the title indicates, this book is only a guide and is not intended to be a comprehensive treatise on library-based anthropological research techniques. It is simply an introduction to the mechanics and resources of library use in order to assist students in making efficient and thorough information searches. At the same time the student will acquire some grasp of the flavor and importance of research so that its depth and value are more fully appreciated.

Large and, to some extent, intermediate sized academic libraries with their millions of books and specialized services can be both confusing and intimidating. Learning to navigate in a library is a problem for most students either entering or returning to college, for the upper division student beginning to concentrate on a major field of study, as well as for the graduate student whose undergraduate library was smaller and less complex. It is hoped the information contained in the following chapters will make such navigation less difficult.

Much of the information presented in this book is applicable to other fields. The use of the library, the development of a research project, and the writing of the final paper are activities common to all social science disciplines. However, anthropological research is anthropological in character. Thus, the special properties of research in this field are given special attention.

Chapter 1 provides a summary statement about anthropology as an academic pursuit and identifies some of the research dimensions of the discipline. Chapter 2 identifies the basic services available for undergraduate students at most academic libraries. Chapter 3 expands upon the first chapter and discusses some of the characteristics of the information needs of anthropology and anthropologists. This chapter also describes the process of library-based anthropological research. The importance of topic selection and the process of research paper writing are also discussed. Chapter 4 describes the use of the local library catalog as an essential stage of library research. Chapters 5 through 22 identify a variety of other library resources and how they may be used during library-based anthropological research. The reader should be generally aware that a library may not have some of the resources identified, although most library reference works held at collegiate and university libraries should be included.

The resource chapters are arranged in a standardized format. Each chapter contains a summary description of the type of resource being considered and its potential use in a research project. This is followed by appropriate subject headings to locate additional resources. The largest part of any chapter is devoted to an annotated list of resources arranged by anthropological subdiscipline, region, and then region by subdiscipline. For example, in Chapter 11 general handbooks dealing with cultural/social anthropology (nos. 11.3-11.5) are presented before area handbooks about Africa (nos. 11.16-11.20). Handbooks about the anthropology of Africa (no. 11.21) are presented last.

The process of library research for student anthropologists need not be a complicated process. A wide variety of simple methods of library research can be used by students with limited time and purpose. The goal of the descriptive chapters is to lead the student researcher on an abbreviated tour of the basic kinds of library reference works and the range of materials available within these resource categories.

1

What Is Anthropology?

Nancy Johnson Black

When undergraduate students are asked what comes to mind when they think of anthropology, their responses usually range from 200,000 year old Neanderthals to exotic locations such as Papua New Guinea, and extend to Hollywood's swashbuckling version of the archaeologist, Indiana Jones. These aspects reflect some aspects of the discipline that have been popularized in recent years. While it is encouraging to see that the discipline conjures up some kind of mental image for undergraduates, it is somewhat disconcerting as an anthropologist to realize that students are often disappointed because I do not wear a pith helmet or sarong, and am not wrapped in a python.

The roots of anthropology go back as far as the Greeks in the fourth century B.C., although the discipline with its recognized body of knowledge, theory, and professionalism did not emerge as a distinct field until the late nineteenth century. Many scholars credit the Greek historian Herodotus (488-425 B.C.), who studied Egyptian and Persian civilizations, as the founder of anthropology. Indeed, the name of the discipline is derived from the Greek *anthropos*, human, and *logos*, account, conveying the efforts to describe and explain the regularities in human behavior.

According to the American Anthropological Association, the largest professional organization of anthropologists in the world, more than 300 colleges and universities in the United States alone offer an undergraduate major degree in anthropology and many more offer anthropology courses. In 1988, approximately 4,000 undergraduate students received degrees in anthropology, and some 375 doctoral degrees in anthropology were awarded.

There is general agreement among social scientists about the definition of anthropology. The discipline can be characterized as the study of human phenomena in its biological, social, and cultural aspects. As a social science, anthropology is concerned with the scientific study of the complexity of human life through time and space. Because of the diversity of humankind and the broad scope of its examination, anthropologists have had some difficulty reaching consensus about many aspects of their discipline, and the definition of culture is no exception. Most anthropologists would agree however with the early definition of culture advanced by the nineteenth century English scholar

Edward B. Tylor. Culture is viewed as a complex of commonly shared beliefs, values, customs, behavior, and artifacts, which are transmitted by humans over generations through learning. Culture may be thought of simply as information or ideas about how people behave or why people believe what they do and also helps to understand the dynamic and changing aspects of culture.

Traditional Subdisciplines of Anthropology

Since the beginning of twentieth, anthropology has developed into an increasingly complex and segmented academic discipline. There are four subdisciplines which constitute the major areas of concern and research among contemporary anthropologists:

Archaeology

Prehistoric archaeology is the systematic retrieval and interpretation of the physical remains left by human beings, including their cultural and skeletal remains. Archaeology is concerned with the history and behavior of prehuman and human populations through time and space based on material remains of past life and activities, such as fossil relics, artifacts, implements, inscriptions, interments, and so forth.

Cultural/Social Anthropology

Cultural/social anthropology is the dominant subfield, and is concerned with the description and analysis of contemporary societies and the underlying patterns of human behavior, past and present. Ethnography is the description of the sociocultural system of a single group. Ethnology is the comparative study of ethnographic descriptions for the purpose of generalizing about the nature of human groups.

Anthropological Linguistics

The two primary concerns of linguistic anthropology are to establish the evolutionary relationships between human language and systems of animal communication, and to understand the multiple social functions of human linguistic behavior. Both approaches yield valuable information about the ways in which people communicate as well as the ways in which they understand the external world. Anthropological linguistics subsumes the study of human language and animal communication (or the evolutionary development of human speech); language universals (or discovering characteristics common to all languages); language and world view (or exploring the ways in which the structure and form of a language determines the perceptual reality of its speakers); language classification (or the classification of languages into different families to determine linguistic relationships); writing systems (or the examination of the various origins of writing systems, their spread, and decipherment); and language in society (or the study of trade languages and language standardization in sociocultural context).

Biological/Physical Anthropology

Biological or physical anthropology has many common interests with the natural and biological sciences from its examination of *Homo sapiens* as a species. Research concerns include our biological origins, evolutionary history, and genetic diversity as well as the physical variation, growth, and development of primates. Several branches of physical anthropology exist including: primatology, or the study of living nonhuman primates; human paleontology, or the search for fossil remains of early human species; forensic anthropology, or the identification of victims of murders and accidents; and population genetics, or the study of hereditary differences within and between populations.

Relationships with Other Social Sciences

There are many similarities between anthropology and other social sciences. Sociology has many similar concerns and the two are usually differentiated by the study of modern versus traditional societies. However, anthropologists are clearly working in urban and industrial fields, conventionally the domain of sociologists. The concept of the state and of its origins in political science has been developed by anthropologists, and anthropology has examined various economic concepts and problems with a more comparative perspective. Similarly, anthropology has influenced the development of a system of cross-cultural psychiatry or ethnopsychiatry within psychology, and psychology has offered anthropology new hypotheses for an interpretation of the concept of culture.

The connection with history has been a close one because anthropology was originally based on an evolutionist perspective. Anthropology has offered to historians new techniques of research on the analysis and criticism of oral tradition and has stimulated the development of ethnohistory. Both cultural anthropology and human geography place great importance on humans as they use space or act to transform the environment. It is significant that many early anthropologists, especially European, were originally geographers.

In summary, anthropologists may be identified primarily as social/cultural anthropologists who study the social, symbolic, and material lives of humans past and present, or as biological/physical anthropologists who study humanity as a biological phenomenon. Anthropologists tend to specialize within their subdivision and often will focus on a specific theoretical area, geographic region, or the comparative study of a limited number of human societies. The discipline has traditionally been associated with non-Western groups and exotic locations. However, more recently anthropologists have turned their attention to the study of peasant villages and cities within the context of larger regions and a world system. Activist anthropologists have called attention to the plight of indigenous people in the contemporary world. One only need think of global issues that concern us all such as the destruction of tropical forests in Latin America and southeast Asia, and the systematic extermination and ethnocide of many indigenous and ethnic groups to realize the relevance of anthropological subject matter to our own lives.

2

Libraries as Sources of Anthropological Information

The library, typically located at the center of a college or university campus, reflects the concept that all branches of knowledge gravitate around a central source of information. The traditional role of the library has been to collect, organize, and store books, journals, and other materials. Most important, the modern academic library is an information center where the student can go and find answers to specific questions. To fulfill these various roles, the library offers a number of services that can aid you in locating the information desired.

You should be familiar with the range of services provided by the campus library. Although facilities and the range of services offered may vary from campus to campus, there is usually one main library building. There may be other libraries devoted to specific programs such as natural sciences, humanities, medicine, law, and some of these may be further divided into departmental libraries such as chemistry, journalism, physics, or education.

Basic Library Services

Most campus libraries provide a series of basic library services. The following section discusses some of the services most commonly available to students:

Reference Area

Begin an investigation of your campus library system in the reference department at the main library. The reference department will probably have a variety of library brochures, maps, and other guides to familiarize you with the services being offered by your campus library. Most of the major reference material will be found here as well. Reference books are specialized library resources to assist your in obtaining information and in using the resources of the library. They are usually available to all library users on open shelves within a designated area, typically near the reference department. Reference librarians provide assistance finding the reference materials that will answer your specific needs, or they will refer you to the person who can help you. You should never hesitate to ask a reference librarian for assistance.

Library Catalog

The catalog, probably the most important resource in your library, is a record of all books and other materials cataloged in a library. Because the information in a library catalog is presented in a standardized way, you will need to understand the format and the various pieces of information. The use of a library catalog is discussed further in Chapter 4.

Computerized Searching

A major use of computers is to search through various indexes and abstracts to locate pertinent titles of articles and books. Given the time and financial costs required to establish these computer search programs, libraries typically do not establish their own systems but use services of commercial firms for this purpose. Chapter 20, Online Databases, contains detailed information regarding computerized searching of anthropological literature.

Interlibrary Loan

All libraries would like to own everything a patron needs, but budget and space limit the size of any collection. Most academic and public libraries in the United States participate in systems through which they may borrow books and journals from other libraries. Most circulating books may be borrowed, and parts of them may be photocopied. Libraries will typically not loan entire journals or reference books, and sections of these may be photocopied. There is usually no charge for borrowing books, although photocopy costs may be charged. The charge for photocopies will vary from one library to another because fees are set by the lending library.

You must submit a written request on an interlibrary loan form. These forms should be completed with all the information requested. Different information will be requested for a book and a journal. In both cases, you will be asked to provide the source in which you found the citation. Missing information will cause a delay in getting the material. When you wish to get material through interlibrary loan, be certain to submit your request well in advance of the date when you need the materials. Interlibrary loan requests usually take two to six weeks, and sometimes longer.

Library Instruction

Most libraries provide some kind of instruction in the use of the library. This instruction may take various forms: booklets about the library; tours by librarians; self-guided tours using either a booklet or a cassette player; informal instruction by a librarian on how to use various reference works; guest lectures by librarians as requested by instructors; and credit courses on the use of materials in a particular field. You should explore the instruction offerings provided by your campus library as early as possible in your collegiate career.

Closed Stacks

Some libraries allow you to go to the book shelves; others do not. In order to get books in libraries whose stacks are closed, you must fill out a call slip and give it to a library employee who will find the book and give it to you. A call slip usually asks for basic information that you must copy from the catalog record for the book.

Special Collections

Most libraries will have a designated areas for special collections. Such collections can include rare books; state, local, and federal documents; university archives; and local history. Special collections are essentially libraries within libraries and frequently have special restrictions on the use of their materials. The holdings of special collections are not always given in the library catalog.

Microforms

To save space and increase usefulness, many materials have been preserved on microforms, microfilm, or microfiche. The most common resources on microforms are periodicals and others include old and rare books. A microform comes in the form of a reel of film with one or two pages per frame. A microfiche is a card-shaped piece of film containing up to 100 printed pages, greatly reduced. Reading either requires the use of a special viewer, usually kept in a separate area in the library.

Audiovisual Materials

Many libraries contain media sections that house films, videotapes, photographs, slides, and sound recordings. If your topic concerns the anthropology of the performing or visual arts, or architecture, you will often find materials useful to your research on the audiovisual collection.

Reserve

Some books and journals are placed "on reserve" in a special area of the library because they are in high demand by students. Materials on reserve can often be used only for a limited amount of time (usually as short as an hour) and often may only be used in the library (although there are usually special arrangements for taking materials overnight or whenever the library is closed). Checkout procedures and hours when the library is open vary at different libraries, so you will need to find out the special regulation sat your library. Stiff fines are usually imposed for keeping reserve materials past the time limit.

Circulation

All libraries have a procedure for borrowing materials. Since circulation policies will vary from one library to another, you will need to find out what circulation rules and regulations apply at your library. In addition to checking out books, the circulation department can trace missing titles, hold books for you when they are returned by someone else, inform you when books must be returned, and notify you when materials are overdue.

Photocopying Services

Most academic libraries provide photocopy equipment and services to permit patrons to copy a page or pages from books, journals, and other materials. The library will have coin-operated photocopy machines or a copy center staffed with personnel who will make the copy for you. There are charges for making copies. Because of United States copyright law, books may not be copied in their entirety. If you have any questions about the legality of making or using photocopies, ask a librarian for detailed information.

Carrels

A carrel is a private study area in the library. Some libraries will assign advanced undergraduate students, graduate students, and faculty members a carrel for a quarter, semester, or academic year. Carrels are especially useful for the student who is writing a thesis because research materials can be kept in the carrel until the work is finished. Location inside the library makes these study areas convenient to reference and reserve materials. Unfortunately, most libraries have a limited number of carrels and assignment is competitive.

3

Library Research in Anthropology

The Nature of Library Research in Anthropology

Very little research has been published about the information gathering needs and problems of anthropologists. In 1968, Diana Amsden, a librarian and anthropology doctoral student, published the summary results of a questionnaire sent to determine the information gathering patterns of professional anthropologists (Amsden 1968). Among other things, the survey indicated that lists of references in books and articles, and conversations with other anthropologists, were the most commonly used information gathering techniques. Book reviews, publishers, announcements of forthcoming publications, notes, and correspondence with other anthropologists, were frequently mentioned. The least common techniques include seminar presentations, the library catalog, as well as indexing and abstracting services.

Although the response to the questionnaire was low and therefore statistically unreliable, the results do reflect the character, methods, and problems of anthropologists, especially in university and museum situations. The high average number of hours spent in obtaining information, twelve hours available at the time, suggested to Amsden a need for improvement in these aids. It was also seen to indicate the need for improved instruction in library based research methods.

The survey also identified several problems common to most anthropologists attempting to obtain information, including the inadequacy of local library collections and the decentralization of library materials. Such problems are probably familiar to most students as well. The need for finding more efficient means of obtaining foreign and unpublished materials was noted, as was the need for improved indexing and abstracting services.

More recent studies (Choi 1983, 1988; Clark and Clark 1982; Currier 1976; Garfield 1984; Hartmann 1995; MacLeod 1985; Perkins 1973; Rana 1982; Spurling 1973; Stenstrom and McBride 1979), in conjunction with the patterns identified by Amsden, suggest the following characteristics of the information gathering techniques of anthropologists.

- Anthropologists use material from a wide range of disciplines outside of anthropology.

- Foreign-language materials are important for anthropological research.

- The accumulated knowledge of anthropology, at least as published in journals, maintains continuing importance for the discipline,

- Anthropologists use a variety of literature in their research, although books and journals publishing original research are used most often.

Anthropologists apparently do not express concern about the need for rapid dissemination of research findings. Some anthropologists noted "that there was nothing of importance in their field that they could not await a year or two to read" (Handler 1989:42). This sense of development in the field is highly variable and is a function of the nature of one's research.

The traditional emphasis on fieldwork continues to make anthropology unique among the social sciences. Other social sciences incorporate some fieldwork methodologies, but anthropology relies fieldwork as the primary information gathering technique. Fieldwork by anthropologists continues among relatively isolated societies, as well as in urban areas and in the various institutions of modern society. The tradition of fieldwork requires that sufficient research in the literature be completed before an anthropologist enters the field (Bernard 1988).

Structure of Anthropological Inquiry

Anthropology, as with other social sciences, has a body of literature that includes both scholarly and popular material (Haas 1977; Kane 1984; Kelly 1970; Nelson 1979; Ogburn 1989; Perry 1984; Perry and Nelson 1983; Westerman 1994).

Primary Sources

A primary or original source is a fundamental, authoritative document used in the preparation of a subsequent work. The most common primary sources used by anthropologists are field notes, and archival and museum collections. Graduate theses are another source of primary data that often does not get published.

Secondary Sources

Secondary sources include any material other than primary sources used in the preparation of a written work. The type of secondary information needed will vary with career stage. The heaviest users of research libraries are graduate students establishing command of their discipline's literature. Younger scholars will also be the ones with the most need to keep up with the field systematically. Senior researchers have developed small niches they know well and can depend on informal means for current awareness.

Library Reference Literature
Although essentially a form of secondary literature, library reference sources are a special kind of resource not always considered by anthropologists. The two leading anthropological libraries produce the most important current general reference sources. *Anthropological literature* is international in scope, covers all disciplines, and is an index to periodical literature at Tozzer Library, Harvard University. The annual *Bibliographic guide to anthropology*, also based on the collection at Tozzer Library, provides current bibliographic coverage to the book literature of anthropology. The Museum of Mankind Library in London combines the Royal Anthropological Institute collection and the holdings of the Department of Ethnography library at the British Museum. It produces the annual *Anthropological index to current periodicals in the Museum of Mankind Library* which is similar to Anthropological Literature but with an emphasis of the Old World.

Lengthy reviews of the literature for current anthropological issues are found in the Annual review of anthropology. Review articles also appear frequently in leading journals such as *American antiquity, American ethnologist,* and *Current anthropology,* as well as *Reviews in anthropology.* The best available abstracting service is *Abstracts in anthropology.*

Quantitative and documentary materials are often used to supplement the field observations of the anthropologist. The types of primary sources used include census data, birth, death, and marriage records, legal codes, and tax rolls. American research libraries seldom collect such material, usually available only in the field.

Archaeologists and ethnographers make use of a wide variety of government produced information. Much current archaeological research in the United States follows the mandates of cultural resource management statutes. Yet these valuable surveys and site reports are usually not collected by libraries (Schmidt 1984).

Systematic cross-cultural comparison is considered valuable by most anthropologists. Correlation analyses using data in the Human Relations Area Files (HRAF) are its most systematic expression (Barry 1980; Clarke and Henige 1984; Ember and Ember 1988; Sutton 1991). Anthropologists make relatively little usage of machine-readable data files, although archaeologists have gone further than cultural/social anthropologists in computer-assisted analysis of quantitative data. Large scale data bases of sites and artifactual data have been compiled by museums and state and federal agencies, and some interinstitutional data sharing is underway. *World cultures,* a quarterly electronic journal and database, offers articles, programs, and data sets on microcomputer diskettes (Bernard and Jones 1984; Brody and Lambert 1984; Clarke and Henige 1984; Clement and Ogburn 1995; Cohen-Williams and Hendon 1995; Droessler and Wilke 1984; Kibbee 1987; LaGrange 1989; Lavell 1995; Levinson 1988, 1989; Still 1996).

Research Strategies for
Library Research in Anthropology

Research, one of the basic tools, of all scholarship, is the result of careful investigation of a selected topic and is intended to display an understanding of the topic as well as the ability to express yourself in a scholarly manner.

Anthropological study is usually based on empirical, methodological, or theoretical foundations obtained from library research. Anyone who plans to conduct field research must first discover legitimate subdivisions in order to limit research parameters. A thorough search of the literature points out what previous work has been done. Only then can efficient and productive work be done.

Much of the research carried out by students beginning in anthropology will depend heavily upon library resources and services. For the beginning student researcher these resources may appear voluminous, complex, and highly specialized. However, by following the logical progression in library research you will discover that most of the obstacles can be overcome.

The Research Process

Research can take many forms and involve many kinds of sources of information. All research should begin with a strategy, that is, the development of an organized and systematic approach to the subject or problem. The procedure outlined below is useful for basic research on almost any topic.

- *Understand the assignment.*

Be certain that you clearly understand whether the instructor expects a report or an evaluation. A report requires skill in choosing sources, in abstracting material from them, and in documenting borrowed material. The main purpose is to report the results of your reading. An evaluation not only presents information but also analyzes it. To write an evaluation you must be thoroughly familiar with a topic, reach certain conclusions on the basis of reading, and support conclusions with material from various authorities. An evaluation requires considerable originality and imagination.

A research paper is usually assigned several weeks in advance and work should begin as soon as possible. If your instructor suggests dates when the various phases should be completed, keep up with this schedule or stay ahead of it. Many students have faith in the value of desperate all-night sessions to meet an assignment, but a successful research paper grows slowly through continued effort. To collect and organize your material will require more time than you expect. Start working on your paper as soon as its is assigned.

- *Select a topic.*

Select a general area of interest. Your choice of a subject is critical. Selecting the wrong subject will make your research drudgery; selecting a suitable one will make it an exciting challenge.

Define and refine the topic to a sufficient size. The search for a topic is a main concern while doing exploratory reading in dictionaries, encyclopedias, handbooks, and yearbooks. Be alert for some aspect of a subject that may interest you. Note the term and concepts encountered during your reading; they may prove useful in later research. You will probably narrow a subject several times before reducing it to its proper scope.

- *Establish a list of potential subject headings.*

Subject headings are the controlled terms used to list books in the library catalog. The *Library of Congress Subject Headings* (LCSH) lists authorized terms or headings for a topic; note the indicators for broader terms (BT), narrower terms (NT), and related terms (RT). A book form of the *Library of Congress Subject Headings* is usually available in the reference area.

- *Identify books on the topic.*

After you set limits on your topic, determine whether bibliographies exist for your topic. Use the library catalog to identify books on a topic.

- *Find articles in periodicals.*

Use indexes such as Anthropological literature or Anthropological index to identify articles on your topic. The list of subject headings defined above may be useful in identifying headings for articles. Use the library catalog to locate the titles and call numbers of the periodicals in which the needed articles appear.

Using Additional Sources

At any point in your research you may need to use additional sources for more information, to check the accuracy of information, to locate primary materials, or to find government publications. These may include biographical and statistical sources, as well as atlases and other formats. The reference staff can assist you or refer you to the appropriate division or department of the library.

Compiling a working bibliography is often a test of topic selection. As you collect sources pertaining to your topic, you may discover that there is less material than you expected; therefore, you must expand the topic or abandon it. Students frequently complain there is not enough material in the campus library to develop a specific topic. Usually such complaints are not justified. Books and articles on related subjects should provide enough material.

Consulting with a Librarian

Librarians are usually available to assist students working on research papers. If you decide to consult with a librarian about your research you should remember that a librarian can help you best if you know:

- Your subject, which you have narrowly defined to a realistic research project.

- The end result you want your research to achieve; a persuasion to a point of view, a clear description of an event, or a soundly developed predictive model you want adopted.

- The audience for which the research is intended: fellow students, faculty, etc.

You may be led in different directions depending on these three factors. You save yourself, and the librarian, a lot of time and frustration by being as specific as possible. There are obviously times when you may need to be general, for example, when you are beginning a term paper in an area of research unfamiliar to you. You might explain your situation to the librarian as: "I have an assignment for my anthropology class to write a ten-page term paper on some aspect of the Central American refugee situation in the southeastern United States." The librarian now knows your general subject, the purpose and audience, and the length of your final product.

Library Research Materials

The kinds of library research materials available for anthropology are similar to those for other disciplines, and they serve similar purposes for a given subject. Efficient use of these materials is dependent upon a basic understanding of the purposes of each kind of reference source, the organization and arrangement of the material, and the distinguishing features. Before using library reference work, you should examine the table of contents and preliminary pages which explain the purpose, the plan and arrangement, and any special features.

There are two kinds of reference works: those which contain the needed information (e.g., dictionaries, encyclopedias, handbooks, biographical dictionaries, atlases, etc.), and those which direct the user to where the desired information can be found (e.g., indexes and bibliographies). Chapters 5 through 23 identify and describe representative reference sources useful to the beginning student. These include the following kinds of materials:

Published Catalogs of
Specialized Libraries and Archives

The contents of specialized libraries and archives are important since they expand the range of library resources available to the student. Catalogs and guides to specialized libraries and archives of interest to anthropology students are identified in Chapters 5 (Libraries) and 6 (Archives).

Guides to the Literature of
Anthropology and Related Fields

A guide not only provides a list of appropriate titles of books and journals, giving the author, publisher, place and year of publication, but it usually gives an annotation of some kind. An annotation is a short description of the usefulness of the work, indicating such information as the number of pages, presence of an index or bibliography, the time period or type of material included, or other significant information that can be briefly stated.

Guides are especially important for beginning research because they:

- Cover a specific subject area.

- Suggest several types of reference sources with specific titles under each.

- Provide a brief description or annotation of the individual titles recommended.

- Suggest ways of carrying out research in a specific subject field, including using the library and its catalog to its fullest potential.

- Includes lists of professional societies and journals affiliated with a field of research.

Guides to the literature of anthropology and related fields of interest to anthropology students are identified in Chapter 7.

Bibliographies

A bibliography is a list. It may be found at the end of a journal or encyclopedia article, graduate thesis or dissertation, book report, term paper, etc. It may be an entire book itself. Usually the contents and form are restricted in some manner. These sources are invaluable because they identify the literature of a specific field. They provide descriptive and critical information which the library catalog cannot and point out materials which may be in the library collection but are not listed in the catalog (e.g., periodical articles, chapters or edited volumes, etc.). Subject and regional bibliographies of interest to anthropology students are identified in Chapters 8 and 9.

Dictionaries and Encyclopedias

A dictionary provides specialized definitions and explanations of terminology and concepts. An encyclopedia gives a summary treatment of the various aspects of a subject, including definition, description, background, and relevant bibliographical references. Encyclopedias elaborate on a theme more extensively than do dictionaries. Rather than concentrate on meanings, spellings, hyphenations, and so forth, the longer articles in an encyclopedia provide more scope for the subject in terms of its history and application. The articles in encyclopedias are usually written by specialists. Dictionaries and encyclopedias of interest to anthropology students are identified in Chapter 10.

Handbooks

A handbook is usually confined to one subject area and is concise in the material covered. Handbooks of interest to anthropology students are presented in Chapter 11.

Annual Reviews and Book Reviews

An annual review or yearbook usually provides current information in a brief and concise update. Book reviews are critical statements and are extremely useful for determining the potential importance of a book. Annual reviews and book review sources of interest to anthropology students are presented in Chapter 12.

Indexes and Abstracts

Indexes indicate where periodical articles on a subject can be found, and abstracts are digests or summaries of periodical articles and other kinds of literature. Usually an abstract of an article provides you with enough information to decide whether the entire work should be read.

There is much important research published in journals and other periodicals. Because of the temporal delay usual in the publication of books, the periodical literature is the place to find the latest developments in theory and the most recent analysis of empirical research. For these kinds of reasons it is important that you learn how to make efficient use of the periodical literature as early as possible in your career.

At the present time the number of useful periodicals in anthropology is increasing rapidly. Listings of some of the more useful ones appear in Chapter 14, Journal Literature. Because of this proliferation it is essential to make use of the various guides to periodicals in pursuing any research project. Those guides most useful to the anthropology student are the author/subject indexes of anthropology and other guides to more general social science journals (see Chapter 13, Indexes and Abstracts).

When using these indexes, the student should carefully read the introductory material to understand how the entries are presented and an explanation of the abbreviations used. There is usually a list of the periodicals surveyed by the index. Finally, the student should be aware that the library may not have all of the journals listed in an index. Thus, it is desirable to have a general idea of the library's holdings before going to the periodical indexes so that time is not wasted taking down references to articles in journals not available in the library.

More sophisticated indexing services are provided by abstracts. Similar to periodical indexes, abstracts provide the names of journals, the authors, pages, and dates. In addition, an abstract is an index to books as well as periodical articles. The most useful feature of an abstracting service is the summary which it provides for each citation. Indexes and abstracts of interest to anthropology students are identified in Chapter 13.

Periodicals

Professional journals provide current articles, essays, book reviews, and other material relating specifically to the subject of a given branch of knowledge. Periodicals of interest to anthropology students are identified in Chapter 14.

Biographical Information

Biographical dictionaries are collections of sketches of varying length about the life of an individual and may include bibliographies and critical evaluations for a body of work. Biographic sources of interest to anthropology students is presented in Chapter 15.

Directories of Organizations and Associations

A directory lists names and addresses of organizations and institutions. It may provide other pertinent information as well, such as the purpose, dues, and officers of an organization. Directories are usually updated periodically to maintain their accuracy. Directories of organizations and associations of interest to anthropology students is presented in Chapter 16.

Government Documents

Government publications include all the kinds of sources mentioned above but are published by government agencies. Information about government documents of interest to anthropology students is presented in Chapter 17.

Atlases and Cartographic Materials

An atlas provides geographical and physical features of an area as well as political and socioeconomic information. Atlases and other cartographic materials of interest to anthropology students is presented in Chapter 18.

Theses and Dissertations

The results of anthropological research often first appear in theses and dissertations before formal publication. These material are usually available through interlibrary loan services and offer an excellent source of current research activity. Guides to theses and dissertations of interest to anthropology students is presented in Chapter 19.

Online Databases

Information about online databases of interest to anthropology students is presented in Chapter 20.

Internet

The Internet is an emerging resource of great significance for the information needs of anthropologists. Information about the Internet of interest to anthropology students is presented in Chapter 21.

Anthropological Films and Photography

Films, videotapes, and other audiovisual materials are increasingly used in anthropology to record field data, to document endangered peoples, and for classroom simulations of fieldwork. Guides to anthropological films and photography of interest to anthropology students are identified in Chapter 22.

Human Relations Area Files

The Human Relations Area Files is a unique research sources for anthropology students. Published on microfiche, the Human Relations Area Files makes available both published and unpublished books, journal articles, and manuscripts pertaining to selected cultural groups and topics of importance worldwide. Information about the Human Relations Area Files of interest to anthropology students are presented in Chapter 23.

Writing the Paper

Writing is not a mechanical process that can be done in a sequence of fixed steps. You will undoubtedly develop a procedure of your own for producing a research paper. Use the following suggestions as a basis and vary them to suit your own work habits.

Rough Draft

When you have developed an outline and are confident that you have sufficient notes, you are ready to write a rough draft. Arrange your notes in groups to correspond to the main divisions of your outline.

When you have divided your notes into piles, work through each group to determine the subdivisions. When your notes are arranged in the order you will use them, you are ready to begin writing. If possible, a first draft should be written at a single sitting. Do not linger over the choice of words. If you come to a concept that is difficult to express, leave enough space and proceed. A rough draft gains in unity if composed in this way.

Leave wide margins for revisions. Some students will triple-space a rough draft. Revise your draft frequently and do not be overly concerned about the neatness at this stage. Whether or not a second draft is needed will depend on your writing habits. If you revise extensively, you may need to make an intermediate draft. The second draft will probably closely resemble the final paper in content.

Final Draft

If time permits, put the rough draft aside for a few days before revising it. Preparing the final draft should be a creative revision, not mechanical recopying. Unlike the first draft, which can be produced in one sitting, the final draft should be revised and copied a few paragraphs at a time. The advantage of piecemeal revision is that you are able to concentrate on details. Copy the text of the paper slowly. Keep reading ahead in the rough draft so that ideas can be integrated more closely. The following aspects of the paper should be considered in revision:

- Check spelling, punctuation, and capitalization.

- Vary sentence structure, arrangement, and length.

- Unify each paragraph by a clear topic sentence.

- Add whatever transitional words and phrases are needed to clarify the paper.

- Eliminate unnecessary words.

- Check the accuracy of each quotation.

Anthropological Citations and References

References or citations are important to give proper credit to the work of others and to permit readers of your paper to find literature you have cited.

Direct Citations

"The persistence of indigenous languages should be no more construed as an indicator of 'traditional Indian-ness' than the presence of craft production" (Cook 1982:18).

The information in parentheses provides the necessary reference data:

Cook	Last name of the author or authors of the citation.
1982	Year in which the article or book containing the quotation was published.
18	Number of the page on which the quotation is found; if the quotation extends more than one page, list all page numbers; e.g., (Cook 1982:18-20).

With this information the reader can find the full reference in your list of references.

Indirect Citations

Indirect citations are references which give credit for a particular idea or concept that are not directly quoted. For example,

It has been stated that the survival of indigenous languages is not an indicator of the persistence of traditional craft production (Cook 1982:18).

Cook (1982:18) has stated that the survival of indigenous languages is not an indicator of the persistence of traditional craft production.

The same information content is provided in each example of direct and indirect citations.

Bibliography Format

You must fully document your research paper. There should be a bibliographic entry for each reference included in the text of your paper. Conversely, there should not be items in your list of references which are not referred to within your text. Thus, if your paper summarizes information extracted from several general works, it is appropriate to include in the text a statement that" The following information is drawn from Doe (1995), Jones (1996), and Smith (1995)." Then each of these works is included in your list of references. The purpose of the bibliography is to provide all the information necessary for another person to find each citation.

There are several forms of bibliographic citation, and there is no inherent reason to use one form, rather than another, except for the sake of clear communication and consistency. Unless instructed otherwise, all works used should be cited in the following format suggested by the American Anthropological Association.

Single author articles in journals
Frison, George C.
1968   A functional analysis of certain chipped stone tools. *American antiquity* 33:149-155.

Double author articles in journals
Johanson, D., and T. White
1979   A systematic assessment of early African hominids. *Science* 203:779-781.

Multiple author works in journals
Berlin, B., J.S. Boster, and J.P. O'Neill
1981   The perceptual bases of ethnobiological classification: evidence from Aguauna Jivaro ornithology. *Journal of ethnobiology* 1:95-98.

Edited volumes
Ladd, John, ed.
1973   *Ethnical relativism.* Wadsworth, Belmont, California.

Articles in edited volumes
Polanyi, Karl
1958   The economy as instituted process. In *Trade and markets in the early empires.* Karl Polanyi, Conrad Arensberg, and H.W. Pearson, eds. pp. 243-270. Free Press, Glencoe Illinois.

Authored books
Murdock, George P.
1959   *Africa: its peoples and their culture.* McGraw-Hill, New
        York.

Separate articles with identical authorship published in the same year
Mandelbaum, David G.
1939a   Agricultural ceremonies among three tribes of Travancore.
        Ethnos 4:114-128.
1939b   The Jewish way of life in Cochin. *Jewish social studies*
        1:423-460.

Theses and dissertations
Bailey, Robert C.
1982   The Socioecology of Efe Pygmy men in the Ituri forest, Zaire.
        Ph.D. dissertation, Department of Anthropology, Harvard
        University, Cambridge, Massachusetts.

References Cited

Amsden, Diana. 1968. Information problems of anthropologists. *College and research libraries* 29(2):117-131.

Barry, Herbert. 1980. Description and uses of the Human Relations Area Files. In: *Handbook of cross-cultural psychology.* H.C. Triandis and J.W. Berry, eds. pp. 445-478. Boston: Allyn and Bacon.

Bernard, H. Russell. 1988. *Research methods in cultural anthropology.* Newbury Park, California: Sage.

Bernard, H. Russell, and Roy Jones. 1984. Machine readable data files in the social sciences: an anthropologist and a librarian look at the issues. *Behavioral and social sciences librarian* 3:15-23.

Brody, Fern, and Maureen Lambert. 1984. Alternative databases for anthropological searching. *Database* 7:28-32.

Choi, Jin M. 1988. An analysis of authorship in anthropology journals, 1963 and 1983. *Behavioral and social sciences librarian* 6(3-4): 85- 94.

Choi, Jin M. 1988. Citation analysis of intra- and interdisciplinary communication patterns of anthropology in the U.S.A. (1963- 1983). *Behavioral and social sciences librarian* 6(3-4):65-84.

Clark, Barton M., and Sharon E. Clark. 1982. Core journals in anthropology: a review of methodologies. *Behavioral and social sciences librarian* 2:95-110.

Clarke, Jack A., and David P. Henige. 1984. The Human relations area files (database): two perspectives. *Behavioral and social sciences librarian* 3: 45-52.

Clement, Elaine, and Joyce L. Ogburn. 1995. Searching GeoRef for archaeology. *Behavioral and social sciences librarian* 14(1):1-10.
Cohen-Williams, Anita, and Julia A. Hendon. 1995. Internet resources for anthropology. *College and research libraries news* 2: 87-90.
Currier, Margaret. 1976. Problems in anthropological bibliography. *Annual review of anthropology* 5:15-34.
Droessler, Judith B., and Candy Wilke. 1984. Physical anthropology literature: online access. *Reference services review* 12:22-26.
Ember, Carol R., and Melvin Ember. 1988. *Guide to cross-cultural research using the HRAF archive*. New Haven: HRAF Press.
Garfield, Eugene. 1984. Anthropology journals: what they cite and what cites them. *Current anthropology* 25:514-528.
Hartmann, Jonathan. 1995. Information needs of anthropologists. (revision of a master's research paper, Kent State University). *Behavioral and social sciences librarian* 13(2):13-24.
Haas, Marilyn L. 1977. Anthropology: a guide to basic sources. *Reference services review* 5:45-51.
Handler, Mark. 1989. Anthropology. In: *Information needs in the social sciences: an assessment.* pp. 41-48. Mountain View, California: Program for Research Information Management, Research Libraries Group.
Kane, Deborah. 1984. Resources in psychological anthropology. *Collection building* 5:23-40.
Kelly, Gail M. 1970. Anthropology. In: *A Reader's guide to the social sciences.* B.F. Hoselitz, ed. pp. 41-90. New York: Free Press.
Kibbee, Jo. 1987. Tradition meets technology: searching folklore online. *Database* 9:24-26.
LaGrange, Marie-Salome. Les systemes experts et la recherche en archeologie et sciences humaines: un point de vue pragmatique. *Documentaliste* 26:11-15, 1989.
Lavell, Cherry. A database of radiocarbon dates for archaeology. *The Indexer* 19:173-176, 1995.
Levinson, David. 1989. The Human Relations Area Files. *Reference services review* 17:83-86, 90.
MacLeod, Stephen. 1985. Anthropology. In: *Selection of library materials in the humanities., social sciences, and sciences.* P.A. McClung, ed. pp. 167-187. Chicago: American Library Association.
Nelson, Bonnie R. 1979. Anthropological research and printed library catalogs. *Reference quarterly* 19:159-170.
Ogburn, Joyce L. 1989. Anthropology. In: *The Social sciences: a cross-disciplinary guide to selected sources.* N.L. Herron, ed. pp. 144-157. Englewood, Colorado: Libraries Unlimited.

Perkins, David. 1973. *Bibliographic control for recently published books in anthropology.* Unpublished M.A. thesis, California State University, Northridge.

Perry, Larry S. 1984. Anthropology and archaeology: a selective interdisciplinary guide to the reference literature: periodical indexes. *Reference services review* 12:33-39.

Perry, Larry S., and Bonnie R. Nelson. 1983. Anthropology: Haas revisited. *Reference services review* 11:67-70.

Rana, R.P. 1982. A trend in citation patterns in anthropology. *Annals of library science and documentation* 29:170-175.

Schmidt, Nancy J. 1981. New periodicals in cultural anthropology. *Behavioral and social sciences librarian* 2:57-93.

Schmidt, Nancy J. 1984. NTIS reports on contract archaeology: their bibliographic characteristics and place in an academic library collection. *American antiquity* 49:586-599.

Spurling, Norman K. 1973. *Information needs and bibliographic problems of the anthropology departments at U.N.C. and Duke University.* Washington, D.C.: ERIC Document Reproduction Service.

Stenstrom, Patricia, and Ruth B. McBride. 1979. Serials use by social science faculty: a survey. *College and research libraries* 40:426-431.

Still, Gael M. 1996. The anthropology of online search strategy formation: a study of four countries. (United Kingdom, United States, Australia and Canada). *Online and CDROM review* 20:59-66.

Sutton, Ellen D. 1991. The Human relations area files and Cross-Cultural CD: enhanced access to selected subjects. *Reference services review* 19(1):57-70.

Westerman, R. C. 1994. *Fieldwork in the library: a guide to research in anthropology and related area studies.* Chicago: American Library Association.

4

Library Catalog

Barbara Walden

The catalog is the primary reference source in any library. You will need to use it at all stages of your research, starting with it at the very beginning and returning to it along the way. A library catalog is designed to make possible the location of a book even though you may have only partial information concerning it. For example, you may wish to collect information for a paper on the folktales of the Salishan Indians of the Northwest Coast of North America. Perhaps you recall the name Franz Boas from a class discussion of the topic. Under Boas, Franz you will find a reference to a book titled *Folktales of the Salishan and Sahaptin Tribes,* published in 1917 by the American Folklore Society. Or, if you do not know an author's name or book title, by looking under a general subject heading such as **Salishan Indians** you will locate the Boas volume as well as others on the same topic. In a computerized catalog you may retrieve similar results with a keyword search of **Boas, folktales,** or **Salishan.**

The catalog of the library you use may be on cards, on microfilm or microfiche, or stored in a computer. In many libraries, older materials are still recorded in a card catalog, while newer items are listed in the computer. Since anthropologists must deal with both the old and the new, you should not hesitate to ask the staff in any library you use to explain where older and newer materials are recorded. Also, you need to be aware that the library catalog may not have information about all the materials a library owns. Materials in special formats such as archives, maps, government materials, or electronic data files are not always fully represented in a library's catalog, and these practices are not always the same from one library to another. So you should not hesitate to ask about what is not recorded in the catalog you are using.

Nowadays, most libraries in the United States and Canada will have a computerized catalog. In some computerized catalogs you may find listed holdings not only for the library you are in, but also for other libraries with which your library has cooperative borrowing agreements. On the same computer screen as the catalog you may also find other resources to facilitate your library research, such as electronic encyclopedias and dictionaries, databases of information about periodical articles, and other information which increasingly brings together in computerized form a wealth of information about your subject. Some library catalogs even include direct linkages to computerized versions of books and journals. Because changes in a computerized environment can occur steadily and rapidly, the scope of materials accessible through the library's catalog, as well as the type of resources accessible along with the catalog on the computer screen, will not remain constant. Here again, you should ask questions about the scope of the catalog and what other resources are included on the computer screen. If you are accessing the computerized catalog remotely rather than in the library, take advantage of the help screens to find out more. Some library catalogs may even include a form for you to send in an e-mail inquiry. The rest of this chapter will deal with the basics of searching electronic catalogs and card catalogs. Information about other things you may find on the library's computer screen, such as databases of periodical articles, are covered in other sections of this guide.

Searching an Online Library Catalog

No matter what form the catalog takes, items are usually listed in it by author, by subject (assigned subject headings) and by title. An electronic catalog usually will offer additional means of searching, such as by keyword or call number, and additional ways of refining your search, such as by date of publication.

Author Searching

Author searches find authors, editors, associations, companies, composers, performers, government bodies, and so forth. To search for an individual as author, in most catalogs you enter the surname first. For example, to find Claude Levi-Strauss, type **a=levi strauss c** and press **ENTER/RETURN**.

If the surname is not located, especially in a computerized catalog, try varying the spelling or spacing in the name. Computers are very precise about spacing, and the conventional library spelling of a surname may be spelled differently too. In a computerized catalog you can try truncating or entering the first few letters of the surname followed by a truncation symbol, usually *, ?, or $. For example, you may enter **Le Roy** or **Le Roy La*** instead of **Le Roy Ladurie Emmanuel.**

If you truncate or use a form of the name other than the conventional one, you may occasionally find a "search under" or "see" notice. This will instruct you what form of the author's name will work in the catalog. For example:

LADURIE EMMANUEL LE ROY
1 *Search Under: LE ROY LADURIE EMMANUEL

To search for an organization, institution, or corporation as author, enter the name of the organization or institution. For example, **a=national geographic soc** and press **ENTER/RETURN**.

To search for a government agency as author, enter the government name, followed by the agency name. For example, **a=united states bureau of indian affairs** will find all the publications of the various subdivisions of the Bureau of Indian Affairs.

Title Searching

Title searches find titles of books, journals, magazines, recordings, series, and so forth. To search by title, simply enter t=[title] and press **ENTER/RETURN**. For example, **t=handbook of american indians north of mexico.** Omit any initial articles, such as a, an, or the, in any language, and if desired, you may enter only the first few words.

If you need several books on a single subject, search for one using the author or title approach and note the subject headings used. For example, if you know that Garold Barney has written about the Ghost Dance, the full bibliographic record in the catalog (below) provides several related subject terms, such as **Ghost Dance, Indians of North America—Great Plains--Religion, Mormon Church--Great Plains--Influence** and **Mormons--Great Plains** assigned to it.

Author: Barney, Garold D.
Title: Mormons, Indians, and the Ghost Dance religion of 1890 / Garold D. Barney.
Published: Lanham, MD : University Press of America, c1986.
Description: ix, 248 p. : ill. ; 24 cm.
Subjects, Library of Congress (Use s=):
Ghost dance
Indians of North America--Great Plains--Religion
Mormon Church--Great Plains--Influence
Mormons--Great Plains

Check the catalog under these subject headings to find other similar materials.

Subject Searching

Very often, the subject approach will be your first stop as you begin to discover what the library has on your topic. Searches by subject must use standardized subject terminology found in the *Library of Congress Subject Headings* (LCSH). These volumes are usually located near electronic catalog terminals or elsewhere in the reference section of your library. Here you will find not only the assigned subject term for your subject, but also information about other possible subject terms which are related, broader, or narrower than the one you have in mind.

For example, if you enter the search term s=**mohave apache indians,** you will the message:

MOHAVE APACHE INDIANS
1 *Search Under: YAVAPAI INDIANS

This message indicates that the correct search term is **Yavapai Indians.** Often the catalog will provide a direct route to this correct term. In this example, you just type "1" to go to the right place.

If you enter the search term s=**apache indians,** you will find other related topics listed as well.

APACHE INDIANS
***Search Also Under:**
1 MESCALERO INDIANS
2 MOGOLLON INDIANS

If you are remotely searching an electronic catalog, the catalog itself may contain references to correct standardized subject terms and other related terms.

You will want to be creative in your subject approach to the catalog. One of the most common errors in using the library catalog and other indexes is neglecting related topics. When you are investigating a specific subject, it assumes a distorted importance for you: you may think that any book relating to your subject should be in the catalog under the subject heading. Use your imagination and look under related headings as well. For example, if you are writing a paper on Salishan Indians also look under related headings such as **Indians of North America--Northwest Coast of North America** or **Indians of North America--Northwest, Pacific.**

Some of these subheadings are standardized, while others relate specifically to the topics listed. Browse through the various subheadings for your topic in order to locate more information.

Other Searching Options
in a Computerized Library Catalog

The process of searching a computerized catalog may vary depending on which library you are using. Attempts are only now beginning to bring standardization to computerized catalogs; however nearly all computerized catalogs offer a variety of searching capabilities in addition to the basics of author, title, and established subject terminology. Additional searching options may include key word, call number, location or format of the material, date of publication, etc.

In the examples in this section, the format of the search commands is that used in the computerized catalog of University of Minnesota and several other large libraries; check the help screens or ask a librarian to help you with search commands in a computerized catalog which is new to you.

Keyword Searching

Keyword searches look for a word or words anywhere in a bibliographic record and may find items which cannot be located by **a=** , **t=** , or **s=** . For example, **k=salishan** will retrieve all items with Salishan in the record.

Combining Keywords

Depending on the catalog available, you may be able to combine search terms and refine your search by using 'Boolean operators' such as **and, with, or, not,** and **adj** (adjacent to). Ask a librarian or use the help screens if you need guidance in doing this.

The **and** *Operator*

The **and** logical operator finds records containing both terms anywhere in a bibliographic record. For example, **k=salishan and women** yields an autobiography of a Salishan woman in which both search terms appear as part of the subject headings.

Author: Mourning Dove, 1888-1936.
Title: Mourning Dove : a **Salishan** autobiography / edited
                 by Jay Miller.
Published: Lincoln : University of Nebraska Press, c1990.
Description: xxxix, 265 p. : ill. ; 23 cm.
Subjects, Library of Congress (Use s=):
                 Mourning Dove, 1888-1936.
                 Salishan Indians--Biography
                 Salishan Indians--**Women**
                 Salishan Indians--Social life and customs

Entering **k=dove and salishan** would have produced the same result.

The **or** *Operator*

The **or** logical operator finds all records including either one term or another or both. Use this operator sparingly, as it may yield numerous irrelevant results. If you enter **k-salishan or women** you will get all records with either the word **salishan** or **women**, and most of them may not pertain to your subject. The or operator is most useful when you need to search for synonyms, such as **k= marijuana or marihuana or cannabis.**

The **not** Operator

The **not** logical operator excludes records containing the specified term. For example, **k=central america not costa rica.**

Positional Operators

Positional operators, such as **adj, adj#, near, near#,** and **with,** determine the spatial relationship between terms within the bibliographic record.

The adj *Operator*

The **adj** operator requires terms to be adjacent and in the same order. For example, **k=cremation adj vessel.**

The adj# *Operator*

The **adj#** operator requires terms to be within a specific number of words and in the same order. For example, **k=maya adj3 vessel.**

The near *Operator*

The **near** operator requires terms to be next to each other, in any order. For example, **k=waste near management.**

The near# *Operator*

The **near** operator requires terms to be within a specific number of words, in any order. For example, **k=lowland near5 maya.**

The with *Operator*

The **with** operator terms must be in the same sentence, in any order. For example, **k=maya with religion,** will retrieve items with **maya** and **religion** in the title, as well as items with **maya** and **religion** in an assigned subject term.

Field Labels

Field labels are used to limit a search to a particular segment such as author, title, subject, or conference name. For example, **k=willey.au. and sabloff.au,** retrieves titles co-written by Gordon Willey and Jeremy Sabloff, or **k=(iroquois.ti. or mohawk.ti.) with longhouse,** retrieves titles that contain either the word **Iroquois** or **Mohawk** and the word **longhouse.** Also, **k=philadelphia.cn. same archaeology,** retrieves conference proceedings with archaeology and Philadelphia in the conference name.

Truncating Search Terms

Use the truncation symbol (usually ***, ?,** or **$**) to locate all items beginning with the stem entered. For example, **k=mesoamer?** Finds **Mesoamerica, Mesoamerican, Mesoamericanization,** etc. Similarly, **k=maya?1** finds one additional character only, such as **maya, mayan,** and **mayas.**

Date Searching

Use the **.yr** field labels to search by date. For example, **k=circumcision and 1997.yr.,** finds records with the term **circumcision** anywhere in the record and a 1997 publication date.

Language Searching

Use the first three letters of the language name, except for Japanese (jpn) and ancient Greek (grc). For example, **k=structuralism and fre.la.**, finds French language materials with the word **structuralism** anywhere in the . record. Do not use **eng.la.** to limit to English, as this will overload the capacity of the system.

Format Searching

Publication type may be used to limit searches by serials (**s**), maps (**p**), visual materials (**f**), computer files (**d**), manuscripts (**u**), or musical scores and sound recordings (**m**). For example, **k=linguistics.su. and s.fmt**, finds linguistics journals. A search of **k=fre.la. and s.fmt.**, finds journals in French.

Stop Words

Stop words are so common that they cannot be searched in a **k=** search. Examples include **an, at, by, for, in, many, more, no, not, of, on, or, the to, and with.**

Call Number Browsing

Use **c=** to browse Library of Congress or Dewey Decimal call numbers. For example, **c=F2270.1 .E3 G83** (Library of Congress) or **c=72C C729** (Dewey Decimal). If the call number includes a date, leave a space before the date, as in **c=571.7 B632 1951.** Use **co=** to browse all other call number types, such as **co=microfilm news 12** (microform), **co=cd-rom 52** (compact discs), or **co=diss** (disserations).

Call Number Approach and
Library Classification Systems

Libraries expend great effort to bring materials on similar subjects together using classification systems. If you know the outlines of the classification scheme used by your library, you can browse in the subjects that relate to your topic, either by using the computerized catalog or by going to the place where the books on your subject are shelved.

Dewey Decimal Classification System

The Dewey Decimal Classification System may be more widely used than the Library of Congress system in smaller academic and public libraries. This system is also followed by a majority of the libraries in English-speaking countries now or formerly part of the British Commonwealth of Nations. In addtion, it is perhaps the most important single system of library classification world wide and is used in almost every nation on the globe.

000 General Works
100 Philosophy
200 Religion
300 Social Sciences
400 Language
500 Pure Science
600 Technology, Applied Science, Useful Arts
700 The Arts
800 Literature, Belles Lettres
900 History; Biography

Library of Congress Classification System

The second classification system which is in general use, particularly in large libraries and academic libraries, is the Library of Congress classification system. Instead of a numerical category classification the Library of Congress scheme uses a system of letter designators.

A	General Works
B	Philosophy; Religion
C	History: Auxiliary Sciences
D	History: General and Old World; Topography
E-F	History: America
G	Geography; Anthropology, Folklore
H	Social Sciences
J	Political Science
K	Law
L	Education
M	Music
N	Fine Arts
P	Philology and Literature
Q	Science
R	Medicine
S	Agriculture
T	Technology
U	Military Science
V	Naval Science
Z	Bibliography and Library Science

Appendix A provides a detailed breakdown of the Library of Congress classification scheme pertaining to anthropology and related subjects.

Other Library Classification Systems

Sometimes special libraries or divisions within a library may have special classification schemes for some material. Most often these are nonbook materials such as photographs, newspaper clippings or other special materials.

5

Published Catalogs of Specialized Libraries

Published library and archival catalogs are important bibliographic resources not usually considered by students. These catalogs are essentially specialized bibliographies and make it possible for you to identify material in specialized libraries without having to travel great distances to physically check library catalogs. More importantly, many of these catalogs use subject headings specially designed for anthropology, and contain detailed references to articles in professional journals or edited volumes.

The importance of published library catalogs is well known to anthropologists. The massive catalog of the Tozzer Library at the Peabody Museum of Archaeology and Ethnology at Harvard University, with its supplements, has become the main bibliography and index for the discipline. The Tozzer Library catalog uses author and subject arrangements developed for anthropologists, and provides both a retrospective periodical index for a field where periodical indexing is particularly poor, as well as subject access to books that might never be found using Library of Congress subject headings.

Published library catalogs are indispensable tools for compiling a working bibliography. This chapter lists some of the major library collections in anthropology for which published catalogs are available. Chapter 6 identifies some important guides to archives and manuscript collections.

For additional published catalogs of specialized libraries, consult the library catalog under the appropriate subject with the subdivision *Bibliography.* For example,

Anthropology -- Bibliography -- Catalogs
Latin America -- Bibliography -- Catalogs
Indians of North America -- Bibliography -- Catalogs

Anthropology
5.1   Harvard University. Peabody Museum of Archaeology and Ethnology. Library. *Catalogue: subjects.* Boston: G.K. Hall, 1963. 27 v.; 51 microfilm reels; *First supplement,* 1970. 6 v.; *Second supplement,*

1971. 3 v.; *Third supplement*, 1975. 4 v.; *Fourth supplement*, 1979. 4
v.; *Catalogue: authors*. Boston: G.K. Hall, 1963. 26 v.; *First
supplement*, 1970. 6 v.; *Second supplement*, 1971. 2 v.; *Third
supplement*, 1975. 3 v.; *Fourth supplement*, 1979. 3 v. GN24 .H372
1963; *Index to subject headings*. rev. ed. Boston: G. K. Hall, 1971.
237 p. GN24 .H372x 1963; *Index to anthropological subject headings*.
2 rev. ed., 1981. 177 p. Z695.1 .A63 T69 1981.

    *Author and subject catalogues of the Tozzer Library: formerly the
Library of the Peabody Museum of Archaeology and Ethnology,
Harvard University* [Microform]. 2 ed. Boston: G.K. Hall, 1988. 1,116
microfiches: negative. GN761 .T69x 1988.

    The coverage of this preeminent library (now known as Tozzer
Library) emphasizes the Americas, especially Mexican and Central
American archaeology, ethnography, and linguistics, although
holdings cover the world. It is probably the most comprehensive
anthropology library in the United States, if not the world, and the
catalog appropriately reflects the broad research interests of the faculty
and museum staff at Harvard University. The subject catalog uses a
classified arrangement that is primarily geographic with subject
divisions and subdivisions. The author catalog includes personal
names of authors, editors, and translators, as well as the names of
museums, professional societies, journals, and the contents of
monographic series. There are included also works about authors and
critical replies to their works, but not book reviews. *Festschriften*
(collections of articles written in honor of an esteemed individual) and
conference proceedings are included and periodical; articles have been
included individually since the late nineteenth century.

    This catalogue contains entries for monographs and serials
catalogued through June 1986. From July 1986 forward, catalogued
entries can be found in *Bibliographic guide to anthropology and
archaeology* (Boston: G.K. Hall. v.1 - , 1988 - . 1/yr). This catalogue
also contains citations to periodical articles through June 1983, after
which time they can be found in *Anthropological Literature*.

Colonialism and European Expansion

5.2   Biblioteca Civica Berio di Genova. *Catalogo della Raccolta
Colombiana*. 2. ed. Boston, G. K. Hall, 1963. 151 p. 016.973 C717g.

    Contains one of the world's greatest collections of material
pertaining to the voyages and discoveries of Columbus and other early
explorers of the Western Hemisphere.

5.3   Great Britain. Colonial Office. Library. *Catalogue of the Colonial
Office Library, London*. Boston: G.K. Hall, 1964. 15 v.; *First*

Supplement, 1963-1967, 1967. 894 p.; *Second supplement, 1976-1971, 1972; Accessions to the Library [of the Foreign and Commonwealth Office]. May 1971-June 1977.* Boston: G.K. Hall, 1979. 4 v. Z921 .G66 G73.

Includes an extensive social and policy sciences library collection relating to the dependent territories of the British Empire and later, the independent countries of the British Commonwealth. The catalog of the Colonial Office Library includes three departments: the Colonial Office, the Commonwealth Relations Office, and the Department of Technical cooperation. In 1968 the library was merged with the Foreign Office library to form the Foreign and Commonwealth Office Library.

5.4   Great Britain. Foreign Office. Library. *Catalogue of the Foreign Office Library, 1926-1968.* Boston: G.K. Hall, 1972. 8 v. Z921 .G682 1972.

Emphasis is on British external affairs, especially the politics, government, history, economic development, and international relations of foreign countries.

5.5   New York (N.Y.) Missionary Research Library. *Dictionary catalog of the Missionary Research Library, New York.* Boston: G.K. Hall, 1968. 17 v. Z7817 .N54 1968.

Includes more than 273,000 entries on missions and missionaries worldwide, especially the theory and practice of missions, history of missionary societies, ethnographic studies, etc. During much of the nineteenth century missions furnished the primary point of contact between the United States and countries of Africa, Asia, and South America, making early mission reports of interest to anthropologists. The emphasis of the collection is Protestant missions outside of the United States, but there is also material on missions from Europe, Roman Catholic missions, and work among Native Americans.

5.6   Royal Commonwealth Society. Library. *Subject catalogue of the Royal Commonwealth Society, London.* Boston: G. K. Hall, 1971. 7 v. Z7164 .C7 R83.

Supplements the *Subject catalogue of the Library of the Royal Empire Society* (London, 1930. 4 v.) and the *Biography catalogue of the Library of the Royal Commonwealth Society.* Includes: v. 1. British Commonwealth and Europe, Asia, in general, Mideast, India; v. 2. Asia, other Asian areas, Africa, Africa in general, North Africa; v. 3. Africa: West Africa, East Africa; v. 4. Africa, noncommonwealth Africa, including former foreign colonies, Republic of South Africa, other southern African countries; v. 5. The Americas; v. 6. Australia, New Zealand, Pacific; v. 7. Biography, voyages and travels, World War I, World War II.

Ethnographic Art

5.7   Robert Goldwater Library. *Catalog of the Robert Goldwater Library of Primitive Art, the Metropolitan Museum of Art.* Boston, Massachusetts: G.K. Hall, 1982. 4 v. N5310.8 .U6 N484 1982.

Probably the largest and most definitive library collection of materials relating to the study of ethnographic art; contains 47,000 entries with arrangement by five major geographic regions; subdivided by country and ethnic/linguistic group.

Linguistics

5.8   Center for Applied Linguistics. Library. *Dictionary catalog of the Library of the Center for Applied Linguistics, Washington, D.C.* Boston: G. K. Hall, 1974. 4 v. P129 .C46 1974.

Includes material related to the teaching of English as a second language, teaching of African and Asian languages in the United States, surveys of neglected languages, linguistic documentation, language acquisition, and Native American language education policy.

Race Relations

5.9   Institute of Race Relations. Library. *Library catalogue of the Institute of Race Relations, London.* Boston: G.K. Hall, 1981. 6 v. Z921 .L5958 1981.

Comprehensive collection of materials on race relations, including material on biological theories of race.

Africa

5.10   International African Institute. Library. *Cumulative bibliography of African studies.* Boston: G. K. Hall, 1973. 2 v. *Author catalog.* 4 microfilm reels; *Classified catalog.* 6 microfilm reels. Z3509 .I57 1973.

Includes approximately 100,000 books and articles listed in the bibliography published in the quarterly journal *Africa* from 1929 to 1970, and in the *International African Bibliography* during 1971 and 1972. The primary focus is tropical Africa although coverage includes continental Africa, Madagascar, and other adjoining islands.

5.11   London. University. School of Oriental and African Studies. Library. Library *Catalogue of the School of Oriental and African Studies.* Boston: G.K. Hall, 1963. 28 v.; *First supplement,* 1968. 16 v.; *Second supplement,* 1973. 16 v.; *Third supplement,* 1979. 19 v.; *Fourth supplement,* 1978-1984. 363 microfiche. Z3009 .L63.

Approximately 1,300,000 entries relating to areas of interest of the School of Oriental and African Studies, including linguistics, archaeology, ethnography, and geography.

5.12   Musée de l'Homme (Museum National d'Histoire Naturelle). Bibliothèque. *Catalogue systématique de la section Afrique.* Boston, G. K. Hall, 1970. 2 v. DT3 .P37 1970.

Includes entries for approximately 8,000 volumes and periodical titles arranged geographically by subdivisions. The catalog is especially rich in ethnographic material.

5.13   Northwestern University (Evanston, Illinois). Library. *Catalog of the African collection.* Boston: G. K. Hall, 1962. 2 v. 016.96 N8195.

5.14   Northwestern University (Evanston, Illinois). Melville J. Herskovits Library of African Studies. *The Africana conference paper index, compiled and published by the Melville J. Herskovits Library of African Studies, Northwestern University.* Boston: G.K. Hall, 1982. 2 v. DT1.5 .M45 1982.

Includes more than 12,000 conference papers, mostly written in English or French, presented throughout the world since 1945. Arranged through a register of conferences, with author and keyword indexes.

5.15   Northwestern University (Evanston, Illinois). Melville J. Herskovits Library of African Studies. *Catalog of the Melville J. Herskovits Library of African Studies, Northwestern University Library, and Africana in selected libraries, Evanston, Illinois.* Boston: G.K. Hall, 1972. 8 v.; 8 microfilm reels; *First supplement,* 1978. 6 v. DT3 M45 1972.

Includes approximately 60,000 volumes, 600 periodicals and newspapers, as well as rare books, microfilms and microfiche, manuscripts, maps. phonograph records, photographs, on all aspects of sub-Saharan or tropical Africa.

5.16   Washington, D.C. Library of Congress. African Section. *Africa south of the Sahara; index to periodical literature, 1900-1970.* Boston: G. K. Hall, 1971. 4 v.; *First supplement,* 1973; 8 microfilm reels; *Second supplement,* 1974. 3 v.; 3 microfilm reels, 1981; *Third supplement,* 1985. 306 p. DT348 .A34.

A catalog of journal articles at the Library of Congress on Africa, published in African, Asian, European, and North American journals. There is extensive coverage for anthropology, especially ethnography and linguistics.

Africa --- Ethnographic Art
5.17   Washington, D.C. Smithsonian Institution. National Museum of African Art. *Catalog of the Library of the National Museum of African Art Branch of the Smithsonian Institution Libraries.* Boston: G.K. Hall, 1991. 2 v.

Africa --- Linguistics
5.18   *African language materials in the Boston University Libraries.* Gretchen Walsh and Jenny Hochstadt, comps. 2 ed. Boston: Boston University, African Studies Center, 1988. 73, 24 p. Z3501 .A1 V3 1972.

Entries are arranged by language, with a section dealing with entire language groups or groups of languages.

Africa --- South
5.19   University of Rhodesia. Library. *Catalogue of the C. M. Doke Collection on African Languages in the Library of the University of Rhodesia.* Boston: G. K. Hall, 1972. 546 p. Z7106 .U54.

Includes approximately 3,000 entries pertaining to African languages.

Africa --- West
5.20   University of Ibadan. Library. *Africana catalogue of the Ibadan University Library, Ibadan, Nigeria.* Boston: G. K. Hall, 1973. 2 v. DT3 .I23 1973.

An important general collection on Nigeria, including the Africana Collection of Herbert Macaulay, founder of Nigerian nationalism, and Henry Carr, Nigerian educator and book collector.

Asia
5.21   New York Public Library. Reference Department. *Dictionary catalog of the Oriental collection.* Boston: G. K. Hall, 1960. 16 v.; 30 microfilm reels; *First supplement,* 1976. 8 microfilm reels. PJ307 .N4.

Includes some 65,000 volumes relating to the Orient, defined to include the Middle East, including North Africa, and the Far East. The collection is strong in the ancient Near East (Egypt, Mesopotamia, etc.); the civilizations of India, Iran, Armenia, Georgia, Turkey, Central Asia, Southeast Asia, China, and Japan; Islam, Buddhism, and other religions; Sanskrit; and Korea and Malaya.

Asia — East

5.22   Harvard University. Harvard-Yenching Library. *Catalog of Protestant missionary works in Chinese.* Boston: G.K. Hall, 1980. 339 p.; 1 microfilm reel. Z7757 .C6 H37.

Catalog of Chinese language editions of the Bible, catechisms, hymnals, prayer books, and so forth, from 1810 to 1927.

5.23   University of Chicago. Far Eastern Library. *Classified catalog and subject index.* Boston: G.K. Hall, 1973. 18 v.; 12 microfilm reels; *First supplement,* 1981. 4 v.; 12 microfilm reels; *Author-title catalog of the Chinese collection,* 1973. 8 v.; 16 microfilm reels; *First supplement,* 1981. 4 v. *Author-title catalog of the Japanese collection,* 1973. 4 v.; 8 microfilm reels; *First supplement,* 1981. 4 v. Z881 .C5365.

This collection was initially compiled in China with an emphasis on basic reference tools, scholarly journals, and research materials for the study of Chinese literature, history, and institutions, especially of the ancient period. The collection has expanded to include the Laufer Collection of East Asian languages, microfilms of 3,000 rare books from the national library of Bejing, and materials in Japanese and on modern Chines social sciences and literature.

Asia — South

5.24   India Office Library. *Catalogue of European printed books.* Boston: G. K. Hall, 10 v. Z3209 .G7.

The India Office Library was founded in 1801 as the Library of the Honourable East India Company, and is strong in the art and archaeology, history, philosophy and religion, linguistics, ethnography, economics, and politics of South Asia, including the Indo-Pakistan subcontinent, and the neighboring countries of Afghanistan, Tibet, Sri Lanka (Ceylon), Burma, and Malaysia.

5.25   Minnesota. University. Ames Library of South Asia. *Catalog of the Ames Library of South Asia, University of Minnesota.* Boston: G.K. Hall, 1980. 16 v.; 16 microfilm reels. DS340 .A44 1980.

Contains approximately 90,000 books, periodicals, manuscripts, pamphlets, maps, newspapers, and microforms on South Asia.

Asia — Southeast

5.26   Cornell University. Libraries. *Southeast Asia catalog.* Boston: G.K. Hall, 1976. 7 v.; *First supplement,* 1983. 3 v. Z3221 .C86.

Contains approximately 150,000 entries in European and Asian languages relevant to Burma, Cambodia, Indonesia, Laos, Malaysia-

Singapore-Brunei, the Philippines, Portuguese Timor, Thailand, and Vietnam. It is the largest and most comprehensive collection of its kind in the United States.

5.27   Singapore. University. Library. *Catalogue of the Singapore/Malaysia collection.* Boston: G. K. Hall, 1968. 757 p.; *Supplement, 1968-1972,* 1974. 324 p. Z3250 .S56.

Includes an extensive collection of library materials relating to the development of the Malayan states, Singapore, and the Bornean regions (excluding Brunei and Indonesian Borneo) from their pre-colonial roots through independence.

5.28   Washington, D.C. Library of Congress. Orientalia Division. *Southeast Asia subject catalog.* Boston: G.K. Hall, 1972. 6 v.; 9 microfilm reels. Z3221 .U525.

Comprises a catalog maintained for 25 years by the Southeast Asia section of the Orientalia Division; "it is essentially a subject catalog of bibliographic citations to books, pamphlets, journal articles, theses, microforms, and other materials dealing with Southeast Asia, and written primarily in Western languages."

Europe

5.29   Brotherton Library. *Catalogue of the Romany collection formed by D. U. McGrigor Phillips and presented to the University of Leeds.* Edinburgh: T. Nelson, 1962. 227 p. Z5118 .G5 L4.

Contains over 1,200 books and pamphlets, manuscripts, music, correspondence, playbills, etc., relating to Gypsies.

Latin America

5.30   Florida. University. Libraries. *Catalog of the Latin American Collection.* Boston: G. K. Hall, 1973. 13 v.; 26 microfilm reels; *First supplement,* 1979. 7 v.; 7 microfilm reels. F1408 .F66.

Includes some 120,000 books, pamphlets, periodicals, and government documents, with particular strengths on Brazil and the Caribbean area.

5.31   Ibero-Amerikanisches Institut (Berlin, Germany). *Schlagwortkatalog des Ibero-Amerikanisches Instituts, Prüssischer Kulturbesitz in Berlin; Subject catalog of the Ibero-American Institute, Prussian Cultural Heritage Foundation in Berlin.* Boston: G.K. Hall, 1977. 30 v.; 30 microfilm reels. F1408 .I24 1977.

One of the world's leading libraries in Latin American studies; includes some 300,000 volumes, including books and periodical articles and the important 25,000 volume Walter Lehmann Collection of Latin American Archaeology and Ethnology.

5.32 Texas. University, Austin. Library. Latin American Collection. *Catalog of the Latin American collection*. Boston: G. K. Hall, 1969. 31 v.; 31 microfilm reels; *First supplement*, 1971. 5 v.; 10 microfilm reels; *Second supplement*, 1973. 3 v.; 6 microfilm reels; *Third supplement*, 1975. 8 v.; 16 microfilm reels; *Fourth supplement*, 1977. 3 v.; 3 microfilm reels. F1408 .U55 1969.

Catalog of a major Latin American collection with 175,000 volumes in all disciplines, including anthropology, from the fifteenth century to the present. The greatest strength is Mexico; continued by: *Bibliographic guide to Latin American studies* (Boston: G.K. Hall, 1979 -).

5.33 Tulane University. Latin American Library. *Catalog of the Latin American Library of the Tulane University Library, New Orleans*. Boston, Mass., G. K. Hall, 1970. 9 v.; *First supplement*, 1973. 2 v.; 4 microfilm reels; Second supplement, 1975. 2 v.; 4 microfilm reels; *Third supplement*, 1978. 2 v.; 2 microfilm reels. F1408 .T85 1970.

Formerly the library of the Middle American Research Institute, includes materials from all of Latin America, with historical strengths in Mexico, Central America, and the Caribbean.

5.34 Washington, D.C. Pan American Union. Columbus Memorial Library. *Index to Latin American periodical literature, 1929-1960*. Boston, G. K. Hall, 1962. 8 v.; *First supplement*, 1968. 2 v.; *Second supplement*, 1980. 2 v. F1401 .C58.

An index to periodical articles in the economic, political, governmental, social, and cultural fields from more than 3,000 periodicals.

Latin America — Caribbean
5.35 Institute of Jamaica. Kingston. Reference Library. *The Catalogue of the West India Reference Library*. Millwood, New York: Kraus International Publications, 1980. 2 v. F1608 .W47 1980.

Includes comprehensive coverage for Jamaica and the English-speaking Caribbean; especially strong in the subjects of slavery and the slave trade, sugar cane, the plantation economy, and African retentions in the culture and social life of the West Indies.

5.36 Miami. University, Coral Gables. Cuban and Caribbean Library. *Catalog of the Cuban and Caribbean Library, University of Miami,*

Coral Gables, Florida. Boston: G. K. Hall, 1977. 6 v. F2161. U55 1977.

Coverage includes the Greater and Lesser Antilles, the Guyanas, Venezuela, Colombia, and Central America, excluding El Salvador.

Latin America — Mexico and Central America

5.37   México. Biblioteca Nacional de Antropología e Historia. *Catálogos de la Biblioteca Nacional de Antropología e Historia, México; Catalogs of the National Library of Anthropology and History, Mexico.* Boston: G.K. Hall 1972 10 v.; 20 microfilm reels. GN24 .B53 1972.

Catalog specializing in the anthropology and history of Mexico, northern Central America, and to a lesser extent, the rest of Latin America; especially strong in Mexican anthropology and archaeology, with many entries listed under the names of specific archaeological sites.

Latin America — South America

5.38   Catholic University of America, Washington, D.C. Oliveira Lima Library. *Catalog of the Oliveira Lima Library, the Catholic University of America.* Boston: G. K. Hall, 1970. 2 v. DP517 .O45 1970.

Important collection of 50,000 volumes on the Luso-Brazilian world assembled by the historian Manuel de Oliveira Lima.

5.39   Perú. Biblioteca Nacional. Lima. *Catálogo de autores de la Colección Peruana, Biblioteca Nacional del Perú.* Boston: G. K. Hall, 1979. 6 v.; 6 microfilm reels. F3408 .B53 1979.

Middle East

5.40   Chicago. University. Oriental Institute. Library. *Catalog of the Oriental Institute Library, University of Chicago.* Boston: G. K. Hall, 1970. 16 v.; *First supplement (Catalog of the Middle Eastern Collection, formerly the Oriental Institute Library, University of Chicago),* 1977. 962 p. Z1013 .C43.

The Oriental Institute Library aims "to collect all useful printed material on every aspect of the Near East," especially the ancient Near East and medieval Islam. The catalog contains some 300,000 entries and is especially strong in Assyriology, Egyptology, and Islam. Coverage of Middle Eastern ethnography is not comprehensive.

5.41   Jerusalem. Ecole Biblique et Archeologique Française. Bibliotheque. *Catalogue de la Bibliotheque de l'Ecole Biblique et Archeologique Française; Catalog of the Library of the French Biblical and*

Archeological School, Jerusalem, Israel. Boston: G. K. Hall, 1975 13 v.

Subjects covered include Judaism, Christian antiquity, papyrology, linguistics, epigraphy, numismatics, archaeology, Assyriology, Egyptology, geography, Oriental history, and Biblical theory. This catalog is of interest to archaeologists concerned with the ancient Near East.

5.42   Utah. University. Middle East Library. *Arabic Collection: Aziz S. Atiya Library for Middle East Studies.* Salt Lake City: University of Utah Press, 1968. 841 p.; *Supplement,* 1971. Z3013 .U76.

List of materials at the Middle East Library, University of Utah.

North America

5.43   Minnesota Historical Society. *Chippewa and Dakota Indians; a subject catalog of books, pamphlets, periodical articles, and manuscripts in the Minnesota Historical Society.* St. Paul: Minnesota Historical Society, 1969. 131 p. E99 .C6 M5 1969.

Some 2,000 subject entries are reproduced from the public catalog of the Minnesota Historical Society library; divided into two parts, printed materials and manuscripts.

5.44   Museum of the American Indian, Heye Foundation. Huntington Free Library and Reading Room, New York. *Dictionary catalog of the American Indian Collection, Huntington Free Library and Reading Room, New York.* Boston: G. K. Hall, 1977. 4 v. E58 .H86 1977.

Includes more than 35,000 volumes on the art, archaeology, ethnography, history, and current affairs of all Native Americans in the Western Hemisphere; especially strong in holdings of anthropological papers of universities and museums in the United States, Canada, and Latin America; in journals of most historical and archaeological societies in the United States; in manuscripts, codices, and field notes of anthropologists associated with the Museum of the American Indian, Heye Foundation; in United States and Canadian government reports; and in Native American language dictionaries and bibles, autobiographies and biographies, and newspapers.

5.45   Newberry Library, Chicago. Edward E. Ayer Collection. *Dictionary catalog of the Edward E. Ayer Collection of Americana and American Indians in the Newberry Library.* Boston: G. K. Hall, 1961. 16 v. *First supplement,* 1970. 3 v.; 3 microfilm reels; *Second supplement,* 1980. 4 v. E18 .E39.

Includes some 100,000 volumes, with special strengths including Native Americans from prehistory to the present; contact between Native Americans and Europeans, including eighteenth and nineteenth century books of travel; and description; voyages and travels during the period of exploration and early settlement; and cartography from the fifteenth through eighteenth-centuries; and Hawaii, the Philippines, and adjacent Oceania.

5.46   New York (City) Public Library. Reference Department. *Dictionary catalog of the history of the Americas.* Boston: G. K. Hall, 1961. 28 v. *First supplement,* 1973. 9 v. Z1201 .N4.

Includes more than 100,000 volumes relating to the development of the New World from ancient times top the present. Entries for Indians of the Americas are extensive, comprising two full volumes, as are holdings for archaeology.

5.47   United States. Department of the Interior. Library. *Biographical and historical index of American Indians and persons involved in Indian affairs.* Boston: G. K. Hall, 1966. 8 v. Z1209 .U494.

This collection of books, journal articles, and government documents, was originally developed in the Bureau of Indian Affairs, and is now incorporated into the library of the Department of the Interior. Includes various lists, such as lists of different Indian agencies; alphabetical listing of Indian agents with dates and place of appointments; bibliography of books and articles about various battles. Entries usually refer to publications printed in the second half of the nineteenth or first quarter of the twentieth centuries.

5.48   United States. Department of the Interior. Library. *Dictionary catalog of the Department Library.* Boston, G. K. Hall, 1967. 37 v. *First supplement,* 1968. 4 v.; *Second supplement,* 1971. 2 v.; *Third supplement,* 1973. 4 v.; *Fourth supplement,* 1975. 8 v. 019 Un3.

The Library of the Department of the Interior was founded in 1949 with the merger of five agency libraries, including the Bureau of Indian Affairs. This important catalog also contains material from the Bureau of Land Management, National Park Service, and Bureau of Reclamation.

North America --- Arctic and Sub-Arctic
5.49   Arctic Institute of North America. Library. *Catalogue of the Library of the Arctic Institute of North America, Montreal.* Boston: G. K. Hall, 1968. 4 v.; *First supplement,* 1971. 902 p.; *Second supplement,* 1974. 2 v.; *Third supplement,* 1980. 3 v. Z6005 .P7 A73.

One of the largest polar libraries in the world, includes the physical, biological, and social sciences, technology, and general interest materials.

5.50   Dartmouth College. Library. Stefansson Collection. *Dictionary catalog of the Stefansson Collection on the Polar regions in the Dartmouth College Library.* Boston: G. K. Hall, 1967. 8 v. 016.998 .D255.
Materials are primarily historical and contain records of exploration; includes tape-recorded lectures, interviews, diaries, and correspondence.

5.51   Scott Polar Research Institute. Library. *The Library catalogue of the Scott Polar Research Institute, Cambridge, England.* Boston: G.K. Hall, 1976. 19 v.; *First supplement, 1981* 5 v.
Contains books, journals, journal articles, conference proceedings, pamphlets, and unpublished theses and dissertations devoted to the Arctic.

North America --- Northwest

5.52   British Columbia. Provincial Archives. Library. *Dictionary catalogue of the Library of the Provincial Archives of British Columbia, Victoria.* Boston: G. K. Hall, 1971. 8 v. Z1392 .N7 P76 1971.
Contains approximately 170,000 entries, including ethnography and archaeology, relating to British Columbia, Canada west of the Great Lakes, and Northwest and Yukon Territories, Arctic exploration, and the adjacent states of Alaska, Idaho, Montana, Oregon, and Washington.

5.53   Washington (State). University. Seattle. Library. *The Dictionary catalog of the Pacific Northwest Collection of the University of Washington Libraries, Seattle.* Boston: G. K. Hall, 1972. 6 v.
Important source on the Pacific Northwest states of Alaska, Idaho, Montana, Oregon, and Washington, especially the history of early exploration, fur trade, missionary movements, and immigration.

North America --- Southeast

5.54   Florida. University. Gainesville. Libraries. *Catalog of the P. K. Yonge Library of Florida History.* Boston: G. K. Hall, 1977. 4 v.; 8 microfilm reels. F311 .A17 F58.
Collection on the history of Florida, includes materials on colonial history, archaeology and ethnography, and an important administrative manuscript collection.

North America --- West

5.55   Yale University. Library. Yale Collection of Western Americana.
Catalog of the Yale Collection of Western Americana. Boston: G.K.
Hall, 1962 4 v.; 4 microfilm reels. Z1251 .W5 Y35 1962.

One of the nation's largest collections of rare books relating to the
American West; covers the trans-Mississippi West, including the
Canadian Northwest and Alaska, from the earliest discovery to the
passing of the frontier.

Oceania

5.56   Bernice Pauahi Bishop Museum. Library. *Dictionary catalog of the
Library.* Boston: G. K. Hall, 1964. 9 v. *First supplement,* 1967. 676 p.;
1 microfilm reel; *Second supplement,* 1969. 239 p.; 1 microfilm reel.
Z881 .H784.

The only American museum devoted entirely to the anthropology
and natural history of the Pacific region; emphasis is given to early
Pacific voyages, texts in Pacific languages, manuscripts, maps, and
photographs.

5.57   California. University, Santa Cruz. Library. *Catalog of the South
Pacific collection.* Santa Cruz: University Library, University of
California, Santa Cruz, 1985 2 v. Z4001 .C28 1978.

Includes approximately 9,000 items covering political, cultural,
and economic development of Polynesia, Melanesia, Micronesia,
Australia, and New Zealand.

Oceania --- Australasia

5.58   Guam. Nieves M. Flores Memorial Library. *Union catalog of the
Guam Public Library, Guam and Pacific area materials: collections
of the Guam Public Library and the Micronesian Area Research
Center.* Agana, Guam: Nieves M. Flores Memorial Library, 1974. 464
p. Z4741 .N54 1974.

Important collection of more than 220,000 items relating to the
Australasian and South Pacific region, including the East Asian
archipelago and Antarctica; especially strong for anthropology and
native peoples of the area, particularly Maoris and Australian
aborigines.

Oceania --- Hawaii

5.59   Hawaii. University, Honolulu. Library. Hawaiian Collection.
Dictionary catalog of the Hawaiian collection. Boston, G. K. Hall,
1963. 4 v. Z4709 .H22.

Probably the world's largest library collection in Hawaii, with
strengths in early accounts of voyages and travels, and anthropology.

6

Guides to Archives and Manuscript Collections

Guides to archives and manuscript collections are an important source frequently ignored by students. These guides can help you identify research material appropriate to your project. Because archives are not always accessible or available to the general public, it is frequently necessary to make an appointment before considering a research visit. Local restriction regarding the photocopying of materials, and the use of computers, pens, and cameras, should be investigated in advance.

For additional published catalogs of specialized archives, consult the library catalog under the appropriate subject with the subdivision *Manuscripts*. For example,

Anthropology -- Manuscripts -- Catalogs
Latin America -- Manuscripts -- Catalogs
Indians of North America -- Manuscripts -- Catalogs

Anthropology

6.1   National Anthropological Archives. *Catalog to Manuscripts at the National Anthropological Archives, Department of Anthropology, National Museum of Natural History, Smithsonian Institution, Washington, D.C.* Boston: G.K. Hall, 1975. 4 v. E77 .N38x 1975.

Includes 40,000 documents collected by the Bureau of American Ethnology between 1879 and 1965 in three divisions: an alphabetical file on the Indians of North America north of Mexico; a smaller geographical file on peoples of Mexico, Central America, and non-North American areas; and a numerical file indicating the subject under which entries have been filed in the two other divisions. Subject approach is by tribe, linguistic group, or name of individual. See also: James R. Glenn, *Guide to the National Anthropological Archives, Smithsonian Institution* (Washington, D.C.: National Anthropological Archives, 1992. 314 p.).

6.2   Silverman, Sydel, and Nancy J. Parezo, eds. 1995. *Preserving the Anthropological Record.* 2 ed. New York: Wenner-Gren Foundation for Anthropological Research. 254 p. GN14 .P75 1995.

Papers presented at a symposium Preserving the Anthropological Record: Issues and Strategies, sponsored by the Wenner-Gren Foundation and held February 28 through March 4, 1992 in Rancho Santa Fe, California. Contents include: Sydel Silverman, Introduction; Mary Elizabeth Ruwell, The National Anthropological Archives; Joan Warnow-Blewett, Discipline history centers in the sciences; Donald Tuzin, The Melanesian Archive; Don D. Fowler and Douglas R. Givens, Preserving the archaeological record; John van Willigen, The records of applied anthropology; Thomas H. Wilson and Nancy J. Parezo, The role of museums in preserving the anthropological record; Nancy J. Parezo, Nathalie F.S. Woodbury, and Ruth J. Person, Saving the past for the future: guidelines for anthropologists; Mary Elizabeth Ruwell, The physical preservation of anthropological records; Robert V. Kemper, The potentials and problems of computers; Shepard Krech III, and William C. Sturtevant, The future uses of the anthropological record; Sydel Silverman, and Nancy J. Parezo, The next steps.

6.3   Van Keuren, David K. *The Proper study of mankind: an annotated bibliography of manuscript sources on anthropology and archeology in the Library of the American Philosophical Society.* Philadelphia: American Philosophical Society, 1986. Q11 .P83x no.10 1986.

Africa
6.4   Pearson, J. D. *A guide to manuscripts and documents in the British Isles relating to Africa.* London; New York: Mansell, 1993-1994. 2 v. CD1048 .A3 P43 1993.

6.5   South, Aloha. *Guide to Federal archives relating to Africa.* Waltham, Massachusetts: Crossroads Press, 1977. 556 p. DT1 .S68x 1977.

Describes Africa-related documents in the National Archives of the United States.

6.6   South, Aloha. *Guide to non-federal archives and manuscripts in the United States relating to Africa.* London: Zell, 1988. 2 v. CD3002 .S68 1989.

Africa -- South Africa
6.7   Botha, C. Graham. *A Brief guide to the various classes of documents in the Cape archives for the period 1652-1806.* Cape Town: Cape Times Limited, 1918. 85 p. 016.9687 C17.

6.8   Botha, C. Graham. *The Public archives of South Africa, 1652-1910.*
        New York: B. Franklin, 1969. 108 p. 968 B648p.
        Guide to the archives of Natal, Orange Free State, and the
        Transvaal, first published in 1928.

Asia

6.9   Pearson, J. D. *Oriental manuscripts in Europe and North America: a
        survey.* Bibliotheca Asiatica, 7. Zug: Inter Documentation , 1971. 515
        p. Z6605.O7 P42.

Asia --- East

6.10   Matthews, Noel, and M. Doreen Wainwright. *A Guide to manuscripts
        and documents on the British Isles relating to the Far East.* London:
        Oxford University Press/School of Oriental and African Studies, 1977.
        182 p. CD1048 .A77 .M37.
        A survey of English, Welsh, Scots, and Irish depositories.

Asia --- South

6.11   Low, D. A., J.C. Iltis, and M. Doreeen Wainwright. *Government
        archives in South Asia: a guide to national and state archives in
        Ceylon, India and Pakistan.* London: Cambridge University Press,
        1969. 355 p. CD2081 .L6.

6.12   Pearson, J. D. *A Guide to manuscripts and documents in the British
        Isles relating to South and South-East Asia.* London: Mansell, 1990.
        337 p. Z6605.O7 P42.
        A supplement to M.D. Wainwright and N. Matthews, *A Guide to
        Western manuscripts and documents in the British Isles relating to
        South and South East Asia* (London: Oxford University Press, 1965.
        532 p. CD1048 .A8 .W3).

6.13   Wijayaratne, D. J., S. Ananda, and C.H.B. Reynolds. *Catalogue of the
        Sinhalese manuscripts in the India Office Library.* London: India
        Office Library and Records, 1981. 73 p. Z6621.B86 C6.

Asia --- Southeast

6.14   Korn, V.E. *Collection of documents from the Department of Oriental
        Manuscripts, the Royal Institute for Anthropology, Leiden,
        Netherlands.* Leiden, Netherlands: Koninklijk Instituut vour Taal-,
        Land- en Volkenkunde, 1973; Zug: Inter Documentation, 1975. 1594
        microfiche.
        Important collection of documents pertaining to Indonesia,
        Sumatra, and Bali, assembled by Victor Emanuel Korn (1892-1969);

includes: *Guide to the Microfiche Edition of the Korn Collection: The Archives of Professor Victor Emanuel Korn Now in the Royal Institute of Linguistics and Anthropology, Leiden, the Netherlands* (Zug, Switzerland: Inter Documentation, 1975. 56 p.).

Europe --- West

6.15   Biblioteca Nacional (Spain). *Inventario general de manuscritos de la Biblioteca Nacional*. Madrid: Ministerio de Educación Nacional, Dirección General de Archivos y Bibliotecas, Servicio de Publicaciones, 1953-1984. 10 v. 016.1 M26i.

6.16   Foster, Janet, and Julia Sheppard. *British archives: a guide to archive resources in the United Kingdom*. 3 ed. Basingstoke, England: Macmillan; New York: Stockton Press, 1995. 627 p. CD1040 .F67 1995.

6.17   Matilla Tascón, Antonio. *Breve guía de los principales archivos de Madrid*. Madrid: Asociación Nacional de Bibliotecarios, Archiveros y Arqueologos, Sección de Archivos, 1958. 16 p.
        For a more comprehensive guide see: *Guía de los archivos de Madrid* (Madrid: Dirección General de Archivos y Bibliotecas, Servicio de Publicaciones del Ministerio de Educación Nacional, 1952. 592 p. 946.2 M26 Sp5).

6.18   Simpson, Donald H. *The Manuscript catalogue of the Library of the Royal Commonwealth Society*. London: Mansell, 1975. 193 p. DA16 .R69 1975. DA16 .R69x 1975.

Europe --- East

6.19   Grimsted, Patricia K. *Archives and manuscript repositories in the USSR: Estonia, Latvia, Lithuania, and Belorussia*. Princeton, New Jersey: Princeton University Press, 1981. 929 p. CD1735 .B34 G74.

6.20   Grimsted, Patricia K. *Archives and manuscript repositories in the USSR: Moscow and Leningrad*. Princeton, New Jersey: Princeton University Press, 1972. 436 p. CD 1711 G7.
        Continued by: P.K. Grimsted, *Archives and manuscript repositories in the USSR: Moscow and Leningrad: supplement* (Zug: Inter Documentation, 1976).

6.21   Grimsted, Patricia K. *Archives and manuscript repositories in the USSR: Ukraine and Moldavia*. Princeton, New Jersey: Princeton University Press, 1988. CD 1735 U4 G75 1988.

6.22   Grimsted, Patricia K. *Archives in Russia 1993: a brief directory.*
        Washington, D.C.: International Research and Exchanges Board,
        1993. CD1711 .A733x 1993.

6.23   Grimsted, Patricia K. *A Handbook for archival research in the USSR.*
        New York: International Research and Exchanges Board; Washington,
        D.C.: Kennan Institute for Advanced Russian Studies, 1989. 430 p.
        CD1711 .G68 1989.

6.24   Horecky, Paul L, and David H. Kraus. *East Central and Southeast
        Europe: a handbook of library and archival resources in North
        America.* Santa Barbara, California: Clio Press, 1976. 467 p. DJK9
        .E27x 1976.

Latin America

6.25   *Archivo General de Indias de Sevilla: guía del visitante.* Madrid.
        1958. 016.98 Sp 1ar.
            A dated but still useful general guide to the holdings of the
        Archivo General de Indias in Seville, Spain. More current guides to
        specialized parts of the collection are currently being issued,
        including: *Calendar of the Papeles de Cuba, 1781-1821; Spanish
        Florida borderlands calendar of the P.K. Yonge Library of Florida
        History* (Gainesville: The P.K. Yonge Library of Florida History,
        1984. 12 microfilm reels); C. García del Pino, and A. Melis Cappa.
        *Catálogo parcial de los fondos de la sección XI, Cuba, del Archivo
        General de Indias* (La Habana: Editorial ORBE, 1978. 215 p.
        016.97291 Sp15g); J. González, *Catálogo de mapas y planos de Santo
        Domingo* (Madrid: Dirección General de Archivos y Bibliotecas, 1973.
        447 p.); L. Hanke, *Guía de las fuentes en el Archivo General de
        Indias para el estudio de la administración virreinal española en
        México y en el Perú: 1535-1700* (Köln; Wien: Bohlau, 1977. 3 v. 946
        H194); A. Heredia Herrera, *Catálogo de las consultas del Consejo de
        Indias* (Madrid: Dirección General de Archivos y Bibliotecas, 1972;
        Sevilla: Diputación Provincial de Sevilla, 1983-1984. 2 v. CD1862
        .A55 1983); L.A. Musso Ambrosi, *El Río de la Plata en el Archivo
        General de Indias de Sevilla: guía para investigadores* (2 ed.
        Montevideo, 1976. 224 p. 982 M977); Br. Nectario Maria. *Catálogo
        de los documentos referentes a la antigua provincia de Maracaibo,
        existentes en el Archivo General de Indias de Sevilla* (Caracas:
        Universidad Católica Andrés Bello, Instituto de Investigaciones
        Historicas, 1973. 399 p. F2331.M28 N43x 1973); Br. Nectario Maria.
        *Indice de documentos referentes a los obispos de Venezuela
        (1532/1816) existentes en el Archivo General de Indias de Sevilla*

(Caracas: Universidad Católica Andrés Bello, Instituto de
Investigaciones Históricas, 1975. 298 p. 282.86 N282); J. Ortiz de la
Tabla, M. Fernández Martínez, and A. Rivera Garrido. *Cartas de
cabildos hispanoamericanos: Audiencia de Quito (siglos
XVI-XIX)*(Sevilla: Consejo Superior de Investigaciones Científicas,
Escuela de Estudios Hispano-Americanos de Sevilla: Asesoría Quinto
Centenario, Consejería de Cultura y Medio Ambiente, Junta de
Andalucía, 1991. 506 p. F3733 .O78x 1991); J. Ortiz de la Tabla, and
Bibiano Torres, *Cartas de cabildos hispanoamericanos: audiencia de
Guatemala* (Sevilla: Escuela de Estudios Hispanoamericanos, 1984.
524 p. F1466.4 .C3x 1984); A.J. Parejas Moreno, *Documentos para la
historia del Oriente boliviano, siglos XVI y XVII: catálogo de
documentos de la sección V (Audiencia de Charcas) del Archivo
General de Indias* (La Paz, Bolivia: Talleres-Escuela de Artes Gráficas
del Colegio Don Bosco, 1981. 144 p. F3322 .P33x 1982); H.
Rutimann, *Computerization project of the Archivo General de Indias,
Seville, Spain: a report to the Commission on Preservation and
Access, 1992* (Washington, D.C.: The Commission on Preservation
and Access, 1992. 17 p. Z699.5 .A7 R8x N 1992); W.R. Shepherd,
*Guide to the materials for the history of the United States in Spanish
archives* (Washington, D.C.: Carnegie institution of Washington,
1907. 107 p. 016.973 Sh4); J.A. Susto Lara, *Panamá en el Archivo
General de Indias* (Panamá: Imprenta Nacional, 1927. 48 p. 986
Su82); V. Tau Anzoategui, *Libros registros-cedularios de Charcas,
1563-1717: catálogo*. Buenos Aires: Instituto de Investigaciones de
Historia del Derecho, 1992-1994. F3322 .L53x 1992; B. Torres
Ramírez, J. Gil-Bermejo García, and E. Vila Vilar, *Cartas de cabildos
hispanoamericanos: audiencia de Panamá: estudio preliminar y
edición* (Sevilla: Escuela de Estudios Hispanoamericanos, 1978. 432 p.
016.9862 T636); J. Vázquez Machicado, *Catálogo descriptivo del
material del Archivo de Indias referente a la historia de Bolivia* (La
Paz: Ministerio de Educación y Cultura, Instituto Boliviano de
Cultura, 1989. 525 p. F3322 .V39x 1989); E. Vila Vilar, and M.J.
Sarabía Viejo, *Cartas de cabildos hispanoamericanos: audiencia de
México* (Sevilla: Escuela de Estudios Hispano-Americanos, Consejo
Superior de Investigaciones Científicas, Excma. Diputación Provincial
de Sevilla, 1985-1990. 2 v. CD1859.S3 C37x 1985).

6.26   Canedo, Lino G. *Los archivos de la historia de América*. México:
        Instituto Panamericano de Geografía e Historia, 1961. 906 P191
        no.225.

6.27   Canedo, Lino G. *Los archivos históricos de Venezuela.* Maracaibo: Universidad del Zulia, Facultad de Humanidades y Educación, 1966. 147 p. 016.987 G586.

6.28   Canedo, Lino G. *De México a la Alta California, una gran epopeya misional.* México: Editorial Jus, 1969. 240 p. 975 G586.

6.29   Germany. Staatliche Archivverwaltung. *Übersicht über Quellen zur Geschichte Lateinamerikas in Archiven der Deutschen Demokratischen Republik.* Potsdam: Staatliche Archivverwaltung, 1971. 122 p. CD941 .G83 v.2(2).
        Latin American historical materials in archives located in the former German Democratic Republic.

6.30   Grieb, Kenneth. *Research guide to Central America and the Caribbean.* Madison, Wisconsin: University of Wisconsin Press, 1985. 431 p. F2161 .R47x 1985.
        Identifies Central American and Caribbean archival sources.

6.31   Nauman, Ann K. *A handbook of Latin American & Caribbean national archives; Guía de los archivos nacionales de América Latina y el Caribe.* Detroit, Michigan: Blaine Ethridge Books, 1983. 127 p. CD3680 .N38 1983.

6.32   Walne, Peter. *A Guide to manuscript sources for the history of Latin America and the Caribbean in the British Isles.* London: Oxford University Press; Institute of Latin American Studies, University of London, 1973. 580 p. CD1048.L35 G84 1973).

Latin America --- Caribbean

6.33   Ingram, K. E. *Manuscripts relating to Commonwealth Caribbean countries in United States and Canadian repositories.* St. Lawrence, Barbados: Caribbean Universities Press, 1975. 422 p. CD3002 .I53.

Latin America --- Mexico and Central America

6.34   Luján Múñoz, Jorge. *Guía del Archivo General de Centro América.* Ciudad de Guatemala: Ministerio de Educación, Archivo General de Centro América, 1982. 48 p. CD3691 .A73 1982.
        General guide to the Archivo General de Centro America in Guatemala City.

6.35   Rio, Ignacio del. *A Guide to the Archivo Franciscano of the National Library of Mexico.* México: Instituto de Investigaciones Bibliográficas,

Universidad Nacional Autónoma de México; Washington: Academy of American Franciscan History, 1975. 016.2713 R476.
Archival guide to materials on the Franciscan in Mexico and the southwestern United States.

6.36   *Microfilm collection of manuscripts on Middle American cultural anthropology.* Chicago: University of Chicago Library, Dept. of Photographic Reproduction, 1962. 9 p.
Guide to an important microfilm collection of manuscripts pertaining to the indigenous peoples of Mexico and Central America.

6.37   Spores, Ronald. *Colección de documentos del Archivo General de la Nación para la etnohistoria de la Mixteca de Oaxaca en el siglo XVI.* Vanderbilt University Publications in Anthropology, no. 41. Nashville, Tennessee, 1992. 104 p. F1219.8 .M59 C655x 1992.
Listing of documents in the Archivo General de la Nación, Mexico City, pertaining to the Indians of the Oaxaca region of southern Mexico.

6.38   Szewczyk, David M. *The Viceroyalty of New Spain and early independent Mexico: a guide to original manuscripts in the collections of the Rosenbach Museum & Library.* Philadelphia: Rosenbach Museum and Library, 1980. 139 p. 016.972 R723.
Catalog of manuscripts covering the period between 1540-1810 in Mexico curated at the Rosenbach Museum and Library.

6.39   Weeks, John M. *Maya ethnohistory: a guide to Spanish colonial documents at Tozzer Library, Harvard University.* Vanderbilt University Publications in Anthropology, 34. Nashville, 1987. 121 p. F1435 .T76x 1987.
Guide to documents dealing with the Maya Indians, 1520-1800.

6.40   Weeks, John M. *Mesoamerican ethnohistory in United States libraries: reconstruction of the William E. Gates collection of historical and linguistic manuscripts.* Culver City, California: Labyrinthos, 1990. 247 p. PM3008 .W44x 1990.

6.41   Weeks, John M. *Middle American Indians: a guide to the manuscript collection at Tozzer Library, Harvard University.* New York: Garland, 1985. 244 p. F1219 .T697x 1985.
Guide to the manuscript collection at Tozzer Library dealing with the ethnography, linguistics, ethnohistory, and archaeology of Mesoamerican Indians.

Latin America --- South America

6.42   Horna, Hernan. *Colombian archival sources on colonial Peru.*
Washington, D.C.: United States National Section, Pan American
Institute of Geography and History, 1971. 39 p. F3444 .H67x 1971.

6.43   Szewczyk, David M. *A Calendar of the Peruvian and other South
American manuscripts in the Philip H. & A. S. W. Rosenbach
Foundation, 1536-1914.* Philadelphia: The Philip H. & A. S. W.
Rosenbach Foundation, 1977. 190 p. 016.985 P537.

Middle East

6.44   Blumhardt, James F., and D.N. MacKenzie. *Catalogue of Pashto
manuscripts in the libraries of the British Isles: Bodleian Library, the
British Museum, Cambridge University Library, India Office Library,
John Rylands Library, School of Oriental and African Studies, and
Trinity College, Dublin.* London: Trustees of the British Museum,
1965. 147 p. Z6605.P97 B5.

6.45   *Catalogue of the Urdu, Punjabi, Pashto, and Kashmiri manuscripts
and documents in the India Office Library and Records.* London:
India Office Library and Records; British Library, 1990. 180 p. Z6621
.B85 I4 1990.

6.46   Gacek, Adam. *Catalogue of the Arabic manuscripts in the Library of
the School of Oriental and African Studies, University of London.*
London: Library of the School of Oriental and African Studies,
University of London, 1981. 306 p.

6.47   Matthews, Noe, and M. Doreen Wainwright. *A Guide to manuscripts
and documents in the British Isles relating to the Middle East and
North Africa.* Oxford; New York: Oxford University Press, 1980. 482
p. CD1048.N4 M37.

North America

6.48   *Directory of archives and manuscript repositories in the United
States.* 2 ed. Phoenix: Oryx Press, 1988. 853 p. CD3020 .D49 1988.
Provides information on 4,500 archive and manuscript collections.

6.49   *Guide to the National Archives of the United States.* Washington,
D.C.: National Archives and Records Administration, 1987. 896 p.
CD3023 .U53 1987.
Briefly describes various collections by branch of government,
bureau, or agency.

6.50   *National union catalog of manuscript collections.* Washington, D.C.:
         Library of Congress, 1959/61-1991/1993. Z6620 .U5 N3.
         National inventory of manuscript collections based on information
         submitted by reporting libraries.

6.51   Smith, Allen. *Directory of oral history collections.* Phoenix: Oryx
         Press, 1988. 141 p. D16.14 .S65x 1988.
         Details oral history collections in United States libraries,
         museums, societies, and associations.

North America --- Anthropology

6.52   Butler, Ruth L. *A Check list of manuscripts in the Edward E. Ayer
         collection.* Chicago: The Newberry Library, 1937. 295 leaves.
         Z6621.C53 A2.
         Listing of manuscripts at the Newberry Library relating to North
         and Middle American Indians.

6.53   Freeman, John F. *A Guide to manuscripts relating to the American
         Indian in the library of the American Philosophical Society.* Memoirs
         of the American Philosophical Society, 65. Philadelphia: American
         Philosophical Society, 1966. 491 p. Z1209 .F7.
         Continued by: Daythal Kendall, *A Supplement to A guide to
         manuscripts relating to the American Indian in the library of the
         American Philosophical Society* (Philadelphia: American
         Philosophical Society, 1982. 168 p. Z1209 .F7 Suppl.).

6.54   Hill, Edward E. *Guide to records in the National Archives of the
         United States relating to American Indians.* Washington, D.C.:
         National Archives and Records Service, General Services
         Administration, 1981. 467 p. E93 .H5x 1982.
         The National Archives of the United States has available for
         purchase a 962 reel set of microfilm of correspondence received by the
         Bureau of Indian Affairs between 1834 and 1880. This volume opens
         up the entire collection to students and scholars. The introduction
         identifies the variety of entries under which data may be found; a
         jurisdictional index identifies agencies; the tribal index provides the
         official list of Indian tribes from the perspective of the United States
         government; arranged chronologically by pre-Federal records, Indian
         treaties (1789-1871), and Bureau of Indian Affairs materials.

6.55   Morgan, Dale L., and George P. Hammond. *A Guide to the
         manuscript collections* [at the Bancroft Library, University of

California, Berkeley]. Berkeley: Bancroft Library; University of California Press, 19631972. 2 v. 016.97 C128g.
Includes: v. 1. *Pacific and Western manuscripts (except California),* deals with the history of the American West, with an emphasis on the nineteenth century; arranged by state or geographical region; detailed index of names, organizations, places, and subjects; v. 2. *Manuscripts relating chiefly to Mexico and Central America,* is arranged in alphabetical order by author, title, or subject; detailed indeed of persons, places, and subjects.

North America — Arctic

6.56   Bershad, Sonia S. *A Calendar of letters and documents in the collection of the Arctic Institute of North America, University of Calgary.* Calgary: Arctic Institute of North America, 1980. 90 leaves. Z6611 .S4 S36 1982.

6.57   Holland, Clive. *Manuscripts in the Scott Polar Research Institute, Cambridge, England: a catalogue.* New York: Garland, 1982. 815 p.

North America — East

6.58   *Iroquois Indians: a documentary history: guide to the microfilm collection.* Woodbridge, Connecticut; Reading, England: Research Publications, 1984. 419 p. E99 .I7 I74x 1985.
"This temporary guide is intended for use in conjunction with Iroquois Indians: A Documentary History," "Introduction by Mary A. Druke; "The documents included were compiled by a project begun in September 1978 at the D'Arcy McNickle Center for the History of the American Indian at the Newberry Library."

6.59   Judkins, Russell A. *Handbook for Archival Research in the Dr. Charles E. Bartlett Iroquois Collection.* Geneseo: State University of New York, Department of Anthropology and the Geneseo Foundation. 37, 1989. 34 p. E99 .I9 I76 1987.

6.60   Judkins, Russell A. *Iroquois studies: a guide to documentary and ethnographic resources from western New York and the Genesee Valley.* Geneseo: Department of Anthropology, State University of New York and the Geneseo Foundation, 1987. 63 p. E99.I7 J8x 1987.

6.61   Trautmann, Thomas R., and Karl Sanford Kabelac. *The Library of Lewis Henry Morgan.* Transactions of the American Philosophical Society, v. 84 (6-7). Philadelphia: American Philosophical Society, 1994. 336 p. Q11 .P6 v. 84(6-7).
Catalog and register of the papers of Lewis Henry Morgan (1818-1881) at the Department of Rare Books and Special Collections, University of Rochester Library.

6.62   White, Bruce M. *The Fur trade in Minnesota: an introductory guide
        to manuscript sources.* St. Paul: Minnesota Historical Society, 1977.
        61 p. HD9944.U46 M65.

North America — Northwest Coast

6.63   Carriker, Robert C. *Guide to the microfilm edition of the Pacific
        Northwest Tribes Missions Collection of the Oregon Province archives
        of the Society of Jesus.* Wilmington, Delaware: Scholarly Resources,
        1987. 97 p.

6.64   *Guide to Pacific Northwest Native American materials in the Melville
        Jacobs Collection and in other archival collections in the University
        of Washington Libraries.* Seattle: University of Washington Libraries,
        University of Washington, 1982. 113 p.

North America — Southeast

6.65   Anderson, William L., and James A. Lewis. *A Guide to Cherokee
        documents in foreign archives.* Metuchen, New Jersey: Scarecrow
        Press, 1983. 751 p. E99.C5 A77x 1983.
        Description of approximately 8,000 entries in 25 archives in
        Canada, France, Great Britain, Mexico, and Spain.

6.66   Chepesiuk, Ronald, and Arnold Shankman. *American Indian archival
        material: a guide to holdings in the Southeast.* Westport, Connecticut:
        Greenwood Press, 1982. 325 p. E77 .C45x 1982.
        Guide to archival and manuscript materials on North American
        Indians located in Alabama, Florida, Georgia, Kentucky, Louisiana,
        Mississippi, North Carolina, South Carolina, Tennessee, Virginia, and
        West Virginia.

6.67   Davis, Mary B. *Field notes of Clarence B. Moore's Southeastern
        archaeological expeditions, 1891-1918: a guide to the microfilm
        edition.* Bronx, New York: Huntington Free Library, Library, Museum
        of the American Indian, 1987. 32 p. C115 .M66 F43 1987.
        Microfilm publication of the field notes of Clarence Bloomfield
        Moore (1852-1936) on the archaeology and prehistory of the
        Southeast.

6.68   Kutsche, Paul. *A Guide to Cherokee documents in the northeastern
        United States.* Metuchen, New Jersey: Scarecrow Press, 1986. 531 p.
        E99.C5 K8x 1986.

North America — West

6.69   *Guide to the microfilm edition of the Washington Matthews papers:
        ten rolls; the Wheelwright Museum of the American Indian.*
        Albuquerque: University of New Mexico Press, 1985. 109 p. E76.45
        .M37 W43x 1985.

Bibliographic guide to the Washington Matthews (1843-1905) papers pertaining to the Navajo, Hidatsa, and other American Indian groups.

6.70   Powell, John Wesley. 1971. *Anthropology of the Numa: John Wesley Powell's Manuscripts on the Numic Peoples of Western North America, 1868-1880*. Don D. Fowler and Catherine S. Fowler, eds. Smithsonian contributions to anthropology, no. 14. Washington, D.C.: Smithsonian Institution Press.

6.71   Shears, Brenda L. *Field notes and maps of the Hendricks-Hodge Archaeological Expedition, 1917-1923: a guide to the microfilm edition*. Bronx, New York: Huntington Free Library and Reading Room, Museum of the American Indian, Heye Foundation, 1987. 17 p.
Publication of field notes of the Hendricks-Hodge Archaeological Expedition (1917-1923) at Hawikku site in the Zuni region of New Mexico.

6.72   Withington, Mary C. *A Catalogue of manuscripts in the collection of western Americana founded by William Robertson Coe, Yale University Library*. New Have: Yale University Press, 1952. 398 p. 016.9744 Y12.

North America --- Linguistics
6.73   Butler, Ruth L. *A Bibliographical check list of North and Middle American Indian linguistics in the Edward E. Ayer collection*. Chicago: The Newberry Library, 1941. 2 v. PM108 .E39x 1941.

6.74   McQuown, Norman A. 1989. *Catalogue of American Indian Language Manuscripts and Printed Books in the British (Museum) Library in London*. Microfilm collection of Manuscripts on Cultural Anthropology, ser. XXVIII, no. 152. Chicago: University of Chicago Library. 373 p.

Oceania
6.75   Cook, John, Nancy Lane, and Michael Piggott. *A Guide to Commonwealth government information sources*. Sydney: Pergamon Press, 1988. 89 p. J905 .C66x 1988.
A guide to Australian information sources, including archives.

6.76   *Guide to collections of manuscripts relating to the Pacific Islands*. Canberra: Pacific Manuscripts Bureau, Australian National University, 1968.
Annotated guide to the Oceanic and Melanesian items microfilmed by the Pacific Manuscripts Bureau.

6.77   *Guide to collections of manuscripts relating to Australia*. Canberra: National Library of Australia, 1965. 2 v. 016.994 C1.

6.78   Nunn, G. Raymond. *Asia and Oceania: a guide to archival and manuscript sources in the United States.* London; New York: Mansell, 1985. 5 v. DS5 .A78x 1985.

7

Guides to the Literature of Anthropology and Related Fields

Guides to the literature of anthropology and related fields can often lead you to sources that may have been neglected. These reference sources can identify many kinds of materials, including encyclopedias, dictionaries, journals, bibliographies, indexes, abstracts, and so forth. This chapter identifies some of the more useful guides to the literature of anthropology and related social sciences. Each title identified is selective, but should be sufficient for you to locate a variety of reference and other materials on many topics and areas.

For additional research guides to the literature of anthropology and related fields, consult the library catalog under the appropriate subject with the subdivision *Bibliography*. For example,

> *Anthropology --- Bibliography*
> *Latin America --- Bibliography*
> *Indians of North America --- Bibliography*

General Social Science

7.1   Li,Tze-chung. *Social science reference sources: a practical guide.* 2 ed. Westport, Connecticut: Greenwood Press, 1990. 590 p. H61 .L5x 1990.

The work is divided into three parts: Social sciences ion general; Subdisciplines of the social sciences; and Bibliographical services in the social sciences. In the first part the author discusses the nature of the social sciences, bibliographical needs of social scientists, general social science and statistical reference sources, government publications, and bibliographic data bases. The second section covers reference sources in eight social science disciplines: cultural anthropology, economics and business, education, history, law, political science, psychology, and sociology. The final section is limited to the problems of bibliographic control in the social sciences.

7.2   Webb, William H. *Sources of information in the social sciences: a guide to the literature.* 3 ed. Chicago: American Library Association, 1986. 777 p. H61 .S666x. 1986.
       The most comprehensive guide available for a variety of social sciences. Each discipline is introduced and described in a lengthy historical and bibliographic essay, followed by an annotated list of reference sources and a list of periodicals.

7.3   White, Carl M. *Sources of information in the social sciences, a guide to the literature.* 2 ed. Chicago: American Library Association, 1973. 702 p. H51 .W44x. 1973.
       The standard guide to the literature of the social sciences, including anthropology. Chapters include a bibliographic essay explaining the history and methodology of the discipline, and an annotated list of significant reference works.

The following guides pertain to the literature of anthropology and related social science disciplines.

Anthropology

7.4   Brown, Samuel R. *Finding the source in sociology and anthropology: a thesaurus-index to the reference collection.* New York: Greenwood Press, 1987. 269 p. HM51 .B76x 1987.
       Arranged by subject and serves as a guide to a variety of reference sources in anthropology.

7.5   Frantz, Charles. *The Student anthropologist's handbook: a guide to research, training, and career.* Cambridge, Massachusetts: Schenkman, 1972. 228 p. GN42 .F7.
       Introductory chapters on the nature of anthropology and the field as a profession, are followed by sections on field and laboratory research, use of libraries and museums, reference works and aids to library research, and a consideration of cultural areas and regional studies.

7.6   Kibbee, Josephine Z. *Cultural anthropology: a guide to reference and information sources.* Englewood, Colorado: Libraries Unlimited, 1991. 205 p. GN42 .K53x 1991.

7.7   Westerman, R. C. *Fieldwork in the library: a guide to research in anthropology and related area studies.* Chicago: American Library Association, 1994. 357 p. GN42 .W47x 1994.

Archaeology

7.8   Woodhead, Peter. *Keyguide to information sources in archaeology.*
London; New York: Mansell, 1985. 219 p. CC120 .W66 1985.
Guide to documentation, reference aids, important organizational
sources around the world. Part 1 is an overview of archaeology and its
literature, relationships to other subjects, careers, organizations in the
field, and education. Part 2 is a bibliographical listing of sources of
information beginning with general archaeology, archaeological
science, and regional sections. Part 3 lists selected worldwide
organizations worldwide as contact points for additional information.

7.9   Woodhead, Peter, and Geoffrey Stansfield. *Keyguide to information
sources in museum studies.* 2 ed. London; New York: Mansell, 1994.
224 p. AM5 .W66x 1994.

Biological/Physical Anthropology

7.10   Gray, J. Patrick, ed. *A Guide to primate sociobiological theory and
research.* HRAF Theoretical Information Control System, Guide 6.
New Haven: HRAF Press, 1984. 597 p. GN365.9 .G85 1984.

7.11   Wolfe, Linda D. *Field primatology: a guide to research.* Garland
Reference Library of Social Science, 356. New York: Garland, 1987.
288 p. QL737 .P9 W654 1987.

Economics

7.12   Andreano, Ralph L., Evan I. Farber, and Sabron Reynolds. *The
Student economist's handbook: a guide to sources.* Cambridge,
Massachusetts: Schenkman, 1967. 169 p. 016.33 An25.
Excellent overview of sources relating to economics; includes
chapters on statistics, library use, government documents, periodical
literature and indexes, and annotated bibliographies of major
statistical sources.

7.13   Fletcher, John. *Information sources in economics.* 2 ed. London;
Boston: Butterworths, 1984. 339 p. HB71 .I53 1984.

Education

7.14   Berry, Dorothea M. *A Bibliographic guide to educational research.* 3
ed. Metuchen, New Jersey: Scarecrow Press, 1990. 500 p. LB17 .B47x
1990.
Contains more than 250 references with descriptive annotations.

History

7.15   Howe, George F. *Guide to historical literature*. New York:
        Macmillan, 1961. 962 p. D5 .A43x 1961.
        Although dated, remains one of the most complete and
        authoritative books on the literature of history. It includes information
        on many different types of sources such as chronologies, atlases,
        bibliographies, and indexes, and is arranged by subject and country.

7.16   Poulton, Helen J. *The Historian's handbook: a descriptive guide to
        reference works*. Norman: University of Oklahoma Press, 1972. 304 p.
        D5 .P68x 1972.
        Useful for the beginning researcher although lacks the detail of
        Guide to historical literature.

7.17   Prucha, Francis P. *Handbook for research in American history: a
        guide to bibliographies and other reference works*. Lincoln: University
        of Nebraska Press, 1987. 289 p. E178 .P75x 1987.
        Useful guide to bibliographic and reference works in American
        history.

Political Science

7.18   Holler, Frederick L. *Information sources of political science*. 4 ed.
        Santa Barbara, California: ABC-Clio, 1986. 417 p. JA66 .H64 1986.

7.19   Merritt, Richard L., and Gloria J. Pyszka. *The Student political
        scientist's handbook*. Cambridge, Massachusetts: Schenkman; New
        York: Harper and Row, 1969. 171 p. 320.7 M553.

Psychology

7.20   Sarbin, Theodore R., and William C. Coe. *The Student psychologist's
        handbook: a guide to sources*. Cambridge, Massachusetts:
        Schenkman; New York: Harper and Row, 1969. 104 p. 150.72 Sa71.

Sociology

7.21   Aby, Stephen H. *Sociology: a guide to reference and information
        sources*. Littleton, Colorado: Libraries Unlimited, 1987. 231 p. HM51
        .A2x 1987.
        A general guide to the specialized reference literature of
        sociology.

7.22   Bart, Pauline, and Linda Frankel. *The Student sociologist's handbook*.
        4 ed. New York: Random House, 1986. 291 p. HM68 .B37 1986.

Africa

7.23   Baker, Philip. *International guide to African studies research; Etudes africaines: guide international de recherches.* 2 ed. London; New York: International African Institute; H. Zell, 1987. 264 p. DT19.8 .B35x 1987.

7.24   Bhatt, Purnima M. *Scholars' guide to Washington, D.C. for African studies.* Washington, D.C.: Smithsonian Institution Press, 1980. 347 p. DT3 .B52x 1980.
        Organized into two sections: Washington, D.C. based library, archival, museum, sound, map, pictorial, and machine-readable data base collections; and academic, cultural, and professional organizations that may be of assistance to researchers.

7.25   Duignan, Peter. *Guide to research and reference works on Sub-Saharan Africa.* Stanford, California: Hoover Institution Press, Stanford University, 1971. 1102 p. DT351 .D85x 1971.
        Lists some 3,100 research and reference works and introduces organizations, libraries, and archives.

7.26   Hartwig, Gerald W, and William M. O'Barr. *The Student Africanist's handbook; a guide to resources.* Cambridge, Massachusetts: Schenkman; New York: Halsted Press, 1974. 152 p. DT3 .H37x 1974.
        Includes chapters on the nature of African studies; a brief overview of the societies, cultures, and modern nations of Africa; general reference and disciplinary sources; bibliography of African regions and countries; aids for intensive research and special topics.

7.27   Skurnik, W. A. E. *Sub-Saharan Africa: a guide to information sources.* Detroit: Gale Research, 1977. 130 p. DT351 .S477x 1977.

Asia

7.28   Nunn, Godfrey R. *Asia, reference works: a select annotated guide.* London: Mansell, 1980. 365 p. DS35.2 .N86x 1980.
        Provides an annotated listing, arranged by country, of significant reference works relating to Asia, excluding the Middle East and Central Asia.

7.29   Nunn, Godfrey R. *Asia: a selected and annotated guide to reference works.* Cambridge, Massachusetts: M.I.T. Press 1971. 223 p. 016.016915 N923.

Asia --- East

7.30   Berton, Peter, and Eugene Wu. *Contemporary China; a research guide.* Stanford, California: Hoover Institution on War, Revolution, and Peace, 1967. 695 p. DS777.55 .B47x 1967.

Useful, though dated, guide for mainland China since 1949, as well as Taiwan and Hong Kong from 1949.

7.31   Herbert, P. A, and T. Chiang. *Chinese studies research methodology.* Hong Kong: Chinese Materials Center, 1982. 269 p. DS734.95 .H47x 1982.

Intended for students writing honors and postgraduate theses in the field of Chinese studies. Part 1 contains a brief survey of Chinese studies and major Chinese collections, and comments on standard and regional historical sources. Part 2 a basic research methodology manual that also gives information on transcription, Chinese dictionary arrangement, etc.; Part 3 is a selected bibliography of reference tools, including bibliographies, library catalogs, indexes, and atlases.

7.32   Kim, Han-Kyo, and Hong Kyoo Park. *Studies on Korea, a scholar's guide.* Honolulu: University Press of Hawaii, 1980. 438 p. DS902 .S7x 1980.

7.33   Kim, Hong N. *Scholars' guide to Washington D.C. for East Asian studies: China, Japan, Korea, and Mongolia.* Washington, D.C.: Smithsonian Institution Press, 1979. 413 p. DS503 .K55x 1979.

Organized into two sections: Washington, D.C. based library, archival, museum, sound, map, pictorial, and machine-readable data base collections; and academic, cultural, and professional organizations that may be of assistance to researchers.

Asia --- South

7.34   Pearson, J.D. *South Asian bibliography: a handbook and guide.* Sussex, England: Harvester Press; Atlantic Highlands, New Jersey: Humanities Press, 1979. 381 p. Z3185 .S65.

Handbook of bibliographies, finding aids, and reference works compiled by scholars of the South Asia Library Group.

Asia --- Southeast

7.35   Johnson, Donald C. *A Guide to reference materials on Southeast Asia, based on the collections in the Yale and Cornell University libraries.* New Haven: Yale University Press, 1970. 160 p. DS521 .J64x 1970.

7.36   Johnson, Donald C. *Southeast Asia: a bibliography for undergraduate libraries.* Williamsport, Pennsylvania: Bro-Dart, 1970. 59 p. DS521 .S675x 1970.

Europe

7.37   Dillon, Kenneth J. *Scholars' guide to Washington, D.C. for Central and East European studies: Albania, Austria, Bulgaria, Czechoslovakia, Germany (FRG & GDR), Greece (Ancient & Modern), Hungary, Poland, Romania, Switzerland, Yugoslavia.* Washington, D.C.: Woodrow Wilson International Center for Scholars, 1980. 329 p. DK9 .D54x 1980.
        Organized into two sections: Washington, D.C. based library, archival, museum, sound, map, pictorial, and machine-readable data base collections; and academic, cultural, and professional organizations that may be of assistance to researchers.

7.38   Grant, Steven A. *Scholar's guide to Washington, D.C. for Russian/Soviet studies: the Baltic States, Byelorussia, Central Asia, Moldavia, Russia, Transcaucasia, the Ukraine.* 2 ed. Washington, D.C.: Kennan Institute for Advanced Russian Studies of the Woodrow Wilson International Center for Scholars: Smithsonian Institution Press, 1983. 416 p. DK17 .G7x 1983.
        Organized into two sections: Washington, D.C. based library, archival, museum, sound, map, pictorial, and machine-readable data base collections; and academic, cultural, and professional organizations that may be of assistance to researchers.

7.39   Pitschmann, Louis A. *Scholars' guide to Washington, D.C., for northwest European studies.* Washington, D.C.: Woodrow Wilson International Center for Scholars: Smithsonian Institution Press, 1984. 436 p. DL5 .P5x 1984.
        Organized into two sections: Washington, D.C. based library, archival, museum, sound, map, pictorial, and machine-readable data base collections; and academic, cultural, and professional organizations that may be of assistance to researchers.

Latin America

7.40   Grow, Michael. *Scholars' guide to Washington, D.C., for Latin American and Caribbean studies.* 2 ed. Washington, D.C.: Woodrow Wilson Center Press; Baltimore: Johns Hopkins University Press, 1992. 427 p. F1408 .G76x 1992.
        Organized into two sections: Washington, D.C. based library, archival, museum, sound, map, pictorial, and machine-readable data

base collections; and academic, cultural, and professional organizations that may be of assistance to researchers.

7.41   McNeil, R.A., and B.G. Valk, eds. *Latin American studies: a basic guide to sources.* 2 ed. Lanham, Maryland: Scarecrow Press, 1990. 470 p. F1408 .L39x 1990.

Thirty-seven chapters describe the types of resources and research techniques available for the social sciences and the humanities.

Latin America --- Mexico and Central America

7.42   McGlynn, Eileen A. *Middle American anthropology: directory, bibliography, and guide to the UCLA Library collections.* Los Angeles: Latin American Center, University of California, 1975. 131 p. F1434 .M44x 1975.

Includes international directory of individuals and institutions, and bibliography of reference books, serials, monographs, and rare and non-rare books; based on the collections at the University of California at Los Angeles.

Middle East

7.43   Binder, Leonard. *The Study of the Middle East: research and scholarship in the humanities and the social science: a project of the Research and Training Committee of the Middle East Studies Association.* New York: Wiley, 1976. 648 p. 956 St94.

Includes a bibliographic survey and assessment of research and scholarship on Middle Eastern anthropology.

7.44   Grimwood-Jones, Diana. *Middle East and Islam: a bibliographical introduction.* rev. ed. Zug, Switzerland: Inter Documentation, 1979. 429 p. BP161.2 .M5x 1979.

Includes a section on anthropology.

7.45   Simon, Reeva S. *The Modern Middle East: a guide to research tools in the social sciences.* Boulder, Colorado: Westview Press, 1978. 283 p. DS44 .S56x 1978.

Selective guide for students doing research on the nineteenth and twentieth century Middle East; arranged by reference material with five main divisions: Bibliography, Periodicals, Primary source material, Reference sources, and Report literature.

North America

7.46   Haas, Marilyn L. *Indians of North America: methods and sources for library research.* Hamden, Connecticut: Library Professional

Publications, 1983. 163 p. E77 .H12x 1983.

A useful guide for beginning students about to start research on North American Indians; includes chapters on Subject headings, classification systems, and call numbers; Indexes, Abstracts; On-line data bases; Library catalogs; Handbooks, encyclopedias, dictionaries; Directories, catalogs, and dissertation sources; and Archives and government documents.

7.47   Hirschfelder, Arlene B., Mary G. Byler, and Michael A. Dorris. *Guide to research on North American Indians.* Chicago: American Library Association, 1983. 330 p. E77 .H57 1983.

7.48   Salzmann, Zdenek, and Joy Salzmann. *Guide to Native Americans of the Southwest.* Boulder, Colorado: Westview Press, 1997. 136 p.

A comprehensive introduction to indigenous cultures of the American Southwest (Arizona, New Mexico, Colorado, and Utah); provides individual sections on the main prehistoric and contemporary peoples of the region, their lifeways, art, and cultural monuments.

8

Subject Bibliographies

A bibliography is essentially a list of books and articles or essays. It may be found at the end of a journal article, thesis or dissertation, book, term paper, and so forth. Usually the contents and form are restricted in some manner. Bibliographies are very useful because someone has already done some searching and has compiled the information. Sometimes an entire book may be a bibliography, compiled by an individual or some larger group or organization. In addition, a library may have a list of its holdings published as the Library of Congress in Washington, D.C., does in the *National Union Catalog*. There are many specialized subject bibliographies of potential interest to anthropologists. These are located throughout the holdings of a library collection as well as in the reference area.

One form of subject bibliography that has assumed importance in recent years is the reproduction of catalogs of special collections in large libraries (see Chapter 5). Often representing a body of materials on a subject acquired over a long period of years, they are significant not only for the rich collections they record, but for including information on periodical articles and chapters in edited volumes. One outstanding example is the *Author and Subject Catalogues* of the Tozzer Library, formerly the Library of the Peabody Museum of Archaeology and Ethnology, at Harvard University. Other examples include bibliographies of individual authors which provide complete descriptions of a scholar's works, his contributions to scholarly journals and other collections, together with sources of biography and criticism. The increased amount of publication and disciplinary specialization have led to the production of bibliographies restricted to increasingly narrow subjects.

One type of bibliography that deserves special consideration is the guide to the literature in a broad subject field. These guides have developed as a result of the increased number and complexity of reference materials in various fields and are intended to guide the beginning research worker in the selection of pertinent sources. Many of them include the following characteristics:

- Overview of a subject area
- Description of the nature of research in the subject area
- Exhaustive listing of reference titles

- Lists of significant texts and syntheses in the field
- Lists of pertinent journals in the field, including indexing, abstracting, and review journals
- Lists of libraries, museums, and other repositories of outstanding collections
- Lists of societies and associations in the field

There are numerous books concerned with anthropology published each year. Since it would be impossible to include the titles of all the bibliographies published over a long period of time, a selection is included in the following two chapters.

The range of coverage provided by specialized subject bibliographies is illustrated in this chapter. The list is not meant to be comprehensive, but is highly selective. These bibliographies, as well as the titles listed in Chapter 9, are selective in that they signify major titles for a specific subject. All bibliographies reflect the bias of the compiler or compilers, their depth of knowledge of the subject, the amount of writing on the subject, and the time and place in which it was compiled.

For additional subject bibliographies, consult the library catalog under the appropriate subject with the subdivision *Bibliography*. For example,

Cree Indians --- Bibliography
Ethnobotany --- Bibliography
Mead, Margaret, 1901-1978 --- Bibliography
Missions --- California --- Bibliography

Guides to the Bibliographic Literature of Anthropology
8.1   Smith, Margo L., and Yvonne M. Damien, eds. *Anthropological bibliographies: a selected guide*. South Salem, New York: Redgrave, 1981. 307 p. GN25 .A58x 1981.
         A basic guide to the literature of anthropological bibliography compiled by the Library-Anthropology Resource Group in Chicago. Includes more than 3,000 bibliographies in books, articles, filmographies, and discographies, with an emphasis on recent publications. Some entries are annotated, and indexes provide access by personal name, geographic area, ethnic group, language, and subject.

Anthropology
8.2   *Bibliographic guide to anthropology and archaeology*. Boston: G.K. Hall, 1987- . 1/yr. GN1 .B52x.
         A current bibliography of books and edited volumes received by Tozzer Library at Harvard University. Arrangement is by author, title,

Tozzer Library at Harvard University. Arrangement is by author, title, and subject. It is the annual supplement to the *Author and Subject Catalogues of the Peabody Museum of Archaeology and Ethnology, Harvard University.*

Anthropology — Biobibliography

8.3   Gordan, Joan, ed. *Margaret Mead: the complete bibliography, 1925-1975.* The Hague: Mouton, 1976. 202 p. GN21 .M36 M42.

Includes 1,397 citations to printed sources, chronologically listed, with notes on variant language editions and reprints; separate notations for records, tapes and cassettes, films, and videotapes; personal name and subject indexes.

8.4   Lapointe, François, and Claire C. Lapointe. *Claude Levi-Strauss and his critics: an international bibliography of criticism (1950-1976), followed by a bibliography of the writings of Claude Levi-Strauss.* New York: Garland, 1977. 219 p. GN21.L4 L36x 1977.

Includes books, reviews, and unpublished theses on Levi-Strauss, works giving a general presentation, titles devoted to a single work of Levi-Strauss, materials comparing him with other figures, and works arranged by subject; also, a chronological bibliography of his writings, including translations, published through 1975; author and personal name indexes.

8.5   Leach, Edmund R. *Edmund Leach: a bibliography.* Royal Anthropological Institute of Great Britain and Ireland, Occasional Paper, 42. London: Royal Anthropological Institute of Great Britain and Ireland, 1990. 79 p. GN21 .L36 L43x 1990.

Based on Sir Edmund Leach's compilation of his own publications, amended with other citations after his death by Heather Weston at the request of the Royal Anthropological Institute's Council.

8.6   Nordquist, Joan. *Claude-Levi Strauss: a bibliography.* Santa Cruz, California: Reference and Research Services Press, 1987. 60 p. GN21 .L4 N66 1987.

Articles and books by Levi-Strauss translated into English are divided into four sections: books by Levi-Strauss, with reviews and critical essays; essays by Levi-Strauss, with critical essays; lists about Levi-Strauss and his work; and selected articles about his work, including articles in books published from 1970 and journal articles published from 1979.

Archaeology

8.7   American School of Prehistoric Research. *Old World bibliography.* Cambridge, Massachusetts. v. 1-8, 1948-1955. 016.302 Am35. "Recent publication mainly in Old World Palaeolithic archaeology and palaeoanthropology."

8.8   *COWA surveys and bibliographies.* Cambridge, Massachusetts: Council for Old World Archaeology. 1957-1971. 913 C1.

8.9   Hand, Richard A. 1994. *A Bookman's guide to archaeology: a compilation of over 7,000 books pertaining to the scientific study of prehistoric and historic people, their artifacts, inscriptions and monuments with prices and annotations, both bibliographical and descriptive.* Metuchen, New Jersey: Scarecrow Press, 1994. 1,022 p. CC165 .H287x 1994.

8.10   Heizer, Robert F., Thomas R. Hester, and Carol Graves. *Archaeology, a bibliographical guide to the basic literature.* New York: Garland, 1980. 434 p. CC165 .H44x 1980.

    Includes over 4,800 English language references published before 1979. Emphasis is given to the Americas, although coverage exists for Africa, Asia, and Europe.

8.11   Picken, Frances. *A Worldwide archaeological sample.* New Haven, Connecticut: Human Relations Area Files, 1983. 2 v. (274 leaves). CC165 .P52x 1983.

    Selective bibliography covering archaeological site data from 29 prehistoric sequences (Americas, 7; Europe, 7; Eastern Asia, 6; Western Asia, 5; Africa, 4). The purpose of the volume is to provide prehistoric data to be used in global comparisons of data.

Archaeology --- Gender

8.12   Bacus, Elisabeth A., *et al. A Gendered past: a critical bibliography of gender in archaeology.* Museum of Anthropology, University of Michigan, Technical Reports, 25. Ann Arbor, 1993. 172 p. GN799 .W66 G46x 1993.

Archaeology --- Historical

8.13   Cotter, John L. *Bibliography of historical sites archaeology.* Ann Arbor: University Microfilms, 1972. 3 . .

    Includes sections on historical sites artifacts and excavation reports.

8.14   Hulan, Richard, and Stephen S. Lawrence. *A Guide to the reading and study of historic site archaeology*. Museum of Anthropology, University of Missouri, Museum Brief 5. Columbia, 1970. 127 p. E51 .M87 no. 5 1976.

Archaeology --- Laboratory Techniques
8.15   Ellis, Linda. *Laboratory techniques in archaeology: a guide to the literature, 1920-1980*. New York: Garland, 1982. 419 p. CC75 .E4x 1982.

Archaeology --- Pottery
8.16   Oppelt, Norman T. *Southwestern pottery: an annotated bibliography and list of types and wares*. 2 ed. Metuchen, New Jersey: Scarecrow Press, 1988. 325 p. E78 .S7 O67x 1988.

Archaeology --- Underwater
8.17   Ruppe, Carol. *Underwater archaeology: a bibliographic guide*. Tempe: Department of Anthropology, Arizona State University, 1974. 32 p. CC77 .U5 R86x 1974.

Biological/Physical Anthropology
8.18   Comas, Juan, and Maria Villanueva. *Human biology (1929-1978): ensayo histórico bibliográfico*. México: Universidad Nacional Autónoma de México, 1982. 397 p. GN1.H8 C6x 1982.

8.19   Fay, George E. *A Bibliography of fossil man*. Magnolia, Arkansas: Department of Sociology and Anthropology, Southern State College, 1959-1964. 2 v. 016.302 F29.
       Coverage extends from 1845 to 1963; continued by G.E. Fay, *A bibliography of fossil man; Supplement 1* (Greeley: Colorado State College, Museum of Anthropology, 1969. 2 v.).

8.20   Finnegan, Michael, and M.A. Faust. *Bibliography of human and non-human non-metric variation*. Amherst: Department of Anthropology, University of Massachusetts, 1974. 133 p. GN62.8 .F56x 1974 .

8.21   Musiker, Reuben, comp. *The Australopithecinae: bibliography*. Cape Town. University of Cape Town Libraries, 1969. 49 p. 016.3011 M973.

Biological/Physical Anthropology --- History
8.22   Spencer, Frank. *Ecce homo: an annotated bibliographic history of*

physical anthropology. New York: Greenwood Press, 1986. 495 p.
GN60 .S64x 1986.

Selective bibliography of books and articles dealing with
primatology, paleoanthropology, and other aspects of physical
anthropology; arranged in four major sections: ancient times through
the seventeenth century, eighteenth, nineteenth, and twentieth
centuries.

8.23   Spencer, Frank. *History of physical anthropology: an encyclopedia.*
New York: Garland, 1996. 2 v. GN50.4 .H57 1982.

Biological/Physical Anthropology --- Primatology

8.24   Akins, Faren R., *et al. Behavioral development of nonhuman
primates: an abstracted bibliography.* New York: IFI/Plenum, 1980.
304 p. 599.8 B3935.

8.25   Ruch, Theodore C. *Bibliographia primatologica: a classified
bibliography of primates other than man.* Springfield, Illinois;
Baltimore: C.C. Thomas, 1941. Z7996 .P85 R899b 1941.

Includes sections on: Anatomy, embryology and quantitative
morphology; physiology, pharmacology and psychobiology; primate
phylogeny and miscellanea.

8.26   Swanson, Janice C., *et al. Environmental enrichment information
resources for nonhuman primates: 1987-1992.* Beltsville, Maryland:
U.S. Department of Agriculture, National Agricultural Library;
Bethesda: National Institutes of Health, National Library of Medicine;
Seattle: Primate Information Center, University of Washington, 1992.
105 p. Government Publication A 17.2: E 89 x.

Contents include: How to use this document; General; Regulatory;
Facility design/development; Plans/programs; Enrichment
techniques/devices; Training; Well-being assessment; Behavior;
Breeding; Miscellaneous; Great apes; Family: *Pinged;* Chimpanzees;
Gorillas; Orangutans; Lesser apes; Family: *Hylobatidae;* Gibbons; Old
World monkeys; Family: *Cercopithecidae;* Baboons; Macaques; Other
Old World monkeys; New World monkeys; Marmosets and tamarins;
Family: *Callitrichidae;* Cebid monkeys; Family: *Cebidae;* Prosimians;
Lemurs; Family: *Lemuridae;* Other prosimians; Primate information
sources; Journals containing primate information.

Cultural Anthropology --- Applied Anthropology

8.27   Cernea, Michael M. 1994. *Sociology, anthropology, and development:
an annotated bibliography of World Bank publications, 1975-1993.*

Washington, D.C.: World Bank, 1994. 301 p. Z7164 .S68 C47.

8.28   Downing, Theodore E., and Gilbert Kushner, eds. *Human rights and anthropology.* Cambridge, Massachusetts: Cultural Survival, 1988. 200 p. GN33.6 .H85x 1988.

8.29   Tippett, Alan R., comp. *Bibliography for cross-cultural workers.* South Pasadena, California: William Carey Library, 1971. 252 p. GN315 .T57x 1971.

8.30   Van Willigen, John. *Anthropology in use: a bibliographic chronology of the development of applied anthropology.* Pleasantville, New York: Redgrave, 1980. 150 p. GN397.5 .V3x 1980.
        Organized chronologically with author and geographic indexes.

Cultural Anthropology --- Asian-Americans
8.31   Matsuda, Mitsugu. *The Japanese in Hawaii: an annotated bibliography of Japanese Americans.* Honolulu: Social Sciences and Linguistics Institute, University of Hawaii; University Press of Hawaii, 1975. 304 p. DU624.7 .J3 M38x 1975.

8.32   Ong, Paul M., William Wong Lum. *Theses and dissertations on Asians in the United States, with selected references to other overseas Asians.* Davis: Asian American Studies, Department of Applied Behavioral Sciences, University of California, 1974. 113 p. E184 .O6 .O54x 1974.
        Lists 1,372 items in topical arrangement with key word and author indexes.

8.33   Saito, Shiro. *Filipinos overseas: a bibliography.* Staten Island, New York: Center for Migration Studies, 1977. 156 p. DS665 .S2x 1977.

8.34   Saito, Shiro. *Philippine-American relations: a guide to manuscript sources in the United States.* Westport, Connecticut: Greenwood Press, 1982. 256 p. 016.9914 P538.

Cultural/Social Anthropology --- Cross-Cultural Studies
8.35   Bonta, Bruce. *Peaceful peoples: an annotated bibliography.* Metuchen, New Jersey: Scarecrow Press, 1993. 288 p. GN378 .B66x 1993.
        Interesting bibliography of cross-cultural studies of peace (philosophy) and aggressiveness (psychology).

Cultural/Social Anthropology --- Culture Change

8.36   Keesing, Felix M. *Culture change: an analysis and bibliography of anthropological sources to 1952.* Stanford: Stanford University Press, 1953. 242 p. GN24 .K44x 1953.
Lists 4,212 entries and includes a chronological analysis of the progress of anthropological thought and a critique of research.

8.37   Kerri, James N. *American Indians (U.S. & Canada): a bibliography of contemporary studies and urban research.* Monticello, Illinois: Council of Planning Librarians, 1973. 165 p. HT166 .C6x 376-377.

Cultural/Social Anthropology --- Economic Anthropology

8.38   Pas, H. T. van der. *Economic anthropology 1940-1972: an annotated bibliography.* Oosterhout: Anthropological Publications, 1973. 221 p. GN448 .P37x 1973.
Arranged chronological and by author, and Includes extensive annotations; author index.

Cultural/Social Anthropology --- Educational Anthropology

8.39   Burnett, Jacquetta H. *Anthropology and education: an annotated bibliographic guide.* New Haven: HRAF Press; Council on Anthropology and Education, 1974. 159 p. LB45 .B87x 1974.

8.40   Rosenstiel, Annette. *Education and anthropology: an annotated bibliography.* New York: Garland, 1977. 646 p. LB45 .R67x 1977.
International bibliography of over 3,400 books, articles, dissertations, etc., pertaining to the development, trends, theoretical issues, and methodology of anthropology and education.

Cultural/Social Anthropology --- Ethnographic Art

8.41   Berlo, Janet C. *The Art of pre-Hispanic Mesoamerica: an annotated bibliography.* Boston: G.K. Hall, 1985. 272 p. F1219.3 .A7 B38x 1985.
Contains 1,533 entries in English, Spanish, German, French, and Italian, with brief descriptive and critical annotations; detailed subject and place name index provides access through specific archaeological sites, subjects, symbolic elements, media, deities, and techniques.

8.42   Burt, Eugene C., ed. *African art five-year cumulative bibliography: mid-1983 through 1988.* Seattle: Data Arts, 1990. 170 p. N7380 .Z99 A43x 1990.

8.43   Burt, Eugene C. *An Annotated bibliography of the visual arts of East Africa.* Bloomington: Indiana University Press, 1980. 371 p. N7397 .B8x 1980.

8.44   Burt, Eugene C. *Bibliography of ethnoarts bibliographies.* rev. ed. Seattle: Data Arts, 1990. 40 p. N5311 .B877x 1990.

8.45   Burt, Eugene C., comp. *Bibliography of tribal arts bibliographies: Africa, the Americas, Oceania.* Seattle: Data Arts, 1985. 47 p. Z5956.P68 B85y 1985.
        List based on a series of articles published in the *Tribal Arts Review* during 1985 and 1986.

8.46   Burt, Eugene C. *Ethnoart: Africa, Oceania, and the Americas: a bibliography of theses and dissertations.* New York: Garland, 1988. 212 p. N5311 .B88 1988.

8.47   Burt, Eugene C. *Native American art: five-year cumulative bibliography: mid-1983 through 1988.* Seattle: Data Arts, 1990. 157 p. E98 .A7 N38x 1990.

8.48   Burt, Eugene C. *Oceanic art five-year cumulative bibliography: mid-1983 through 1988.* Seattle: Data Arts, 1990. 55 p. N7399.7 .O24x 1990.

8.49   Burt, Eugene C. *Serials guide to ethnoart: a guide to serial publications on visual arts of Africa, Oceania, and the Americas.* New York: Greenwood Press, 1990. 368 p. N5310.7 .B87 1990.

8.50   Parezo, Nancy J., Ruth M. Perry, and Rebecca S. Allen. 1990. *Southwest Native American arts and material culture: a guide to research.* Studies in Ethnic Art, 1. New York: Garland, 1990. 3 v. E78 .S7 P37x 1991.

8.51   *Tribal and ethnic art.* Oxford, England; Santa Barbara, California: Clio Press, 1982. 99 p. N5311 .T73x 1982.
        "Contains 900 abstracts of books, available dissertations, periodical articles, and exhibition catalogues with essays or texts, published between 1972 and 1979."

Cultural/Social Anthropology --- Ethnomusicology
8.52   Frisbie, Charlotte J. *Music and dance research of Southwestern United States Indians: past trends, present activities, and suggestions for*

future research. Detroit: Information Coordinators, 1977. 109 p. 781.7173 F917.
Contains bibliographic essays arranged by decade from 1880 to 1976.

8.53 Kunst, Jaap. *Ethnomusicology: a study of its nature, its problems, methods and representative personalities to which is added a bibliography.* 3 ed. The Hague: M. Nijhoff, 1974. 303 p. 781 K963c.

8.54 Nettl, Bruno. *Reference materials in ethnomusicology: a bibliographic essay.* 2 ed. Detroit: Information Coordinators, 1967. 54 p. ML128 .E8 N5 1967.

8.55 Schuursma, Ann. *Ethnomusicology research: a select annotated bibloiography.* Garland Library of Music Ethnology, 1. New York: Garland, 1992. 173 p. ML128 .E8 S4 1992.

Cultural/Social Anthropology --- Ethnoscience
8.56 Conklin, Harold C. *Folk classification: a topically arranged bibliography of contemporary and background references through 1971.* rev. ed. New Haven: Department of Anthropology, Yale University, 1980. 521 p. GN468.4 .C66x 1980.
Includes approximately 5,000 references to analyses of specific systems of folk classifications, discussions and comparisons of such analyses, and theoretical and practical background on classification in general.

Cultural/Social Anthropology --- Folklore
8.57 Aarne, Antti. *The Types of the folktale: a classification and bibliography.* 2 ed. Helsinki: Suomalainen Tiedeakatemia, 1973. 588 p. GR1 .F55 no.74.
Antti Aarne's *Verzeichnis der Marchentypen,* possibly the most important source for the study of folklore; translated and enlarged by Stith Thompson.

8.58 Brunvand, Jan H. *Folklore: a study and research guide.* New York: St. Martin's Press, 1976. 144 p. GR66 .B78x 1976.

8.59 MacGregor-Villareal, Mary. *Brazilian folk narrative scholarship: a critical survey and selective annotated bibliography.* Garland Folklore Library, 8. New York: Garland, 1994. 264 p. GR133 .B6 M27x 1994.

8.60   Sienkewicz, Thomas J. *World mythology: an annotated guide to collections and anthologies.* Lanham, Maryland: Scarecrow Press, 1996. 480 p. BL311 .S54x 1996.

Provides bibliographic access to English-language translations, retellings, and summaries of myths from cultures around the world, including Africa, Asia, Oceania, and the Americas.

Cultural/Social Anthropology --- Hispanic-Americans

8.61   Robinson, Barbara J., and J. Cordell Robinson. *The Mexican American: a critical guide to research aids.* Greenwich, Connecticut: JAI Press, 1980. 287 p. E184.M5 R6x 1980.

8.62   Talbot, Jane M., and Gilbert R. Cruz. *A Comprehensive Chicano bibliography, 1960-1972.* Austin, Texas: Jenkins, 1973. 375 p. E184.M5 T3x 1973.

8.63   Trejo, Arnulfo D. *Bibliografía chicana: a guide to information sources.* Detroit: Gale, 1975. 193 p. E184 .M5 T74x 1975.

8.64   Woods, Richard D., comp. *Mexican autobiography: an annotated bibliography; La autobiografía mexicana: una bibliografía razonada.* New York: Greenwood Press, 1988. 228 p. CT553 .W66x 1988.

8.65   Woods, Richard D. *Reference materials on Mexican Americans: an annotated bibliography.* Metuchen, New Jersey: Scarecrow Press, 1976. 190 p. E184 .M5 W66.

Cultural/Social Anthropology --- History of Anthropology

8.66   Erickson, Paul A. *History of anthropology bibliography.* Halifax, Nova Scotia, Canada: Department of Anthropology, Saint Mary's University, 1984. 142 p. GN17.Z99 E74x 1984.

Updated by annual supplements of *History of anthropology bibliography* (Halifax, Nova Scotia: Department of Anthropology, Saint Mary's University, v. 1- , 1985- . 1/yr.).

8.67   Kemper, Robert V., and John F.S. Phinney. *The History of anthropology: a research bibliography.* New York: Garland, 1977. 212 p. GN17 .K45x 1977.

Classified bibliography of more than 2,400 entries arranged in five primary sections: General sources on the history of anthropology (52 entries); Background (546 entries); Modern anthropology, i.e., post-1900 (1,786 entries); Related social sciences (39 entries); and Bibliographical sources (16 entries). Each section is subdivided by subject, geographic area, and personality; author index. A useful beginning guide for the student of the history of anthropology.

8.68 Voget, Fred W. *A History of ethnology.* New York: Holt, Rinehart, and Winston, 1975. 879 p. GN17 .V63.
General, historical review of the development of anthropology with an extensive list of sources and indexing.

Cultural/Social Anthropology --- Medical Anthropology
8.69 Driver, Edwin D. *The sociology and anthropology of mental illness: a reference guide.* rev. ed. Amherst: University of Massachusetts Press, 1972. 487 p. GN17 .V63 1972.

8.70 Favazza, Armando R., and Mary Oman. *Anthropological and cross-cultural themes in mental health: an annotated bibliography, 1925-1974.* Columbia: University of Missouri Press, 1977. 386 p. 061 M69 v.65.
Includes 3,600 English-language entries in chronological arrangement based on 68 journals, with descriptive abstracts; author and subject indexes. Continued by: A.R. Favazza, and A.D. Faheem, *Themes in cultural psychiatry: an annotated bibliography, 1975-1980* (Columbia: University of Missouri Press, 1982. 194 p. 016.61689 F277).

8.71 Harrison, Ira E., and Sheila Cosminsky. *Traditional medicine: implications for ethnomedicine, ethnopharmacology, maternal and child health, mental health, and public health: an annotated bibliography of Africa, Latin America, and the Caribbean.* New York: Garland, 1976-1984. 229, 327 p. GN477 .H36x 1976.
Includes a general section followed by sections on Africa and the Latin American/Caribbean area; each section is subdivided by topics such as health care delivery, mental health, ethnomedicine, etc.; author indexes at end of sections and country index at end of volume.

Cultural/Social Anthropology --- Methods --- Fieldwork
8.72 Gravel, Pierre B., Robert B. Marks Ridinger. *Anthropological fieldwork: an annotated bibliography.* New York: Garland, 1988. 241 p. GN346 .G7x 1988.

8.73 Stein, Evan. *The Use of computers in folklore and folk music: a preliminary bibliography.* Washington, D. C.: Library of Congress, Archive of Folk Song, 1979. 12 p. ML128.E8 S75x 1979.

Cultural/Social Anthropology --- Methods --- Village Studies

8.74   Moore, Mick, John Connell, and Claire M. Lambert, comps. *Village studies data analysis and bibliography.* Epping: Bowker Institute of Development Studies, Village Studies Programme at University of Sussex, 1976-1978. 2 v. Z7165.I6 I54 1976.

Bibliography of single village studies undertaken between 1950 and 1975 as part of the Village Studies Programme at the Institute of Development Studies. The term "village studies" refers to life in a single village based on research conducted there. Contents include: v. 1. India, 1950-1975; v. 2. Africa, Middle East and North Africa, Asia (excluding India), Pacific Islands, Latin America, West Indies and the Caribbean, 1950-1975.

Cultural/Social Anthropology --- Political Anthropology

8.75   Divale, William T. *Warfare in primitive societies: a bibliography.* rev. ed. Santa Barbara, California: ABC-Clio, 1973. 123 p. GN497 .D58x 1973.

Part 1 is divided into 16 theoretical or topical sections (e.g., biological; factors, demographic factors, scalping, war rituals, etc.) and Part 2 comprises sections on seven major regions and lists sources on warfare of various peoples of these regions.

Cultural/Social Anthropology --- Race and Ethnic Relations

8.76   Bentley, G. Carter. *Ethnicity and nationality: a bibliographic guide.* Seattle: University of Washington Press, 1981. 381 p. GN495.6 .B46x 1981.

8.77   Buenker, John D., and Nicholas C. Burckel. *Immigration and ethnicity: a guide to information sources.* Detroit: Gale, 1977. 305 p. JV6465 .B8x 1977.

Approximately 1,400 books, articles, and doctoral dissertations emphasizing non-American Indian and African-American immigration to the United States.

8.78   Cashman, Marc, ed. *Bibliography of American ethnology.* Rye, New York: Todd Publications, 1976. 304 p. E184.A1 C347x 1976.

Arranged according to General Ethnology, American Indians, Black Americans, and Other Minorities.

8.79   Kinloch, Graham C. *Race and ethnic relations: an annotated bibliography.* New York: Garland, 1984. 250 p. E184.A1 K54x 1984.

8.80   Kinloch, Graham C. *Social stratification: an annotated bibliography.*
        New York: Garland, 1987. 357 p. HT609 .K548x 1987.

8.81   Oaks, Priscilla. *Minority studies: a selective annotated bibliography.*
        Boston: G. K. Hall, 1975. 303 p. E184.A1 O2x 1975.

Cultural/Social Anthropology --- Religion

8.82   Choquette, Diane. *New religious movements in the United States and
        Canada: a critical assessment and annotated bibliography.* Westport,
        Connecticut: Greenwood Press, 1985. 235 p. BL2525 .C46x 1985.

8.83   Cornell University. Libraries. *Witchcraft: Catalogue of the Witchcraft
        Collection in Cornell University Library.* Millwood, New York: KTO
        Press, 1977. 644 p.

8.84   Diehl, Katharine S. *Religions, mythologies, folklores: an annotated
        bibliography.* 2 ed. New York: Scarecrow Press, 1962. 573 p. 016.2
        D563a.

8.85   Melton, J. Gordon, and Isotta Poggi. *Magic, witchcraft, and paganism
        in America: a bibliography: compiled from the files of the Institute for
        the Study of American Religion.* New York: Garland, 1992. 408 p.
        016.2 D563a.

8.86   Mitchell, Robert C. , and Harold W. Turner. *A comprehensive
        bibliography of modern African religious movements.* Evanston,
        Illinois, Northwestern University Press, 1966. 132 p. BL2400 .M5x
        1966.

8.87   Porter, Jack N., comp. *Jews and the cults: bibliography.* Fresh
        Meadows, New York: Biblio Press, 1981. 49 p. BM534 .P67x 1981.
            Annotated bibliography of relations among Judaism and Christian
        sects.

8.88   Richmond, Mary L. H. *Shaker literature: a bibliography.* Hancock,
        Massachusetts: Shaker Community; Hanover, New Hampshire:
        University Press of New England, 1977. 2 v. BX9771 .R53x 1977.

8.89   Springer, Nelson P. , and A.J. Klassen. *Mennonite bibliography,
        1631-1961.* Scottdale, Pennsylvania: Herald Press, 1977. 2 v.
        BX8121.2 .S67x 1977.
            Includes 28,000 entries arranged by subject; v. 1. International,
        Europe, Latin America, Asia, Africa; v. 2. North America; indexes.

8.90   Turner, Harold W. *Bibliography of new religious movements in primal societies.* Boston: G. K. Hall, 1977-1992. 6 v. BL80.2 .T87x 1977.
        Includes Black Africa and North America.

8.91   Weigle, Marta, comp. *A Penitente bibliography.* Albuquerque: University of New Mexico Press, 1976. 162 p. BX3653.U6 W398x 1976.
        Annotated list of materials dealing with the Hermanos Penitentes of the American Southwest.

8.92   Zaretsky, Irving I., and Cynthia Shambaugh. *Spirit possession and spirit mediumship in Africa and Afro-America: an annotated bibliography.* New York: Garland, 1978. 443 p. BF1242.A35 Z37x 1978.
        International bibliography of 2,054 titles written between mid-nineteenth century and 1977.

Cultural/Social Anthropology --- Urban Anthropology

8.93   Van Willigen, John. *The Indian city: a bibliographic guide to the literature on urban India.* New Haven: Human Relations Area Files, 1979. 2 v. Z5942 .V36.

Cultural/Social Anthropology --- Women

8.94   Ballou, Patricia K. *Women: a bibliography of bibliographies.* 2 ed. Boston, Massachusetts: G.K. Hall, 1986. 268 p. HQ1121 .B28x 1986.
        Annotated bibliography of English language books, articles, essays, and dissertations published since 1970.

8.95   Byrne, Pamela R., and Suzanne R. Ontiveros, eds. *Women in the Third World: a historical bibliography.* Santa Barbara, California: ABC-Clio Information Services, 1986. 152 p. HQ1870.9 .B96x 1986.

8.96   Goodwater, Leanna. *Women in antiquity: an annotated bibliography.* Metuchen, New Jersey: Scarecrow Press, 1975. 171 p. HQ1134 .G6x 1975.

Linguistics

8.97   Blass, Birgit A., Dora E. Johnson, and William W. Gage. *A Provisional survey of materials for the study of neglected languages.* Washington, D.C.: Center for Applied Linguistics, 1969. 414 p. P121 .B467x 1969.
        Annotated list of over 2,000 items representing 382 languages and dialects.

8.98   Gazdar, Gerald, Ewan Klein, and Geoffrey K. Pullum. *A Bibliography of contemporary linguistic research.* New York: Garland, 1978. 425 p. P121 .G39x 1978.

8.99   Gipper, Helmut, and Hans Schwarz. *Bibliographisches Handbuch zur Sprachinhaltsforschung.* Köln: Westdeutscher Verlag, 1962-1989. 8 v. P121 .G48x 1962.

8.100   Gordon, W. Terrence. *Semantics: a bibliography, 1986-1991.* Metuchen, New Jersey; London: Scarecrow Press, 1992. 280 p. P325 .G674x .
        Continues: W.T. Gordon, *Semantics: a bibliography, 1965-1978* (Metuchen, New Jersey: Scarecrow Press, 1980. 307 p.); and W.T. Gordon, *Semantics: a bibliography, 1979-1985* (Metuchen, New Jersey: Scarecrow Press, 1987. 292 p.).

8.101   Hewes, Gordon W. *Language origins: a bibliography.* 2 ed. The Hague: Mouton, 1975. 2 v. P116 .H4x 1975.
        Includes more than 11,000 entries, including works from anthropology as well as psychology, philosophy, speech pathology, animal communication behavior, and linguistics.

8.102   Wares, Alan C. *Bibliography of the Summer Institute of Linguistics.* Dallas, Texas: Summer Institute of Institute, 1992. 603 p. P116 .H4x 1975.
        Compilation of works dealing with linguistics, ethnography, and applied anthropology, published by members of the Summer Institute of Linguistics; includes technical articles arranged by author, and vernacular works arranged by country.

Linguistics --- Methods

8.103   Pop, Sever. *Bibliographie des questionnaires linguistiques.* Louvain: Commission d'Enquete Linguistique, 1955. 168 p. 016.4 P81.
        Chronological listing of questionnaires used in linguistic field research.

8.104   Wellisch, Hans H. *Transcription and transliteration: an annotated bibliography on conversion of scripts.* Silver Spring, Maryland: Institute of Modern Languages, 1975. 133 p. P226 .W4x 1975.

9

Regional Bibliographies

Bibliographies listed in Chapter 8 have a subject or topical emphasis. In this chapter, bibliographies with a more regional or geographical emphasis are identified. For additional regional bibliographies, consult the library catalog under the appropriate subject with the subdivision *Bibliography*. For example,

Latin America -- Bibliography
Indians of North America -- Bibliography

Africa

9.1   Bischof, Phyllis, *et al. Bibliographies for African studies, 1987-1993*. London New York: Hans Zell Publishers, 1994. 176 p. DT351 .B53x 1994.

Some 1,000 bibliographies published as books, articles, parts of edited volumes, etc., relating to Sub-Saharan Africa; continues: Y. Scheven, *Bibliographies for African studies, 1970-1975* (Waltham, Massachusetts: Crossroads Press, 1977. 159 p.); Y. Scheven, *Bibliographies for African studies, 1976-1979* (Los Angeles, California: Crossroads Press, 1980. 142 p.); Y. Scheven, Bibliographies for African studies, 1980-1983 (Oxford, England: Hans Zell; New York: Saur, 1984. 300 p.); and Y. Scheven, *Bibliographies for African studies, 1970-1986* (London; New York: Hans Zell, 1988. 615 p.).

9.2   Forde, C. Daryll. *Select annotated bibliography of tropical Africa.* New York, 1956; New York: Kraus, 1969. 1 v. 016.96 In8.

9.3   Glazier, Kenneth M. *Africa south of the Sahara; a select and annotated bibliography, 1964-1968.* Stanford, California: Hoover Institution Press, 1969. 139 p. 016.967 G469af.

Lists 200 English-language books published or reissued between

1964 and 1968, with brief annotations; continues K.M. Glazier, *Africa south of the Sahara, 1958-1963* (Stanford, California: Hoover Institution on War, Revolution, and Peace, Stanford University, 1964).

9.4   Hess, Robert L., and Dalvan M. Coger. *Semper ex Africa ... A bibliography of primary source for nineteenth-century tropical Africa as recorded by explorers, missionaries, traders, travelers, administrators, military men, adventurers, and others.* Stanford, California: Hoover Institution on War, Revolution, and Peace, 1972. 800 p. DT351 .H47x 1972.

9.5   Panofsky, Hans E. *A bibliography of Africana.* Westport, Connecticut: Greenwood Press, 1975. 350 p. DT3 .P28x 1975.
    A basic handbook for students of Africa; sections include: The Study of Africa; Bibliographies and serials; Guide to resources by subject and discipline; Guide to resources in non-African areas; Guide to resources in African nations; and On collecting and disseminating Africana.

9.6   Pearson, J. D. *International African bibliography, 1973-1978: books, articles, and papers in African studies.* London; New York: Mansell, 1982. 343 p. DT3 .P388x 1982.
    A cumulation of the International African Institute's quarterly *International African bibliography,* for the period 1973 to 1978. Organization is generally geographical, with each region or country subdivided into categories, ranging from general to specific disciplines, such as archaeology.

Africa -- Archaeology

9.7   *Africa since 1914: a historical bibliography.* Santa Barbara, California: ABC-Clio Information Services, 1985. 402 p. DT351 .A365x 1985.

9.8   Anderson, Irene. *Rock paintings and petroglyphs of South and Central Africa, 1959-1970: a bibliography.* Johannesburg: Department of Bibliography, Librarianship and Typography, University of Witwatersrand, 1971. 25 p.

9.9   Craig, Barbara J. *Rock paintings and petroglyphs of South and Central Africa, a bibliography of prehistoric art.* Cape Town: School of Librarianship, University of Cape Town, 1947. 58 p. 016.30243 C844.

9.10   Friede, H. M. *A Select bibliography of Southern African archaeo-metallurgical literature, 1822-1982.* Johannesburg: University of the Witwatersrand, 1983. 8 leaves.

9.11   Movius, Hallam L. *A Bibliography of Early Man, Pleistocene studies and Palaeolithic archaeology in southern, equatorial, and eastern Africa.* New York: Wenner-Gren Foundation for Anthropological Research, 1954. 126 p.

9.12   Ridinger, Robert B.M. *African archaeology: a selected bibliography.* New York: G.K. Hall; Toronto: Maxwell Macmillan Canada; Maxwell Macmillan International, 1993. 311 p. GN861 .R53x 1993.

9.13   Seeley, J. A. *Conservation in Sub-Saharan Africa: an introductory bibliography for the social sciences.* Cambridge: African Studies Centre, Cambridge University, 1985. 207 p. Z5863.P7 S43y 1985.

9.14   Vogel, Joseph O. *Great Zimbabwe: the Iron Age in South Central Africa.* Research Guides to Ancient Civilizations, 2. New York: Garland, 1994. 299 p. DT3025 .G84 V64x 1994.

Africa -- Cultural/Social Anthropology

9.15   *Ethnographic survey of Africa: Central Africa, Belgian Congo.* London: International African Institute, 1954-1960. pt. 1-5.
        Multivolume collection of basic African ethnographies published by the International African Institute; contents include: 1. J. Vansina, *Les tribus Ba-Kuba et les peuplades apparentees* (1954. 64 p.); 2. H. van Geluwe, *Les Bira et les peuplades limitrophes* (1957. 165 p.); 3. H. van Geluwe, *Mamvu-Mangutu et Balese-Mvuba* (1957. 195 p.); 4. H. Burssens, *Les peuplades de l'entre Congo-Ubangi (Ngbandi, Ngbaka, Mbandja, Ngombe, et Gens d'Eau)* (1958. 219 p.); 5. H. van Geluwe, *Les Bali et les peuplades apparentees* (1960. 130 p.).

9.16   *Ethnographic survey of Africa: East Central Africa.* London: International African Institute, 1950-1977, pt. 1-18.
        Contents include: 1. M. Douglas, *Peoples of the Lake Nyasa region* (London: Oxford University Press, 1950. 131 p.); 2. W. Whiteley, *Bemba and related peoples of Northern Rhodesia; J. Slaski, Peoples of the lower Luapula Valley* (1950. 100 p.); 3. A.H.J. Prins, *The Coastal tribes of the North-Eastern Bantu* (1952. 138 p.); 4. A. Butt, *The Nilotes of the Anglo-Egyptian Sudan and Uganda* (1952. 198 p.); 5. J. Middleton, *The Central tribes of the north-eastern Bantu; the Kikuyu, including Embu, Meru, Mbere, Chuka, Mwimbi,*

Tharaka, and the Kamba of Kenya (1953. 300 p.); 6. G.W.B.
Huntingford, *The Northern Nilo-Hamites* (1953. 111 p.); 7. P.
Gulliver, and P.H. Gulliver. *The Central Nilo-Hamites* (1953. 106 p.);
8. Huntingford, G.W.B., *The Southern Nilo-Hamites* (1953. 152 p.); 9.
P.T.W. Baxter, and A. Butt, *The Azande, and related peoples of the
Anglo-Egyptian Sudan and Belgian Congo* (1953. 152 p.); 10. J. S. La
Fontaine, *The Gisu of Uganda* (1959. 68 p.); 11. M.C. Fallers. *The
Eastern lacustrine Bantu (Ganda and Soga)*(1960. 86 p.); 12. A.H.J.
Prins, *The Swahili-speaking peoples of Zanzibar and the East African
Coast: Arabs, Shirazi and Swahili* (1967. 146 p.); 13. B.K. Taylor, *The
Western lacustrine Bantu (Nyoro, Toro Nyankore, Kiga, Haya, and
Zinza, with sections on the Amba and Konjo)*(1962. 159 p.); 14. M.
d'Hertefelt, *Les anciens royaumes de la zone interlacustre
meridionale, Rwanda, Burundi, Buha* (1962. 252 p.); 15. R.G. Willis,
*The Fipa and related peoples of south-west Tanzania and north-east
Zambia* (1966. 82 p.); 16. T.O. Beidelman, *The Matrilineal peoples of
Eastern Tanzania: Zaramo, Luguru, Kaguru, Ngulu, etc.* (1967. 94 p.);
17. R.G. Abrahams, *The Peoples of Greater Unyamwezi, Tanzania
(Nyamwezi, Sukuma, Sumbwa, Kimbu, Konongo)*(1967. 92 p.); 18. S.F.
Moore and P. Puritt, *The Chagga and Meru of Tanzania* (1977. 140
p.).

9.17   *Ethnographic survey of Africa. North Eastern Africa.* London:
       International African Institute, 1955-1974. pt. 1-4.
          Contents include: 1. I.M. Lewis, *Peoples of the Horn of Africa:
       Somali, Afar, and Saho* (1955. 200 p.); 2. G.W.B. Huntingford, *The
       Galla of Ethiopia: the kingdoms of Kafa and Janjero* (London. 1955.
       156 p.); 3. E. Cerulli, *Peoples of south-west Ethiopia and its
       borderland* (1956. 148 p.); 4. W.A. Shack, *The Central Ethiopians
       Amhara, Tigrina and related peoples* (1974. 152 p.);

9.18   *Ethnographic survey of Africa: Southern Africa.* London:
       International African Institute, 1952-1954. pt. 1-4.
          Contents include: 1. H. Kuper, *The Swazi* (1952. 89 p.); 2. V.G.J.
       Sheddick, *The Southern Sotho* (1953. 87 p.); 3. I. Schapera, *The
       Tswana* (1953. 80 p.); 4. H. Kuper, A.J.B. Hughes, and J. van Velsen,
       The Shona and Ndebele of southewrn Rhodesia (1954. 131 p.).

9.19   *Ethnographic survey of Africa. West Central Africa.* London:
       International African Institute, 1951-1953. pt. 1-4.
          Contents include: 1. M. McCulloch, *The Southern Lunda and
       related peoples (Northern Rhodesia, Belgian Congo, Angola* (1951.
       110 p.); 2. M. McCulloch, *The Ovimbundu of Angola* (1952. 50 p.); 3.

V.W. Turner, *The Lozi peoples of north-western Rhodesia* (1952. 62 p.); 4. M.A. Jaspan, *The Ila-Tonga peoples of north-western Rhodesia* (1953. 72 p.).

9.20   *Ethnographic survey of Africa. Western Africa.* London: International African Institute, 1950-1960. pt. 1-15.

        Contents include: 1. M. Manoukian, *Akan and Ga-Adangme peoples of the Gold Coast* (London: Oxford University Press, 1950. 112 p.); 2. M. McCulloch, *The Peoples of Sierra Leone Protectorate* (1950. 102 p.); 3. C.D. Forde, *The Ibo and Ibibio-speaking peoples of south-easterm Nigeria* (London: Oxford University Press, 1950. 94 p.); 4. C.D. Forde, *The Yoruba-speaking peoples of south-western Nigeria* (1951. 102 p.); 5. M. Manoukian, *Tribes of the northern territories of the Gold Coast* (1951. 102 p.); 6. M. Manoukian, *The Ewe-speaking people of Togoland and the Gold Coast* (1952. 63 p.); 7. H.D. Gunn, *Peoples of the plateau area of Northern Nigeria* (1953. 110 p.); 8. L. Bohannon, and P. Bohannon, *The Tiv of central Nigeria* (1953. 100 p.); 9. M. McCulloch, *Peoples of the central Cameroons: Tikar* (1954. 174 p.); 10. C.D. Forde, *Peoples of the Niger-Benue confluence* (1955. 160 p.); 11. E. Ardener, *Coastal Bantu of the Cameroons (the Kpe-Mboko, Duala-Limba and Tanga-Yasa groups of the British and French trusteeship territories of the Cameroons)*(1956. 116 p.); 12. H.D. Gunn, *Pagan peoples of the central area (the Butawa, Warjawa, etc., of the Bauchi-Kano borderland; the Kurama, etc., the Katab Group, the Kadara, etc., of Zaria Province)*(1956. 146 p.); 13. R.E. Bradbury, *The Benin kingdom and the Edo-speaking peoples of south-western Nigeria: together with a section on the Itsekiri* (1964. 210 p.); 14. D.P. Gamble, *The Wolof of Senegambia, together with notes on the Lebu and the Serer* (1957. 110 p.); 15. H.D. Gunn, *Peoples of the middle Niger region, northern Nigeria* (1960. 138 p.).

9.21   Hambly, Wilfrid D. *Source book for African anthropology.* Anthropological Series, 26. Chicago: Field Museum of Natural History, 1937. 2 v. DT15 .H3x 1968.

        Includes an extensive bibliography on pp. 728-866; continued by W.D. Hambly, *Source book for African anthropology. Supplement. Bibliography of African anthropology* (Fieldiana: Anthropology, 37(2). Chicago: Field Museum of Natural History, 1952).

9.22   Wieschhoff, H. A. *Anthropological bibliography of Negro Africa.* American Oriental series, v. 23. New Haven: American Oriental Society, 1948. 461 p. 016.30196 W637.

Continued by: N. Mylius, *Afrika Bibliographie, 1943-1951* (Wien: Verein Freunde der Völkerkunde, 1952. 237 p.).

Africa -- Demography

9.23   Gregory, Joel W., Dennis D. Cordell, and Raymond Gervais. *African historical demography: a multidisciplinary bibliography.* Los Angeles, California: Crossroads Press, 1984. 248 p. HB3661.A3 G73x 1984.

9.24   Ware, Helen R.E. *Population and development in Africa south of the Sahara: a review of the literature, 1970-1978.* Mexico City: International Review Group of Social Science Research on Population and Development, 1978. 115 p. HB3661 .A3 W37.

Africa -- Development

9.25   Cook, Gillian P. *Development in Africa south of the Sahara 1970-1980: a select annotated bibliography.* Cape Town: University of Cape Town Libraries, 1984. 410 p. HC800 .C6x 1984.

9.26   Ofori, Patrick E. *Land in Africa: its administration, law, tenure, and use: a select bibliography.* Nendeln, Liechtenstein: KTO Press, 1978. 200 p. HD963 .O3x 1978.

Africa -- Ethnomusicology

9.27   Thieme, Darius. *African music: a briefly annotated bibliography.* Washington, D.C.: Music Division, Library of Congress, 1964. 55 p. 016.78 Un3af.

9.28   Varley, Douglas H. *African native music: an annotated bibliography.* London: Royal Empire Society, 1936. 116 p. 016.325 R812 no.8.

Africa --- Folklore

9.29   Gorog, Veronika. *Bibliographie annotée litterature orale d'Afrique noire.* Paris: Conseil International de la Langue Française, 1992. 367 p.

9.30   Scheub, Harold. *African oral narratives, proverbs, riddles, poetry, and song.* Boston: G. K. Hall, 1977. 393 p. GR350 .S3x 1977.
        International bibliography of more than 5,800 collections appearing as separate publications or as contributions to periodicals.

Africa -- Linguistics

9.31   *African language and literature collection, Indiana University*

Libraries. Bloomington: African Studies Program, Indiana University Libraries, 1994. 515 p. PL8005 .I53x 1994.

9.32 Der-Houssikian, Haig. *A Bibliography of African linguistics.* Edmonton, Alberta; Champaign, Illinois: Linguistic Research. 1972, 96 p. PL8005 .D4x 1972.

9.33 Murphy, John D., and Harry Goff, comp. *A Bibliography of African languages and linguistics.* Washington: Catholic University of America Press, 1969. 147 p. PL8005 .M8x 1969.

Africa -- Medical Anthropology

9.34 Luijk, J. N. van. *Selected bibliography of sociological and anthropological literature relating to modern and traditional medicine in Africa south of the Sahara.* Leiden: Afrika-Studiecentrum, 1969. 62 p.

Excludes coverage of South Africa and former Portuguese and Spanish colonies.

Africa -- Religion

9.35 Mitchell, Robert C., and Harold W. Turner, comp. *A Comprehensive bibliography of modern African religious movements.* Evanston, Illinois: Northwestern University Press, 1966. 132 p. BL2400 .M5x 1966.

9.36 Ofori, Patrick E. *Black African traditional religions and philosophy: a select bibliographic survey of the sources from the earliest times to 1974.* Nendeln: Kraus-Thomson, 1975. 421 p. BL2466 .O35x 1977.

Books, dissertations, and journal articles in a subject arrangement; regional sections are subdivided by country and subject.

9.37 Ofori, Patrick E. *Christianity in tropical Africa: a selective annotated bibliography.* Nendeln, Liechtenstein: Kto Press, 1977. 461 p. BR1360 .O36x 1977.

9.38 Ofori, Patrick E. *Islam in Africa south of the Sahara: a select bibliographic guide.* Nendeln, Liechtenstein: Kto Press, 1977. 223 p. BP64 .A4 S85x 1977.

9.39 Zoghby, Samir M. *Islam in sub-Saharan Africa: a partially annotated guide.* Washington, D.C.: Library of Congress, 1978. 318 p. BP64 .A4 S87x 1978.

Includes 2,682 annotated entries arranged by historical period, region, and subject.

Africa --- Technology
9.40   Lawal, Ibironke O. *Metalworking in Africa south of the Sahara: an annotated bibliography.* Westport, Connecticut: Greenwood Press, 1995. 270 p. TS205 .L39x 1995.

Africa -- Urbanization
9.41   O'Connor, Anthony M. *Urbanization in tropical Africa, an annotated bibliography.* Boston: G. K. Hall, 1981. 381 p. HT148 .S8 O2x 1981.

9.42   Verhaegen, P. *L'Urbanisation de l'Afrique noire: son cadre, ses causes et ses consequences economiques, sociales et culturelles.* Bruxelles: Centra de Documentation Economique et Sociale Africaine, 1962. 385 p. 016.96 C333 No.9.

Africa -- Central
9.43   Bruel, Georges, and Danielle de Lame. *Bibliographie de l'Afrique equatoriale francaise.* Paris: E. Larose, 1914. 326 p. 016.96 B83.

Africa -- Central --- Cultural/Social Anthropology
9.44   Hertefelt, Marcel d'. *Bibliographie de l'Afrique sud-saharienne, sciences humaines et sociales, 1979.* Tervuren, Belgique: Musée Royal de l'Afrique Centrale, 1983. 479 p.
        Continued by M. d'Hertefelt and A. Bouttiaux, *Bibliographie de l'Afrique sud-saharienne, sciences humaines et sociales, 1981-1983, periodiques* (Tervuren: Musée Royal de l'Afrique Centrale, 1986. 543 p.).

9.45   Hertefelt, Marcel d', and Danielle de Lame. *Société, culture et histoire du Rwanda: encyclopedie bibliographique 1863-1980/87.* Tervuren, Belgique: Musée Royal de l'Afrique Centrale, 1987. 2 v.

9.46   Jones, Ruth. *South-east Central Africa and Madagascar: general, ethnography/sociology, linguistics.* London: International African Institute, 1961. 53 leaves. 016.9676 In8s.
        Bibliography of entries selected for their anthropological significance comprise an excellent beginning source for Central Africa and Madagascar.

Africa -- Central -- Ethnographic Art
9.47   Bieduyck, Daniel P. *The Arts of Central Africa: an annotated bibliography.* Boston: G.K. Hall, 1987. 300 p. NX589.6 .C6 B5x.

Africa -- Central -- Pygmies

9.48   Liniger-Goumaz, Max. *Pygmées et autres races de petite taille (Boschimans-Hottentots-Negritos, etc.); bibliographie générale. Pygmies and other short-sized races.* Geneve: Editions du Temps, 1968. 338 p. 016.3015 L648.
Includes some 3,300 entries arranged by author with subject and geographical index.

Africa -- East

9.49   Blackhurst, Hector. *East and northeast Africa bibliography.* Lanham, Maryland: Scarecrow Press, 1996. 360 p. DT365.18 .B53x 1996.
Useful general bibliography on Dijouti, Eritrea, Ethiopia, Somalia, Sudan, Kenya, Tanzania, and Uganda; author and subject indexes.

9.50   Ofcansky, Thomas P. *British East Africa, 1856-1963: an annotated bibliography.* New York: Garland, 1985. 474 p. DT423 .O33x 1985.

Africa -- East --- Cultural/Social Anthropology

9.51   McCall, Michael K. *Indigenous technical knowledge in farming systems of eastern Africa: a bibliography.* Ames, Iowa: Technology and Social Change Program, Iowa State University, 1994. 101 p. Z5075 .A353 M33x 1994.

Africa --- East -- Linguistics

9.52   Garsse, Yvan van. *Ethnological and anthropological literature on the three Southern Sudan provinces: Upper Nile, Bahr el Ghazal, Equatoria.* Sint Niklaas Waas: Parlaan, 1972. 83 leaves. GN652.S93 G37x 1972.

9.53   Jones, Ruth. *East Africa: general, ethnography/sociology, linguistics and related subjects (based on the bibliographical card index of the International African Institute.* London: International African Institute, 1960. 69 leaves. 016.9676 In8e.

9.54   Killick, Tony. *The Economies of East Africa, a bibliography: 1974-1980.* Boston: G.K. Hall, 1984. 294 p. HC860 .K5x 1984.

9.55   Molnos, Angela. *Cultural source materials for population planning in East Africa.* Nairobi: East African Publishing House, 1972-1973. 4 v. H62.5 .A3413 C87.
Publication of A. Molnos, *Bibliography on family life in East Africa* (Nairobi: Programme for Better Family Living, East Africa,

Food and Agriculture Organization of the United Nations, 1972. 67 leaves. HQ692.4 .B52x 1972), a listing of citations selected in advance of publication from *Cultural source materials for population planning in East Africa, v. 4: Bibliography*, compiled by A. Molnos and published in 1973 . Issued with Krystall, A. *Annotated bibliography on family life in Kenya* (Nairobi, 1974).

9.56   Molnos, Angela. *Development in Africa: planning and implementation a bibliography (1946-1969) and outline with some emphasis on Kenya, Tanzania, and Uganda.* Nairobi: East African Academy, Research Information Centre, 1970. 120 p. Z3516 .M64.

9.57   Molnos, Angela. *Sources for the study of East African cultures and development; a bibliography of social scientific bibliographies, abstracts, reference works, catalogues, directories, writings on archives, bibliographies, book production, libraries, and museums. With special reference to Kenya, Tanzania, and Uganda, 1946-1966 (1967-1968).* Nairobi: East African Research Information Centre, 1988. 54 p. DT365 .M6 1969.

9.58   Molnos, Angela. *Die sozialwissenschaftliche Erforschung Ostafrikas 1954-1963 (Kenya, Tanganyika/Sansibar, Uganda).* Berlin, New York: Springer-Verlag, 1965. 304 p.

9.59   Wilding, Richard. *A Bibliography of the history and peoples of the Swahili-speaking world: from earliest times to the beginning of the 20th century.* Nairobi: Lamu Society, 1976. 98 p. DT365.4 .W55x 1976.

Africa --- East --- Linguistics
9.60   Molnos, Angela. *Language problems in Africa; a bibliography (1946-1967) and summary of the present situation, with special reference to Kenya, Tanzania and Uganda.* Nairobi: East African Research Information Centre, 1988. 62 p.

9.61   Spaandonck, Marcel van. *Practical and systematical Swahili bibliography; linguistics, 1850-1963.* Leiden: E.J. Brill, 1965. 61 p. 016.49692 Sp11.

9.62   Whiteley, Wilfred H. *A Linguistic bibliography of East Africa.* rev. ed. Kampala: East African Swahili Committee and East African Institute of Social Research, 1958. 215 p. 016.496 W587.

9.63   Wilding, Richard. *Swahili bibliography of the East African coast.*
        Nairobi: Lamu Society, 1990. 1 v.

9.64   Zocli, Ernest. *Bibliographie de la langue swahili.* Abidjan, Côte
        d'Ivoire: Institut Africain pour le Developpement Economique et
        Social, 1974. 41 leaves.

Africa -- North
9.65   Blackhurst, Hector. *East and Northeast Africa bibliography.* Lanham,
        Maryland; London: Scarecrow Press, 1996. 301 p. DT365.18 .B53x
        1996.

Africa -- North -- Cultural/Social Anthropology
9.66   Ait-Chaalal, Amine. *Le Maghreb: reperes bibliographiques,
        chronologie, documents.* Louvain-la-Neuve: Centre d'Etudes et de
        Recherches sur le Monde Arabe Contemporain, 1993. 40 p.

9.67   Akture, Sevgi, Isil Karabay, and Hulya Ozdil. *The Middle Eastern and
        North African cities: a selected bibliography (1970-1992).* Ankara:
        O.D.T.U. Mimarlik Fakultesi, 1983. 202 p.

9.68   Cigar, Norman L. *North African architecture.* Monticello, Illinois:
        Vance Bibliographies, 1978. 6 p.

9.69   Davis, Lenwood G. *Urbanization in the Middle East, with some
        references to North Africa: an introductory survey.* Monticello,
        Illinois: Council of Planning Librarians, 1978. 20 p. HT166 .C6x
        1539.

9.70   Miller, E. Willard. *Northern and western Africa: a bibliography of the
        Third World.* Monticello, Illinois: Vance Bibliographies, 1981. 96 p.
        JF1351 .P83x P-818.

9.71   Rebuffat, Rene. *Bibliographie de l'Afrique du Nord antique:
        periodiques et series.* Paris: Presses de l'Ecole Normale Superieure,
        1980. 94 p.

9.72   Scheffler, Thomas. *Ethnisch-religiose Konflikte und gesellschaftliche
        Integration im Vorderen und Mittleren Orient: Literaturstudie.* Berlin:
        Das Arabische Buch, 1990. 251 p.

Africa --- North --- Women
9.73   Bullwinkle, Davis. *Women of northern, western, and central Africa: a*

bibliography, 1976-1985. New York: Greenwood Press, 1989. 601 p. HQ1787 .B86x 1989.

9.74   Hadraoui, Touria. *Etudes feminines: repertoire et bibliographie.* Casablanca Morocco: UNU/Wider; Le Fennec, 1991. 255 p.

9.75   Otto, Ingeborg. *Frauenfragen im Modernen Orient: eine Erganzungsbibliographie; Women in the Middle East and North Africa: a supplementary bibliography.* Hamburg: Deutsches Ubersee-Institut, Ubersee-Dokumentation, Referat Vorderer Orient, 1989. 126 p. HQ1784 .O8x 1982.

9.76   Tauzin, Aline. *Femmes, famille, Société au Maghreb et en emigration: 700 travaux et documents inedits: repertoire.* Paris: Karthala, 1990. 188 p. HQ1795.5 .T38 1990.

Africa --- North --- Linguistics
9.77   Johnson, Dora E. *Languages of the Middle East and North Africa.* Arlington, Virginia: Center for Applied Linguistics, 1976. 54 p.

Africa -- North -- Berbers
9.78   Brenier-Estrine, Claude. *Bibliographie berbere annotée, 1993-1994.* Aix-en-Provence: Institut de recherches et d'etudes sur le monde arabe et musulman, 1995. 199 p.

Africa--- South
9.79   Kalley, Jacqueline A. *The Transkei region of southern Africa, 1877-1978: an annotated bibliography.* Boston: G. K. Hall, 1976. 218 p. DT846.T7 K344x 1980.

9.80   Musiker, Naomi. *South African history: a bibliographical guide with special reference to territorial expansion and colonization.* New York: Garland, 1984. 297 p. DT766 .M984x 1984.

9.81   Musiker, Reuben. *South African bibliography: a survey of bibliographies and bibliographical work.* 3d ed. New York: Mansell, 1996. 142 p. DT753 .M8724x 1996.
        Bibliography of bibliographies with coverage for Namibia, Botswana, Lesotho, and Swaziland.

9.82   Musiker, Reuben, and Naomi Musiker. *Southern Africa bibliography.* Lanham, Maryland: Scarecrow Press, 1996. 264 p. DT1019 .M87 1996.

Selective bibliography of books and monographs on Angola, Botswana, Lesotho, Malawi, Namibia, Mozambique, South Africa, Swaziland, Zambia, and Zimbabwe published since 1945; arranged by subject and contains author, title, and subject indexes.

Africa --- South --- Biological/Physical Anthropology

9.83   Meyer, Ann. *Hominids of the Lower and Middle Pleistocene: the Australopithecinae and Homo habilis; a bibliography.* Johannesburg: University of the Witwatersrand, Department of Bibliography, Librarianship and Typography, 1968. 41 p.

Africa --- South --- Cultural/Social Anthropology

9.84   Kalley, Jacqueline A. *South Africa under apartheid: a select and annotated bibliography.* New York: Greenwood Press, 1989. 544 p. DT1757 .K35x 1989.

9.85   Rip, Sheila. *Bibliography of Southern African research on ageing, 1970-1988.* Pretoria: Human Sciences Research Council, 1989. 64 p.

9.86   Rita-Ferreira, Antonio. *Bibliografia etnologica de Moçambique (das origens a 1954).* Lisboa: Junta de Investigaçoes do Ultramar. 1961. 254 p. 016.301967 R51.
        Approximately 1,000 annotated book and articles arranged by region and ethnic group.

9.87   Schapera, Isaac. *Select bibliography of South African native life and problems.* London: Oxford University Press, 1941. DT763 .S33x 1941; New York: Kraus, 1969. 249 p. DT763 .S33x 1941 Suppl.
        Supplement: Modern status and conditions: bibliography, 1939-1949. Cape Town, 1950; *Supplement 2: Modern status and conditions: bibliography, 1950-1958.* Cape Town, 1958; *Supplement 3: Modern status and conditions: bibliography, 1959-1963.* Cape Town, 1964. 51 p.; *Supplement 4: Modern status and conditions: bibliography, 1964-1980.* Cape Town, 1974. 39 p.
        Briefly annotates books, articles, and reports arranged in sections: physical anthropology, archaeology, ethnology, modern status and conditions, and linguistics.

9.88   Scholtz, P. L. *Race relations at the Cape of Good Hope, 1652-1795: a select bibliography.* Boston: G. K. Hall, 1981. 124 p. DT834 .S35x 1981.

9.89   *South African women: a select bibliography.* Johannesburg: South
        African Institute of International Affairs, 1996. 307 p.

9.90   Strohmeyer, Eckhard, and Walter Moritz. *Umfassende Bibliographie
        der Völker Namibiens (Sudwestafrikas) und Sudwestangolas;
        Comprehensive bibliography of the peoples of Namibia (South West
        Africa) and Southwestern Angola.* Kampala: Starnberg (Germany):
        Vertrieb, Max-Planck-Institut zur Erforschung der
        Lebensbedingungen der Wissenschaftlich-technischen Welt, 1975-
        1982. 2 v. GN656.N35 S78x.

Africa --- South --- Textiles

9.91   Levy, June R. *African traditional garb of the native tribes of Southern
        Africa: a bibliography.* Johannesburg: University of the
        Witwatersrand, Department of Bibliography, Librarianship and
        Typography, 1972. 74 p. GN418 .L49x 1972.

Africa, South --- Bantu

9.92   Bastin, Y. *Bibliographie bantoue selective.* Tervuren: Musée Royal de
        l'Afrique Centrale, 1975. 56 p. GN654 .A3 no.24.

9.93   Doke, Clement M. *Bantu: modern grammatical, phonetical, and
        lexicographical studies since 1860.* London: International African
        Institute, 1945. 119 p. 016.4963 D685.

9.94   Kamasa, Rwakazina. *L'art oral traditionnel Bantu: elements
        bibliographiques.* Lubumbashi: Centre de Linguistique Theorique et
        Appliquée, Universite Nationale du Zaire, 1973. 53 leaves.

9.95   Viljoen, R. A. *Bibliografie oor die Bantoes in die Republiek van
        Suid-Afrika. Bibliography on the Bantu in the Republic of South
        Africa.* Pretoria: National Bureau of Educational and Social Research,
        1966. 45 p. 016.968 Un3.

Africa --- South --- Sotho

9.96   Neser, L. *Southern Sotho ethnography: a classified bibliography.*
        Kwa-Dlangezwa, South Africa: University of Zululand, 1984. 95 p.

Africa --- South --- Zulu

9.97   Galloway, Margaret H. *Zululand and the Zulus; a bibliography.* Cape
        Town: University of Cape Town Libraries, 1969 16 p. 016.9683 G138.

9.98   Neser, L. *Zulu ethnography: a supplementary bibliography.*
Kwa-Dlangezwa, South Africa: University of Zululand, 1980. 71 p.
DT878.Z9 N48x 1976 Suppl.
Supplement to Neser, L., *Zulu ethnography: a classified
bibliography* (Kwa-Dlangezwa: KwaZula Documentation Centre;
University of Zululand, 1976. 92 p. 016.968 Un3).

Africa --- West
9.99   Amedekey, E. Y. *The Culture of Ghana: a bibliography.* Accra:
Ghana Universities Press, 1970. 215 p. DT510 .A64x 1973.

Africa --- West --- Archaeology
9.100   Shaw, Thurstan, and Joel Vanderburg. *A Bibliography of Nigerian
archaeology.* Ibadan: Ibadan University Press for the Institute of
African Studies, University of Ibadan, 1969. 68 p. 016.9669 Sh28.

Africa --- West --- Cultural/Social Anthropology
9.101   Aguolu, Christian C. *Nigeria: a comprehensive bibliography in the
humanities and social sciences, 1900-1917.* Boston: G. K. Hall, 197.
620 p. DT515.22 .A46x 1973.

9.102   East, Rupert M. *A Vernacular bibliography for the languages of
Nigeria.* Zaria: Literature Bureau, 1941. 85 p.

9.103   Ita, Nduntuei O. *Bibliography of Nigeria: a survey of anthropological
and linguistic writings from the earliest times to 1966.* London: F.
Cass, 1971. 273 p. GN653 .I83x 1971.
Includes more than 5,400 books, articles, and other materials
about ethnography, linguistics, archaeology, and historical and
sociological studies.

9.104   Jones, Ruth. *West Africa: general, ethnography, sociology, linguistics.*
London: International African Institute. 1958. 116 leaves. 016.966
In8.
Bibliography of items selected for their anthropological
importance comprises an excellent beginning source for West Africa.

9.105   Lucas, David. *An Annotated bibliography of the Nigerian fertility and
family planning literature up to 1982.* Canberra: Demography
Department, Research School of Social Sciences, Australian National
University, 1986. 119 p.

9.106 Olafioye, A. O. *Social life and customs in Nigeria: a selective bibliography.* Lagos: National Library of Nigeria, 1969. 25 p.

Africa --- West --- Ethnographic Art

9.107 Ben-Amos, Paula. *Bibliography of Benin art.* Primitive Art Bibliographies, 6. New York: Museum of Primitive Art, 1968. 17 p. N7399 .N52 B46x 1968.

9.108 Cole, Herbert M. *Bibliography of Yoruba sculpture.* Primitive Art Bibliographies, 3. New York: Museum of Primitive Art, 1964. 11 p.

9.109 Owerka, Carolyn. *A Bibliography of Yoruba art.* New York: Pace Editions, 1982. 40 p.

Africa --- West --- Women

9.110 Coles, Catherine M., Barbara Entwhisle, and Margaret Hardner. *Nigerian women in development: a research bibliography.* Los Angeles: Crossroads Press, 1986. 170 p. HQ1240.5 .N6 C65x 1986.

Africa --- West --- Ashanti

9.111 Afre, S. A. *Ashanti Region of Ghana: an annotated bibliography, from earliest times to 1973.* Boston: G. K. Hall, 1975. 494 p. DT507 .A335x 1975.
More than 2,500 annotated entries arranged with subdivisions.

Africa --- West --- Hausa

9.112 Powe, Edward L. *Hausa studies: a select bibliography of dissertations and theses submitted to northern Nigerian universities.* Kano, Nigeria: Department of Library Science, Bayero University, 1984. 17 p. .

9.113 Salamone, Frank A., and James A. McCain. *The Hausa people, a bibliography.* New Haven, Connecticut: Human Relations Area Files, 1983. 295 leaves. DT515.45 .H38 S24x 1983.

Africa --- West --- Ibo

9.114 Anafulu, Joseph C. *The Ibo-speaking peoples of southern Nigeria: a selected annotated list of writings, 1627-1970.* München: Kraus International, 1981. 321 p. DT515.45 .I33 A5x 1981.

Africa --- West --- Yoruba

9.115 Baldwin, David E., and Charlene M. Baldwin. *The Yoruba of southwestern Nigeria: an indexed bibliography.* Boston: G. K. Hall, 1976. 269 p. 016.96692 B193.

Lists books, articles, and other publications on southwestern Nigeria as well as literary works by Yoruba authors.

9.116   Issah, Hali S. *Yoruba customs and institutions: an annotated bibliography*. Marina, Lagos: Concept Publications, 1988. 66 p.

9.117   Ombu, Jigekuma A. *The Benin Kingdom 1550-1970: an enumerative bibliography*. Dresden: Staatliches Museum für Völkerkunde, 1995. 205 p.

9.118   Stanley, Janet. *Ife, the holy city of the Yoruba: an annotated bibliography*. Ile-Ife, Nigeria: University of Ife Press, 1982. 228 p.

Asia
9.119   *Cumulative bibliography of Asian studies, 1941-1965: author bibliography*. Boston, Massachusetts: K. Hall, 1969. 4 v. Z3001 .C93; *Cumulative bibliography of Asian studies, 1941-1965: subject bibliography*. Boston, Massachusetts: G. K. Hall, 1970. 4 v. Z3001 .C94.

Cumulates a series of publications begun in 1934 as *Lists by the American Council of Learned Societies Devoted to Humanistic Studies' Commission in Far Eastern Studies*, continued 1936-1940 as the Council's *Bulletin of Far Eastern Bibliography*, and from 1941 issued in the *Journal of Asian Studies*; continued by *Cumulative bibliography of Asian studies, 1966-1970: author bibliography* (Boston, Massachusetts: G. K. Hall, 1973. 3 v.) and *Cumulative bibliography of Asian studies, 1966-1970: subject bibliography* (Boston: G. K. Hall, 1972. 3 v.).

Asia --- Central
9.120   Lee, Don Y. *An Annotated bibliography on inner Asia: premodern*. Bloomington, Indiana: Eastern Press, 1983. 183 p. DS786 .L4x 1983.

Asia --- Central --- Archaeology
9.121   Lee, Don Y., and Jane Workman, eds. *An Annotated archaeological bibliography of selected works on Northern and Central Asia*. Bloomington, Indiana: Eastern Press, 1983. 94 p. GN851 .L43x 1983.

Asia --- Central --- Cultural/Social Anthropology
9.122   Andrei, Bishop of Sukhumi, and N.V. Nikol'skago. *Naiboliee vazhnyia statisticheskiia viedieniia ob inorodtsakh Vostochnoi Rossii i Zapadnoi Sibiri, podverzhennykh vliianiiu islama*. Kazan': Tip. Gubernskago pravleniia, 1912. 320 p.

Russian language bibliography of ethnic Bashkir, Udmurts, Mordvins, Tatars, Chuvash, and Mari.

9.123 Baldaev, R. L., and N.N. Vasil'ev. *Ukazatel' bibliografii po mongolovedeniiu na russkom iazyke, 1824-1960.* Leningrad, 1962. 88 p.
Russian-language bibliography on the Mongols of Central Asia.

9.124 *Bibliografiia po sovetskomu mongolovedeniiu; Mongol studies in the Soviet Union: a bibliography of Soviet publications 1981-1986 in Russian.* Bloomington, Indiana Research Institute for Inner Asian Studies, 1988. 95 p.

9.125 Iorish, I. I. *Materialy o mongolakh, kalmykakh i buriatakh v arkhivakh Leningrada: istoriia, pravo, ekonomika.* Moskva: Nauka, 1966. 204 p. 016.9517 Io7.
Bibliography, in Russian, on the Mongols, Kalmyks, and Buriats of Central Asia.

Asia — East

9.126 Kerner, Robert J. *Northeastern Asia: a selected bibliography; contributions to the bibliography of the relations of China, Russia, and Japan, with special reference to Korea, Manchuria, Mongolia and eastern Siberia, in Oriental and European languages.* Berkeley: University of California Press, 1939; New York: Burt Franklin, 1969. 2 v. DS504.5 .K47x 1939.
Includes 14,000 entries, mostly in Asian languages or Russian, covering the geography, history, international relations, economics, culture and civilization, social conditions, and other aspects of the region.

9.127 Koh, Hesung Chun. *Social science resources on Korea: a preliminary computerized bibliography.* New Haven: Human Relations Area Files, 1968. 2 v. 016.9519 K823.

9.128 Lust, John. *Western books on China published up to 1850 in the Library of the School of Oriental and African Studies, University of London: a descriptive catalogue.* London: Bamboo, 1987. 331 p. DS706 .U55x 1987.

9.129 Kamachi, Noriko, John K. Fairbank, and Chuzo Ichiko. *Japanese studies of modern China since 1953: a bibliographical guide to historical and social science research on the nineteenth and twentieth*

centuries: supplementary volume for 1953-1969. Cambridge,
Massachusetts: East Asian Research Center, Harvard University;
Harvard University Press, 1975. 603 p. DS706 .K35x 1975.

9.130   Tsien, Tsuen-hsuin. *China: an annotated bibliography of
bibliographies.* Boston: G.K. Hall, 1978. 604 p. Z3106 .T87.

9.131   Wolff, Ernst. *Chinese studies: a bibliographic manual.* San Francisco:
Chinese Materials Center, 1981. 152 p. Z3106 .W6.

Asia --- East --- Archaeology
9.132   Vanderstappen, Harrie A., ed. *The T. L. Yuan bibliography of western
writings on Chinese art and archaeology.* London: Mansell, 1975. 606
p. N7340 .Y83x 1975.

Asia --- East --- Cultural/Social Anthropology
9.133   Anderson, T. V., and D.G. Savinov. *Etnografiia narodov Vostochnoi
Sibiri i Dal'nego Vostoka: literatura, opublikovannaia v 1944-1975.*
Leningrad: Izd-vo Leningradskogo Universiteta, 1983. 96 p.
DK771.E27 A52x 1983.
          Other Russian language bibliographies covering Siberia include:
A.P. Okladnikov, *Etnografiia narodov Altaia i Zapadnoi Sibiri*
(Novosibirsk: Nauka, 1978. 219 p.) and I.N. Gemuev and I.S.
Khudiakov, *Etnografiia narodov Sibiri* (Novosibirsk: Nauka, Sibirskoe
otd-nie, 1984. 149 p.).

9.134   Beardsley, Richard K. *Bibliographic materials in the Japanese
language on Far Eastern archaeology and ethnology.* Center for
Japanese Studies Bibliographical Series, 3. Ann Arbor: University of
Michigan Press, 1950. 74 p. 016.30195 B38.

9.135   Beardsley, Richard K., and Nakano Takashi. *Japanese sociology and
social anthropology: a guide to Japanese reference and research
materials.* Ann Arbor: University of Michigan Press, 1970. 276 p.
Z7165.J3 B4.
          Dated but still useful guide to the literature.

9.136   Izumi, Seiichi. *Cultural anthropology in Japan, by the Committee for
the Publication of Cultural Anthropological Studies in Japan.* Tokyo:
Tokyo Electrical Engineering College Press, 1967. 112 p. 016.3015
C899.
          Bibliography in Japanese and English of selected books and
articfles published in Japan between 1960 and 1964.

Asia --- East --- Linguistics

9.137   Jakobson, Roman. *Paleosiberian peoples and languages: a bibliographical guide.* New Haven: HRAF Press, 1957; Westport, Connecticut: Greenwood, 1981. 222 p. 016.3015 C899.
Includes 1,898 entries dealing with the peoples of northeast Asia (Gilyak, Chukchee, Yakaghir, and Tenisei).

Asia --- East --- Religion

9.138   Cohen, Alvin P. *Publications on religions in China, 1981-1989.* Amherst: University of Massachusetts at Amherst, 1991. 73 p. Z7757 .C6 .T55.

9.139   Thompson, Laurence G. *Chinese religion: publications in Western languages, 1981 through 1990.* Ann Arbor: Association for Asian Studies; Los Angeles: Ethnographic Press, Center for Visual Anthropology, University of Southern California, 1993. 288 p. BL1802 .T46x 1993.
Continues: L.G. Thompson, *Chinese religion in Western languages: a comprehensive and classified bibliography of publications in English, French, and German through 1980* (Tucson: Association for Asian Studies; University of Arizona Press, 1985. 302 p.); L.G. Thompson, *Studies of Chinese religion: a comprehensive and classified bibliography of publications in English, French, and German through 1970* (Encino, California: Dickenson, 1976. 190 p.)

9.140   Yu, David C., and Laurence G. Thompson. *Guide to Chinese religion.* Boston, Massachusetts: G.K. Hall, 1985. 200 p. BL1802 .T46x 1993.

Asia --- East --- Women

9.141   Koh, Hesung Chun. *Korean and Japanese women: an analytic bibliographical guide.* Westport, Connecticut: Greenwood Press, 1982. 903 p. BL1802 .T46x 1993.

Asia --- East --- Ainu

9.142   Gusinde, Martin, and Chie Sano. *An Annotated bibliography of Ainu studies by Japanese scholars.* Nagoya, Japan: Nanzan University, 1962. DS832 .G8 1962.

Asia --- East --- Chinese

9.143   Skinner, G. William, Winston Hsieh, and Shigeaki Tomita. *Modern Chinese society: an analytical bibliography.* Stanford, California: Stanford University Press, 1973. 3 v. HN733 .M63 1973.

Asia --- East --- Koreans

9.144   Koh, Hesung Chun. *Korea: an analytical guide to bibliographies.* New Haven: Human Relations Area Files Press, 1971. 334 p. DS902 .K64x 1971.

9.145   Koh, Hesung Chun. *Korean family and kinship studies guide, with a section on women.* New Haven: Human Relations Area Files, 1980. 548 leaves. 016.3041 K823.

Asia --- East --- Yi (Lolo)

9.146   Dessaint, Alain Y. *Minorities of Southwest China: an introduction to the Yi (Lolo) and related peoples and an annotated bibliography.* New Haven: HRAF Press, 1980. 373 p. DS730 .D45.

Includes a brief survey of the linguistics, history, and ethnography of the Yi (Lolo) people, the fourth largesty minority in China, and related gropups in Yunan, Szechwan, Kweichow, and neighboring Vietnam, Laos, Thailand, Burma, and India.

Asia --- South

9.147   Chaudhuri, Sibadas. *Bibliography of Tibetan studies; being a record of printed publications mainly in European languages.* Calcutta: Asiatic Society, 1973. 232 p. Z3107 .T5 C46.

Sopme 2,000 entries, including citations in Western languages and romanized Japanese, arranged in subject categories, including archaeology, ethnology, and linguistics.

9.148   Chaudhuri, Sibadas. *Index to the publications of the Asiatic Society, 1788-1953.* Calcutta: Asiatic Society, 1956-1957. Z5055.I58 A753.

Bibliography of publications of the Asiatic Society in Calcutta; continued by S. Chaudhuri, *Index to the publications of the Asiatic Society: first supplement, 1954-1968* (Calcutta: Asiatic Society, 1971).

9.149   Goonetileke, H. A. I. *A Bibliography of Ceylon: a systematic guide to the literature on the land, people, history and culture published in Western languages from the sixteenth century to the present day.* Zug, Switzerland: Inter Documentation 1970-1983. Z3211 G6.

General bibliography of Sri Lanka with sections of interest to anthropologists on physical anthropology and ethnology of racial and tribal groups, social organization, cultural and social exchange, folk religion and popular religious cults.

9.150   Gustafson, W. Eric. *Pakistan and Bangladesh: bibliographic essays in social science.* Islamabad: University of Islamabad Press, 1976. 364 p.

DS376.9 P34.
Collection of bibliographic essays on the social sciences, including anthropology, deriving from the National Seminar on Pakistan and Bangladesh, which has met at the South Asian Institute, Columbia University, since 1970.

9.151   Hedrick, Basil C., *et al. A Bibliography of Nepal.* Metuchen, New Jersey: Scarecrow Press, 1973. 302 p. Z3207 .N4 B53.
More than 3,000 entries in subject categories, including anthropology, archaeology, and sociology.

9.152   Nelson, David N. *Bibliography of South Asia.* Lanham, Maryland: Scarecrow Press, 1994. 484 p. Z3185 .N45 1994.
Introductory bibliography of recently published materials on South Asia, Afghanistan, Bangladesh, Bhutan, India, Maldives, Nepal, Pakistan, and Sri Lanka.

9.153   Scholberg, Henry. *Bibliography of Goa and the Portuguese in India.* New Delhi: Promilla; Atlantic Highlands, New Jersey: Humanities Press, 1982. 413 p. DS498 .S36 1982.
Bibliography covers the period 1497-1961, from the time Vasco de Gama sailed from Portugal until Jawaharlal Nehru annexed the Portuguese possessions in 1961.

Asia --- South --- Archaeology
9.154   *Annual bibliography of Indian archaeology.* Leiden. v.1-23, 1926-1972. Z5133 .I4I6.
International bibloiography of scholarly writings dealing with the archaeology and prehistory of India and contiguous territories to the east.

9.155   Chaudhuri, Sibadas. *Bibliography of studies in Indian epigraphy, 1926-50.* Baroda: Oriental Institute, 1966. 113 p. Z7049.I3 C5.

9.156   Roy, Ashim K., and N.N. Gidwani. *Indus Valley civilization: a bibliographic essay.* New Delhi: Oxford & IBH, 1982. 264 p. DS425 .R69 1982.
Includes an essay on the development of Indus Valley civilization and a list of Harappan sites, as well as a selected bibliography of journal and newspaper articles, books, and dissertations, published in English, prior to 1979.

Asia --- South --- Biological/Physical Anthropology
9.157   Reid, Russell M. *Bibliography of the physical anthropology of the peoples of India, III.* Coconut Grove, Miami, Florida: Field Research Projects, 1972. Z5115 .R443.

Asia --- South --- Cultural/Social Anthropology
9.158   Cekki, Danesa A. *The Social system and culture of modern India: a research bibliography.* New York: Garland, 1975. 843 p. Z7165 I6 C5.

Includes almost 5,000 entries organized to include anthropology and social psychology.

9.159   Fürer-Haimendorf, Elizabeth von. *An Anthropological bibliography of South Asia, together with a directory of recent anthropological fieldwork.* Paris: Mouton, 1958-1970. 3 v. Z5115 .F83.

Includes books, articles, and dissertations dealing with the cultural and social aspects of anthropology in India, Pakistan, Nepal, Sikkim, Bhutan, and Sri Lanka; coverage: v. 1: 1940-1954; v.2: 1955-1959; v.3: 1960-1964; continued by: Helen A. Kanitkar, *An Anthropological bibliography of South Asia; together with a directory of anthropological field research compiled by Elizabeth von Furer-Haimendorf* (The Hague: Mouton, v.1 - , 1976 -).

9.160   Goonetileke, H.A.I., and Samuel Devasirvadham. *Mass communication in Sri Lanka: an annotated bibliography.* Singapore: Asian Mass Communication Research and Information Centre, 1978. 77 p.

9.161   Mandelbaum, David G. *Materials for a bibliography of the ethnology of India.* Berkeley: Department of Anthropology, University of California, 1949. 220 leaves. DS430 .Z9 M27 1949.

9.162   Padmanabha, P. *Indian census and anthropological investigations.* rev. ed. Delhi: Controller of Publications, 1983. 190 p.

9.163   Perkins, David, Norman E. Tanis, and Harish Vaish. *India and its people: a bibliography.* Ann Arbor: University Microfilm International, 1980. 461 p. Z3206 .P47.

9.164   Ray, Shyamal K. *Bibliography of anthropology of India; including index to current literature, 1960-1964.* Calcutta: Anthropological Survey of India, 1976. 323 p. Z5115 .R39.

International classified bibliography of books and articles, mostly in English, arranged by broad subjects of anthropological interest; author, ethnic group, and geographical indexing.

9.165 Satyaprakash. *Muslims in India: a bibliography of their religious, socio-economic, and political literature.* Gurgaon, Haryana: Indian Documentation Service, 1985. 279 p. Z3208.E85 S27 1985.

9.166 Sharma, Jagdish S. *Indian socialism: a descriptive bibliography.* Delhi: Vikas Publishing. House, 1975. 349 p. Z7164.S67 S44.

9.167 Sharma, Jagdish S. *India's minorities: a bibliographical study.* Delhi: Vikas Publishing House, 1975. 192 p. Z3208.M54 S47.

9.168 Wood, Hugh B. *Nepal bibliography.* Eugene, Oregon: American-Nepal Education Foundation, 1959. 108 p. Z3207 .N4 W6.
       Emphasis on historical, social, political, and cultural aspects of life in Nepal.

Asia --- South --- Linguistics
9.169 Agesthialingom, S., and S. Sakthivel. *A Bibliography of Dravidian linguistics.* Annamalainagar: Annamalai University, 1973. 362 p. PL4601 .A62.

Asia --- South --- Tribal India
9.170 Agesthialingom, S., and S. Sakthivel. *A Bibliography for the study of Nilgiri hill tribes.* Annamalainagar: Annamalai University, 1973. 60 p. Z5115 .A44.
       Ethnographic bibliography for the Nilgiri Hills tribes, Tamil Nadu.

9.171 Misra, P.K., *et al. Tribes of southern region: a select bibliography.* New Delhi: Inter-India; New York: Apt Books, 1986. 171 p.

9.172 Patel, A.A. *Bibliography on scheduled castes and scheduled tribes.* New Delhi: Social Studies Division, Office of the Registrar General, India, Ministry of Home Affairs, 1982. 561 p. Z3208.E85 B52x 1982.

9.173 Prasad, Maheshwari. *Tribal geography: an introductory bibliography: a selected and partially annotated bibliography of literature pertaining to tribes.* New Delhi: Classical Publications, 1979. 203 p. Z5111 .P73.

9.174   Sen, Sipra. *Arunachal Pradesh and the tribes: select bibliography.*
Delhi, India: Gian Publishing House, 1986. 232 p. Z5111 .P73.

9.175   Sen, Sipra. *The Tribes of Meghalaya.* Delhi, India: Mittal
Publications, 1985. 170 p. Z5115 .S46 1985.
Includes an introductory study of the Scheduled Tribes of
Meghalaya.

9.176   Sen, Sipra. *Tribes of Nagaland.* Delhi, India: Mittal Publications,
1987. 283 p. Z5115 .S47 1987.
Includes an introductory study of Scheduled Tribes of Nagaland.

9.177   Sen, Sipra. *Tribes of Tripura: description, ethnology, and
bibliography.* New Delhi: Gyan Publishing House, 1993. 346 p. Z5115
.S47 T85 1993.

9.178   Sharma, Rajendra N., and Santosh Bakshi. *Tribes and tribal
development: a select bibliography.* New Delhi: Uppal, 1984. 489 p.
Z7165.I6 S523 1984.

9.179   Troisi, J. *The Santals: a classified and annotated bibliography.* New
Delhi: Manohar Book Service, 1976. 234 p. Z3208.E85 T76.
More than 500 books, articles, and government reports in English,
Santali, and Italian, on the Santals of Bihar and Bengal.

Asia --- South --- Urbanism
9.180   Van Willigen, John. *The Indian city: a bibliographic guide to the
literature on urban India.* New Haven: Human Relations Area Files,
1979. 2 v. HQ1742 .V36 1979.
Approximately 3,800 books, articles, coference papers, theses, and
dissertations published between the mid-nineteenth century and 1973.

Asia --- South --- Women
9.181   Pandit, Harshida. *Women of India: an annotated bibliography.* New
York: Garland, 1985. 278 p. HQ1742 .P32 1985.

9.182   Sakala, Carol. *Women of South Asia a guide to resources.* Millwood,
New York: Kraus International Publications, 1980. 517 p. HQ1735.3
.S3 1980.
Approximately 4,600 books, articles, dissertations, and
audiovisual materials for India, Pakistan, Bangladesh, Sri Lanka, and
Nepal. Includes a series of reports on libraries, government archives,
and records of women's organizations in South Asia.

Asia --- Southeast

9.183   Ayal, Eliezer B. *The Study of Thailand: analyses of knowledge, approaches and prospects in anthropology, art history, economics, history, and political science.* Athens: Ohio University Center for International Studies, Southeast Asia Program, 1978. 257 p. DS570.98 .S78 1978.

9.184   Cheeseman, Harold A.R. *Bibliography of Malaya.* London, New York: Longmans, Green, 1959. 234 p. Z3246 .C5.

9.185   Cotter, Michael. *Vietnam: a guide to reference sources.* Boston: G. K. Hall, 1977. 272 p. DS556.3 C68 1977.
        Approximately 1,500 references sources divided into sections for general reference and major disciplines.

9.186   Heussler, Robert. *British Malaya: a bibliographical and biographical compendium.* New York: Garland, 1981. 193 p. DS592 .H4 1981.

9.187   Johnson, Donald C. *A Guide to reference materials on Southeast Asia, based on the collections in the Yale and Cornell University libraries.* New Haven: Yale University Press, 1970. 160 p. DS521 .J64x 1970.

9.188   Johnson, Donald C. *Index to Southeast Asian journals, 1960-1974: a guide to articles, book reviews, and composite works.* Boston: G. K. Hall, 1977. 811 p. DS501 .J64 1977.
        Classified arrangement of articles, with sections for book reviews; continued by D.C. Johnson, *Index to Southeast Asian journals, 1975-1979: a guide to articles, book reviews, and composite works* (Boston: G.K. Hall, 1982. 265 p.).

9.189   Karni, Rahadi S. *Bibliography of Malaysia and Singapore.* Kuala Lumpur: Penerbit Universiti Malaya, 1980. 649 p. .

9.190   Kemp, Herman C. *Annotated bibliography of bibliographies on Indonesia.* Koninklijk Instituut voor Taal-, Land-en Volkenkunde, Bibliographical Series, 17. Leiden: KITLV Press, 1990. 433 p. DS615 .K46x 1990.

9.191   Sukanda-Tessier, Viviane, and Haris Sukanda Natasasmita. *Bibliographie d'une documentation indonesienne contemporaine, 1950-1970.* Paris: Ecole Francaise d'Extreme-Orient, 1974. 480 p. 016.992 Su45.

9.192   Trager, Frank N. *Burma: a selected and annotated bibliography.* New Haven: Human Relations Area Files Press, 1973. 356 p. DS527.4 .T73 1973.
Lists more than 2,000 entries dealing with Burma.

Asia --- Southeast --- Cultural/Social Anthropology

9.193   Cotter, Conrad P. *Bibliography of English language sources on human ecology: Eastern Malaysia and Brunei.* Honolulu: Department of Asian Studies, University of Hawaii, 1965. 2 v. DS646.36 .C68 1965.
Includes coverage of Brunei, Sabah, and Sarawak.

9.194   Embree, John F. *Bibliography of the peoples and cultures of mainland Southeast Asia.* New Haven: Yale University, Southeast Asia Studies, 1950; New York: Russell and Russell, 1972. 821 p. DS521 .E43 1950.
Bibliography of books and articles in English arranged by region, tribal group, and subject.

9.195   Kennedy, Raymond. *Bibliography of Indonesian peoples and cultures.* New Haven: Yale University Press; London: H. Milford, Oxford University Press, 1945. 212 p. GN635 .I65 1962.
Revised edition: R. Kennedy, T.W. Maretski, and H.T. Fischer, *Bibliography of Indonesian peoples and cultures* (New Haven: Southeast Asia Studies, Yale University; Human Relations Area Files, 1962. 207 p.).

9.196   Koentjaraningrat. *Anthropology in Indonesia: a bibliographical review.* The Hague: Nijhoff, 1975. 343 p. 016.992 K819.
Detailed review of cultural/social antrhropology of Indonesia, followed by a list of references.

9.197   LeBar, Frank M. *Ethnic groups of insular Southeast Asia.* New Haven: Human Relations Area Files Press, 1972-1975. 2 v. GN635 .S58 L42.
Includes: v.1. Indonesia, Andaman Islands, and Madagascar; v.2. Philippines, Formosa, Sulu Sangihi, and Botel Tobago.

9.198   LeBar, Frank M., G.C. Hickey, and J.K. Musgrave. *Ethnic groups of mainland Southeast Asia.* New Haven: Human Relations Area Files Press, 1964. 228 p. DS509.5 I4 1964.
Concise ethnographic descriptions with selective bibliographies for approximately 150 groups.

9.199   Marston, John. *An Annotated bibliography of Cambodia and Cambodian refugees.* Minneapolis: Southeast Asian Refugee Studies

Project, Center for Urban and Regional Affairs, University of Minnesota, 1987. 121 p. DS554.8 .A56 1987.

9.200 Nagelkerke, Gerard A. *The Chinese in Indonesia: a bibliography, 18th century, 1981.* Leiden, Netherlands: Library of the Royal Institute of Linguistics and Anthropology, 1982. 238 p. DS563.5 .I57 1974.

9.201 Pelzer, Karl J. *West Malaysia and Singapore: a selected bibliography.* New Haven: Human Relations Area Files Press, 1971. 394 p. DS592 .P45 1971.

9.202 Suzuki, Peter. *Critical survey of studies on the anthropology of Nias, Mentawei and Engano.* Gravenhage: M. Nijhoff, 1958. 87 p. DS647 .S9 1958.
Bibliography on Indonesian ethnology commissioned by the Netherlands Institute for International Cultural Relations.

9.203 Teeuw, A. *A Critical survey of studies on Malay and Bahasa Indonesia.* Gravenhage: M. Nijhoff, 1961. 176 p. 016.4992 T229.

Asia --- Southeast --- Demography
9.204 Saw, Swee-Hock. *The Demography of Malaysia, Singapore, and Brunei: a bibliography.* Hong Kong: Centre of Asian Studies, University of Hong Kong; Oxford University Press, 1970. 39 p. 016.3125 Sa96.

Asia --- Southeast --- Philippines
9.205 Saito, Shiro. *The Philippines; a review of bibliographies.* Occasional Papers, 5. Honolulu: East-West Center Library, 1966. 80 leaves. Z3291 .A1 S3.

9.206 *Selected bibliography of the Philippines, topically arranged and annotated.* New Haven, Connecticut: Human Relations Area Files, 1956. 138 p. 016.9914 C432.

9.207 Wernstedt, Frederick L., *et al. Philippine studies: geography, archaeology, psychology and literature; present knowledge and research trends.* De Kalb: Center for Southeast Asian Studies, Northern Illinois University, 1974. 104 p. 991.4 P5375.

**Asia --- Southeast --- Philippines ---
Cultural/Social Anthropology**
9.208 Saito, Shiro. *Filipinos overseas: a bibliography.* Staten Island, New

York: Center for Migration Studies, 1977. 156 p. DS665 .S2x 1977.

9.209   Saito, Shiro. *Philippine ethnography: a critically annotated and selected bibliography.* Honolulu: University Press of Hawaii, 1972. 512 p. DS655 .S25x 1972.
Approximately 4,300 classified entries relating to Philippine cultural and social anthropology.

Asia --- Southeast --- Philippines --- Linguistics

9.210   Asunción-Lande, Nobleza C. *A Bibliography of Philippine linguistics.* Papers in International Studies, Southeast Asia series, 20. Athens: Ohio University, Center for International Studies, 1971. 147 p. PL5506 .A8x 1971.

9.211   Ward, Jack H. *A Bibliography of Philippine linguistics and minor languages; with annotations and indices based on works in the Library of Cornell University.* Ithaca: Southeast Asia Program, Cornell University, 1971. 549 p. 016.499211 W213.

Asia --- Southeast --- Hmong

9.212   Olney, Douglas P. *A Bibliography of the Hmong (Miao) of Southeast Asia and the Hmong refugees in the United States.* 2 ed. Minneapolis: Southeast Asian Refugee Studies Project, Center for Urban and Regional Affairs, University of Minnesota, 1983. 75 p. DS509.5 .H66 O46x 1983.
Continued by J. Christina Smith, *The Hmong: an annotated bibliography, 1983-1987* (Minneapolis: Southeast Asian Refugee Studies Project, Center for Urban and Regional Affairs, University of Minnesota, 1988. 67 p).

Asia --- Southeast --- Mon-Khmer

9.213   Shorto, H. L. *Bibliographies of Mon-Khmer and Tai linguistics.* London, New York: Oxford University Press, 1963. 87 p. 016.49593 Sh81.
Bibliography on Mon-Khmer and Tai languages.

Europe --- East

9.214   Gates-Coon, Rebecca. *Eastern European bibliography.* Lanham, Maryland: Scarecrow Press, 1993. 187 p. 016.49593 Sh81.
Selective bibliography that documents the formative impact of the earlier history of the region.

9.215   Horecky, Paul L. *East Central Europe: a guide to basic publications.*
Chicago: University of Chicago Press, 1969. 956 p. DJK9 .H672x
1969.

9.216   Horecky, Paul L. *Southeastern Europe: a guide to basic publications.*
Chicago: University of Chicago Press, 1969. 755 p. DR10 .X1 H67x
1969.
Guide to the standard sources for Albania, Bulgaria, Greece,
Romania, and Yugoslavia.

9.217   Schaffner, Bradley L. *Bibliography of the Soviet Union, its
predecessors and successors.* Lanham, Maryland: Scarecrow Press,
1995. 583 p. DK17 .S3x 1995.
Provides subject access to works on the social, political, and
cultural development of the fifteen successor states of the Soviet
Union.

9.218   Sullivan, Helen F., and Robert H. Burger. *Russia and the former
Soviet Union: a bibliographic guide to English language publications,
1986-1991.* Englewood, Colorado: Libraries Unlimited, 1994. 380 p.
DK17 .S85x 1994.
Continues: S.M. Horak, *Russia, the USSR, and Eastern Europe: a
bibliographic guide to English language publications, 1964-1974*
(Littleton, Colorado: Libraries Unlimited, 1978. 488 p.); S.M. Horak,
*Russia, the USSR, and Eastern Europe a bibliographic guide to
English language publications, 1975-1980* (Littleton, Colorado:
Libraries Unlimited, 1982. 279 p.); S.M. Horak, *Russia, the USSR,
and Eastern Europe: a bibliographic guide to English language
publications, 1981-1985* (Littleton, Colorado: Libraries Unlimited,
1987. 273 p.).

Europe --- East --- Archaeology
9.219   Field, Henry. *Bibliography of Soviet archaeology and physical
anthropology 1936-1967.* Coconut Grove, Florida, 1967. 21 p.
016.947 F455.

Europe --- East --- Cultural/Social Anthropology
9.220   Bunakova, O. V., and R.V. Kamenetskaia. *Bibliografiia trudov
Instituta etnografii im. N. N. Miklukho Maklaia, 1900-1962.*
Leningrad: Nauka, 1967. 281 p. Z511 B8.
Includes approximately 5,100 entries with author and subject
indexes.

9.221   Fischer, George, and Walter Schenkel. *Social structure and social change in Eastern Europe; guide to specialized studies published in the West since World War II in English, French, and German.* New York: Foreign Area Materials Center, 1970. 100 p. Z7165 .E82.

9.222   Hagar, Helmut. *A Bibliography of works published by Estonian ethnologists in exile, 1945-1965.* Stockholm: Institutum Litterarum Estonicum, 1965. 63 p. 016.3015 H12.

9.223   Halpern, Joel M. *Bibliography of English language sources on Yugoslavia.* 2 ed. Amherst: Department of Anthropology, University of Massachusetts, 1969. 134 p. DR305 .H35x 1969.

9.224   Horak, Stephan M. *Guide to the study of the Soviet nationalities: non-Russian peoples of the USSR.* Littleton, Colorado: Libraries Unlimited, 1982. 265 p. DK33 .G788 1982.

9.225   Kerner, Robert J. *Slavic Europe: a selected bibliography in the western European languages.* Cambridge, Massachusetts: Harvard University Press, 1918. 402 p. D449 .K47x 1918.

9.226   Rank, Aino. *Ethnology 1945-1975.* Stockholm: Estonian Scientific Institute, 1975. 58 p. Z2533 .F65 no.5.

9.227   Rank, Aino. *A Bibliography of works published by Estonian historians in exile 1945-1969; history, archaeology, history of art, music, the Church and law.* Stockholm: Institutum Litterarum Estonicum, 1969. 56 p. Z2533 .F65x No.3.

9.228   Sanders, Irwin T., Roger Whitaker, and Walter C. Bisselle. *East European peasantries: social relations: an annotated bibliography of periodical articles.* Boston: G.K. Hall, 1976-1981. 2 v. HN373 .S26 1976.
         Bibliography of periodical articles dealing with the countries of formerly Communist East Europe and Greece in the Mugar Library, Boston University.

9.229   Shennikov, A.A. *Etnografiia narodov Vostochnoi Evropy: sbornik statei.* Leningrad: Geogr. o-vo SSSR, 1977. 159 p.
         Russian language bibliography of East European ethnology.

9.230   Titova, Zoia D. *Etnografiia. Bibliografiia russkikh bibliografii po etnografii narodov SSSR (1851-1969).* Moskva: Kniga, 1970. 143 p.

GN585 .S65 T58 1970.
Annotated listing of 734 items arranged by region.

Europe --- West --- Archaeology

9.231   *Bibliographie zur archaologischen Germanenforschung.* Berli: VEB
Deutscher Verlag der Wissenschaften, 1966. 220 p.
Bibliography of German archaeology and prehistory prepared by
the Universitat. Institut fur Ur- und Fruhgeschichte at the University
of Berlin.

9.232   Bonser, Wilfrid. *An Anglo-Saxon and Celtic bibliography, 450-1087.*
Oxford, England: B. Blackwell, 1957. 2 v. Z2017 .B6.

9.233   Bonser, Wilfrid. *A Romano-British bibliography, 55 BC-449 AD.*
Oxford, England: B. Blackwell, 1964. 2 v. Z2017 .B62.

9.234   Bonser, Wilfrid, and June Troy. *A Prehistoric bibliography.* Oxford,
England: B. Blackwell, 1976. 425 p. GN805 .B66 1976.
Bibliography dealing with the archaeology and prehistory of Great
Britain.

9.235   Gerlach, Gudrun, and Rolf Hachmann. *Verzeichnis vor- und
fruhgeschichtlicher Bibliographien.* Berlin: de Gruyter, 1971. 269 p.

9.236   Hachmann, Rolf. *Ausgewahlte Bibliographie zur Vorgeschichte von
Mitteleuropa.* Wiesbaden: Steiner, 1984. 390 p. GN803 .A87 1984.
Bibliography of prehistoric central Europe.

9.237   Montandon, Raoul. *Bibliographie generale des travaux
palethnologiques et archeologiques.* Geneve, Lyon: Georg,
1917-1921. 3 v.
Bibliography of Palaeolithic archaeology in France.

9.238   Schmider, Beatrice. *Bibliographie analytique de prehistoire pour le
paleolithique superieur europeen: publications parues entre 1850 et
1968, conservees a la Bibliotheque du Musée de l'Homme.* Paris:
Centre de Documentation Sciences Humaines, 1975. 2 v. GN772.2 .A1
S34.
Bibliography of European Palaeolithic archaeology.

Europe --- West --- Cultural/Social Anthropology

9.239   Bonser, Wilfrid. *A Bibliography of folklore as contained in the first
eighty years of the publications of the Folklore Society.* London:

Folklore Society; William Glaisher, 1961. 126 p. 395B B645.

9.240 Lange, Peter M. *Studies on Italy, 1943-1975: select bibliography of America and British materials in political science, economics, sociology, and anthropology.* Torino: Fondazione Giovanni Agnelli, 1977. 183 p. HC305 .L34.

9.241 Ripley, William Z. *A Selected bibliography of the anthropology and ethnology of Europe.* Boston: Trustees of Boston Public library, 1899. 160 p.
Approximately 2,000 book and article entries, arranged by author; subject index.

9.242 Sweet, Louise E., and Timothy O'Leary. *Circum-Mediterranean peasantry: introductory bibliographies.* New Haven: Human Relations Area Files Press, 1969. 106 p. Z7165 .M38 S8.
Preliminary bibliographic guide to the anthropological literature for Albania, Algeria, the Eastern Islands, Egypt, France, Greece, Israel, Italy, Jordan, Lebanon, Libya, Morocco, Portugal, Spain, Syria, Tunisia, Turkey, the Western Islands, and Yugoslavia.

9.243 Theodoratus, Robert J. *Europe: a selected ethnographic bibliography.* New Haven: Human Relations Area Files, 1969. 544 p. Z5117 .T5.
Includes approximately 8,000 books and articles emphasizing the nineteenth and twentieth century materials.

9.244 Weeks, John M., and Martha L. Brogan. *The Social anthropology of Western Europe: a selective bibliography of books in Humanities/Social Sciences Libraries, University of Minnesota.* Minneapolis: Humanities/Social Sciences Libraries and Western European Area Studies Center, University of Minnesota, 1988. 124 p. GN575 .W44 1988.

Europe --- West --- Linguistics
9.245 Price, Glanville. *The Present position of minority languages in Western Europe: a selective bibliography.* Cardiff: University of Wales Press, 1969. 81 p. Z7006 .P75.

Europe --- West --- Greeks
9.246 Vlachos, Evangelos. *An Annotated bibliography on Greek migration.* Athens: Social Sciences Centre, 1966. 127 leaves.

9.247   Vlachos, Evangelos. *Modern Greek society: continuity and change: an annotated classification of sources.* Fort Collins: Colorado State University, Department of Sociology and Anthropology, 1969; New York: AMS Press, 1980. 177 p.
        Includes introductory essays and bibloiographies in topical arrangement.

Europe --- West --- Gypsies

9.248   Binns, Dennis. *A Gypsy bibliography: a bibliography of all recent books, pamphlets, articles, broadsheets, theses and dissertations pertaining to Gypsies and other travellers that the author is aware of at the time of printing.* Chorltonville, Manchester: Dennis Binns Publications, 1982. 110 p.

Europe --- West --- Irish

9.249   Danaher, Kevin. *A Bibliography of Irish ethnology and folk tradition.* Dublin: Mercier Press, 1978. 95 p. GN585 .I7 D3 1978.

Europe --- West --- Sami (Lapps)

9.250   *Bibliografia samiid birra 1960-1969.* Ohcejohka/Utsjoki: Samiraddi, 1980. 203 p.
        Bibliography prepared by the Nordic Sami Council in English, Finnish, Lapp, Spanish, and Swedish.

9.251   *Sami bibliografia: callosat Norggas 1945-1987; Samisk bibliografi: utgivelser i Norge 1945-1987; Sami bibliography: publications in Norway 1945-1987.* Trondheim: Universitetsbiblioteket i Trondheim, 1989. 336 p.

9.252   Thomasson, Lars. *De svenska samerna och renskotseln i Sverige. Bibliografiska anteckningar for aren 1960-69.* Umea: Lansmuseet, 1971. 149 p. 068 Sk96 no.9.

Europe --- West --- Spaniards

9.253   González Olle, Fernando. *Manual bibliográfico de estudios españoles.* Pamplona: Ediciones Universidad de Navarra, 1976. 1,375 p. Z2681 .G66.

Latin America

9.254   *Bibliographic guide to Latin American studies.* Boston: G. K. Hall, v.1 - , 1978 - . 1/yr. Z1610 .B52.
        "Consists of publications cataloged by the Latin American Collection of the University of Texas, with additional entries from the

Library of Congress."

Latin America --- Race Relations

9.255   Levine, Robert M. *Race and ethnic relations in Latin America and the Caribbean an historical dictionary and bibliograph.* Metuchen, New Jersey: Scarecrow Press, 1980. 252 p. F1419 .A1 L48 1980.

Dictionary of terms pertaining to relations among ethnic and racial groups; includes an extensive bibliograpohy of 1,342 books and articles arranged geographically.

Latin America --- Women

9.256   Knaster, Meri. *Women in Spanish America: an annotated bibliography from pre-conquest to contemporary times.* Boston: G. K. Hall, 1977. 696 p. HQ1460.5 .K59 1977.

Includes some 2,400 annotated entries.

9.257   Stoner, K. Lynn. *Latinas of the Americas: a source book.* New York: Garland, 1989. 692 p. HQ1460.5 .S76x 1989.

Latin America --- Caribbean Area

9.258   Brown, Enid. *Suriname and the Netherlands Antilles.* Lanham, Maryland: Scarecrow Press, 1992. 293 p. F2408 .B76x 1992.

Provides over 1,000 published and unpublished English-language works written on Suriname and the Netherlands Antilles.

9.259   Carvajal, Manuel J. *The Caribbean, 1975-1980: a bibliography of economic an rural development.* Metuchen, New York: Scarecrow Press, 1993. 897 p. HC151 .C298x 1993.

Over 5,300 entries on economic and rural development in the Caribbean, except Cuba and Puerto Rico.

9.260   Comitas, Lambros. *Caribbeana 1900-1965, a topical bibliography.* Seattle: Research Institute for the Study; University of Washington Press, 1968. 909 p. 016.91729 C735.

Includes approximately 7,000 enties for books, monographs, reports, articles, theses, and government documents on non-Spanish speakling Caribbean Islands and adjacent mainland countries.

9.261   Covington, Paula H. *Latin America and the Caribbean: a critical guide to resources.* New York: Greenwood Press, 1992. 924 p. F1408 .L3846x 1992.

9.262   Goslinga, Marian. *A Bibliography of the Caribbean*. Lanham, Maryland: Scarecrow Press, 1996. 368 p. F2161 .G67x 1996.

More than 3,600 entries divided into historical materials listed chronologically, reference materials listed according to format, and contemporary works arranged by subject area. Includes materials in the social sciences and humanities in English, Spanish, French, and Dutch pertaining to a region from Belize, Guyana, Suriname, and French Guiana.

9.263   Jordan, Alma, and Barbara Comissiong. *The English-speaking Caribbean: a bibliography of bibliographies*. Boston: G.K. Hall, 1984. 411 p. F2161 .J78x 1984.

9.264   *Notes bibliographiques caraibes*. Basse-Terre, Guadeloupe, no. 1 - , 1977 - . F2161 .N67x.

Creoles and Pidgins, English, and French.

9.265   Laguerre, Michel S. *The Complete Haitiana: a bibliographic guide to the scholarly literature, 1900-1980*. Millwood, New York: Kraus International, 1982. 2 v. F1915 .L33 1982.

Includes books, articles, essays, dissertations and theses, and government publications arranged in eleven major topical headings subdivided into 65 sections.

9.266   Mevis, Rene. *Inventory of Caribbean studies: an overview of social research on the Caribbean conducted by Antillean, Dutch, Surinamese scholars in the period 1945-1973; with an index of Caribbean specialists and a bibliography*. Leiden: Caribbean Department, Royal Institute of Linguistics Anthropology, 1974. 181 p. 016.9729 M573.

Continued by: Theo M.P. Oltheten, *Inventory of Caribbean studies: an overview of social scientific publications on the Caribbean by Antillean, Dutch and Surinamese authors in the period 1945-1978/79* (Leiden: Smitts Drukkers-Uitgevers B.V. Caribbean; Department of Caribbean Studies, Royal Institute of Linguistics and Anthropology, 1979. 280 p.).

9.267   Nagelkerke, Gerard A. *Netherlands Antilles, a bibliography, 17th century-1980*. Leiden, Netherlands: Dept. of Caribbean Studies, Royal Institute of Linguistics and Anthropology; The Hague: Smits Drukkers-Uitgevers, 1982. 422 p. F2141 .N3 1982.

"This bibliography gives a survey of the collection of books, articles, manuscripts, etc., relating to the Netherlands Antilles kept in the library of the Royal Institute of Linguistics and Anthropology

(KITLV) in Leiden;" text in Dutch with introduction in Dutch, English, and Papiamento; continues: G.A. Nagelkerke, *Literatuur-overzicht van de Nederlandse Antillen vanaf de 17e eeuw to 1970: literatuur aanwezig in de bibliotheek van het Koninklijk Instituut voor Taal-, Land- en Volkenkunde te Leiden* (Leiden: De Bibliotheek, 1973. 147 p.).

9.268   Nagelkerke, Gerard A. *Suriname, a bibliography, 1940-1980.* Leiden, Netherlands: Department of Caribbean Studies, Royal Institute of Linguistics and Anthropology, 1980. 336 p. F2408 .N34x 1980.

Latin America --- Caribbean Area --- Archaeology

9.269   Acosta Saignes, Miguel. *Zona circuncaribe: período indígena.* México: Instituto Panamericano de Geografía e Historia, 1953. 101 p. 906 P191 no.162.

9.270   Chevrette, Valerie. *Annotated bibliography of the Precolumbian art and archaeology of the West Indies.* New York: Library, Museum of Primitive Art, 1971. 18 p. F1619 .C54 1971.

9.271   Myers, Robert A. *Amerindians of the Lesser Antilles: a bibliography.* New Haven: Human Relations Area Files, 1981. 158 leaves. F2001 .M9 1981.

  Classified bibliography of approximately 1,300 references to archaeological, historical, and linguistic research on the Ciboney, Arawak, and Carib peoples of the eastern Caribbean.

9.272   Pagán Perdomo, Dato. *El arte rupestre en el área del Caribe: inventario del arte rupestre en Santo Domingo: bibliografía sumaria del area.* Santo Domingo: Ediciones Fundación García-Arevalo, 1978. 93 p. F1909 .P328 1978.

9.273   Weeks, John M., and Peter J. Ferbel. *Ancient Caribbean.* New York: Garland, 1994. 325 p. F1619 .W44x 1994.

**Latin America --- Caribbean Area ---
Biological/Physical Anthropology**

9.274   Clermont, Norman. *Bibliographie annotée de l'anthropologie physique des Antilles.* Montreal: Centre de Recherches Caraibes, 1972. 51 p. 016.3013 C597.

Latin America --- Caribbean Area ---
Cultural/Social Anthropology

9.275   Hall-Alleyne, Beverley, Garth White, and Michael Cooke. *Towards a bibliography of African-Caribbean studies, 1970-1980.* Kingston: African-Caribbean Institute of Jamaica, 1982. 37 p. F2169 .H3 1982. Bibliography of African influences in the Caribbean area.

9.276   Sued Badillo, Jalil. *Bibliografía antropológica para el estudio de los pueblos indígenas en el Carib.* Santo Domingo: Ediciones Fundación García-Arévalo, 1977. 579 p. F1619 .S93 1977.
         International bibliography covering the Caribbean Islands and surrounding countries of Central and South America.

Latin America --- Caribbean Area --- Women

9.277   Cohen Stuart, Bertie A. *Women in the Caribbean: a bibliography.* Leiden: Department of Caribbean Studies, Royal Institute of Linguistics and Anthropology, 1979. 163 p. HQ1501 .C6x 1979.
         Approximately 650 entries dealing with Surinam, French Guiana, and Guyana, the Bahamas, and Bermuda.

9.278   Massiah, Joycelin. *Women in the Caribbean: an annotated bibliography: a guide to material available in Barbados.* Cave Hill, Barbados: Institute of Social and Economic Research (Eastern Caribbean), University of the West Indies, 1979. 133 leaves. HQ1501 .M37x 1979.

9.279   *Rural women: a Caribbean bibliography with special reference to Jamaica.* San Jose: Committee for Rural Women and Development, Inter-American Institute of Agricultural Sciences (IICA), 1980. 29 p. HQ1518 .R87x 1980.

Latin America --- Mexico and Central America

9.280   Markman, Sidney D. *Colonial Central America: a bibliography including materials on art and architecture, cultural, economic, and social history, ethnohistory, geography, government, indigenous writings, maps and plans, urbanization, bibliographic and archival documentary sources.* Tempe: Center for Latin America Studies, Arizona State University, 1977. 345 p. F1428 .M24x 1977.

9.281   McGlynn, Eileen A. *Middle American anthropology: directory, bibliography, and guide to the UCLA Library collections.* Los Angeles: Latin American Center, University of California, 1975. 131 p. F1434 .M44x 1975.

9.282   Welch, Thomas L., and Myriam Figueras. *Travel accounts and descriptions of Latin America and the Caribbean, 1800-1920: a selected bibliography.* Washington, D.C.: Columbus Memorial Library, Organization of American States, 1982. 293 p. F1409 .W4x 1982.

Latin America --- Mexico and Central America --- Anthropology

9.283   Bernal, Ignacio. *Bibliografía de arqueología y etnografía.* México: Instituto Nacional de Antropología e Historia, 1962. 634 p. F1434 .B47x 1962.

Includes approximately 13,000 entries arranged by region and subject.

9.284   Lines, Jorge A. *Anthropological bibliography of aboriginal Costa Rica.* San Jose: Tropical Science Center, 1967. 196 p. F1545 .L65155x 1967.

9.285   Lines, Jorge A., and Michael D. Olien. *Anthropological bibliography of aboriginal El Salvador.* San Jose: Tropical Science Center, 1965. 114 p. F1485 .L56x 1965.

9.286   Lines, Jorge A. *Anthropological bibliography of aboriginal Guatemala, British Honduras.* San Jose: Tropical Science Center, 1967. 396 p. F1465 .L56x 1967.

9.287   Lines, Jorge A., Edwin M. Shook, and Michael D. Olien. *Anthropological bibliography of aboriginal Honduras.* San Jose: Tropical Science Center, 1966. 190 p. F1505 .L56x 1966.

9.288   Lines, Jorge A., Edwin M. Shook, and Michael D. Olien. *Anthropological bibliography of aboriginal Nicaragua.* San Jose: Tropical Science Center, 1965. 98 p. F1525 .L56x 1965.

9.289   Shook, Edwin M., Jorge A. Lines, and Michael D. Olien. *Anthropological bibliography of aboriginal Panama.* San Jose: Tropical Science Center, 1965. 79 p. F1563 .S56x 1965.

Latin America --- Mexico and Central America --- Archaeology

9.290   Berlo, Janet C. *The Art of pre-Hispanic Mesoamerica: an annotated bibliography.* Boston: G.K. Hall, 1985. 272 p. F1219.3 .A7 B38x 1985.

9.291 Howard-Reguindin, Pamela F., and Ann E. Smith. *Author index to the publications of the Middle American Research Institute, Tulane University, 1926-1985.* New Orleans: Middle American Research Institute, Tulane University, 1985. 33 p. F1434 .H68x 1985.

9.292 Kendall, Aubyn. *The Art and archaeology of pre-Columbian Middle America: an annotated bibliography of works in English.* Boston: G. K. Hall, 1977. 324 p. F1219.3 .A7 K4x 1977.

9.293 Kendall, Aubyn. *The Art of pre-Columbian Mexico: an annotated bibliography of works in English.* Austin: Institute of Latin American Studies, University of Texas at Austin, 1973. 115 p. F1219.3 .A7 K43x 1973.

9.294 Lee, Thomas A. *New World Archaeological Foundation: obra, 1952-1980.* Provo, Utah: New World Archaeological Foundation; College of Family, Home, and Social Sciences, Brigham Young University, 1981. 142 p. F1219.7 .L43 1981.

9.295 Magee, Susan F. *Mesoamerican archaeology: a guide to the literature and other information source.* Austin: Institute of Latin American Studies, University of Texas at Austin, 1981. 71 p. F1219.7 .M34x 1981.

.9.296 Saville, Marshall H. *Bibliographic notes on Xochicalco, Mexico.* New York, Museum of the American Indian, Heye Foundation, Indian Notes and Monographs, 6(6). New York, 1928. 301.82 N48ind v. 6(6).

9.297 Strecker, Matthias. *Rock art of east Mexico and Central America: an annotated bibliography.* 2 ed. Los Angeles: Institute of Archaeology, University of California, Los Angeles, 1982. 81 p. F1219 .S77x 1982.

Latin America --- Mexico and Central America --- Biological/Physical Anthropology

9.298 Comas, Juan, and Santiago Genovés T. *La antropología física en México, 1943-1959: inventario y programa de investigaciones.* México: Universidad Nacional Autónoma de México, 1960. 66 p.

Latin America --- Mexico and Central America --- Cultural/Social Anthropology

9.299 Ewald, Robert H. *Bibliografía comentada sobre antropología social guatemalteca, 1900-1955.* Guatemala: Seminario de Integración Social Guatemalteca, 1956. 132 p. 016.30182 Ew14S.

9.300   Ojeda Diaz, Maria de los Angeles. *Indice de los trabajos sobre Mesoamérica de Eduard Seler*. México: Biblioteca Nacional de Antropología e Historia, 1978. 26 p. E57 .S46 O35x 1978.
Biobibliography of German ethnohistorian Eduard Seler (1849-1922).

9.301   Parra, Manuel G., and Wigberto Jiménez Moreno. *Bibliografía indigenista de México y Centroamérica (1850-1950)*. México: Instituto Nacional Indigenista, 1954. 342 p. 016.30182 P247.

9.302   Warren, Kay B. *Mesoamerican community studies, 1930-1970: a bibliography*. Princeton: Princeton University Library, 1973. 32 leaves. F1220 .W37x 1973.

Latin America --- Mexico and Central America --- Aztec
9.303   Abrams, H. Leon. *Robert Hayward Barlow, an annotated bibliography with commentary*. Greeley: Museum of Anthropology, University of Northern Colorado, 1981. 32 leaves. F1219.7 .B3 A2x 1981.
Biobibliography of noted Aztec scholar R.H. Barlow (1918-1951).

9.304   Nathan, Michele. *Nahuatl sources in the Tulane University Latin American Library: an annotated bibliography*. New Orleans: Center for Latin American Studies, Tulane University, 1975. 50 p. PM4069 .N372 1975.

9.305   Welch, Thomas L., and Rene L. Gutierrez. *The Aztecs: a bibliography of books and periodical articles*. Washington, D.C.: Columbus Memorial Library, Organization of American States, 1987. 169 p. F1219 .W456 1987.

Latin America --- Mexico and Central America --- Maya
9.306   Hellmuth, Nicholas M. *A Bibliography of the 16th-20th century Maya of the Southern lowlands: Chol, Chol Lacandon, Yucatec Lacandon, Quejache, Itza, and Mopan, 1524-1969*. Greeley: Museum of Anthropology, University of Northern Colorado, 1970. 114 leaves. F1435 .H4 1970.

9.307   Saville, Marshall H. *Bibliographic notes on Palenque*. New York, Museum of the American Indian, Heye Foundation, Indian Notes and Monographs, 6(5). New York, 1928. 301.82 N48ind v.6(5).

9.308   Saville, Marshall H. *Bibliographic notes on Quirigua, Guatemala.*
New York, Museum of the American Indian, Heye Foundation, Indian
Notes and Monographs, 6(1). New York, 1919. 301.82 N48ind v.6(1).

9.309   Saville, Marshall H. *Bibliographic notes on Uxmal.* New York,
Museum of the American Indian, Heye Foundation, Indian Notes and
Monographs, 9(2). New York, 1921. 301.82 N48ind v. 9.

9.310   Tozzer, Alfred M. *A Maya grammar, with bibliography and
appraisement of the works noted.* Papers of the Peabody Museum of
American Archaeology and Ethnology, Harvard University, 9.
Cambridge, Massachusetts, 1921. 301 p. E51 .H337 v.9.
Includes an excellent bibliography of primary sources for the
study of Maya languages.

9.311   Valle, Rafael H. *Bibliografía maya.* México: Instituto Panamericano
de Geografía e Historia, 1937-1941; New York: B. Franklin, 1971.
404 p. Z1210 .M4 V3.
Comprehensive bibliography of the Maya.

9.312   Ventur, Pierre. *Maya ethnohistorian: the Ralph L. Roys papers.*
Nashville: Vanderbilt University, 1978. 153 p. F1435.6 .R69 V4x
1978.
Bibliography of the work of ethnohistorian Ralph Loveland Roy
(1879-1965).

9.313   Vogt, Evon Z. *Bibliography of the Harvard Chiapas Project-the first
twenty years, 1957-1977.* Cambridge, Massachusetts: Peabody
Museum of Archaeology and Ethnology, Harvard University, 1978. 75
p. F1221 .T9 1978.
Discusses the methodology and problems, names the 138
participants, and lists some 400 books, articles, and unpublished
reports about the Tzotzil Maya resulting from the Harvard Chiapas
Project.

9.314   Weeks, John M. *Maya civilization.* New York: Garland, 1993. 369 p.
F1435 .W43 1993.

9.315   Welch, Thomas L., and Rene L. Gutierrez. *The Mayas: a bibliography
of books and periodical articles.* Washington, D.C: Columbus
Memorial Library, Organization of American States, 1991. 236 p.
F1435 .W35x 1991.

9.316   White, Anthony G. *Mayan architecture: a selected bibliography.*
Monticello, Illinois: Vance Bibliographies, 1984. 5 p. F1435.3 .A6
W44 1984.

Latin America --- Mexico and Central America --- Olmec
9.317   Jones, Julie. *Bibliography for Olmec sculpture.* New York: Museum of
Primitive Art Library, 1963. 8 p. Z1210 .O4 J6 1963.

Latin America --- South America
9.318   Goodman, Edward J. *The Exploration of South America: an annotated
bibliography.* New York: Garland, 1983. 174 p. E101 .G65 1983.
Includes 915 entreies dealing with the history of exploration of
South America from the Spanish conquerors to the discovery of Machu
Picchu.

9.319   Levine, Robert M. *Brazil since 1930: an annotated bibliography for
social historians.* New York: Garland, 1980. 336 p. F2508 .L48x
1980.
Continues: R.M. Levine, *Brazil, 1822-1930: an annotated
bibliography for social historians* (New York: Garland, 1983. 487 p.).

Latin America --- South America --- Archaeology
9.320   Dubelaar, C. N. *The Petroglyphs in the Guianas and adjacent areas of
Brazil and Venezuela: an inventory with a comprehensive
bibliography of South American and Antillean petroglyphs.* Los
Angeles: Institute of Archaeology, University of California, Los
Angeles, 1986. 326 p. F2230.1 .P48 D83 1986.

9.321   Silverman, Helaine. *Ancient Peruvian art: an annotated bibliography.*
New York: G.K. Hall, 1996. 250 p. F3429.3 .A7 S55 1996.
Annotated bibliography of books, journal articles, and exhibition
catalogs and historiographical essay on the study of ancient Peruvian
art; sites considered include Chavín, Moche, Cuzco, Chan Chan,
Wari, Tiahuanaco, and others.

Latin America --- South America --- Cultural/Social Anthropology
9.322   Baldus, Herbert. *Bibliografia comentada de etnología brasileira,
1943-1950.* Rio de Janeiro: Souza, 1954. 142 p. GN564 .B7 1954.

9.323   Baldus, Herbert. *Bibliografia crítica da etnología brasileira.* Sao
Paulo: Comissao do IV Centenario da Cidade de Sao Paulo, Servico de
Comemoracoes Culturais, 1954. 859 p. F2510 .B3 1970.

9.324   Baldus, Herbert. *Bibliografia crítica da etnología brasileira.*
         Hannover: Kommissionverlag Munstermann-Druck, 1968 - . GN4
         .V6
         Introductory matter in Portuguese, English, and German.

9.325   Bernal Villa, Segundo. *Guía bibliográfica de Colombia de interés*
         para el antropologo. Bogota: Ediciones Universidad de los Andes,
         1969. 782 p. Z1731 .B44.
         Extensive bibliography with an emphasis on cultural anthropology
         although some attention is given to archaeology, linguistics,
         geography, and History.

9.326   Fuchs, Helmuth. *Bibliografia básica de etnología de Venezuela.*
         Sevilla, 1964. 251 p. F2319 .F83 1964.

9.327   Larrea, Carlos M. *Bibliografia científica del Ecuador.* 3 ed. Quito:
         Ccrporación de Estudios y Publicaciones, 1968. 289 p. Z7407 .S6 L33
         1968.
         Author listing of books and periodical articles.

9.328   Mareski, Sofia, and Oscar H. Ferraro. *Bibliografia sobre datos y*
         estudios económicos en el Paraguay. Asunción: Centro Paraguayo de
         Documentación Social, 1972. 82 leaves. HC222 .M37 1972.
         Author listing on some 975 entries with subject index.

9.329   Martínez, Héctor, Miguel Cameo C., and Jesús Ramírez S.
         Bibliografia indígena andina peruana (1900-1968). Lima: Centro de
         Estudios de Población y Desarrollo, 1969. 157 p. F3429 .M3 1969.
         Some 1,700 entries arranged by a general section and sections for
         northern, central, and southern areas of Peru, each with geographical
         and topical subdivisions.

9.330   Nagelkerke, Gerard A. *Suriname, a bibliography, 1940-1980.* Leiden,
         Netherlands: Department of Caribbean Studies, Royal Institute of
         Linguistics and Anthropology, 1980. 336 p. F2419 .N33 1977.

9.331   O'Leary, Timothy J. *Ethnographic bibliography of South America.*
         New Haven: Human Relations Area Files, 1963. 387 p. GN562 .O44
         1963.
         Listing of some 24,000 books and articles covering the
         ethnographic literature of continental South America through 1961.

9.332   Pollak-Eltz, Angelina. *Bibliografia afrovenezolana.* Caracas:
         Universidad Católica Andrés Bello," Instituto de Investigaciones
         Históricas, 1976. 25 p. F2310 .P6 1983.
         Continued by: A. Pollak-Eltz, *Nuevos aportes a la Bibliografia*
         afrovenezolana: datos recolectados desde la publicación de la
         Bibliografia afrovenezolana en la revista Montalbán no. 5, Caracas,
         1976 (Caracas: Centro de Religiones Comparadas, Universidad
         Católica Andrés Bello, 1983. 16 p.).

9.333   Schwab, Federico. *Bibliografia etnológica de la Amazonia peruana,*
         1542-1942. Lima: Companía de impresiones y publicidad, 1942. 76 p.
         F3429 .S39 1942.

9.334   Welch, Thomas L. *The Indians of South America: a bibliography.*
         Washington, D.C.: Columbus Memorial Library, Organization of
         American States, 1987. 594 p. F2229 .W4 1987.

Latin America — South America —
Government Relations
9.335   Fuerst, Rene. *Bibliography of the indigenous problem and policy of*
         the Brazilian Amazon region, 1957-1972. IWGIA Document, 6.
         Copenhagen: International Work Group for Indigenous Affairs;
         Geneva: Documentation and Information Center for Indigenous
         Affairs in the Amazon Region, 1972. 44 p. F2519.3 .G6 X58 1972.

Latin America — South America —
Linguistics
9.336   Key, Harold H., and Mary Key. *Bolivian Indian tribes: classification,*
         bibliography, and map of present language distribution. Norman:
         Summer Institute of Linguistics of the University of Oklahoma, 1967.
         128 p. F3320 .K4 1967.

Latin America — South America —
Literature
9.337   Cardozo, Lubio. *Bibliografia de la literatura indígena venezolana.*
         Mérida: Universidad de los Andes, Centro de Investigaciones
         Literarias, 1970. 122 p. 016.898 C179.

9.338   Niles, Susan A. *South American Indian narrative, theoretical and*
         analytical approaches: an annotated bibliography. New York:
         Garland, 1981. 183 p. F2230.1 .F6 1981.

Latin America --- South America ---
Aymara

9.339 Rivet, Paul, and Georges Crequi-Montfort. *Bibliographie des langues aymara et kicua.* Paris: Institut d'Ethnologie, 1951-1956. 4 v. 301.06 P218 v.51.

Latin America --- South America ---
Chono

9.340 Cooper, John M. *Analytical and critical bibliography of the tribes of Tierra del Fuego and adjacent territory.* Washington, D.C.: United States Government Printing Office, 1917. 233 p. E51 .U6 no.63.
Coverage includes Chono, Ona (Selknam), Alacaluf, and Yahgan Indians.

Latin America --- South America --- Inca

9.341 Welch, Thomas L., and René L. Gutiérrez. *The Incas: a bibliography of books and periodical articles.* Washington, D.C.: Columbus Memorial Library, Organization of American States, 1987. 145 p. F3429 .W46 1987.

Latin America --- South America ---
Maroons

9.342 Price, Richard. *The Guiana Maroons: a historical and bibliographical introduction.* Baltimore: Johns Hopkins University Press, 1976. 184 p. F2431 .N3 1976.
Lists 1,330 entries and includes an evaluative essay of the literature.

Latin America --- South America ---
Toba

9.343 Miller, Elmer S. *A Critically annotated bibliography of the Gran Chaco Toba.* New Haven: Human Relations Area Files, 1980. 2 v. F2823 .T7 1980.
Listing of materials about the Guaicuran-speaking Toba (Natekebit) Indians of the Gran Choco.

Middle East

9.344 Allworth, Edward. *Soviet Asia, bibliographies: a compilation of social science and humanities sources on the Iranian, Mongolian, and Turkic nationalities, with an essay on the Soviet-Asian controversy.* New York: Praeger, 1975. 686 p. DK855.4 .A64 1975.
Lists some 5,200 bibliographies published in Czarist Russia and the former Soviet Union between 1850 and 1970.

9.345   Anderson, Margaret. *Arabic materials in English translation: a bibliography of works from the pre-Islamic period to 1977.* Boston: G. K. Hall, 1980. 249 p. PJ7692 .E1 A5 1980.

9.346   Atiyeh, George N. *The Contemporary Middle East, 1948-1973: a selective and annotated bibliography.* Boston: G. K. Hall, 1975. 664 p. DS44 .A85 1975.
        Emphasis is given to social conditions and related subjects; brief annotations.

9.347   Dotan, Uri. *A Bibliography of articles on the Middle East, 1959-1967.* Tel Aviv: Tel Aviv University, Shiloah Center for Middle Eastern and African Studies, 1970. 227 p. Z3013 .D67.

9.348   Field, Henry. *Bibliography of southwestern Asia.* Coral Gables, Florida: University of Miami Press, 1953-1962. 7 v. QH179 .F5.
        Provides areal coverage from Istanbul to the Hindu Kush on the north, and from Aden to the Makran Coast on the south; subject indexing provided by: H. Field, and Bernard J. Clifton, *Subject index to Bibliographies on Southwestern Asia, I-V* (Coral Gables, Florida: University of Miami Press, 1959-1961).

9.349   Rossi, Peter M., and Wayne E. White. *Articles on the Middle East, 1947-1971: a cumulation of the bibliographies from the Middle East journal.* Ann Arbor, Michigan: Pierian Press, 1980. 4 v. DS44 .R6 1980.

9.350   Sinor, Denis. *Introduction a l'etude de l'Eurasie centrale.* Wiesbaden: Harrassowitz, 1963. 371 p. 016.95 Si67.

Middle East --- Guides

9.351   Elwell-Sutton, L.P. *Bibliographical guide to Iran: the Middle East Library Committee guide.* Sussex, England: Harvester Press; Totowa, New York: Barnes and Noble Books, 1983. 462 p. DS254.5 .B5 1983.

9.352   Grimwood-Jones, Diana, Derek Hopwood, and J.D. Pearson. *Arab-Islamic bibliography: the Middle East Library Committee guide: based on Giuseppe Gabrieli's Manuale di bibliografia musulmana.* Hassocks, England: Harvester Press; Atlantic Highland, New Jersey: Humanities Press, 1977. 292 p. BP161.2 .M5 1979.
        A basic bibliographic guide to the literature of the Middle East.

9.353   Hopwood, Derek, and Diana Grimwood-Jones. *Middle East and Islam:*
         a bibliographical introduction. Zug, Switzerland: Inter
         Documentation, 1972. 368 p. Z3013 .M58.
         Continued by: Diana Grimwood-Jones, *Middle East and Islam: a*
         bibliographical introduction (rev. ed. Zug, Switzerland: Inter
         Documentation, 1979. 429 p.); P. Auchterlonie, *Middle East and*
         Islam: a bibliographical introduction: supplement, 1977-1983 (Zug,
         Switzerland: IDC, 1986. 244 p.).

9.354   Littlefield, David W. *The Islamic Near East and North Africa: an*
         annotated guide to books in English for non-specialists. Littleton,
         Colorado: Libraries Unlimited, 1977. 375 p. DS44 .L54x 1977.

9.355   Silverberg, Sanford R. *Middle East bibliography.* Lanham, Maryland:
         Scarecrow Press, 1992. 599 p.
         Contains over 4,400 book entries, most of which were published
         after 1980.

9.356   Simon, Reeva S. *The Modern Middle East: a guide to research tools*
         in the social sciences. Boulder: Westview Press, 1978. 283 p. DS44
         .S56x 1978.

9.357   Zuwiyya, Jalal. *The Near East (South-west Asia and North Africa); a*
         bibliographic study. Metuchen, New Jersey: Scarecrow Press, 1973.
         392 p. DS44 .Z89x 1973.

Middle East --- Archaeology
9.358   Bachatly, Charles. *Bibliographie de la prehistoire egyptienne*
         (1869-1938). Le Caire, 1942. 77 p. 016.962 B122.

9.359   Battersby, Harold R. *Anatolian archaeology: a bibliography.* New
         Haven: Human Relations Area Files, 1976. 2 v. DS155 .B38 1976.

9.360   Berghe, Louis vanden. *Bibliographie analytique de l'archeologie de*
         l'Iran ancien. Leiden: Brill, 1979. 329 p. DS261 .B47 1979.

9.361   *Bibliographie analytique de l'assyriologie et de l'archeologie du*
         Proche-Orient. Leyde: E.J. Brill, v.1 - , 1956 - . 1/yr. Z7055 .B5.
         Published by the Rencontre Assyriologique Internationale and
         issued in two sections, L'Archeologie and La Philologie, which appear
         in alternate years.

9.362   Mathaf al-Misri, Maktabah. *Catalogue de la Bibliotheque du Musée egyptien du Caire, 1927- 1958, par Dia' Abou Ghazi et Abd el-Mohsen el-Khachab.* Le Caire: Organisme General des Imprimeries Gouvernementales, 1966 - .

9.363   Pearson, J. D. *A Bibliography of Pre-Islamic Persia.* London: Mansell, 1975. 288 p. DS266 .P43 1975.
         More than 7,000 entries arranged according to four major subjects.

9.364   Porter, Bertha, and Rosalind L.B. Moss. *Topographical bibliography of ancient Egyptian hieroglyphic texts, reliefs, and paintings.* Oxford: Clarendon Press, 1927. 016.4931 P833.
         Bibliography of ancient Egyptian antiquities and hieroglyphic writing.

9.365   Shron, G. S. *Otechestvennye publikatsii po koptologii i greko-rimskomu Egiptu: bibliograficheskii ukazatel'.* Leningrad: Biblioteka Akademii Nauk SSSR, 1989. 159 p.
         Russian language bibliography on the Egyptian Copts.

9.366   Weeks, Kent R. *An Historical bibliography of Egyptian prehistory.* Winona Lake, Indiana: American Research Center in Egypt by Eisenbrauns, 1985. 138 p. GN865 .E3 W44 1985.

Middle East --- Cultural/Social Anthropology

9.367   Banuazizi, Ali. *Social stratification in the Middle East and North Africa: a bibliographic survey.* London; New York: Mansell, 1984. 248 p. HN656 .S6 1984.

9.368   Hanifi, M. Jamil. *Annotated bibliography of Afghanistan.* 4 ed. New Haven: HRAF Press, 1982. 545 p. DS351.5 .H3 1982.

9.369   Hansen, Gerda, and Rolf-Dieter Preisberg. *Wirtschaft, Gesellschaft und Politik der Staaten der Arabischen Halbinsel: eine bibliographische Einfuhrung; Economy, society and politics of the countries of the Arabian Peninsula: a bibliographic introduction.* Hamburg: Deutsches Orient-Institut, 1976. 271 p. HC497 .A6 H3 1976.

9.370   Patai, Raphael. *Jordan, Lebanon, and Syria: an annotated bibliography.* New Haven: HRAF Press, 1957. 289 p. DS44 .P3 1957.

9.371   Sweet, Louise E. *The Central Middle East; a handbook of anthropology and published research on the Nile Valley, the Arab Levant, southern Mesopotamia, the Arabian Peninsula, and Israel.* New Haven: HRAF Press, 1971. 323 p. DS57 .C44 1971.
Includes detailed regional surveys and critically annotated bibliographies.

9.372   Suzuki, Peter T. *Social change in Turkey since 1950; a bibliography of 866 publications.* Heidelberg: High Speed Press Center, 1969. 108 p. 016.9496 Su99.

Middle East --- Religion

9.373   Shinar, Pessah. *Essai de bibliographie selective et annotée sur l'islam maghrebin contemporain: Maroc, Algerie, Tunisie, Libye (1830-1978).* Paris: Editions du Centre National de la Recherche Scientifique, 1983. 506 p. BP64 .A4 N66 1983.

Middle East --- Women

9.374   Al-Qazzaz, Ayad. *Women in the Arab world: an annotated bibliography.* Detroit: Association of Arab-American University Graduates, 1975. 39 p. Z7964.A7 A36.

9.375   Barbar, Aghil M. *The Study of Arab women: a bibliography of bibliographies.* Monticello, Illinois: Vance Bibliographies, 1980. 4 p. JF1351 .P83x P-436.

9.376   Meghdessian, Samira R. *The Status of the Arab woman: a select bibliography compiled ... under the auspices of the Institute for Women's Studies in the Arab World, Beirut University College, Lebanon.* Westport, Connecticut: Greenwood Press, 1980. 176 p. Z7964 .A7 M43.
More than 1,600 books, articles, conference proceedings, theses, and dissertations, primarily in English and French, published since 1950.

9.377   Otto, Ingeborg, and Marianne Schmidt-Dumont. *Frauenfragen im Modernen Orient: eine Auswahlbibliographie; Women in the Middle East and North Africa: a selected bibliography.* Hamburg: Deutsches Orient-Institut, Dokumentations-Leitstelle Moderner Orient, 1982. 247 p. HQ1784 .O8 1982.

9.378   Raccagni, Michelle. *The Modern Arab woman: a bibliography.* Metuchen, New Jersey: Scarecrow Press, 1978. 262 p. HQ1784 .M4 1980.

Nearly 3,000 entries in Western languages and Arabic grouped in geographical sections.

Middle East — Bedouin

9.379 Meir, Avinoam, and Yosef Ben-David. *The Bedouin in Israel and Sinai: a bibliography.* Beersheba: Department of Geography, Ben-Gurion University of the Negev, 1989. 39 p. DS113.7 .M45x 1989.

Middle East — Fellah

9.380 Coult, Lyman H. *An Annotated research bibliography of studies in Arabic, English and French, of the Fellah of the Egyptian Nile, 1798-1955.* Coral Gables: University of Miami Press, 1958. 144 p. HD1538 .E38 1958.

Scholarly bibliography on the culture of the Fellahin.

Middle East — Fezzan

9.381 Ceccherini, Ugo. *Bibliografia della Libia.* Roma: G. Bertero, 1915. 204 p. 016.961 M668.

Includes materials on the sedentary and semisedentary oasis towns of Fezzan.

Middle East — Kabyle

9.382 Lacoste-Dujardin, Camille. *Bibliographie ethnologique de la Grande Kabylie.* Paris: Mouton, 1962. 103 p. 016.94 R244.

Bibliography on the Kabyle, a Berber people of coastal Algeria.

Middle East — Kurds

9.383 Behn, Wolfgang. *The Kurds in Iran: a selected and annotated bibliography.* 2 ed. London: Mansell, 1977. 76 p. DS269 .K87 1977.

More than 250 books and articles, mostly published between 1950 and 1975, relating to the Kurds.

9.384 Hansen, Gerda. *Die Lage der Kurden: Literatur seit 1985.* Hamburg: Deutsches Ubersee-Institut, Ubersee-Dokumentation, Referat Vorderer Orient, 1991. 46 p. DS59 .K86 H36x 1991.

9.385 Musaelian, Zh. S. *Bibliografiia po kurdovedeniiu.* Moskva: Izd-vo vostochnoi lit-ry, Institut Narodov Azii (Akademiia Nauk SSSR), 1963. 183 p. 016.9566 Ak13.

Middle East --- Sudan

9.386   Garsse, Yvan van. *Ethnological and anthropological literature on the three Southern Sudan provinces: Upper Nile, Bahr el Ghazal, Equatoria.* Wien: Institut für Völkerkunde, Universitat Wien, 1972. 83 leaves. GN652 .S93 G37 1972.
More than 1,000 entries arranged by author with subject index.

Middle East --- Tuareg

9.387   Leupen, A. H. A. *Bibliographie des populations touaregues: (Sahara et Soudan centraux).* Leyde: Afrika-Studiecentrum, 1978. 240 p. DT346 .T7 L4 1978.
Topical arrangement of some 1,400 entries.

North America

9.388   Abler, Thomas S., and Sally M. Weaver. *A Canadian Indian bibliography 1960-1970.* Toronto: University of Toronto Press, 1974. 732 p. E78 .C2 A25 1974.

9.389   Krech, Shepard. *Native Canadian anthropology and history: a selected bibliography.* rev. ed. Norman: University of Oklahoma Press, 1994. 212 p. E78 .C2 K74x 1994.

9.390   Hodge, William H. *A Bibliography of contemporary North American Indians: selected and partially annotated with study guide.* New York: Interland, 1976. 310 p. E77 .H694 1976.
Includes 2,600 items in a classified arrangement with an excellent index by tribes, states, areas, and regional groups. Important for its coverage of contemporary issues.

9.391   Hoxie, Frederick E., and Harvey Markowitz. *Native Americans: an annotated bibliography.* Lanham, Maryland: Scarecrow Press, 1991. 324 p. E77 .H68x 1991.
Comprehensive overview of Native American studies, including a range of materials from introductory texts to popular accounts and more advanced scholarship.

9.392   Marken, Jack W. *The Indians and Eskimos of North America: a bibliography of books in print through 1972.* Vermillion, South Dakota: Dakota Press, 1973. 200 p. E77 .M37 1973.

9.393   Murdock, George P., and Timothy J. O'Leary. *Ethnographic bibliography of North America.* 4 ed. New Haven: Human Relations Area Files Press, 1975. 5 v. E77 .M976 1975.

Selective bibliography of some 40,000 entries for books and articles on the indigenous peoples of North America; contents include: v. 1: General North America; v. 2: Arctic and Subsractic; v. 3: Far West and Pacific Coast; v. 4: Eastern United States; and v. 5: Plains and Southwest. Coverage continued by: M. Marlene Martin and Timothy J. Leary, *Ethnographic bibliography of North America: 4 edition supplement 1973-1987* (New Haven: Human Relations Area Files Press, 1990. 3 v.).

Bibliography of native North Americans on disc [computer file]. Santa Barbara, California: ABC-CLIO, 1992 - . 1/yr. 4 computer laser optical discs with documentation.

Contains approximately 60,000 citations to monographs, essays, journal articles, and dissertations on Native North American history, life and culture, from the cumulative eight volumes of the *Ethnographic bibliography of North America* and, in the initial (1992) release, an additional 10,000 new citations. Coverage is from the sixteenth century through year previous to date of issue. Native North Americans include Aleuts; Eskimos or Inuit of Greenland, northern Canada, Alaska, and eastern Siberia; and other native peoples (i.e., "Indians") of Alaska, Canada, the United States, and Mexico north of the northern boundary of Mesoamerica (the area of high cultures in Mexico and Central America). Includes ethnic group and subject index terms. Corresponds to the fourth edition of *Ethnographic bibliography of North America* and its supplement.

9.394   Perkins, David, and Norman Tanis. *California State University, Northridge. Libraries. Native Americans of North America: a bibliography based on collections in the Libraries of California State University, Northridge.* Northridge: California State University, 1975. 558 p. E77 .C15 1975.

9.395   Smith, Dwight L. *The American and Canadian West: a bibliography.* Santa Barbara, California: ABC-Clio, 1979. 558 p. F591 .S596x 1979.
        Includes more than 12,000 descriptive annotations of literature dealing with native Americans; arrangement is by broad topics such as Precolumbian history, Tribal history 1492-1900 (further subdivided by culture area and tribe), and Twentieth century.

9.396   Smith, Dwight L. *Indians of the United States and Canada: a bibliography.* Santa Barbara: ABC-Clio, 1974-1983. 2 v. E77 .I5.
        A compilation of descriptive annotations of literature of the years 1954-1983.

9.397   Swagerty, William R. *Scholars and the Indian experience: critical reviews of recent writing in the social sciences.* Bloomington: D'Arcy McNickle Center for the History of the American Indian, Newberry Library; Indiana University Press, 1984. 268 p. E77 .S36 1984.

9.398   Wolf, Carolyn E., and Nancy S. Chiang. *Indians of North and South America: a bibliography based on the collection at the Willard E. Yager Library-Museum, Hartwick College, Oneonta, New York.* Metuchen, New Jersey: Scarecrow Press, 1977. 576 p. E58 .W85 1977. Continued by: C.E. Wolf, and N.S. Chiang. *Indians of North and South America: a bibliography based on the collection at the Willard E. Yager Library-Museum, Hartwick College, Oneonta, New York; Supplement* (Metuchen, New Jersey: Scarecrow Press, 1988. 654 p.).

North America --- Archaeology
9.399   Anderson, Frank G. *Southwestern archaeology: a bibliography.* New York: Garland,, 1982. 539 p. E78.S7 A53x 1982.
         Extensive bibliography of published works dealing with the archaeology and prehistory of Utah, Arizona, New Mexico, western and southern Colorado, southeastern Nevada and California, Chihuahua and Sonora, and trans-Pecos Texas.

9.400   Bell, Robert E. *Oklahoma archaeology: an annotated bibliography.* 2 ed. Norman: University of Oklahoma Press, 1978. 155 p. 016.9784 B413a.

9.401   Bennett, Gwen P. *A Bibliography of Illinois archaeology.* Springfield: Illinois State Museum; Illinois Archaeological Survey, 1984. 356 p. E78.I3 B46x 1984.

9.402   Davis, R. P. Stephen. *Bibliography of West Virginia archeology.* Morgantown: West Virginia Geological and Economic Survey, 1978. 172 p. 557.96 W52ra no.8.

9.403   Dekin, Albert A. *Arctic archaeology: a bibliography and history.* New York: Garland, 1978. 279 p. E99.E7 D36.

9.404   Kerber, Jordan E. *Coastal and maritime archaeology: a bibliography.* Lanham, Maryland: Scarecrow Press, 1991. 408 p. E99.E7 D36.
         Some 2,800 sources on indigeous coastal peoples including adaptation to various coastal and maritime settings and resources, exploitation of shellfish and formation of shell middens, and excavation and preservation of specific coastal and maritime sites,

such as the Ozette site, Emeryville shellmound, Damariscotta shell heap, and the Boylston Street fishweir site.

9.405   Michael, Ronald L. *Bibliography of literature on Indiana archaeology.* Muncie, Indiana: Departrment of Sociology and Anthropology, Ball State University, 1969. 154 p. 016.973 M582.

9.406   Milisauskas, Sarunas, Frances Pickin, and Charles Clark. *A Selected bibliography of North American archaeological sites.* New Haven, Connecticut: Human Relations Area Files, 1981. 2 v. E77.9 M55 1981.
Includes author, culture period, and site name indexes.

9.407   Schroedl, Alan R. *A Selected bibliography of Utah archeology.* Anthropological Papers, 102. Salt Lake City: University of Utah Press, 1979. 71 p. E78 .U55 1979.

9.408   Snow, Dean R., *Native American prehistory: a critical bibliography.* Bloomington: Newberry Library; Indiana University Press, 1979. 75 p. E77.9 S6 1979.

9.409   Storck, Peter L. *A Preliminary bibliography of early man in Eastern North America, 1839-1973.* Toronto: Royal Ontario Museum, 1975. 110 p. E77.9 .S76 1975.
Contains 1,242 books and journal articles dealing with Paleo-Indian studies.

North America --- Demography
9.410   Dobyns, Henry F. *Native American historical demography: a critical bibliography.* Bloomington: Indiana University Press, 1976. 95 p. E59 .P75 D6 1976.

9.411   Dobyns, Henry F. *Their number become thinned: Native American population dynamics in eastern North America.* Knoxville: University of Tennessee Press; Newberry Library Center for the History of the American Indian, 1983. 378 p. E98.P76 D62 1983.

North America --- Indian-White Relations
9.412   Fenton, William N. *American Indian and white relations to 1830, needs and opportunities for study; an essay.* Chapel Hill: University of North Carolina Press, 1957; New York: Russell and Russell, 1971. 138 p. E77 .F46 1971.
Includes a selective bibliography by L. H. Butterfield, Wilcomb E.

Washburn, and William N. Fenton dealing with Indian-White relations in the humanities and social sciences.

9.413　Kerri, James N. *American Indians (U.S. and Canada): a bibliography of contemporary studies and urban research.* Exchange Bibliography, 376-377. Monticello, Illinois: Council of Planning Librarians, 1973. 165 p. E77 .K47 1973.

9.414　Lydon, James G. *Struggle for empire: a bibliography of the French and Indian War.* New York: Garland, 1986. 272 p. E199 .L93 1986.

9.415　Prucha, Francis P. *A Bibliographical guide to the history of Indian-white relations in the United States.* Chicago: University of Chicago Press, 1977. 454 p. E93 .P7 1977.
　　　Some 9,700 books, articles, and dissertations, published before 1974, arranged by subject.

9.416　Prucha, Francis P. *Indian-white relations in the United States: a bibliography of works published 1975-1980.* Lincoln: University of Nebraska Press, 1982. 179 p. E93 .P78x 1982.

9.417　Prucha, Francis P. *United States Indian policy: a critical bibliography.* Bloomington: Newberry Library; Indiana University Press, 1977. 54 p. E93 .P967 1977.

9.418　Ronda, James P., and James Axtell. *Indian missions: a critical bibliography.* Bloomington: Newberry Library; Indiana University Press, 1978. 85 p. E98 .M6 R5 1978.
　　　Includes an overview of missionary work, followed by a review of denomination, section on the goals of the mission, methods of conversion, and indigenous responses.

9.419　Surtees, Robert J. *Canadian Indian policy: a critical bibliography.* Bloomington: Newberry Library; Indiana University Press, 1982. 107 p. E92 .S9 1982.
　　　Bibliography of French, English, and Canadian government policies.

9.420　Sutton, Imre. *Indian land tenure: bibliographical essays and a guide to the literature.* New York: Clearwater, 1975. 290 p. E98 .L3 S88 1975.
　　　A series of bibliographical essays on: Aboriginal occupancy and territoriality; Land cessions and the establishment of reservations;

Land administration and land utilization; Aboriginal title and land claims; Title clarification and change; Tenure and jurisdiction; Land tenure and culture change; and a final essay comparing the Native American experience with the of other post-colonial indigenous groups.

9.421   Vaughan, Alden T. *Narratives of North American Indian captivity: a selective bibliography.* New York: Garland, 1983. 89 p. E85 .V38 1983.

Listing of captivity narratives written by or about European Americans, and occasionally African Americans, while living among American Indians.

North America — Languages

9.422   Banks, Joyce M., ed. *Books in native languages in the rare book collections of the National Library of Canada; Livres en langues autochtones dans les collections de livres rares de la Bibliotheque Nationale du Canada.* rev. ed. Ottawa: Minister of Supply and Services Canada, 1985. 190 p. PM206 .N3 1985.

Over 500 entries for 58 indigneous languages or dialects.

9.423   Evans, G. Edward. *Bibliography of language arts materials for Native North Americans: bilingual, English as a second language, and native language materials, 1965-1974.* Los Angeles: American Indian Studies Center, University of California, 1977. 283 p. P115 .B56 1977.

9.424   Evans, G. Edward, and Jeffrey Clark. *North American Indian language materials, 1890-1965: an annotated bibliography of monographic works.* American Indian Bibliographic Series, 31. Los Angeles: American Indian Studies Center, University of California, 1980. 154 p. PM206 .E92 1980.

Includes dictionaries, grammars, orthographies, primers, readers, etc. concerning Native American languages north of Mexico.

9.425   Pilling, James C. *Bibliography of the Algonquian languages.* Smithsonian Institution. Bureau of American Ethnology, Bulletin 13. Washington, D.C., 1891; New York: AMS Press, 1973. 614 p. PM600 .P55x 1891.

9.426   Pilling, James C. *Bibliography of the Athapascan languages.* Smithsonian Institution. Bureau of American Ethnology, Bulletin 14. Washington, D.C., 1892; New York: AMS Press, 1973. 125 p. 301.82 Un3b 14.

9.427 Pilling, James C. *Bibliography of the Chinookan languages.*
Smithsonian Institution. Bureau of American Ethnology, Bulletin 15.
Washington, D.C., 1893; New York: AMS Press, 1973. 81 p. 301.82
Un3b 15.

9.428 Pilling, James C. *Bibliography of the Eskimo languages.* Smithsonian
Institution. Bureau of American Ethnology, Bulletin 1. Washington,
D.C., 1887; New York: AMS Press, 1973. 116 p. 301.82 Un3b 1.

9.429 Pilling, James C. *Bibliography of the Iroquoian languages.*
Smithsonian Institution. Bureau of American Ethnology, Bulletin 6.
Washington, D.C., 1888; New York: AMS Press, 1973. 208 p. 301.82
Un3b 6.

9.430 Pilling, James C. *Bibliography of the Muskhogean languages.*
Smithsonian Institution. Bureau of American Ethnology, Bulletin 9.
Washington, D.C., 1889; New York: AMS Press, 1973. 114 p. 301.82
Un3b 9.

9.431 Pilling, James C. *Bibliography of the Salishan languages.*
Smithsonian Institution. Bureau of American Ethnology, Bulletin 16.
Washington, D.C., 1893; New York: AMS Press, 1973. 86 p. 301.82
Un3b 16.

9.432 Pilling, James C. *Bibliography of the Siouan languages.* Smithsonian
Institution. Bureau of American Ethnology, Bulletin 5. Washington,
D.C., 1887; New York: AMS Press, 1973. 87 p. 301.82 Un3b 5.

9.433 Pilling, James C. *Bibliography of the Wakashan languages.*
Smithsonian Institution. Bureau of American Ethnology, Bulletin 19.
Washington, D.C., 1894; New York: AMS Press, 1973. 70 p. 301.82
Un3b 19.

9.434 Singerman, Robert. *Indigenous languages of the Americas: a
bibliography of dissertations and theses.* Lanham, Maryland:
Scarecrow Press, 1996. 346 p. PM108 .S56x 1996.
Accesses more than 1,600 dissertations and master's theses from
American, Canadian, and British institutions covering indigenous
groups in the western hemisphere; includes author, language, dialect,
and tribal indexes.

North America --- Literature

9.435 Beam, Joan, and Barbara Branstad. *The Native American in long fiction: an annotated bibliography.* Lanham, Maryland: Scarecrow Press, 1996. 384 p. PS374 .I49 B42x 1996.

An annotated bibliography of novel-length fictional works by and about Native Americans of the United States published between the 1890s and the 1990s.

9.436 Hirschfelder, Arlene B., comp. *American Indian and Eskimo authors; a comprehensive bibliography.* New York: Association on American Indian Affairs; Interbook , 1973. 99 p. PS153 .I52 H48 1973.

9.437 Jacobson, Angeline. *Contemporary Native American literature: a selected and paretially annotated bibliography.* Lanham, Maryland: Scarecrow Press, 1977. 247 p. PS153.I52 J33x 1977.

9.438 Littlefield, Daniel F., and James W. Parins. *A Biobibliography of Native American writers, 1772-1924.* Metuchen, New Jersey: Scarecrow Press, 1985. 339 p. E77 .L5 1981.

Continued by: D.F. Littlefield, and J.W. Parins, *A Biobibliography of Native American writers, 1772-1924: a supplement* (Metuchen, New Jersey: Scarecrow Press, 1985. 350 p.).

9.439 Littlefield, Daniel F., and James W. Parins. *American Indian and Alaska native newspapers and periodicals.* Westport, Connecticut: Greenwood Press, 1984-1986. 3 v. PN4883 .L57 1984.

Coverage uncludes 1826-1924 (vol. 1), 1925-1970 (vol. 2), and 1971-1985 (vol. 3).

9.440 Rock, Roger O. *The Native American in American literature: a selectively annotated bibliography.* Westport, Connecticut: Greenwood Press, 1985. 211 p. PS173 .I6 R62 1985.

North America --- Social Conditions
9.441 Barrow, Mark V., Jerry D. Niswander, and Robert Fortune. *Health and disease of American Indians north of Mexico: a bibliography, 1800-1969.* Gainesville: University of Florida Press, 1972. 147 p. RA448.5 .B37 1972.

Lists 483 books, articles, and othyer documents arranged by disease categories.

9.442 Gray, Sharon A. *Health of Native people of North America: a bibliography and guide to resources, 1970-1994.* Lanham, Maryland: Scarecrow Press, 1996. 400 p. RA448.5 .I5 G683 1996.

Includes biomediaal and healthcare resources such as associations, publications, dissertations, agency and committee reports, audiovisual materials, and book chapters.

9.443   Hirschfelder, Arlene B. *American Indian stereotypes in the world of children: a reader and bibliography.* Metuchen, New Jersey: Scarecrow Press, 1982. 296 p. 301.82 H616.

9.444   Kelso, Dianne R., and Carolyn L. Attneave. *Bibliography of North American Indian mental health.* Westport, Connecticut: Greenwood Press, 1981. 411 p. RC451.5 .I5 K44 1981.
         Lists 1,363 entries, including published reports and other documents, with extensive indexing.

9.445   Lobb, Michael L., and Thomas D. Watts. *Native American youth and alcohol: an annotated bibliograph.* New York: Greenwood Press, 1989. 165 p. E98 .L7 L63 1989.

9.446   Thornton, Russell, and Mary K. Grasmick. *Bibliography of social science research and writings on American Indians.* Minneapolis: Center for Urban and Regional Affairs, University of Minnesota, 1979. 160 p. E77 .T5x 1979.

9.447   Thornton, Russell, and Mary K. Grasmick. *Sociology of American Indians: a critical bibliography.* Bloomington: Newberry Library, Indiana University Press, 1980. 113 p. E98.S67 .T46 1980.
         Examines the sociological literature on all Native Americans groups north of Mexico.

9.448   Thornton, Russell, Gary D. Sandefur, Harold G. Grasmick. *The urbanization of American Indians: a critical bibliography.* Bloomington: Newberry Library; Indiana University Press, 1982. 87 p. E98 .U72 T47 1982.
         Includes research on both pre- and post-Columbian urbanization; the majority of the entries describe work from the past 50 years on the modern effects of urbanization.

9.449   Wells, Robert N. *Native American resurgence and renewal: a reader and bibliography.* Lanham, Maryland: Scarecrow Press, 1994. 671 p. E93 .N286 1994.
         Examines Native American political and cultural resurgence and contemporary Native American-Anglo relations in the United States.

9.450 Wilson, Terry P. *Teaching American Indian history*. Washington, D.C.: American Historical Association, 1993. 66 p. E76.6 .W55 1993.

North America --- Technology

9.451 Lynas, Lothian. *Medicinal and food plants of the North American Indians; a bibliography*. New York: Library of the New York Botanical Garden, 1972. 21 p. E98 .F7 L96 1972.

9.452 Porter, Frank W. *Native American basketry: an annotated bibliography*. New York: Greenwood Press, 1988. 249 p. E59 .B3 P67 1988.

North America --- Women

9.453 Green, Rayna. *Native American women: a contextual bibliography*. Bloomington: Indiana University Press, 1983. 120 p. E98 .W8 G73 1983.

Consists of an introduction, index, and 672 annotated references about Native American women.

North America --- Arctic and Sub-Arctic

9.454 Helm, June. *The Indians of the subarctic: a critical bibliography*. Bloomington: Newberry Library; Indiana University Press, 1976. 91 p. E99 .A86 H44 1976.

North America --- Arctic and Sub-Arctic --- Aleut

9.455 Jones, Dorothy M., and John R. Wood. *An Aleut bibliography*. Fairbanks: Institute of Social, Economic and Govermental Research, University of Alaska, 1975. 195 p. E99 .A34 J658 1975.

North America --- Arctic and Sub-Arctic --- Athapaskans

9.456 Hippler, Arthur E., and John R. Wood. *The Subarctic Athabascans: a selected annotated bibliography*. Fairbanks: Institute of Social, Economic, and Government Research, University of Alaska, 1974. 331 p. E99 .A86 H57x 1974.

North America --- Arctic and Sub-Arctic --- Eskimo

9.457 Hippler, Arthur E., and John R. Wood. *The Alaska Eskimos: a selected, annotated bibliography*. Fairbanks: Institute of Social and Economic Research, University of Alaska, 1977. 334 p. E99.E7 H545x 1977.

North America --- California

9.458 Heizer, Robert F. *The Indians of California: a critical bibliography*.

Bloomington: Newberry Library, Indiana University Press, 1976. 68 p.
E78 .C15 H427 1976.

9.459 Heizer, Robert F., and Albert B. Elsasser. *A Bibliography of
       California Indians: archaeology, ethnography, Indian history.* New
       York: Garland, 1977. 267 p. E78 .C15 H399 1977.

9.460 Heizer, Robert F., Karen M. Nissen and Edward D. Castillo.
       *California Indian history: a classified and annotated guide to source
       materials.* Ramona, California: Ballena Press, 1975. 90 p. E78 .C15
       H388 1975.

9.461 Oandasan, William. *Bibliography of the tribes of the Covelo Indian
       community in Round Valley of northern California.* Chicago: The
       Newberry Library, 1980. 57 p. E78.C15 C3x 1980.
       Bibliography of the Round Valley Indian Reservation in
       California.

North America --- California --- Chumash
9.462 Anderson, Eugene N. *A Revised, annotated bibliography of the
       Chumash and their predecessors.* 2 ed. Socorro, New Mexico: Ballena
       Press, 1978. 82 p. E99 .C815 A5 1978.

North America --- California --- Digueño
9.463 Almstedt, Ruth. *Bibliography of the Digueño Indians.* Ramona,
       California: Ballena Press, 1974. 52 p. E99 .D5 A46 1974.

North America --- California --- Maidu
9.464 Wilson, Norman L., and Arlean Towne. *Selected bibliography of
       Maidu ethnography and archeology.* Sacramento: State of California,
       Resources Agency, Department of Parks and Recreation, 1979. 78 p.
       016.30182 W695.

North America --- California --- Languages
9.465 Bright, William. *Bibliography of the languages of native California:
       including closely related languages of adjacent areas.* Metuchen, New
       Jersey: Scarecrow Press, 1982. 220 p. PM501 .C2 B7 1982.

North America --- East
9.466 Hirschfelder, Arlene B. *Annotated bibliography of the literature on
       American Indians published in state historical society publications,
       New England and Middle Atlantic states.* Millwood, New York: Kraus
       International Publications, 1982. 356 p. E75 .H5 1982.

Coverage of articles about Native Americans in 37 journals and newsletters published by state historical societies in the following New England and Middle Atlantic states: Connecticut, Delaware, Maine, Maryland, Massachusetts, New Hampshire, New York, New Jersey, Pennsylvania, Rhode Island, and Vermont.

9.467   Rouse, Irving, and John M. Goggin. *An Anthropological bibliography of the eastern seaboard.* New Haven: Eastern States Archaeological Federation at Yale Peabody Museum, 1948-1963. 174 p. 970A Ea77.

9.468   Salisbury, Neal. *The Indians of New England: a critical bibliography.* Bloomington: Newberry Library; Indiana University Press, 1982. 109 p. E78 .N5 S23 1982.

9.469   Tooker, Elisabeth. *The Indians of the Northeast: a critical bibliography.* Bloomington: Newberry Library; Indiana University Press, 1978. 77 p. E78 .E2 T66 1978.
Coverage includes Newfoundland to North Carolina, and the Atlantic seaboard to the Upper Great Lakes.

North America --- East --- Abnaki
9.470   Nelson, Eunice. *The Wabanaki: an annotated bibliography of selected books, articles, documents about Maliseet, Micmac, Passamaquoddy, Penobscot Indians in Maine, annotated by Native Americans.* Cambridge, Massachusetts: American Friends Service Committee; Orono, Maine: American Friends Service Committee, 1982. 108 p. E99 .A13 N44 1982.

North America --- East --- Delaware
9.471   Porter, Frank W. *Indians in Maryland and Delaware: a critical bibliography.* Bloomington: Newberry Library, Indiana University Press, 1979. 107 p. E78 .M3 P6 1979.

9.472   Weslager, C. A. *The Delawares: a critical bibliography.* Bloomington: Newberry Library; Indiana University Press, 1978. 84 p. E99 .D2 W47 1978.

North America --- East --- Iroquois
9.473   Garrow, Larry, Richard Jock, and Ray Cooke. *Mohawk people: past and present: a list of print and visual media on Mohawk history, culture and current events.* Hogansburg, New York: Akwesasne Library Culture Center, 1974. 19 p. E99.M8 .G37.

9.474   Garrow, Larry, Richard Jock, and Ray Cooke. *A Selective bibliography of the Mohawk people.* Minneapolis: National Indian Education Association Library Project, 1974. 49 leaves. E99.M8 G37x 1974a.

9.475   Haas, Marilyn L. *The Seneca and Tuscarora Indians: an annotated bibliography.* Lanham, Maryland: Scarecrow Press, 1994. 465 p. E99 .S3 H33x 1994.
        Includes citations to journal articles, books, theses, and government documents published up to 1992.

9.476   Weinman, Paul L. *A Bibliography of the Iroquoian literature, partially annotated.* New York State Museum and Science Service, Bulletin 411. Albany, University of the State of New York, 1969. 254 p. E99 .I7 1969.

North America --- East --- Malecite
9.477   Herisson, Michel R. P. *An Evaluative ethnohistorical bibliography of the Malecite Indians.* Canadian Ethnology Service, Mercury series. Paper 16. Ottawa: National Museums of Canada, 1974. 260 p. 312.71 N213 no.16.

North America --- East --- Menominee
9.478   Meehan, Patrick J. *The Menominee Indians of Wisconsin.* Monticello, Illinois: Vance Bibliographies, 1978. 14 p. E99 .M44 M43.

North America --- East --- Ojibwa
9.479   Scott, Patricia. *Chippewa and Cree: a bibliography of books, newspaper articles, government documents, and other printed and written matter in various libraries of the United States and Canada.* Rocky Boy, Montana: Rocky Boy School, 1976. 277 p. E99 .C6 S36 1976.

9.480   Tanner, Helen H. *The Ojibwas: a critical bibliography.* Bloomington: Indiana University Press, 1976. 78 p. E99 .C6 T36 1976.

North America --- East --- Potawatomi
9.481   Edmunds, R. David. *Kinsmen through time: an annotated bibliography of Potawatomi history.* Metuchen, New Jersey: Scarecrow Press, 1987. 217 p. E99 .P8 E36 1987.
        Includes some 1,100 sources relating to Potawatomi culture between 1600 and 1908.

North America --- Great Basin

9.482   Stewart, Omer C. *Indians of the Great Basin: a critical bibliography.* Bloomington: Newberry Library; Indiana University Press, 1982. 138 p. E78 .G67 S68 1982.

North America --- Northwest

9.483   Grumet, Robert S. *Native Americans of the Northwest Coast: a critical bibliography.* Bloomington: Newberry Library; Indiana University Press, 1979. 108 p. E78 .N78 G7 1979.

North America --- Northwest --- Ethnographic Art

9.484   Wardwell, Allen, and Lois Lebov. *Annotated bibliography of Northwest Coast Indian art.* New York: Museum of Primitive Art Library, 1970. 25 p. E78 .N78 W27 1970.

North America --- Northwest --- Klamath

9.485   Swartz, B. K. *A Bibliography of Klamath Basin anthropology with excerpts and annotation.* rev. ed. Moscow: University of Idaho, 1968. 156 p. 016.30182 Sw25.

North America --- Northwest --- Yakima

9.486   Schuster, Helen H. *The Yakimas: a critical bibliography.* Bloomington: Newberry Library; Indiana University Press, 1982. 158 p. E99 .Y2 S3 1982.

9.487   Trafzer, Clifford E. 1992. *Yakima, Palouse, Cayuse, Umatilla, Walla Walla, and Wanapum Indians: an historical bibliography.* Metuchen, New Jersey: Scarecrow Press, 1992. 253 p. E78 .N77 T73x 1992.

    This bibliography concentrates on Sehaptin languages of the Columbia Plateau.

North America --- Plains

9.488   Hoebel, E. Adamson. *The Plains Indians: a critical bibliography.* Bloomington: Newberry Library; Indiana University Press, 1977. 75 p. E78 .G734 H588 1977.

    Includes an excellent review of the literature on the Plains Indians.

9.489   Unrau, William E. *The Emigrant Indians of Kansas: a critical bibliography.* Bloomington: Newberry Library, Indiana University Press, 1979. 78 p. E78 .K16 U5 1979.

9.490   Weist, Katherine M., and Susan R. Sharrock. *An Annotated bibliography of Northern Plains ethnohistory.* Missoula, Montana: Department of Anthropology, University of Montana, 1985. 299 p. E78 .G73 1985.

North America --- Plains --- Arapaho

9.491   Salzmann, Zdenek. *The Arapaho Indians: a research guide and bibliography.* New York: Greenwood Press, 1988. 113 p.
Includes 702 books and articles on the Northern and Southern Arapaho. E99 .A7 S25 1988.

North America --- Plains --- Cheyenne

9.492   Powell, Peter J. *The Cheyennes, Maheoo's people: a critical bibliography.* Bloomington: Newberry Library, Indiana University Press, 1980. 123 p. E99 .C53 P5 1980.

North America --- Plains --- Lakota

9.493   Hoover, Herbert T. *The Sioux: a critical bibliography.* Bloomington: Newberry Library; Indiana University Press, 1979. 78 p. E99 .D1 H65 1979.

9.494   Hoover, Herbert T., and Karen P. Zimmerman. *The Sioux and other native American cultures of the Dakotas: an annotated bibliography.* Westport, Connecticut: Greenwood Press, 1993. 265 p. E99 .D1 H66x 1993.

9.495   Marken, Jack W., and Herbert T. Hoover. *Bibliography of the Sioux.* Metuchen, New Jersey: Scarecrow Press, 1980. 370 p. E99 .D1 M3 1980.
Lists 3,367 books, articles, dissertations, and theses about the Dakota.

9.496   Van Balen, John. *The Sioux, a selected bibliography.* Vermillion: Institute of Indian Studies, University of South Dakota, 1978. 168 p. E99 .D1 V188 1978.

North America --- Plains --- Omaha

9.497   Tate, Michael L. *The Upstream people: an annotated research bibliography of the Omaha Tribe.* Metuchen, New Jersey: Scarecrow Press, 1991. 504 p. E99 .O4 T38x 1991.

North America --- Plains --- Pawnee

9.498   Blaine, Martha R. *The Pawnees: a critical bibliography.*

Bloomington: Newberry Library; Indiana University Press, 1980. 109 p. E99 .P3 B55 1980.

North America --- Plains --- Siksika (Blackfeet)

9.499 Dempsey, Hugh A., and Lindsay Moir. *Bibliography of the Blackfoot.* Metuchen, New Jersey: Scarecrow Press, 1989. 245 p. E99 .S54 D46 1989.

9.500 Johnson, Bryan R. *The Blackfeet: an annotated bibliography.* New York: Garland, 1988. 231 p. E99 .S54 J64 1988.

Includes 1,186 entries in English, German, French, Siksika, Spanish, Dutch, and Japanese; also identifies 21 major manuscript collections in the United States and Canada.

North America --- Southeast

9.501 O'Donnell, James H. *Southeastern frontiers: Europeans, Africans, and American Indians, 1513-1840: a critical bibliography.* Bloomington: Newberry Library; Indiana University Press, 1982. 118 p. E78 .S65 O35 1982.

North America --- Southeast --- Languages

9.502 Booker, Karen. *Languages of the aboriginal Southeast: an annotated bibliography.* Lanham, Maryland: Scarecrow Press, 1991. 265 p. PM441 .B66x 1991.

North America --- Southeast --- Catawba

9.503 Blumer, Thomas J. *Bibliography of the Catawba.* Metuchen, New Jersey: Scarecrow Press, 1987. 547 p. E99 .C24 B55 1987.

Includes more than 4,200 briefly annotated entries from newspapers, journals, government reports, legal documents, and private papers.

North America --- Southeast --- Cherokee

9.504 Fogelson, Raymond D. *The Cherokees: a critical bibliography.* Bloomington: Newberry Library; Indiana University Press, 1978. 98 p. E99 .C5 F69 1978.

North America --- Southeast --- Chickasaw

9.505 Hoyt, Anne K. *Bibliography of the Chickasaw.* Metuchen, New Jersey: Scarecrow Press, 1987. 230 p. E99 .C55 H68 1987.

North America --- Southeast --- Choctaw

9.506 Kidwell, Clara S., and Charles Roberts. *The Choctaws: a critical bibliography*. Bloomington: Newberry Library; Indiana University Press, 1980. 110 p. E99 .C8 K5 1980.

North America --- Southeast --- Creek

9.507　Green, Michael D. *The Creeks: a critical bibliography*. Bloomington: Newberry Library; Indiana University Press, 1979. 114 p. E99 .C9 G75 1979.

North America --- Southeast --- Seminole

9.508　Kersey, Harry A. *The Seminole and Miccosukee tribes: a critical bibliography*. Bloomington: Indiana University Press, 1987. 102 p. E99 .S28 K47 1987.

North America --- Southwest

9.509　Dobyns, Henry F., and Robert C. Euler. *Indians of the Southwest: a critical bibliography*. Bloomington: Newberry Library; Indiana University Press, 1980. 153 p. E78 .S7 D58 1980.

9.510　Tate, Michael L. *The Indians of Texas: an annotated research bibliography*. Metuchen, New Jersey: Scarecrow Press, 1986. 514 p. E78 .T4 T3 1986.

North America --- Southwest --- Apache

9.511　Melody, Michael E. *The Apaches: a critical bibliography*. Bloomington: Newberry Library; Indiana University Press, 1977. 86 p. E99 .A6 M46 1977.

North America --- Southwest --- Hopi

9.512　Laird, W. David. *Hopi bibliography: comprehensive and annotated*. Tucson: University of Arizona Press, 1977. 735 p. E99 .H7 L288 1977.

　　　Alphabetical listing of more than 2,900 books, articles, and government and church reports on all aspects of Hopi culture.

North America --- Southwest --- Navajo

9.513　Iverson, Peter. *The Navajos: a critical bibliography*. Bloomington: Indiana University Press, 1976. 64 p. E99 .N3 I94 1976.

9.514　Kluckhohn, Clyde, and Katherine Spencer. *A Bibliography of the Navaho Indians*. New York: J. J. Augustin, 1940. 93 p. 016.30182 K711.

North America — Southwest — Osage
9.515 Wilson, Terry P. *Bibliography of the Osage.* Native American bibliography series, 6. Metuchen, New Jersey: Scarecrow Press, 1985. 162 p. E99.08 .W54 1985.

North America — Southwest — Ute
9.516 Stewart, Omer C. *Ethnohistorical bibliography of the Ute Indians of Colorado.* Boulder: University of Colorado Press, 1971. 94 p. 301.06 C719 no.18.

Includes appendices on the records of the Southern Ute Agency, 1877 through 1952, in the Federal Records Center, Denver, Colorado, and Colorado and out-of-state newspaper articles on Ute Indians.

Oceania
9.517 Cammack, Floyd M., and Shiro Saito. *Pacific Island bibliography.* New York: Scarecrow Press, 1962. 421 p. DU13 .C3 1962.

Includes more than 1,700 entries in several languages dealing with various island groups.

9.518 *Catalog of the South Pacific collection.* Santa Cruz: The Library, University of California, Santa Cruz, 1978. 722 p. DU28.3 .U5 1978.

Includes more than 8,500 entries arrnged by author and title.

9.519 Leeson, Ida. *A Bibliography of bibliographies of the South Pacific.* London, New York: Oxford University Press, 1954. 61 p. DU17 .L44 1954.

Oceania — Cultural/Social Anthropology
9.520 Taylor, C.R.H. *A Pacific bibliography: printed matter relating to the native peoples of Polynesia, Melanesia and Micronesia.* 2 ed. Oxford: Clarendon Press, 1965. 692 p. DU17 .T39 1965.

The basic bibliographic source for Pacific Islands anthropology; arranged by island group and subject. Revision of C.R.H. Taylor, *A Pacific bibliography; printed matter relating to the native peoples of Polynesia, Melanesia, and Micronesia* (Memoirs of the Polynesian Society, 24. Wellington, 1951. 492 p.).

Oceania — Linguistics
9.521 Hollyman, K. J. *A Checklist of Oceanic languages.* Auckland: Linguistic Society of New Zealand, 1960. 32 leaves. PL5001 .H6 1960.

Includes coverage for some 1,500 languages and dialects, with references to linguistic family, the areas where spoken, and bibliographic citations.

9.522   Klieneberger, H. R. *Bibliography of Oceanic linguistics.* London, New
York: Oxford University Press, 1957. 143 p. Z7111 .K5 1957.
Includes books, articles, and reviews dealing with Oceanic
(Polynesian, Micronesian, and Melanesian) languages and
dictionaries, vocabularies, grammars, and other linguistic
contributions.

Oceania --- Australia and New Zealand
9.523   Craig, Beryl F. *Northwest central Queensland: an annotated
bibliography.* Australian Aboriginal Studies, 41. Canberra: Australian
Institute of Aboriginal Studies, 1973. 269 p. DU120 .A8 no.41.

Oceania --- Australia and New Zealand ---
Cultural/Social Anthropology
9.524   Moore, David R. *The Torres Strait collections of A.C. Haddon: a
descriptive catalogue.* London: British Museum Publications, 1984.
109 p. GN667 .T67 M66 1984.

Oceania --- Australia and New Zealand ---
Biological/Physical Anthropology
9.525   Ware, Helen R.E., ed. *Fertility and family formation: Australasian
bibliography and essays, 1972.* Canberra: Department of
Demography, Institute of Advanced Studies, Australian National
University, 1973. 269 p. HB3675 .W37 1973.

Oceania --- Australia and New Zealand ---
Australian Aborigines
9.526   Davidson, R., and L. Reed. *Aboriginal studies on the north coast of
South Wales: a bibliography of source material.* Lismore, N.S.W.:
North Coast Institute of Aboriginal Community Education, 1984. 137
p. GN667 .N5 D38 1984.

9.527   Greenway, John. *Bibliography of the Australian aborigines and the
native peoples of Torres Strait to 1959.* Sydney: Angus and Robertson,
1963. 420 p. GN665 .G74 1963.
Thorough international bibliography of more than 10,000 entries,
primarily in English, dealing with the Australian Aborigines.

9.528   Hill, Marji, and Alex Barlow. *Black Australia: an annotated
bibliography and teacher's guide to resources on Aborigines and
Torres Strait Islanders.* Canberra: Australian Institute of Aboriginal
Studies; Atlantic Highlands, New Jersey: Humanities Press, 1978. 200
p. GN665 .H54 1978.

Includes 547 annotated entries relating to the Australian Aborigines and Torres Straits Islanders; begins with an excellent introduction on ethnocentrism, prejudice, racism, and stereotyping, as well as various summaries throughout on aspects of aboriginal culture, history, and society. Continued by M. Hill and A. Barlow, *Black Australia 2: an annotated bibliography and teacher's guide to resources on Aborigines and Torres Strait Islanders, 1977-82* (Canberra, ACT: Australian Institute of Aboriginal Studies, 1985. 96 p.).

9.529   Moodie, Peter M. *Aboriginal health*. Aborigines in Australian Society, 9. Canberra: Australian National University Press, 1973. 307 p. 614.0994 M77.

9.530   Moodie, Peter M., and E. B. Pedersen. *The Health of Australian Aborigines: an annotated bibliography*. Canberra: Australian Government Publishing Service, 1971. 248 p. 016.6140994 M77 1971.

Oceania --- Australia and New Zealand --- Maoris
9.531   Taylor, C.R.H. *A Bibliography of publications on the New Zealand Maori and the Moriori of the Chatham Islands*. Oxford: Clarendon Press, 1972. 161 p. DU423 .A1 T39 1972.

**Oceania --- Australia and New Zealand ---
Tasmanians**
9.532   Plomley, N. J. B. *An Annotated bibliography of the Tasmanian aborigines*. Royal Anthropological Institute of Great Britain and Ireland, Occasional Paper, 28. London: Royal Anthropological Institute, 1969. 143 p. GN667 .P66 1969.

Oceania --- Melanesia
9.533   Reeves, Susan C., and May Dudley. *New Guinea social science field research and publications 1962-67*. Canberra: New Guinea Research Unit, Australian National University, 1969. 215 p. DU740 .A85 no.32.

**Oceania --- Melanesia --- Cultural/
Social Anthropology**
9.534   Baal, Jan van, K.W. Galis, and R.M. Koentjaraningrat. *West Irian: a bibliography*. Koninklijk Instituut voor Taal-, Land-en Volkenkunde, Bibliographical Series, 15. Dordrecht: Cinnaminson, New Jersey: Floris, 1984. 307 p. DU744 .B3 1984.

9.535 Elkin, A. P. *Social anthropology in Melanesia; a review of research.* London, New York: Oxford University Press, 1953. 166 p. 301.993 E152.

9.536 Galis, Klaas W. *Bibliography of West New Guinea.* New Haven: Yale University, Southeast Asia Studies, 1956. 135 p. DU744 .G3 1956.
English translation of *Bibliographie van Nederlands-Nieuw Guinea.*

9.537 Hays, Terence E. *Anthropology in the New Guinea highlands: an annotated bibliography.* New York: Garland, 1976. 238 p. GN671 .N5 H39 1976.
Books, articles, and theses are grouped into broad subject chapters including: General, including reference works, surveys, and materials by nonanthropologists; Social and cultural anthropology; Linguistics; Prehistory; Physical anthropology; and Physical environment.

9.538 Macintyre, Martha. *The Kula: a bibliography.* Cambridge, New York: Cambridge University Press, 1983. 90 p. DU740.42 .M236 1983.
Includes 625 entries dealing with the kula, an exchange system used by the Massim involving the circulation of necklaces and armshells around a ring of islands off the eastern end of New Guinea.

9.539 Potter, Michelle. *Traditional law in Papua New Guinea; an annotated and selected bibliography.* Canberra: Australian National University, Department of Law, Research School of Social Sciences, 1973. 132 p. 016.34 P853.

Oceania --- Melanesia --- Hawaii
9.540 Hunnewell, James F. *Bibliography of the Hawaiian Islands.* New York: Kraus Reprint, 1962. 75 p. 016.9969 H899.

9.541 Murdoch, Clare G., and Masae Gotanda. *Basic Hawaiiana, selected and annotated.* Honolulu: Hawaii State Library, 1969. 34 p. 016.9969 M941.

Oceania --- Melanesia --- Hawaii -- Archaeology
9.542 Spriggs, Matthew, and Patricia Lehua Tanaka. *Na mea 'imi i ka wa kahiko: an annotated bibliography of Hawaiian archaeology.* Manoa: Social Science Research Institute, University of Hawaii at Manoa; Honolulu: University of Hawaii Press, 1988. 303 p. DU624 .S6 1988.
Includes more than 2,000 entries dealimg with the archaeology and prehistory of Hawaii.

Oceania --- Melanesia --- Hawaii ---
Cultural/Social Anthropology

9.543   Kittelson, David J. *The Hawaiians: an annotated bibliography.*
        Honolulu: Social Science Research Institute, University of Hawaii,
        1985. 384 p. DU624.65 .K58x 1985.
        Briefly annotates 2,712 entries about the Hawaiians.

9.544   Rubano, Judith. *Culture and behavior in Hawaii; an annotated
        bibliography.* Honolulu, Social Science Research Institute, University
        of Hawaii, 1971. 147 p. 016.9969 R821.

Oceania ---Melanesia --- Hawaii --- Linguistics

9.545   Chamisso, Adelbert von, and Samuel H. Elbert. *Uber die Hawaiische
        Sprache.* Amsterdam: Halcyon Antiquariaat, 1969. 79 p. 499.4 C357.

Oceania --- Melanesia --- Ethnographic Art

9.546   Newton, Douglas. *Bibliography of Sepik District art annotated for
        illustrations.* New York: Museum of Primitive Art Library, 1965.
        N7411 .N4 N4 1965.

Oceania --- Melanesia --- Linguistics

9.547   Murane, Elizabeth. *Bibliography of the Summer Institute of
        Linguistics, Papua New Guinea Branch, 1956 to 1975.* Ukarumpa,
        Papua New Guinea: Summer Institute of Linguistics, 1976. 64 p.

Oceania --- Micronesia

9.548   Coppell, William G. *Bibliographies of the Kermadec Islands, Niue,
        Swains Island, and the Tokelau Islands.* Honolulu: Pacific Islands
        Studies Program, University of Hawaii, 1975. 99 p. DU430 .K46 1975.

9.549   Marshall, Mac, and James D. Nason. *Micronesia, 1944-1974: a
        bibliography of anthropological and related source materials.* New
        Haven: HRAF Press, 1975. 337 p. GN669 .M288 1975.

9.550   Snow, Philip A. *A Bibliography of Fiji, Tonga, and Rotuma.* Coral
        Gables: University of Miami Press, 1969. 418 p. DU600 .S66 1969.
        A comprehensive bibliography of some 12,000 entries dating from
        the seventeenth century to the 1960s.

Oceania --- Polynesia

9.551   Du Rietz, Rolf, and Bjarne Kroepelien. *Bibliotheca Polynesiana.*
        Stockholm: Almqvist & Wiksell, 1969. DU510 .D87x 1969.

Oceania --- Polynesia --- Cultural/ Social Anthropology

9.552   Keesing, Felix M. *Social anthropology in Polynesia; a review of research.* London, New York: Oxford University Press, 1953. 126 p. 301.996 K258.

Oceania --- Polynesia --- New Caledonia

9.553   Pisier, Georges. *Bibliographie methodique, analytique et critique de la Nouvelle-Caledonie, 1955-1982.* Noumea: Société d'Etudes Historiques de la Nouvelle-Caledonie, 1983. 350 p. DU720 .P57x 1983.

9.554   O'Reilly, Patrick. *Bibliographie methodique.* Société des Oceanistes, 4. Paris: Musée de l'Homme, 1955. 361 p. 016.9932 Or1.

9.555   O'Reilly, Patrick. *Caledoniens: repertoire bio-bibliographique de la Nouvelle-Caledonie.* 2 ed. Paris: Société des Oceanistes, 1980. 416 p. 920 Or145ca.

Oceania --- Polynesia --- Rapa Island

9.556   Hanson, F. Allan, and Patrick O'Reilly. *Bibliographie de Rapa: Polynesie francaise.* Société des Oceanistes, 32. Paris: Musée de l'Homme, 1973. 53 p. 016.996 H198.

Oceania --- Polynesia --- Solomon Islands

9.557   O'Reilly, Patrick, and Hugh Laracy. *Bibliographie des ouvrages publies par les missions maristes des Iles Salomon.* Société des Oceanistes, 29. Paris: Musée de l'Homme, 1972. 67 p. 016.2662 Or3.
Bibliography of the Marist Brothers and the Solomon Islands.

Oceania --- Polynesia --- Tahiti

9.558   O'Reilly, Patrick, and Edourd Reitman. *Bibliographie de Tahiti et de la Polynesie francaise.* Société des Oceanistes, 14. Paris: Musée de l'Homme, 1967. 1,048 p. 016.996 Or14.
Approximately 10,000 annotated entries dealiong with Tahiti and French Polynesia.

9.559   O'Reilly, Patrick, and Raoul Teissier. *Tahitiens: repertoire bio-bibliographique de la Polynesie francaise.* Société des Oceanistes, 10. Paris: Musée de l'Homme, 1962. 534p. 920 Or145.
Continued by: P. O'Reilly, and R. Teissier, *Tahitiens: repertoire bio-bibliographique de la Polynesie francaise. Supplement* (Paris: Musée de l'Homme, 1966. 103 p.).

9.560   O'Reilly, Patrick, and Raoul Teissier. *Tahitiens: repertoire biographique de la Polynesie francaise.* 2. ed. Société des Oceanistes, 36. Paris: Musée de l'Homme, 1975. 670 p. 920 Or145a.

Oceania --- Polynesia --- Vanuatu

9.561   O'Reilly, Patrick. *Bibliographie methodique.* Société des Oceanistes, 8. Paris: Musée de l'Homme, 1958. 304 p. 016.9934 Or3.

9.562   O'Reilly, Patrick. *Hebridais; repertoire bio-bibliographique des Nouvelles-Hebrides.* Société des Oceanistes, 6. Paris: Musée de l'Homme, 1957. 289 p. 016.9934 Or3h.

10

Dictionaries and Encyclopedias

The specialized dictionaries and encyclopedias listed in this chapter provide detailed definitions and explanations for anthropology and related social science disciplines. The primary goal of a dictionary is obviously to define words. Well-known dictionaries, such as *Webster's Thirds New International Dictionary* or *The Random House Dictionary of the English Language,* are probably familiar to most students. There has been a proliferation of more specialized subject dictionaries in recent years. Unlike general dictionaries, these are not usually concerned with etymology, syllabication, or pronunciation, but rather are intended for those engaged in the study of a specific field. Specialized dictionaries supplement general dictionaries to the extent that they provide the following: newly introduced words in a specialized field; more highly specialized terms; accurate definition sin terms of the subject, more fully treated, and with added descriptive matter when pertinent; illustrative quotations from authorities in the field for clarification; and balanced and unbiased treatment of abstract terms for which there may be a difference of opinion.

The primary search for works that have relevant data on a subject begins with the dictionary and encyclopedia. These basic sources provide succinct statements on terms, styles, and so forth. The works described in this chapter are classified into one of only two categories: dictionaries and encyclopedias. For our purposes, dictionaries define terminology and provide brief data. An encyclopedia is defined as a multivolume illustrated work that includes signed articles and bibliographical data on various subjects and thus provides a general background essential for any kind of research.

For addition dictionaries and encyclopedias, consult the library catalog under the appropriate subject with the subdivision *Bibliography.* For example,

Anthropology --- Dictionaries
Anthropology --- Dictionaries --- Spanish
Human Evolution --- Encyclopedias

Dictionaries
Social Sciences
10.1   Gould, Julius, and William L. Kolb. *A Dictionary of the social sciences.* London: Tavistock; New York: Free Press, 1964. 761 p. H41 .G6 1964.

Compiled under the auspices of the United Nations Educational, Scientific and Cultural Organization (UNESCO) and includes terms and concepts in anthropology, economics, political science, social psychology, and sociology. Each term is thoroughly explained with brief definitions and a discussion of its historical backgrounds or divergent meanings.

10.2   Koschnick, Wolfgang J. *Compact dictionary of the social sciences; Kompaktworterbuch der Sozialwissenschaften.* München: K.G. Saur, 1995. 555 p.

10.3   Koschnick, Wolfgang J. *Standard dictionary of the social sciences; Standardworterbuch fur die Sozialwissenschafte.* München; New York: K.G. Saur, 1984-1992. H41 .K68 1984.

Social Sciences --- Methods

10.4   Miller, P. McC., and M.J. Wilson. *A Dictionary of social science methods.* Chichester, West Sussex; New York: Wiley, 1983. 124 p. H41 .M54 1983.
Defines terms used in the empirical social sciences, including many statistical methods and terms.

Anthropology

10.5   Pearson, Roger. *Anthropological glossary.* Malabar, Florida: R.E. Krieger, 1985. 282 p. GN11 .P43 1985.
Defines some 4,500 terms used in archaeology, biological/physical anthropology, cultural/social anthropology, and linguistics.

10.6   Seymour-Smith, Charlotte, ed. *Dictionary of anthropology.* Boston: G.K. Hall, 1986. 305 p. GN11 .D48 1986b.
Includes more than 2,000 entries for social and cultural anthropology, physical anthropology; also includes biographical entries for some 250 leading figures in the discipline; also published as: *Macmillan dictionary of anthropology* (London: Macmillan Reference Books, 1986).

10.8   Winthrop, Robert H. *Dictionary of concepts in cultural anthropology.* Westport: Connecticut: Greenwood Press, 1991. 347 p. GN307 .W56 1991.

There are times when one may need a foreign language dictionary to clarify the meaning of a term used in anthropology. The following are examples of such dictionaries that are likely to be found in most undergraduate libraries in the United States.

Anthropology -- Chinese

10.9   Hsieh, Chien. *Chung i jen lei hsueh tz`u hui.* Hsiang-kang: Chung wen ta hsueh ch`u pan she, 1980. 88 p.

Anthropology --- French

10.10   *L'Anthropologie.* Les Dictionnaires Marabout Universite, 10.
Vewrviers: Marabout, 1974. 690 p. GN11 .A8 1974.

Anthropology --- German

10.11   Hirschberg, Walter. *Wörterbuch der Völkerkunde, in Verbindung mit
zahlreichen Fachwissenschaftlern.* Stuttgart: A. Kroner, 1965. 508 p.
301.5 H615.

Anthropology -- Malay

10.12   Dewan Bahasa dan Pustaka. *Istilah sosiologi-antropologi,
Inggeris-Malaysia-Inggeris.* Kuala Lumpur: Dewan Bahasa dan
Pustaka, Kementerian Pelajaran Malaysia, 1977. 529 p.

Anthropology -- Polish

10.13   Bielecki, Tadeusz, ed. *Maly slownik antropologiczny.* 2 ed. Warszawa:
Wiedza Powszechna, 1976. 511 p.

Anthropology --- Spanish

10.14   Aguirre Baztan, Angel, and J.L. Acin. *Diccionario temático de
antropología.* 2 ed. Barcelona: Editorial Boixareu Universitaria, 1993.
663 p. GN11 .D46 1988.

10.15   Macazaga Ordono, César. *Diccionario de antropología
mesoamericana.* México: Editorial Innovación, 1985. F1219 .M235
1985.

10.16   Ortíz García, Carmen, and Luis A. Sánchez Gómez. *Diccionario
histórico de la antropología española.* Madrid: Consejo Superior de
Investigaciones Científicas, Departamento de Antropología de España
y América, 1994. 760 p.

Anthropology -- Tamil

10.17   Sakthivel, S. *Glossary of technical terms of anthropology.*
Kothaloothv, Madurai District, Veluchami; 1972. 102 p. GN11 .S24.
1972.

Anthropology -- Urdu

10.18   *Glossary of technical terms (English-Urdu), anthropology; Farhang-i
istilahat, insaniyat.* New Delhi: Bureau of Promotion of Urdu,
Ministry of Education and Culture, Government of India, 1981. 36 p.

There are also specialized dictionaries for the various subdisciplines of
anthropology, as well as dictionaries in non-English languages. The following
are examples of such dictionaries that are likely to be found in most
undergraduate libraries in the United States.

Archaeology

10.19   Adkins, Lesley, and Roy A. Adkins. *The Handbook of British archaeology*. London: Macmillan, 1983. 319 p. DA90 .A6 1982.
First published under title: *A Thesaurus of British archaeology* (Newton Abbot: David and Charles, 1982. DA90 .A6 1982).

10.20   Bahn, Paul G. *Collins dictionary of archaeology*. Santa Barbara, California: ABC-CLIO, 1993. 654 p. CC70 .C54x 1992.

10.21   Bray, Warwick, and David Trump. *The American heritage guide to archaeology*. New York: American Heritage Press, 1970. 269 p. CC70 .B7.
Includes terms, personal and place names, etc., in dictionary arrangement; excludes classic, medieval, and industrial archaeology; also published as *A Dictionary of archaeology* (London: A. Lane, 1970. CC70 .B73 1970), and *The Penguin dictionary of archaeology* (Hammondsworth, Middlesex, England: Penguin Books, 1982).

10.22   Champion, Sara. *A Dictionary of terms and techniques in archaeology*. New York: Facts on File, 1980. 144 p. CC70 .C48 1980b.
Terms used in the scientific and technical aspects of archaeology.

10.23   Fagan, Brian. *The Oxford companion to archaeology*. New York: Oxford University Press, 1996. CC70 .M45 1993.

10.24   Flanagan, Laurence. *Dictionary of Irish Archaeology*. n.p.: Gill and Macmillan, 1992. 221 p. CC70 .M45 1993.

10.25   Jones, W.R. *Dictionary of industrial archaeology*. Herndon, Virginia: Sutton, 1996. 461 p. T37 .J66 1996.

10.26   Mignon, Molly R. *Dictionary of concepts in archaeology*. Westport, Connecticut: Greenwood Press, 1993. 364 p. CC70 .M45 1993.

10.27   Whitehouse, Ruth D. *The Macmillan dictionary of archaeology*. London: Macmillan, 1983. 597 p. CC70 .F32 1983.
Includes entries for terms, sites, persons, etc., with 30 topical divisions; strong European emphasis; also published as *The Facts on File dictionary of archaeology* (New York: Facts on File, 1983. CC70 .F32 1983).

Archaeology --- Arabic

10.28   Aziz, Hilmi, and Muhammad Ghitas. *Qamus al-mustalahat al-athariyah wa-al-fanniyah: Injilizi-Faransi-Arabi*.Dokki, Giza, Egypt: al-Sharikah al-Misriyah al-Alamiyah lil-Nashr-Lunjman, 1993. 198 p. CC70 .A95x 1993.

Dictionary of archaeological and artistic terms in Arabic, English, and French.

10.29　Lapp, Paul W. *Arabic for the beginner in archaeology.* rev. ed. Pittsburgh, Pennsylvania: N.L. Lapp, 1990. 71 p.

Archaeology --- Chinese

10.30　Ho, Hsien-wu. *Chung-kuo wen wu kao ku tzu tien.* Ti 1 pan. Shen-yang shih: Liao-ning ko hsueh chi shu chu pan she, 1993. 838 p.

Archaeology --- Danish

10.31　Rasmussen, Birgit. *Arkologi.* Kobenhavn: Gad, 1979. 207 p. CC70 .R37.

Archaeology --- French

10.32　Rachet, Guy. *Dictionnaire de l'archeologie.* Paris: R. Laffont, 1983. 1,052 p. CC70 .R32 1983.

Archaeology --- French/German

10.33　Jost, Werner. *Deutsch-franzosisches Worterbuch für Kunstgeschichte und Archaologie.* Berlin: E. Schmidt, 1995. 267 p. N33 .J67 1995.

Archaeology --- German

10.34　Apelt, Mary L. *German-English dictionary: art history, archaeology; Deutsch-Englisches Worterbuch fur Kunstgeschichte u. Archaologie.* 2 ed. Berlin: E. Schmidt, 1990. 275 p. N33 .A557 1982.

Archaeology --- Latvian

10.35　Graudonis, Janis. *Arheolo'gijas terminu vardnica.* Riga: Zinatn, 1994. 450 p.

Archaeology --- Malay

10.36　*Istilah arkeologi: bahasa Inggeris-bahasa Malaysia, bahasa Malaysia-bahasa Inggeris.* Kuala Lumpur: Dewan Bahasa dan Pustaka, Kementerian Pendidikan Malaysia, 1988. 107 p.

Archaeology --- Marathi

10.37　Marathe, Ramacandra V. *Ingraji-Marathi puratattva-kosa.* Mumbai: Manjiri Sri. Marathe, 1983. 127 p.

Archaeology --- Polyglot

10.38　Goffer, Zvi. *Elsevier's dictionary of archaeological materials and archaeometry in English with translations of terms in German, Spanish, French, Italian, and Portuguese.* New York: Elsevier, 1996.

10.39 *Unified dictionary of archaeology and history terms (English, French, Arabic); Mujam al-muwahhad li-mustalahat al-athar wa-al-tarikh (Injlizi, Faransi, Arabi).* Tunis: Arab League Educational, Cultural and Scientific Organization, Bureau of Coordination of Arabization, 1993. 187, 56 p. CC70 .U55x 1993.

Archaeology --- Russian

10.40 Bray, Warwick, and David Trump. *Arkheologicheskii slovar.* Moskva: Progress, 1990. 366 p.
    Russian-language translation of *A Dictionary of archaeology* (London: A. Lane, 1970).

10.41 Savvonidi, Nikolai F., V.G. Belousov, and O.E. Alekseeva. *Kartinnyi arkheologicheskii slovar (Anglo-Russkii).* Sankt-Peterburg: Rossiiskaia akademiia nauk, Institut istorii materialnoi kultury, 1995. 64 p.

10.42 Soffer, Olga. *Arkheologicheskii slovar' kamennykh orudii; Archaeological dictionary of stone tools.* Moskva: Institut arkheologii AN SSSR, 1991. 38 p.
    Entries in English with equivalent terms in French, German, Spanish and Russia.

Archaeology --- Spanish

10.43 Bray, Warwick, and David Trump. *Diccionario de arqueología.* Barcelona: Labor, 1976. 275 p.
    Spanish-language translation of *A Dictionary of archaeology* (London: A. Lane, 1970).

Archaeology --- Turkish

10.44 Cambel, Halet, Guven Arsebuk, and Sonmez Kantman. *Cok dilli arkeoloji sozlugu; Multilingual dictionary of archaeological terms; Dictionnaire multilingue d'archeologie; Mehrsprachiges Archaologisches Worterbuch.* Galatasaray, Istanbul: Arkeoloji ve Sanat Yayinlari, 1994. 157 p.

Archaeology --- Vietnamese

10.45 Loofs-Wissowa, H.H.E., Van Minh Pham, and Nguyen M. Long. *Vietnamese-English archaeological glossary with English index.* Canberra: Faculty of Asian Studies, The Australian National University, 1990. 103 p.

Biological/Physical Anthropology

10.46 Heymer, Armin. *Ethological dictionary: German-English-French.* New York: Garland, 1977. 237 p. 591.5 H516.
    Ethology deals with the biology of human behavior, e.g., contact greeting. This dictionary collects over 1,000 terms dealing with ethology and defines them in German, English, and French.

10.47   Stevenson, Joan C. *Dictionary of concepts in physical anthropology.*
         Westport, Connecticut: Greenwood Press, 1991. 432 p. GN50.3 .S74
         1991.

Linguistics

10.48   Crystal, David. *A Dictionary of linguistics and phonetic.* 3 ed. Oxford,
         England; Cambridge, Massachusetts: B. Blackwell, 1991. 389 p. P29
         .C65 1991.

10.49   Crystal, David. *An Encyclopedic dictionary of language and
         languages.* Oxford, England; Cambridge, Massachusetts: B.
         Blackwell, 1992. 428 p. P29 .C68 1992.

10.50   Marciszewski, Witold, ed. *Dictionary of logic as applied in the study
         of language: concepts, methods, theories.* The Hague: M. Nijhoff;
         Hingham, Massachusetts: Kluwer Boston, 1981. 436 p. BC9 .D48.

10.51   Richards, Jack C. *Longman dictionary of applied linguistics.* Harlow,
         Essex, England: Longman, 1985. 323 p. P129 .R5 1985.

Linguistics --- Arabic

10.52   Al Khuli, Muhammad A. *A Dictionary of applied linguistics,
         English-Arabic; with an Arabic-English glossary.* Beirut: Librairie du
         Liban, 1986. 179 p. P29 .K585x 1986.

10.53   Al Khuli, Muhammad A. *A Dictionary of theoretical linguistics:
         English-Arabic, with an Arabic-English glossary.* Beirut: Librairie du
         Liban, 1982. 402 p. P29 .K584x 1982.

10.54   Baalbaki, Ramzi M. *Dictionary of linguistic terms: English-Arabic
         with sixteen Arabic glossaries.* Beirut: Dar el-Ilm lilMalayin, 1990.
         806 p. P29 .B25x 1990.

Linguistics --- Chinese

10.55   Hartmann, R.R.K., F.C. Storck, Chang-chu Huang, Chen-li Li, and
         Chiung chaio Yu. *Yu yen yu yu yen hsueh tz`u tien.* Shang-hai:
         Shang-hai tz`u shu ch`u pan she: Shang-hai tz`u shu ch`u pan she fa
         hsing so fa hsing, 1981. 460 p. P29 .H3412 1981.

Linguistics --- German

10.56   Abraham, Werner. *Terminologie zur neueren Linguistik.* Tübingen:
         Niemeyer, 1974. 555 p. 410.3 T273.

10.57   Welte, Werner. *Moderne Linguistik: Terminologie, Bibliographie; ein
         Handbuch und Nachschlagewerk auf der Basis der
         generativtransformationellen Sprachtheorie.* Munchen: M. Hueber,
         1974. 2 v. 410.3 W466.

Linguistics — Russian

10.58   Akhmanova, O.S. *Slovar' lingvisticheskikh terminov*. Moskva:
Sovetskaia entsiklopediia, 1966. 606 p. 410.3 Ak46.

Linguistics — Spanish

10.59   Abraham, Werner. *Diccionario de terminología lingüística actual.*
Madrid: Editorial Gredos, 1981. 511 p. P29 .T417x 1981.
Spanish-language translation of *Moderne Linguistik:
Terminologie, Bibliographie* (Munchen: M. Hueber, 1974).

Linguistics — Tamil

10.60   Arunabharathi, N. *Glossary of linguistics, English-Tamil*. Madras:
Tamil Nuulagam, 1976. 82 p. P29. A7.

Mythology

10.61   Cotterell, Arthur. *A Dictionary of world mythology.* rev. ed. Oxford,
England: Oxford University Press, 1986. BL303 .C66 1982.
Background information on the principal deities and mythological
figures of West Africa, South and Central Asia, East Asia, Europe,
America, Africa, and Oceania.

Religion

10.62   Brandon, S.G.F. *A Dictionary of comparative religion*. New York:
Scribner, 1970. 704 p. BL31 .D54 1970.

Africa

10.63   *African historical dictionaries.* Metuchen, New Jersey: Scarecrow,
1974 - (in progress).
Each volume contains a brief survey of the history of the country
followed by a dictionary of people and topics; many contain selective
bibliographies. The series includes the following volumes:
1. V.T. Le Vine, and R.P. Nye, *Historical dictionary of Cameroon*
(1974. 198 p.); 2. V.M. Thompson, and R. Adloff, *Historical
dictionary of the People's Republic of the Congo (Congo-Brazzaville)*
(2 ed., 1984. 239 p.); 3. J.J. Grotpeter, *Historical dictionary of
Swaziland* (1975. 251 p); 4. H.A. Gailey, *Historical dictionary of the
Gambia* (2 ed., 1987. 176 p.); 5. R.P. Stevens, *Historical dictionary of
the Republic of Botswana* (1975. 189 p.); 6. M. Castagno, *Historical
dictionary of Somalia* (1975. 213 p.); 7. S. Decalo, *Historical
dictionary of Dahomey (People's Republic of Benin)*(2 ed., 1987. 349
p.); 8. W. Weinstein, *Historical dictionary of Burundi* (1976. 368 p.);
9. S. Decalo, *Historical dictionary of Togo* (3 ed., 1996. 420 p.); 10.
G.M. Haliburton, *Historical dictionary of Lesotho* (1977. 223 p.); 11.
P.J. Imperato, *Historical dictionary of Mali* (3 ed. 1996. 576 p.); 12.
C.P. Foray, *Historical dictionary of Sierra Leone* (1977. 279 p.); 13.
S. Decalo, *Historical dictionary of Chad* (2 ed., 1987. 532 p.); 14.
D.M. McFarland, *Historical dictionary of Upper Volta (Haute
Volta)*(1978. 217 p.); 15. L.S. Kurtz, *Historical dictionary of Tanzania*

(1978. 331 p.); 16. T. O'Toole, *Historical dictionary of Guinea* (3 ed., 1995. 279 p.); 17. J.O. Voll, *Historical dictionary of the Sudan* (1978. 175 p.); 18. R.K. Rasmussen, *Historical dictionary of Rhodesia/Zimbabwe* (1979. 445 p.); 19. J.J. Grotpeter, *Historical dictionary of Zambia* (1979. 410 p.); 20. S. Decalo, *Historical dictionary of Niger* (1979. 358 p.); 21. M. Liniger-Goumaz, *Historical dictionary of Equatorial Guinea* (2 ed., 1988. 238 p.); 22. R. Lobban, and J. Forrest, *Historical dictionary of the Republic of Guinea-Bissau* (2 ed., 1988. 233 p.); 23. L.G. Colvin, *Historical dictionary of Senegal* (1981. 339 p.); 24. W. Spencer, *Historical dictionary of Morocco* (1980. 152 p.); 25. C.A. Crosby, *Historical dictionary of Malawi* (1980. 169 p.); 26. P.M. Martin, *Historical dictionary of Angola* (1980. 174 p.); 27. P. Kalck, *Historical dictionary of the Central African Republic* (1980. 152 p.); 28. A.A. Heggoy, *Historical dictionary of Algeria* (1980. 237 p.); 29. B.A. Ogot, *Historical dictionary of Kenya* (1981. 279 p.); 30. D.E. Gardinier, *Historical dictionary of Gabon* (1981. 254 p.); 31. A.G. Gerteiny, *Historical dictionary of Mauritania* (1981. 98 p.); 32. C.P. Rosenfeld, *Historical dictionary of Ethiopia* (1981, 436 p.); 33. R.B. St John, *Historical dictionary of Libya* (2 ed. 1991. 192 p.); 34. L. Riviere, *Historical dictionary of Mauritius* (1982. 172 p.); 35. T. Hodges, *Historical dictionary of Western Sahara* (1982. 431 p.); 36. J. Wucher King, *Historical dictionary of Egypt* (1984. 719 p.); 37. C.C. Saunders, *Historical dictionary of South Africa* (1983. 241 p.); 38. D.E., and S.E. Holsoe, *Historical dictionary of Liberia* (1985. 274 p.); 39. D.M. McFarland, *Historical dictionary of Ghana* (1985. 296 p.); 40. A. Oyewole, *Historical dictionary of Nigeria* (1987. 391 p.); 41. R.J. Mundt, *Historical dictionary of Cote d'Ivoire (the Ivory Coast)*(2 ed., 1995. 367 p.); 42. R. Lobban, and M. Halter. *Historical dictionary of the Republic of Cape Verde* (2 ed., 1988.171 p.); 43. F.S. Bobb, *Historical dictionary of Zaire* (1988. 349 p.); 44. F. Morton, A. Murray, and J. Ramsay. *Historical dictionary of Botswana* (rev. ed., 1989. 216 p.); 45. K.J. Perkins, *Historical dictionary of Tunisia* (1989. 234 p.); 46. R.K. Rasmussen, and S.C. Rubert, *Historical dictionary of Zimbabwe* (2 ed., 1990. 502 p. DT38.5 .R37 1990); 47. M.J. Azevedo, *Historical dictionary of Mozambique* (1991. 282 p); 48. M. DeLancey, and H.M. Mokeba, *Historical dictionary of the Republic of Cameroon* (2 ed., 1990. 321 p.); 49. S. Selvon, *Historical dictionary of Mauritius* (2 ed., 1991. 295 p.); 50. M. Covell, Maureen. *Historical dictionary of Madagascar* (1995. 408 p.); 51. P. Kalck, *Historical dictionary of the Central African Republic* (2 ed., 1992. 246 p.); 52. S.H. Broadhead, *Historical dictionary of Angola* (2 ed., 1992. 344 p.); 53. C. Fluehr-Lobban, R.A. Lobban, and J.O. Voll, *Historical dictionary of the Sudan* (2 ed., 1992. 527 p.); 54. C.A. Crosby, *Historical dictionary of Malawi* (2 ed., 1993. 243 p.); 55. A.G. Pazzanita, and T. Hodges, *Historical dictionary of Western Sahara* (2 ed., 1994. 641 p.); 56. C.P. Rosenfeld, and E. Rosenfeld, *Historical dictionary of Ethiopia and Eritrea* (2 ed., 1994. 644 p.); 57. J.J. Grotpeter, *Historical dictionary of Namibia* (1994. 724 p.); 58. D.E. Gardinier, *Historical dictionary of Gabon* (2 ed., 1994. 507p.); 59. M. Ottenheimer, and H. Ottenheimer, *Historical dictionary of the Comoro Islands* (1994. 164 p.); 60. L. Dorsey, *Historical dictionary of Rwanda* (1994. 458 p.); 61. S. Decalo, *Historical dictionary of Benin* (3 ed., 1995. 604 p.); 62. R. Lobban, and M. Lopes, *Historical dictionary of the Republic of Cape Verde* (3 ed., 1995. 404 p.); 63. D. Owusu-Ansah, and D.M. McFarland, *Historical dictionary of Ghana* (2 ed., 1995. 477 p.); 64. M.L. Pirouet, *Historical dictionary of Uganda* (1995. 584 p.); 65. A.F. Clark, and L.C. Phillips, *Historical dictionary of Senegal* (2 ed., 1994. 370 p.); 66. P.C. Naylor, and A.A. Heggoy, *Historical dictionary of Algeria* (2 ed. 1994. 488 p.); 67. A. Goldschmidt, *Historical dictionary of Egypt* (2 ed., 1994. 395 p.); 68. A.G. Pazzanita, *Historical dictionary of Mauritania* (2 ed., 1996. 560 p.); 69. S. Decalo, V. Thompson, and R. Adloff, *Historical dictionary of the Congo* (3 ed., 1996. 448 p.); 70. F. Morton, B. Morton, and J. Ramsey, *Historical dictionary of Botswana* (3 ed., 1996. 320 p.); 71. T.K. Park, *Historical dictionary of Morocco* (1996. 544 p.); 72. S. Decalo, *Historical dictionary of Niger* (3 ed., 1996. 576 p.). Forthcoming volumes include Burundi, Chad, Djibouti, Somali, South Africa, and Zaire.

10.64   Balandier, Georges, and Jacques Maquet. *Dictionary of Black African civilization.* New York: L. Amiel, 1974. 350 p. DT352.4 .D5213.

Deals with various aspects of Black African culture and civilization; originally published in French as *Dictionnaire des civilisations africaines* (Paris: Hazan, 1968).

10.65   Biebuyck, Daniel, Susan Kelliher, and Linda McRae. *African ethnonyms: index to art-producing peoples of Africa.* New York: G.K. Hall, 1996. 325 p. GN645 .B53 1996.

A comprehensive index of more than 2,500 names of ethnic groups.

10.66   Olson, James S. *The Peoples of Africa: an ethnohistorical dictionary.* Westport, Connecticut: Greenwood, 1996. 682 p. GN645 .O47 1996.

Asia

10.67   *Asian historical dictionaries.* Metuchen, New Jersey; Lanham, Maryland: Scarecrow, 1989 - (in progress).

Each volume contains a brief survey of the history of the country followed by a dictionary of people and topics; most contain selective bibliographies. The series includes the following volumes: 1. W.J. Duiker, *Historical dictionary of Vietnam* (1989. 285 p); 2. C. Baxter, *Historical dictionary of Bangladesh* (2 ed. 1996. 344 p.); 3. S.J. Burki, *Historical dictionary of Pakistan* (1991. 292 p.); 4. P. Gubser, *Historical dictionary of the Hashemite Kingdom of Jordan* (1991. 164 p.); 5. L.W. Adamec, *Historical dictionary of Afghanistan* (1991. 392 p.); 6. M. Stuart-Fox, and M. Kooyman, *Historical*

dictionary of Laos (1992. 310 p.); 7. K. Mulliner, and L. The-
Mulliner, *Historical dictionary of Singapore* (1991. 285 p.); 8. B.
Reich, *Historical dictionary of Israel* (1992. 421 p.); 9. R.B. Cribb,
Historical dictionary of Indonesia (1992. 739 p); 10. E.V. Roberts,
S.N. Ling, and P. Bradshaw, *Historical dictionary of Hong Kong and
Macau* (1992. 407 p.); 11. A.C. Nahm, *Historical dictionary of the
Republic of Korea* (1993. 336 p.); 12. J.F. Copper, *Historical
dictionary of Taiwan* (1993. 211 p.); 13. A. Car, *Historical dictionary
of Malaysia* (1993. 329 p.); 14. J. Peterson, *Historical dictionary of
Saudi Arabia* (1993. 267 p); 15. J. Becka, *Historical dictionary of
Myanmar* (1995. 352 p.); 16. J.H. Lorentz, *Historical dictionary of
Iran* (1995, 352 p.); 17. R.D. Burrowes, *Historical dictionary of
Yemen* (1995. 528 p); 18. May Kyi Win, and Harold Smith, *Historical
dictionary of Thailand* (1995. 340 p.); 19. A.J.K. Sanders, *Historical
dictionary of Mongolia* (1996. 240 p.); 20. S. Mansingh, *Historical
dictionary of India* (1996. 552 p.); 21. M.C. Peck, *Historical
dictionary of the Gulf Arab States* (1997. 352 p.); 22. D.D. Commins,
Historical dictionary of Syria (1996. 336 p); 22. N. Nazzal, *Historical
dictionary of Palestine* (1997); 24. A.R. Guillermo, *Historical
dictionary of the Philippines* (1997). Forthcoming volumes include
Cambodia, Iraq, Japan, North Korea, Pakistan, and Vietnam.

10.68 *Historical and cultural dictionaries of Asia.* Metuchen, New Jersey:
Scarecrow, 1972-1976).
    Each volume contains a brief survey of the history of the country
followed by a dictionary of people and topics; most contain selective
bibliopgraphies. The series includes the following volumes:
    1. C.L. Riley, *Historical and cultural dictionary of Saudi Arabia*
(1972. 133 p.); 2. B.C. Hedrick, *Historical and cultural dictionary of
Nepal* (1972. 198 p.); 3. E.G. Maring, *Historical and cultural
dictionary of the Philippines* (1973. 240 p.); 4. J.M. Maring,
Historical and cultural dictionary of Burma (1973. 290 p.); 5. M.J.
Hanifi, *Historical and cultural dictionary of Afghanistan* (1976, 141
p.); 6. H.E. Smith, *Historical and cultural dictionary of Thailand*
(1976, 213 p.); 7. D.J. Whitfield, *Historical and cultural dictionary of
Vietnam* (1976, 369 p.); 8. G.T. Kurian, *Historical and cultural
dictionary of India* (1989. 307 p.); 9. J.D. Anthony, *Historical and
cultural dictionary of the Sultanate of Oman and the Emirates of
eastern Arabia* (1976, 136 p.).

Europe
10.69 *European historical dictionaries.* Lanham, Maryland: Scarecrow,
1993 - (in progress).
    Each volume contains a brief survey of the history of the country
followed by a dictionary of people and topics; most contain selective
bibliographies. The series includes the following volumes:
    1. D.L. Wheeler, *Historical dictionary of Portugal* (1993. 316 p.); 2.
M. Heper, *Historical dictionary of Turkey* (1994. 611 p.); 3. G.

Sanford, and A. Gozdecka-Sanford, *Historical dictionary of Poland*
(1994. 365 p.); 4. W.C. Thompson, S.L. Thompson, and J.S.
Thompson, *Historical dictionary of Germany* (1994. 660 p.); 5. T.M.
Veremis, and M. Dragoumis, *Historical dictionary of Greece* (1995.
278 p.); 6. S. Panteli, *Historical dictionary of Cyprus* (1995. 258 p.);
7. I. Scobbie, *Historical dictionary of Sweden* (1995. 341 p.); 8. G.
Maude, *Historical dictionary of Finland* (1995. 384 p.); 9. R.
Stallaerts, and J. Laurens, *Historical dictionary of the Republic of
Croatia* (1995. 387 p.); 10. W.G. Berg, *Historical dictionary of Malta*
(1995. 190 p.); 11. A. Smith, *Historical dictionary of Spain* (1996.
320 p.); 12. R. Hutchings, *Historical dictionary of Albania* (1996. 280
p.); 13. L. Plut-Pregelj, and C. Rogel, *Historical dictionary of
Slovenia* (1996. 450 p.); 14. H.C. Barteau, *Historical dictionary of
Luxembourg* (1996. 392 p.); 15. K.W. Treptow, and M. Popa,
Historical dictionary of Romania (1996. 384 p.); 16. R. Detrez,
Historical dictionary of Bulgaria (1996. 576 p.); 17. K.J. Panton, and
K.A. Cowlard, *Historical dictionary of United Kingdom: 1. England
and the United Kingdom* (1996). Forthcoming volumes include
Estonia, Netherlands, Norway, Russia, Slovakia, and Ukraine.

10.70   *International dictionary of regional European ethnology and folklore.*
Copenhagen: Rosenkilde and Bagger, 1960-1965. 2v. 301.94 In8.
    Published by the International Commission on Folk Arts and
Folklore; includes two parts: General ethnological concepts, by Ake
Hultkrantz, and Folk literature (Germanic), by Laurits Bodker. Vol. 1
is an alphabetically arranged dictionary of ethnological and folkloristic
terms and concepts, arranged by English term with synonyms in
French, German, Spanish, and Swedish; in v. 2 terms are entered
under the various national denominations rather than grouped under
the English equivalent.

Latin America
10.71   *Latin American historical dictionaries.* Metuchen, New Jersey;
Lanham, Maryland: Scarecrow, 1967 - (in progress).
    Each volume contains a brief survey of the history of the country
followed by a dictionary of people and topics; most contain selective
bibliographies. The series includes the following volumes:
    1. R.E. Moore, *Historical dictionary of Guatemala* (rev. ed.,
1973. 285 p.); 2. B.C. Hedrick, *Historical dictionary of Panama*
(1970. 105 p); 3. D.K. Rudolph, *Historical dictionary of Venezuela* (2
ed., 1996. 954 p.); 4. D.B. Heath, *Historical dictionary of Bolivia*
(1972. 324 p.); 5. P.F. Flemion, *Historical dictionary of El Salvador*
(1972. 157 p.); 6. H.K. Meyer, *Historical dictionary of Nicaragua*
(1972. 503 p); 7. S. Bizzarro, *Historical dictionary of Chile* (2 ed.,
1987. 583 p.); 8. C.J. Kolinski, *Historical dictionary of Paraguay*
(1973. 282 p.); 9. K.R. Farr, *Historical dictionary of Puerto Rico and
the U.S. Virgin Islands* (1973. 148 p.); 10. A.W. Bork, *Historical
dictionary of Ecuador* (1973. 192 p.); 11. J.L. Willis, *Historical

dictionary of Uruguay (1974. 275 p.); 12. W. Lux, *Historical dictionary of the British Caribbean* (1975. 266 p.); 13. H.K. Meyer, *Historical dictionary of Honduras* (1976. 399 p.); 14. R.H. Davis, *Historical dictionary of Colombia* (1977. 280 p.); 15. R.I. Perusse, *Historical dictionary of Haiti* (1977. 124 p.); 16. T.S. Creedman, *Historical dictionary of Costa Rica* (2 ed., 1991. 338 p.); 17. I.S. Wright, *Historical dictionary of Argentina* (1978. 1,113 p.); 18. A.L. Gastmann, *Historical dictionary of the French and Netherlands Antilles* (1978. 162 p.); 19. R.M. Levine, *Historical dictionary of Brazil* (1979. 297 p.); 20. M. Alisky, *Historical dictionary of Peru* (1979. 157 p); 21. D.C. Briggs, *Historical dictionary of Mexico* (1981. 259 p.); 22. J. Suchlicki, *Historical dictionary of Cuba* (1988. 368 p.); 23. R.H. Davis, *Historical dictionary of Colombia* (2 ed. 1993. 600 p.); 24. R.A. Nickson, *Historical dictionary of Paraguay* (2 ed., 1993. 685 p.); 25. H.K. Meyer, *Historical dictionary of Honduras* (2 ed., 1994. 708 p.); 26. M. Anthony, *Historical dictionary of Trinidad and Tobago* (1997).

North America

10.72   Davis, Mary B., ed. *Native America in the twentieth century: an encyclopedia.* New York: Garland, 1994. 832 p. E76.2 .N36 1994.
Signed articles provide authoritative information on twentieth-century American Indians and Alaska Natives; entries cover art, communications, daily activities, economic development, education, government policy, health issues, land, law, literature, museums, race relations, Red Power, religion, social issues, etc.

10.73   *Dictionary of Indian tribes of the Americas.* 2 ed. Newport Beach, California: American Indian Publishers, 1993. 3 v.
Coverage of both North and South American Indians; some 1,150 tribal entries are arranged alphabetically.

10.74   Hausman, Gerald. *Turtle Island alphabet: a lexicon of Native American symbols and culture.* New York: St. Martin's Press, 1992. 204 p. E98 .R3 H27 1992.

10.75   LePoer, Barbara L. *A Concise dictionary of Indian tribes of North America.* 2 ed. Algonac, Michigan: Reference Publications, 1991. E76.2 .L44 1991.

10.76   Waldman, Carl. *Encyclopedia of Native American tribes.* New York: Facts on File, 1988. 293 p. E76.2 .W35 1988.

10.77   Wiget, Andrew, ed. *Dictionary of Native American literature.* New York: Garland, 1994. 616 p. PM155 .D53 1994.
Provides a comprehensive and authoritative guide to the oral and written literature of Native Americans; includes tribe and author indexes.

Oceania

10.78   *Oceanian historical dictionaries.* Lanham, Maryland: Scarecrow, 1992 - (in progress).

Each volume contains a brief survey of the history of the country followed by a dictionary of people and topics; most contain selective bibliopgraphies. The series includes the following volumes: 1. J.C. Docherty, *Historical dictionary of Australia* (1992. 302 p.); 2. R.D. Craig, *Historical dictionary of Polynesia* (1993. 326 p.); 3. W.L. Wuerch. and D.A. Ballendorf, *Historical dictionary of Guam and Micronesia* (1994. 206 p.); 4. A. Turner, *Historical dictionary of Papua New Guinea* (1994. 365 p.); 5. K. Jackson, and A. McRobie, *Historical dictionary of New Zealand* (1996. 336 p.).

Encyclopedias

Most students are familiar with general encyclopedias such as *Collier's Encyclopedia, Encyclopedia Americana,* and *Encyclopedia Britannica,* as reference works which contain some information on subjects in almost every field of knowledge. These are usually arranged in alphabetical order and provided with a detailed index. The primary purpose of an encyclopedia includes the following: it is used as a source of answers to factual questions, such as who, what, where, when, and how; as a source of background information; and as a source of direction to additional material in a given subject area. An encyclopedia will usually possess most of the following characteristics: contents arranged alphabetical order; articles of any substance written by specialists; subject specialists used in an editorial capacity; inclusion of living people's biographies; inclusion of illustrations, maps, plans, etc.; provision of bibliographies appended to longer articles; analytical indexing of people, places, and subjects; and numerous cross-references. The value of an encyclopedia for the student approaching a new subject for the first time is the overview, and it is not a proper source for research. Coverage tends to be general and needs to be supplemented by a subject encyclopedia which can deal with subjects more intensively. There are a number of subject specific encyclopedias of interest to students of anthropology.

Social Sciences

10.79   *Encyclopedia of the social sciences.* R.A. Seligman, ed. New York: Macmillan, 1930-1935. 15 v. H41 .E6.

The first comprehensive encyclopedia of the social sciences, projected and prepared under the auspices of ten learned societies. International in scope and treatment although the English-speaking world and western Europe has fuller coverage. Excellent survey of the social sciences as of the 1930s. The introduction has a discussion of the nature and scope of the social sciences, a history of their development, and a country by country survey of their position. The main portion of the work covers important concepts and advances in anthropology, economics, law, political science, social work, and sociology. Brief biographical articles make up 20 percent of the contents. Articles are accompanied by selective bibliographies, cross-references, and a subject index.

10.80   *International encyclopedia of the social sciences.* David L. Sills, ed.
New York: Macmillan, 1968-1980; New York: Free Press, 1979. 18 v.
H 40.A2 I5 1968.
     An excellent encyclopedic summary of the social sciences from
1930 to the 1960s. Produced by some 1,500 scholars from 30
countries, synthesizes concepts, methods, theories, and empirical
findings of ten disciplines (anthropology, economics, geography,
history, law, political science, psychiatry, psychology, sociology, and
statistics). Interdisciplinary and cognate subjects are included: area
studies, behavioral sciences, and major societies of the world, as well
as modern social thought about the arts, religion, and selected
professions. Planned to represent the social sciences of the 1960s, it
reflects development and rapid expansion in these areas. Contributors
were asked to emphasize the analytical and comparative aspects of a
topic rather than historical and descriptive material. It only partially
replaces the *Encyclopedia of the social sciences.* The earlier set
contains some 4,000 biographies whereas the *International
encyclopedia of the social sciences* provides only 600, of which one
half are new. Volume 17 contains a detailed subject index to the set
and an alphabetical and classified list of articles included. Volume 18
is a biographical supplement published in 1980, containing
biographies of 215 persons deceased or retired since publication of the
main set.

10.81   Kuper, Adam, and Jessica Kuper. *The Social science encyclopedia.* 2
ed. London; New York: Routledge, 1996. 923 p. H41 .S63 1996.
     Over 700 articles ranging from 200 words to eight pages
contributed by 500 scholars from 25 countries.

Anthropology
10.82   Carlisle, Richard, ed. *The Illustrated encyclopedia of mankind.* New
York: Marshall Cavendish, 1984. 21 v. GN307 .I44 1984.
     Comprehensive encyclopedia covering more than 500 peoples and
culture groups with contributions by more than 100 specialists in
various fields of cultural anthropology; volumes 1-15 alphabetically
cover individual peoples and cultures of humankind as well as urban
life in six major cities; volumes 6-12 deal with a wide range of general
topics; for example, cultural ecology, trade and commerce, performing
arts, social organization, and so forth.

10.83   Hunter, David E., and Phillip Whitten. *Encyclopedia of anthropology.*
New York: Harper and Row, 1976. 411 p. GN11 .E52.
     Approximately 1,400 entries ranging from a few lines to several
pages, some with brief bibliographies; includes biographies but no
ethnographic articles on cultural groups.

10.84   Levinson, David, ed. *Aggression and conflict: a cross-cultural encyclopedia.* Santa Barbara: ABC-CLIO, 1994. 234 p. HM136 .L46 1994.

10.85   Levinson, David, ed. *Encyclopedia of marriage and the family.* New York: Macmillan Library Reference USA; Simon and Schuster Macmillan, 1995. 2 v. HQ9 .E52 1995.

10.86   Levinson, David, ed. *Encyclopedia of world cultures.* Boston: G.K. Hall, 1991-. 10 v. GN550 .E53 1991.
         A ten-volume reference work containing descriptive summaries for approximately 1,500 cultural groups around the world. Each volume covers a region or regions; to date, contents include: v.1. *North America,* T.J. O'Leary and D. Levinson, eds. (1991. 424 p.); v.2. *Oceania,* T.E. Hays, ed. (1991. 409 p.); v.3. *South Asia,* P. Hockings, ed. (1992. 378 p.); v.4. *Europe (Central, Western, and Southeastern Europe),* L.A. Bennett, ed. (1992. 297 p.); v.5. *East and Southeast Asia,* P. Hockings, ed.; v.6. *Russia and Eurasia/China,* P. Friedrich and N. Diamond, ed.; v.7. *South America,* J. Wilbert, ed. (1994. 425 p.); v.9. Africa and the Middle East, J. Middleton, and A. Rassam, eds. (1995. 445 p.).The final two volumes consist of *Middle America and the Caribbean,* and *Compilation and Indexes.*

10.87   Levinson, David. *Ethnic relations: A cross-cultural encyclopedia.* Santa Barbara: ABC-CLIO, 1994. 293 p. GN496 .L48 1994.

10.88   Levinson, David. *Human environments: a cross-cultural encyclopedia.* Santa Barbara: ABC-CLIO, 1995. 284 p. GF4 .L49 1995.

10.89   Levinson, David, and Melvin Ember. eds. *Encyclopedia of cultural anthropology.* New York: Henry Holt. 4 v. GN307 .E52 1996.
         The first comprehensive encyclopedia of cultural anthropology; contains 340 articles by 310 distinguished anthropologists. Each article includes a current bibliography and thorough cross referencing. Provides frameworks and major organizing concepts, and introduces the major research methods. Covers all philosophical orientations and theoretical perspectives. Covers all the major regions of the world as well as the other fields of anthropology, i.e., linguistics, biological anthropology, and archaeology. Provides a full list of anthropological periodicals and a detailed index of subfields, persons, organizations, concepts, and topics relevant to cultural anthropology.

Archaeology

10.90   Cottrell, Leonard. *The Concise encyclopedia of archaeology.* 2 ed. London: Hutchinson, 1970. 430 p. CC70 .C6 1970.
         Entries for archaeological techniques and discoveries as well as

some biographical information; emphasis on archaeology outside of Greece and Rome, and medieval Europe.

10.91   *Larousse encyclopedia of archaeology.* 2 ed. London; New York: Hamlyn, 1983. 432 p. CC165 .A64213 1983.
English-language translation of *Larousse l'archeologie decouverte des civilisations disparues* (Paris: Librairie Larousse, 1969).

10.92   Meyers, Eric M. *The Oxford encyclopedia of archaeology in the Near East.* New York: Oxford University Press, 1996. 5 v. DS56 .O9 1997.
Includes approximately 1,125 alphabetically arranged entries relating to the archaeology and prehistory of the ancient Near East (Syria-Palestine, Mesopotamia, Anatolia, Iran, Arabia, Egypt, and Cyprus).

10.93   Sherratt, Andrew, ed. *The Cambridge encyclopedia of archaeology.* New York: Crown Publishers, 1980. 495 p. CC165 .C3 1980b.

10.94   Stern, Ephraim, Ayelet Levinzon-Gilboa, and Joseph Aviram. *The New encyclopedia of archaeological excavations in the Holy Land; Entsiklopedyah ha-hadashah la-hafirot arkheologiyot be-Erets.* Jerusalem: Israel Exploration Society; Carta; New York: Simon and Schuster, 1993. 4 v. DS111 .A2 N488 1993.

10.95   Trinder, Barrie Stuart. *The Blackwell encyclopedia of industrial archaeology.* Oxford, England; Cambridge, Massachusetts: Blackwell, 1992. 2 v. T37 .B53x 1992.

Biological/Physical Anthropology

10.96   Jones, Steve, Robert Martin, and David Pilbeam, eds. *The Cambridge encyclopedia of human evolution.* Cambridge, England; New York: Cambridge University Press, 1992. 506 p. GN281 .C345 1992.
Contents include: Patterns of primate evolution; Life of primates; Brain and language; Social organisation; Geological contex; Primate fossil record; Genetics and evolution; Genetic clues of relatedness; Early human behaviour and ecology; Human populations, past and present; Evolutionary future of humankind; and Who's who of historical figures.

10.97   Spencer, Frank, ed. *History of physical anthropology: an encyclopedia.* New York: Garland, 1996. 2 v.
Important encyclopedia summarizes and organizes the basic knowledge, fundamental principles, and development of physical anthropology as a discipline. Coverage includes anthropometry, body composition studies, demography, dental anthropology, dermatoglyphics, forensic anthropology, genetics, growth studies, molecular anthropology, neuroanatomy, paleoanthropology,

paleoprimatology, and primate field studies. Includes extensive bibliographies.

10.98 Tattersall, Ian, Eric Delson, and John A. Van Couvering, eds. *Encyclopedia of human evolution and prehistory.* New York: Garland, 1987. 638 p. GN281 .E53 1988.
Covers human evolution and prehistoric archaeology, including entries on a range of topics such as various fossil and extant primates, methodologies used to study evolution, classic type sites, Paleolithic artifacts, and major workers in the field.

Linguistics

10.99 Crystal, David. *The Cambridge encyclopedia of language.* Cambridge, England; New York: Cambridge University Press, 1987. 472 p. P29 .C64 1987.

10.100 Sebeok, Thomas A. *Encyclopedic dictionary of semiotics.* Berlin; New York: Mouton de Gruyter, 1986. 3 v. P99 .E65 1986.

Mythology and Folklore

10.101 Campbell, Joseph. *Historical atlas of world mythology.* New York: van der Marck Editions; San Francisco: Harper and Row, 1983-1989. BL311 .C26 1983.
Comprehensive encyclopedia of mythology; vol. 1: *The Way of the animal powers,* explores the folkways and mythology of hunter-gatherers and early agriculturalists; vol. 2: *The Way of the seeded earth,* part 1: The sacrifice; part 2: Mythologies of the primitive planters: the North Americas; part 3: Mythologies of the primitive planters: the Middle and Southern Americas; vol. 3: *The Way of the celestial lights,* traces the sky mythologies of the great ancient civilizations; and volume 4: *The way of man,* follows the transformation of mythological structures in the post-Renaissance world.

10.102 Chevalier, Jean, and Alain Gheerbrant. *A Dictionary of symbols.* Oxford, England; Cambridge, Massachusetts: Blackwell, 1994. 1,174 p. GR931 .C4413.

10.103 Cotterell, Arthur. *The Macmillan illustrated encyclopedia of myths and legends.* New York: Macmillan, 1989. 260 p. BL303 .C67 1989.

10.104 *Encyclopaedia of superstitions, folklore, and the occult sciences of the world; a comprehensive library of human belief and practice in the mysteries of life.* Detroit: Gale, 1971. 3 v. 133.03 D228.

10.105 Hertherington, Norriss S., ed. *Encyclopedia of cosmology: historical, philosophical, and scientific foundations of modern cosmology.* New York: Garland, 1992. 704 p. QB980.5 .E53 1993.

10.106 Jobes, Gertrude. *Dictionary of mythology, folklore, and symbols.* Metuchen, New Jersey: Scarecrow Press, 1961-1962. 3 v. GR35 .J6.

10.107 Mercatante, Anthony S. *The Facts on File encyclopedia of world mythology and legend.* New York: Facts on File, 1988. 807 p. BL303 .M45 1988.

10.108 Mercatante, Anthony S., and Robert S. Bianchi, eds. *Who's who in Eygptian mythology.* 2 ed. Lanham, Maryland: Scarecrow Press, 1995. 256 p. BL303 .M45 1988.
        A comprehensive dictionary of Egyptian mythology, arranged alphabetically by major gods, goddesses, myths, and themes.

10.109 Opie, Iona, and Moira Tatem. *A Dictionary of superstitions.* Oxford, England; New York: Oxford University Press, 1989. 494 p. BF1775 .D53 1989.

10.110 Pickering, David. *Cassell dictionary of superstitions.* London: Cassell; New York: Sterling, 1995. 294 p. BF1775 .P44 199.

Africa
10.111 Oliver, Roland, and Michael Crowder, eds. *The Cambridge encyclopedia of Africa.* Cambridge, England; New York: Cambridge University Press, 1981. 492 p. DT3 .C35 1980.

Asia
10.112 Bowring, Richard, and Peter Kornicki, eds. *The Cambridge encyclopedia of Japan.* New York: Cambridge University Press, 1993. 400 p. DS805 .C36 1993.

10.113 Hook, Brian, ed. *The Cambridge encyclopedia of China.* 2 ed. Cambridge, England; New York: Cambridge University Press, 1991. 502 p. DS705 .C35.

10.114 Robinson, Francis, ed. *The Cambridge encyclopedia of India, Pakistan, Bangladesh, Sri Lanka, Nepal, Bhutan, and the Maldives.* Cambridge, England; New York: Cambridge University Press, 1989. 520 p. DS334.9 .C36 1989.

Europe
10.115 Brow, Archie, Michael Kaser and Gerald S. Smith. *The Cambridge encyclopedia of Russia and the former Soviet Union.* 2 ed. Cambridge, England; New York: Cambridge University Press, 1994. 604 p. DK14 .C35 1994.

Latin America
10.116 Collier, Simon, Harold Blakemore, Thomas E. Skidmore, eds. *The Cambridge encyclopedia of Latin America and the Caribbean.* 2 ed.

Cambridge, England; New York: Cambridge University Press, 1992. 479 p. F1406 .C36 1985.

Middle East

10.117   Mostyn, Trevor, and Albert Habib Hourani, eds. *The Cambridge encyclopedia of the Middle East and North Africa.* Cambridge, England; New York: Cambridge University Press, 1988. 504 p. DS44 .C37 1988.

Oceania

10.118   Bambrick, Susan, ed. *The Cambridge encyclopedia of Australia.* Cambridge, England; New York: Cambridge University Press, 1994. 384 p. DU90 .C364 1994.

Other

10.119   Kurian, George T. *The Encyclopedia of the First World.* New York: Facts on File, 1990. 2 v. G63 .K87 1990.

10.120   Kurian, George T. *Encyclopedia of the Third World.* 4 ed. New York: Facts on File, 1992. 3 v. HC59.7 .K87 1992.

Alphabetically arranged by country, includes information on the country's location and area of each country, weather, population, ethnic composition, languages, religions, historical backgrounds, constitution and government, freedom and human rights, civil service, local government and foreign policy, political parties, economy, public finances, currency and banking, agriculture, manufacturing, mining, energy, labor, foreign commerce, transportation and communications, defense, education, legal system, law enforcement, health, food and nutrition, media and culture, and social welfare.

11

Handbooks

A handbook contains a group of miscellaneous facts and serves as a convenient reference source for a specific field of knowledge. Emphasis is usually placed on established knowledge rather than recent advances.

For additional handbooks, consult the library catalog under the appropriate subject with the subdivision *Handbooks, Manuals, Etc.* For example,

> *Anthropology --- Handbooks, Manuals, Etc.*
> *Latin America --- Handbooks, Manuals, Etc.*
> *Indians of North America --- Handbooks, Manuals, Etc.*

Biological/Physical Anthropology --- Anthropometry
11.1   Montagu, Ashley. *A Handbook of anthropometry; with a section on the measurement of body composition.* Springfield, Illinois: Thomas, 1960. 186 p. 573.6 M76h.

Biological/Physical Anthropology --- Fossil Man
11.2   Day, Michael H. *Guide to fossil man.* 4 ed. Chicago: University of Chicago Press, 1986. 432 p. GN282 .D39 1986.

Convenient handbook of paleontological information, emphasizing important sites which have yielded most of the significant fossil hominids. Part I briefly explains the study of fossil bones and teeth, and their variation by age and sex; Part II presents summary descriptive information on hominid fossils, including name of site, location, taxonomic name, geology and stratigraphy, associated finds, dating methods, fossil evidence and descriptive morphology, and bibliographic references.

Cultural/Social Anthropology
11.3   Honigmann, John J., ed. *Handbook of social and cultural anthropology.* Chicago: Rand McNally, 1973. 1,295 p. GN315 .H642; 390 H757.

Survey and discussion of the state of knowledge and a review of research in the various branches of anthropology; each chapter is by a specialist and includes extensive bibliographies.

11.4   Naroll, Raoul, and Ronald Cohen, eds. *A Handbook of method in cultural anthropology.* New York: Columbia University Press, 1970. 1,017 p. GN345 .N37 1973; 301.5 N167ha.
Chapters by specialists on various aspects of methodology. Principal sections include: General problems, The Field work process, Models of ethnographic analysis, Comparative approaches, and Problems of categorization.

Folklore

115   Briggs, Katharine M. *A Dictionary of British folk-tales in the English language, incorporating the F.J. Norton Collection.* London: Routledge and K. Paul, 1970-1971. 2 v. GR141 .B68.

11.6   Kirtley, Bacil F. *A Motif-index of Polynesian, Melanesian, and Micronesian narratives.* New York: Arno Press, 1980. 687 p. GR380 .K49 1980.

11.7   Kirtley, Bacil F. *A Motif-index of traditional Polynesian narratives.* Honolulu: University of Hawaii Press, 1971. 486 p. 303.896 K639.

11.8   Thompson, Stith. *Motif-index of folk-literature; a classification of narrative elements in folktales, ballads, myths, fables, medieval romances, exempla, fabliaux, jest-books, and local legends.* rev. ed. Bloomington: Indiana University Press, 1955-1958. 6 v. GR67 .T52.
Thompson, Stith. *Motif-index of folk literature* [computer file]: *a classification of narrative elements in folk tales, ballads, myths, fables, medieval romances, exempla, fabliaux, jest-books and local legends.* CD-ROM ed. Bloomington: Indiana University Press; Clayton, Georgia: InteLex, 1993. Includes all of the original motif-index edited for errors and bundled with the search software Folio VIEWS.

Linguistics

11.9   Meillet, A., and Marcel S.R. Cohen. *Les langues du monde.* rev. ed. Paris: Centre Nationale de la Recherche Scientifique, 1952. 1,294 p. P121 M487 1952.
Primary reference work in linguistics, covering more than 10,000 languages and dialects worldwide.

11.10   Sebeok, Thomas A. *Current trends in linguistics.* The Hague: Mouton, 1963-1976. 14 v. 408 Se21.
Excellent area survey articles with extensive bibliographies; includes: v.1. *Soviet and East European linguistics;* v.2. *Linguistics in East Asia and South East Asia;* v.3. *Theoretical foundations;* v.4. *Ibero-American and Caribbean linguistics;* v.5. *Linguistics in South Asia;* v.6. *Linguistics in South West Asia and North Africa;* v.7. *Linguistics in Sub-Saharan Africa;* v.8. *Linguistics in Oceania;* v.9. *Linguistics in Western Europe* (2 parts); v.10. *Linguistics in North*

America; v.11. *Diachronic, areal, and typological linguistics;* v.12.
Linguistics and adjacent arts and sciences (4 parts); v.13.
Historiography of linguistics (2 parts); v.14. *Indexes.*

11.11 Sebeok, Thomas A. *Encyclopedic dictionary of semiotics.* Berlin; New York: Mouton de Gruyter, 1986. 3 v. P99 .E65 1986.

11.12 Voegelin, C.F., and F.M. Voegelin. *Classification and index of the world's languages.* New York: Elsevier, 1977. 658 p. P203 .V6; 401.2 V856.

Alphabetically arranged listing of names of groups of related languages; index of all names of groups, subgroups, languages, dialects, and tribes, with cross-references.

Religion
11.13 Weekes, Richard V., ed. *Muslim peoples: a world ethnographic survey.* 2 ed. Westport, Connecticut: Greenwood Press, 1984. 2 v. DS35.625 .A1 M87 1984.

Alphabetical arrangement of brief survey articles on some 190 ethnic groups throughout the world which have been identified as wholly or partially Muslim.

Area Handbooks
11.14 The Foreign Area Studies Division of the Special Operations Research Office serves as a research contractor for the United States Department of the Army and has been prolific in producing influential social science research. Funded by the military the work is affected by the conflict between the management of social science and the management of the government.

Africa: *Algeria, a country study* (5 ed., 1994. 342 p.); *Angola, a country study* (3 ed. 1991. 318 p.); *Kenya, a country study* (3 ed. 1984. 334 p.); *Liberia, a country study* (3 ed. 1985. 340 p.); *Libya, a country study* (4 ed., 1989; 351 p.); *Malawi, a country study* (1989. 353 p.); *Mauritania, a country study* (2 ed. 1990. 218 p.); *Morocco, a country study* (5 ed. 1985. 448 p.); *Mozambique, a country study* (3 ed. 1985. 342 p.); *Nigeria, a country study* (5 ed. 1992. 394 p.); *Rwanda, a country study* (1982. 214 p.); *Somalia, a country study* (4 ed. 1993. 282 p.); *South Africa, a country study* (2 ed. 1982. 464 p.); *Sudan, a country study* (4 ed. 1992. 336 p.); *Tunisia, a country study* (3 ed. 1988. 380 p.); *Uganda, a country study* (2 ed. 1992. 298 p.); *Zaire, a country study* (4 ed. 1994. 394 p.); *Zimbabwe, a country study* (2 ed. 1983. 360 p.).

Asia: *Bangladesh, a country study* (2 ed. 1989. 306 p.); *Burma, a country study* (3 ed. 1983. 326 p); *Cambodia, a country study* (3 ed. 1990. 362 p.); *China, a country study* (4 ed. 1988); *India, a country study* (4 ed., 1985. 688 p.); *Indian Ocean, five island countries* (3 ed. 1995. 412 p.); *Indonesia, a country study* (5 ed. 1993. 462 p.); *Japan, a country study* (5 ed. 1992. 610 p.); *Laos, a country study* (3 ed.

1995. 366 p.); *Malaysia, a country study* (4 ed. 1984. 366 p.);
Mongolia, a country study (2 ed. 1991. 320 p.); *Nepal and Bhutan,
country studies* (3 ed. 1993. 424 p.); *North Korea, a country study* (4
ed. 1994. 346 p.); *Pakistan, a country study* (6 ed. 1995. 398 p.);
Philippines, a country study (4 ed., 1991 386 p.); *Singapore, a country
study* (2 ed. 1991. 328 p.); *South Korea, a country study* (4 ed. 1992.
408 p.); *Sri Lanka, a country study* (2 ed. 1990. 322 p.); *Thailand, a
country study* (6 ed. 1989. 366 p.); *Vietnam, a country study* (1989.
386 p.).

    Europe: *Albania, a country study* (2 ed., 1994. 288 p.); *Armenia,
Azerbaijan, and Georgia, a country studies* (1995. 298 p.); *Austria, a
country study* (2 ed., 1994. 314 p.); *Belarus and Moldova, country
studies* (1995. 254 p.); *Belgium, a country study* (2 ed., 1984. 364 p.);
Bulgaria, a country study (2 ed., 1993. 328 p.); *Cyprus, a country
study* (4 ed. 1993. 304 p.); *Czechoslovakia, a country study* (3 ed.
1989. 421 p); *East Germany, a country study* (3 ed. 1988. 433 p.);
Estonia, Latvia, and Lithuania, country studies (1996. 304 p.);
Federal Republic of Germany, a country study (2nd ed. 1983. 454 p.);
Finland, a country study (2nd ed. 1990. 446 p.); *Greece, a country
study* (4th ed. 1983. 261 p.); *Hungary, a country study* (2 ed., 1990.
320 p.); *Italy, a country study* (2 ed. 1985. 412 p.); *Poland, a country
study* (3 ed. 1994. 356 p.); *Portugal, a country study* (2 ed. 1993. 330
p.); *Romania, a country study* (2 ed. 1991. 356 p.); *Soviet Union, a
country study* (2 ed. 1991. 1,068 p.); *Spain, a country study* (2 ed.
1990. 406 p.); *Yugoslavia, a country study* (3 ed. 1992. 348 p.).

    Latin America: *Argentina, a country study* (3 ed., 1986. 404 p.);
Bolivia, a country study (3 ed., 1991. 354 p.); *Brazil, a country study*
(4 ed., 1983. 410 p.); *Chile, a country study* (3 ed. 1994. 462 p.);
Colombia, a country study (4 ed. 1990. 364 p.); *Costa Rica, a country
study* (2 ed., 1983. 336 p.); *Cuba, a country study* (3 ed. 1985. 368 p.);
Dominican Republic and Haiti, country studies (2 ed. 1991. 456 p.);
Ecuador, a country study (3rd ed. 1991. 306 p.); *El Salvador, a
country study* (2nd ed., 1990. 306 p.); *Guyana and Belize, country
studies* (2nd ed. 1993. 408 p); *Haiti, a country study* (1985.188 p.);
Honduras, a country study (3 ed. 1995. 318 p.); *Islands of the
Commonwealth Caribbean, a regional study* (1989. 771 p.); *Mexico, a
country study* (3 ed. 1985. 472 p.); *Nicaragua, a country study* (3 ed.
1994. 300 p.); *Panama, a country study* (4 ed. 1989. 337 p.); *Panama,
a country study* (4 ed. 1989. 337 p.); *Paraguay, a country study* (2 ed.
1990. 288 p.); *Peru, a country study* (4 ed. 1993. 422 p.); *Uruguay, a
country study* (2 ed. 1992. 302 p.); *Venezuela, a country study* (4 ed.
1993. 276 p.).

    Middle East: *Afghanistan, a country study* (5 ed., 1986); *Egypt, a
country study* (5 ed. 1991. 428 p.); *Iraq, a country study* (4 ed., 1990.
302 p.); *Israel, a country study* (3 ed. 1990. 416 p.); *Jordan, a country
study* (4 ed. 1991. 330 p.); *Lebanon, a country study* (3 ed. 1989. 282
p.); *Persian Gulf States, country studies* (3 ed. 1994. 472 p.); *Saudi
Arabia, a country study* (5 ed. 1993. 354 p.); *Syria, a country study* (3

ed. 1988. 334 p.); *Turkey, a country study* (5 ed. 1996. 458 p.); *The Yemens, country studies* (2 ed., 1986. 378 p.).
Oceania: *Australia, a country study* (1974. 458 p.); *Oceania, a regional study* (2 ed., 1984. 572 p.).

11.15 *World bibliographical series.* Oxford, England; Santa Barbara, California: Clio Press.
This series will cover every country in the world, each in a separate volume comprising annotated entries on works dealing with its history, geography, economy, politics, and with its people and their culture, customs, etc. Volumes published to date include:
Africa: *Algeria* (R.I. Lawless, ed. 1995. 309 p.); *Angola* (R. Black, ed. 1992. 176 p.); *Botswana* (J.A. Wiseman, ed. 1992. 187 p.); *Brunei* (S.C.E. Krausse, and G.H. Krausse. 1988. 249 p.); *Burkina Faso* (S. Decalo, ed. 1994. 132 p.); *Burundi* (M. Daniels, ed. 1992. 135 p.); *Cameroon* (M.W. DeLancey, and P. J. Schraeder, eds. 1986. 201 p); *Cape Verde* (C.S. Shaw, ed. 1991. 190 p.); *Central African Republic* (P. Kalck, ed. 1993. 153 p.); *Chad* (G. Joffe, and V. Day-Viaud, eds. 1995. 188 p.); *The Congo* (R. Fegley, ed. 1993. 68 p.); *Cote d'Ivoire* (M. Daniels, ed. 1996. 231 p.); *Djibouti* (P.J. Schraeder, ed. 1991. 239 p.); *Equatorial Guinea* (R. Fegley, ed. 1991. 118 p.); *Eritrea* (R. Fegley, ed. 1995. 125 p.); *Ethiopia* (S. Munro-Hay, and R. Pankhurst, eds. 1995. 225 p.); *Gabon* (D.E. Gardinier, ed. 1992. 178 p.); *The Gambia* (D.P. Gamble, ed. 1988. 135 p.); *Ghana* (R.A. Myers, ed. 1991. 436 p.); *Guinea-Bissau* (R.E. Galli, ed. 1990. 180 p.); *Kenya* (R.L. Collison, ed. 1982. 157 p.); *Lesotho* (S.M. Willet, and D.P. Ambrose. 1980. 496 p.); *Liberia* (D.E. Dunn, ed. 1995. 207 p.); *Libya* (R.I. Lawless, ed. 1987. 243 p.); *Madagascar* (H. Bradt, ed. 1993 118 p.); *Malawi* (S. Decalo, ed. 2 ed. 1995. 188 p.); *Maldives* (C.H.B. Reynolds, ed. 1993. 93 p.); *Mauritania* (S. Calderini, D. Cortese, and J.L.A. Webb, Jr., eds. 1992. 165 p.); *Mauritius* (P.R. Bennett, ed. 1992. 151 p.); *Morocco* (A.M. Findlay, and A.M. Findlay, eds. rev. ed. 1995. 178 p.); *Mozambique* (C. Darch, ed.1987. 360 p.); *Namibia* (S. Schoeman, and E. Schoeman, eds. 1984. 186 p.); *Niger* (L.F. Zamponi, ed. 1994. 233 p.); *Nigeria* (R.A. Myers, ed.1989. 462 p.); *Rhodesia/Zimbabwe* (O.B. Pollak, and K. Pollak. 1979. 195 p.); *Rwanda* (R. Fegley, ed. 1993. 161 p.); *Senegal* (R. Dilley, and J. Eades, eds. 1994. 284 p.); *Sierra Leone* (M. Binns, and T. Binns, eds. 1992. 235 p.); *Somalia* (M.W. DeLancey, ed. 1988. 191 p.); *South Africa* (G.V. Davis, ed. 1994. 463 p.); *Sudan* (M.W. Daily, ed. 1992. 194 p.); *Swaziland* (B. Nyeko, ed. 1994. 241 p); *Tanzania* (C. Darch, ed. 1985. 316 p.); *Togo* (S. Decalo, ed. 1995. 194 p.); *Tunisia* (A.M. Findlay, A.M. Findlay, and R.I. Lawless, eds. 1982. 251 p.); *Uganda* (R.L. Collison, ed. 1981. 159 p.); *Zaire* (D.B. Williams, R.W. Lesh and A.L. Stamm, eds. 1995.268 p.); *Zambia* (A.M. Bliss, and J.A. Rigg, eds. 1984. 233 p.); *Zimbabwe* (D. Potts, ed.1993. 368 p.).

Asia: *Bhutan* (R.C. Dogra, ed. 1990. 124 p.); *Burma* (P.M. Herbert, ed. 1991. 327 p.); *China* (P. Cheng, ed. 1983. 390 p.); *Hong Kong* (I. Scott, ed. 1990. 248 p.); *India* (I.D. Derbyshire, ed. 1995. 356 p.); *Indian Ocean* (J.J. Gotthold, ed. 1988. 329 p.); *Indonesia* (G.H. Krausse, and S.E. Krausse, eds. 1994. 407 p.); *Japan* (F.J. Shulman, ed. 1990. 873 p.); *Laos* (H. Cordell, ed. 1991. 215 p.); *Macau* (R.L. Edmonds, ed. 1989. 110 p.); *Malaysia* (I. Brown, and R. Ampalavanar, eds. 1986. 308 p.); *Mongolia* (J. Nordby, ed. 1993. 192 p.); *Nepal* (J. Whelpton, ed., 1990. 294 p.); *Pakistan* (D. Taylor, ed. 1990. 255 p.); *Philippines* (J. Richardson, ed. 1989. 372 p.); *Punjab* (D.S. Tatla, and I. Talbot, eds. 1995. 323 p.); *Seychelles* (G. Bennett, ed. 1993. 115 p.); *Siberia and the Soviet Far East* (D.N. Collins, ed. 1991. 217 p.); *Singapore* (S.R. Quah, and J.S.T. Quah, eds. 1988. 258 p.); *Sri Lanka* (V. Samaraweera, ed. 1987. 194 p.); *Taiwan* (W. Lee, ed. 1990. 247 p.); *Thailand* (M. Watts, ed. 1986. 275 p.); *Tibet* (J. Pinfold, ed. 1991.158 p.); *Vietnam* (D.G. Marr, ed. 1992. 393 p.).

Europe: *Albania* (W.B. Bland, ed. 1988. 290 p.); *Andorra* (B. Taylor, ed. 1993. 97 p.); *Austria* (D. Salt, ed. 1986. 318 p.); *Armenia* (V.N. Nersessian, ed. 1993. 304 p.); *The Baltic States: Estonia, Latvia, Lithuania* (I.A. Smith, and M.V. Grunts, eds. 1993. 199 p.); *Belgium* (R.C. Riley, ed. 1989. 271 p.); *Berlin* (I. Wallace, ed. 1993. 160 p); *Bulgaria* (R.J. Crampton, ed. 1989. 232 p.); *Cyprus* (P.M. Kitromilides, and M.L. Evriviades, eds. 1995. 264 p.); *Czechoslovakia* (D. Short, ed. 1986. 409 p.); *Denmark* (K.E. Miller, ed. 1987. 216 p.); *East Germany: the German Democratic Republic* (I. Wallace, ed. 1987. 293 p.); *England* (A. Day, ed. 1993. 591 p.); *Finland* (J.E.O. Screen, ed. 1981. 212 p.); *France* (F. Chambers, ed. 1990. 290 p); *Gibraltar* (G. J. Shields, ed. 1987. 100 p.); *Greenland* (K.E. Miller, ed. 1991. 111 p.); *Hungary* (T. Kabdebo. 1980. 280 p.); *Iceland* (J.J. Horton, ed. 1983. 346 p.); *Irish Republic* (M.O. Shannon, ed. 1986. 404 p.); *Italy* (L. Sponza, and D. Zancani, eds. 1995. 417 p.); *Liechtenstein* (R.A. Meier, ed. 1993. 123 p.); *Luxembourg* (C. Hury, and J. Christophory, eds. 1981. 184 p.); *Malta* (J.R. Thackrah, ed. 1985. 163 p.); *Monaco* (G.L. Hudson, ed. 1991. 193 p.); *The Netherlands* (P.K. King, and M. Wintle. 1988. 308 p.); *Northern Ireland* (M.O. Shannon, ed. 1991. 603 p.); *Norway* (L.B. Sather, ed. 1986.293 p.); *Poland* (G. Sanford, and A. Gozdecka-Sanford, eds. 1993. 250 p.); *Portugal* (P.T.H. Unwin, ed. 1987. 269 p.; *Romania* (A. Deletant, and D. Deletant, eds. 1985. 236 p.); *Russia/U.S.S.R.* (L. Pitman, ed. 1994. 384 p.); *Scotland* (E.G. Grant, ed. 1982. 408 p.); *Slovenia* (C. Carmichael, ed. 1996. 176 p.); *Spain* (G.J. Shields, ed. 1994. 448 p.); *Sweden* (L.B. Sather, and A. Swanson, eds. 1987. 370 p.); *Switzerland* (H.K. Meier, and R.A. Meier, eds. 1990. 409 p.); *Vatican City State* (M.J. Walsh, ed. 1983. 105 p.); *Wales* (G. Huws, D.E. Roberts, eds. 1991. 247 p.); *West Germany, the Federal Republic of Germany* (D.S. Detwiler, and I.E. Detwiler, eds. 1987. 353 p.); *Yugoslavia* (J.J. Horton, ed. 1990. 279 p.).

Latin America: *Argentina* (A. Biggins, ed. 1991. 460 p.); *The Bahamas* (P.G. Boultbee, ed. 1989. 195 p.); *Barbados* (R.B. Potter, and G.M.S. Dann, eds. 1987. 356 p.); *Belize* (P. Wright, and B.E. Coutts, eds. 1993. 307 p.); *Bolivia* (G.M. Yeager, ed. 1988. 228 p.); *Brazil* (S.V. Bryant, ed. 1985. 244 p.); *Chile* (H. Blakemore, ed. 1988. 197 p.); *Colombia* (R.H. Davis, ed. 1990. 204 p.); *Costa Rica* (C.L. Stansifer, ed. 1991. 292 p.); *Cuba* (J. Stubby, L. Haines, and M.F. Haines, eds. 1996. 337 p.); *Dominica* (R.A. Myers, ed. 1987. 190 p.); *Dominican Republic* (K. Schoenhals, ed. 1990. 210 p.); *Ecuador* (D. Corkill, ed. 1989. 155 p.); *El Salvador* (R.L. Woodward, Jr., ed. 1988. 213 p.); *The Falkland Islands, South Georgia and the South Sandwich Islands* (A. Day, ed. 1996. 231 p.); *Grenada* (K. Schoenhals, ed. 1990. 179 p.); *Guatemala* (W.B. Franklin, ed. 1992. 269 p.); *Guyana* (F. Chambers, ed. 1989. 206 p.); *Haiti* (F. Chambers, ed. 1994. 270 p.); *Honduras* (P.F. Howard-Reguindin, ed. 1992. 258 p.); *Jamaica* (K.E. Ingram, ed. 1984. 369 p.); *Martinique* (J. Crane, ed. 1995. 140 p.); *Mexico* (G.D.E. Philip, ed. 1993. 195 p.); *Montserrat* (R. Berleant-Schiller, ed. 1991. 102 p.); *Netherlands Antilles and Aruba* (K. Schoenhals, ed. 1993. 160 p.); *Nicaragua* (R.L. Woodward, Jr, ed. rev. ed. 1994. 295 p.); *Paraguay* (R.A. Nickson, ed. 1987. 212 p.); *Peru* (J.R. Fisher, ed. 1989. 193 p.); *Puerto Rico* (E.E. Cevallos, ed. 1985. 193 p.); *Sao Tome and Principe* (C.S. Shaw, ed. 1994. 183 p.); *St. Kitts-Nevis* (V.P. Moll, ed. 1995. 185 p.); *St. Vincent and the Grenadines* (R.B. Potter, ed. 1992. 212); *Suriname* (R. Hoefte, ed. 1990. 227 p.); *Trinidad and Tobago* (F. Chambers, ed. 1986. 213 p.); *Turks and Caicos Islands* (P. Boultbee, ed. 1991. 97 p.); *Uruguay* (H. Finch, ed. 1989. 232 p.); *Venezuela* (D.A.G. Waddell, ed. 1990. 206 p.); *Virgin Islands* (V.P. Moll, ed. 1991. 210 p.).

Middle East: *Afghanistan* (S. Jones, ed. 1992. 279 p.); *Bahrain* (P.T.H. Unwin, ed. 1984. 265 p.); *Egypt* (R.N. Makar, ed. 1988. 306 p.); *Iran* (R. Navabpour, ed. 1988. 308 p.); *Iraq* (C.H. Bleaney ed. 1995. 237 p.); *Israel and the West Bank and Gaza Strip* (C.H. Bleaney, ed. 1994. 367 p.); *Jordan* (I.J. Seccombe, ed. 1984. 278 p.); *Kuwait* (F.A. Clements, ed. 1996. 340 p.); *Lebanon* (C.H. Bleaney, ed. rev. ed. 1991 230 p.); *Oman* (F.A. Clements. rev. ed. 1994. 346 p.); *Qatar* (P.T.H. Unwin, ed. 1982. 162 p.); *Saudi Arabia* (F.A. Clements, ed. 1988. 354 p.); *Syria* (I.J. Seccombe, ed. 1987. 341 p.); *Turkey* (M. Guclu, ed. 1981. 331 p.); *United Arab Emirates* (F.A. Clements., ed. 1983. 161 p.); *The Yemens: the Yemen Arab Republic and the People's Democratic Republic of Yemen* (G.R. Smith, ed. 1984. 161 p.).

North America: *Alaska* (M.W. Falk, ed. 1995. 219 p.); *Canada* (E. Ingles, ed.1990. 393 p.); *Texas* (J. Marten, ed. 1992. 229 p.); *United States of America* (S.R. Herstein, and N.C. Robbins, eds. 1982. 307 p.).

Oceania: *Australia* (I. Kepars, ed. 1994. 260 p.); *Fiji* (G.E. Gorman, and J.J. Mills, eds. 1994. 207 p); *Hawai'i* (N.J. Morris and L. Dean, eds. 1992. 324 p.); *New Zealand* (R. Grover, ed. 1980. 254 p.); *Pacific Basin and Oceania* (G.W. Fry, and R. Mauricio, eds. 1987.

468 p.); *Papua New Guinea* (F. McConnell, ed. 1988. 378 p.); *Timor, including the islands of Roti and Ndao* (I. Rowland, ed. 1992. 117 p.). **Other:** *The Antarctic* (J. Meadows, W. Mills and H.G.R. King, eds. 1994. 383 p.); *The Arctic* (H.G.R. King, ed. 1989. 272 p.); *Atlantic Ocean* (H.G.R. King, ed. 1985.250 p.).

Africa

11.16   Lystad, Robert A., ed. *The African world: a survey of social research.* New York: Praeger, 1965. 575 p. 916 L997.

A review of social studies and techniques in the African field, intended for students and scholars and as an aid to scholars who are not subject specialists in this area.

11.17   Moroney, Sean, ed. *Africa.* rev. ed. New York: Facts on File, 1989. 2 v. DT3 .H36 1989.

General handbook with survey chapters by specialists on the background, individual countries, and political, economic, social, and cultural affairs.

11.18   Morrison, Donald G. *Black Africa: a comparative handbook.* 2 ed. New York: Paragon House; Irvington Publishers, 1989. 716 p. DT352.8 .M67 1989.

Presents recent comparable information available for independent African nations; e.g., demography, ecology, social and economic development, etc.

11.19   *Peoples of Africa.* New York: Facts on File, 1997. 6 v.

Each of the first five volumes gives a concise profiles of contemporary ethnic groups, specialized topics, and regional profiles. Volume 6 profiles each of the 53 African countries. Volumes include: 1. *Peoples of North Africa;* 2. *Peoples of East Africa;* 3. *Peoples of West Africa;* 4. *Peoples of Central Africa;* 5. *Peoples of Southern Africa;* and 6. *Countries of Africa.*

11.20   Rosenthal, Eric, ed. *Encyclopedia of Southern Africa.* 7 ed. Cape Town: Juta, 1978. 577 p. DT729 .R65 1978.

Includes more than 5,000 articles on southern Africa.

Africa --- Anthropology

11.21   Bernatzik, Hugo A. *Afrika: Handbuch der angewandten Volkerkunde.* Innsbruck: Schlusselverlag, 1947. 2 v. 960 B457.

Handbook of applied anthropology covering North Africa, Sudan, West Africa, East Africa, Congo, Angola-Zambesi area, South Africa, and Madagascar.

Africa --- Linguistics

11.22   Mann, Michael. *A Thesaurus of African languages: a classified and annotated inventory of the spoken languages of Africa.* London; New

York: H. Zell, 1987. 325 p. PL8005 .M36 1987.
Inventories and classifies African languages, including dialects, in sets and subsets; exhaustive listing of languages spoken as home languages by local communities and languages.

Asia

11.23 Franke, Wolfgang. *China Handbuch*. Düsseldorf: Westdeutscher Verlag, 1978. 1,768 columns. 951 F8515ch.

11.24 Sanders, Alan J.K. *The People's Republic of Mongolia: a general reference guide*. London; New York: Oxford University Press, 1968. 232 p. 951.7 Sa56.
Basic handbook with brief descriptions of institutions.

11.25 Taylor, Robert H. ed. *Asia and the Pacific*. New York: Facts on File, 1991. 2 v. DS5 .A79 1991.
General handbook with survey chapters by specialists on the background, individual countries, and political, economic, social, and cultural affairs.

11.26 Wint, Guy. *Asia handbook*. rev. ed. Harmondsworth, England: Penguin, 1969. 735 p. DS5 .W52; 915 W733a.
Contains chapters by specialists on the political, economic, social, and cultural affairs of Asia.

Europe

11.27 Calmann, John, ed. *Western Europe: a handbook*. London, Blond, 1967. 697 p. 940.95 C135.
Includes general and statistical information on individual countries and chapters by specialists on various aspects of European integration.

11.28 Horak, Stephan M., and Richard Blanke, eds. *Eastern European national minorities, 1919-1980: a handbook*. Littleton, Colorado: Libraries Unlimited, 1985. 353 p. DJK26 .H67x 1985.

11.29 Katz, Zev, ed. *Handbook of major Soviet nationalities*. New York: Free Press, 1975. 481 p. DK33 .H35 1975.
A basic reference tool covering Slavs, Baltics, Transcaucasians, Central Asians, and other nationalities.

11.30 Mayne, Richard, ed. *Western Europe*. rev. ed. New York: Facts on File, 1986. 699 p. D907 .W47 1986.
General handbook with survey chapters by specialists on the background, individual countries, and political, economic, social, and cultural affairs.

11.31   Schopflin, George, ed. *The Soviet Union and Eastern Europe.* rev. ed. New York: Facts on File, 1986. 637 p. DK17 .S64 1986.
General handbook with survey chapters by specialists on the background, individual countries, and political, economic, social, and cultural affairs.

Europe --- Anthropology
11.32   Wixman, Ronald. *The Peoples of the USSR: an ethnographic handbook.* Armonk, New York: M.E. Sharpe, 1984. 246 p. DK33 .W59 1984.
Consists of entries arranged in alphabetical order by the names of ethnic groups; includes excellent ethnographic maps.

Latin America
11.33   *Handbook of Latin American studies.* Gainesville: University of Florida Press. v.1 - , 1935 - . 1/yr. F1401 .H3x.
Extensive annotated bibliography of material relating to Latin America; beginning with v. 26, 1964, annual coverage alternates between humanities and social sciences. Beginning with v. 26, 1964, volumes alternate coverage between humanities and social sciences.
Handbook of Latin American studies CD-ROM [computer file]. (Hispanic Division, Library of Congress, ed. Washington, D.C.: Library of Congress, 1995). Provides coverage in CD-ROM format for volumes 1-53 (1936-1994).

11.34   Veliz, Claudio, ed. *Latin America and the Caribbean: a handbook.* New York: Praeger, 1968. 840 p. F1408 .V43 1968b.
General handbook with survey chapters by specialists on the background, individual countries, and political, economic, social, and cultural affairs.

Latin America, Mexico and Central America --- Anthropology
11.35   *Handbook of Middle American Indians.* R. Wauchope, ed. Austin: University of Texas Press, 1964-1976. 16 v. F1434 .H3; 301.82 H191.
Contains essays by specialists on aspects of the anthropology of the various indigenous groups of Mesoamerica; each volume has an extensive bibliography and detailed index; volumes include: 1. *Natural environment and early cultures* (R.C. West, ed. 1964. 570 p.); 2-3. *Archaeology of southern Mesoamerica* (G.R. Willey, ed. 1965. 2 v.); 4. *Archaeological frontiers and external connections* (G.F. Ekholm and G.R. Willey, eds. 1966. 367 p.); 5. *Linguistics* (N.A. McQuown, ed. 1967. 402 p.); 6. *Social anthropology* (M. Nash, ed. 1967. 597 p.); 7-8. *Ethnology* (E.Z. Vogt, ed. 1969. 2 v.); 9. *Physical anthropology* (T.D. Stewart, ed. 1970. 296 p.); 10-11. *Archaeology of northern Mesoamerica* (G.F. Elkholm and I. Bernal, eds. 1971. 2 v.); 12-15. *Guide to ethnohistorical sources* (H.F. Cline, ed. 1972-1975. 4 v.); 16.

Sources cited and artifacts illustrated (M.A.L. Harrison, ed. 1976. 324 p.).

The *Handbook* is continued by *Supplement to the Handbook of Middle American Indians* (V.R. Bricker, ed. Austin: University of Texas Press, 1981- present. F1434 .H3 Suppl.). Volumes published to date include: 1. *Archaeology* (J.A. Sabloff, ed. 1981. 463 p.); 2. *Linguistics* (M.S. Edmonson, ed. 1984. 146 p.); 3. *Literatures* (M.S. Edmonson, ed. 1985. 195 p.); 4. *Ethnohistory* (R.M. Spores, ed. 1986. 232 p.; 5. *Epigraphy* (V.R. Bricker, ed. 1992. 195 p.).

Latin America, South America --- Anthropology

11.36   *Handbook of South American Indians.* J.H. Steward, ed. Smithsonian Institution. Bureau of American Ethnology, Bulletin 143. Washington, D.C., 1946-1959. 7 v. E51 .U6 143; 301.82 Un3b 143.

Contains essays by specialists on aspects of the anthropology of the various indigenous groups of South America; volumes include: 1. *The Marginal tribes* (1946. 624 p.); 2. *The Andean civilizations* (1946. 1,035 p.); 3. *The Tropical forest tribes* (1948. 986 p.); 4. *The Circum-Caribbean tribes* (1948. 986 p.); 5. *The Comparative ethnology of South American Indians* (1949. 818 p.); 6. *Physical anthropology, linguistics and cultural geography of South American Indians* (1950. 715 p.); 7. *Index* (1959. 286 p.).

Latin America, South America --- Linguistics

11.37   Loukotka, Cestmir. *Classification of South American Indian languages.* Los Angeles: University of California, Latin American Center, 1968. 453 p. PM 5008 .L64 1968; 498 L931.

Classification of 117 South American languages.

Middle East

11.38   Adams, Michael. *The Middle East.* New York: Facts on File, 1988. 865 p. DS44 .M495 1988.

General handbook for the Middle East region with survey chapters by specialists on the background, individual countries, and political, economic, social, and cultural affairs.

North America

11.39   Hodgson, Godfrey, ed. *The United States.* New York: Facts on File, 1992. 3 v. E156 .U54 1992.

General handbook with survey chapters by specialists on the background, individual countries, and political, economic, social, and cultural affairs.

11.40   Watkins, Mel, ed. *Canada.* New York: Facts on File, 1993. 701 p. F1008 .C2 1993.

North America --- Anthropology

11.41   Confederation of American Indians, comp. *Indian reservations: a state and federal handbook.* Jefferson, North Carolina: McFarland, 1986. 329 p. E93 .I3828 1986.

Brief overview of many Native American reservations arranged by state and reservation name. Each entry with information about land status, population, culture, government, tribal economy, natural resources, transportation, utilities, and recreational services and opportunities.

11.42   Heard, J. Norman. *Handbook of the American frontier: four centuries of Indian-White relationships.* Native American resources series, 1-3. Metuchen, New Jersey: Scarecrow Press, 1987-1993. 3 v. E76.2 .H43 1987.

Assembles a variety of information about Indian-White relations in the United States. Entries, arranged in alphabetical order, are for individuals or tribes with text ranging from a few lines to several pages. Volumes published to date include: 1. *The Southeastern Woodlands;* 2. *The Northeastern Woodlands;* 3. *The Great Plains.*

11.43   Hodge, Frederick W., ed. *Handbook of American Indians north of Mexico.* Smithsonian Institution. Bureau of American Ethnology, Bulletin 30, 1907-1910. Washington, D.C.; New York: Pageant Books, 1959; St. Clair Shores, Michigan: Scholarly Press, 1968; Totowa, New Jersey: Rowman and Littlefield, 1979. 2 v. E51 .U6 30.

Contains a descriptive list of confederacies, tribes, tribal divisions, and settlements north of Mexico.

11.44   Hodge, Frederick W. *Handbook of Indians of Canada.* Ottawa: C.H. Parmlee, 1913. 632 p. 301.82 H661.

Reprint, with some additional material, of articles relating to Canada in the *Handbook of American Indians north of Mexico.*

11.45   *Handbook of North American Indians.* William C. Sturtevant, ed. Washington, D.C.: Smithsonian Institution Press, 1978-1990. E77 .H25.

Projected to be a twenty-volume encyclopedia summarizing knowledge about all indigenous North American peoples, covering cultures, languages, history, prehistory, and human ecology. The set can be divided into three groups: v. 1-4 provide a continental overview of social and historical matters; v.5-15 describe major cultural areas; and v.16-20 cover technology, linguistics, and biography. Volumes published to date include: 4. *History of Indian-White relations* (W.E. Washburn, ed. 1988. 838 p.); 5. *Arctic* (D. Damas, ed. 1984. 829 p.); 6. *Sub-Arctic* (J. Helm, ed. 1978. 837 p.); 7. *Northwest coast* (W.P. Suttles, ed. 1990. 777 p.); 8. *California* (R.F. Heizer, ed. 1978. 800 p.); 9-10. *Southwest* (A. Ortiz, ed. 1979-1983. 2 v.); 11.*Great Basin* (W.L. D'Azevedo, ed. 1986. 852 p.); 15. *Northeast* (B.G. Trigger, ed. 1978. 924 p.)

11.46   Jenness, Diamond. *The Indians of Canada.* 7 ed. Toronto; Buffalo:
         University of Toronto Press, 1977. 432 p. 301.82 J435.
         A standard source of information on Canadian Indians.

11.47   Kroeber, A.L. *Handbook of the Indians of California.* Smithsonian
         Institution. Bureau of American Ethnology, Bulletin 78. Washington,
         D.C., 1925; Berkeley: California Book Company, 1953; New York:
         Dover Publications, 1976. 995 p. 301.82 Un3b 7.
         Encyclopedic treatment of the Indians of California.

11.48   Ruby, Robert H., and John A. Brown. *A Guide to the Indian tribes of
         the Pacific Northwest.* rev. ed. Norman: University of Oklahoma
         Press, 1992. 289 p. E78 .N77 R79 1992.
         Describes the histories and cultures of more than 150 Pacific
         Northwest Indian groups.

11.49   Stuart, Paul. *Nations within a nation: historical statistics of American
         Indians.* New York: Greenwood Press, 1987. 251 p. E77 .S924 1987.
         Statistical data from various sources are used to create a
         compendium of facts and figures on Native Americans. The majority
         of the tables and charts were prepared from twentieth century sources.
         General categories considered include: Land base and climate;
         Population; Removal, relocation, and urbanization; Vital statistics and
         health; Government activities; Health care and education;
         Employment, earnings, and income; and Indian resources and
         economic development.

11.50   Swanton, John R. *The Indians of the southeastern United States.*
         Smithsonian Institution, Bureau of American Ethnology, Bulletin
         137.Washington, D.C., 1946; Washington, D.C.: Smithsonian
         Institution Press, 1979. 943 p. 301.82 Un3b 137.

11.51   Swanton, John R. *The Indian tribes of North America.* Smithsonian
         Institution, Bureau of American Ethnology, Bulletin 145. Washington,
         D.C., 1952; Washington, D.C.: Smithsonian Institution Press, 1979.
         726 p. E77 .S92 1984.
         Extensive information on Indian tribes arranged by state.

11.52   Wright, Muriel H. *A Guide to the Indian tribes of Oklahoma.*
         Civilization of the American Indian series, 33. Norman: University of
         Oklahoma Press, 1951. 300 p. 301.82 W934.
         Lists 67 Oklahoma tribes in alphabetical order; first issued in
         1951, this handbook is patterned after Hodge's *Handbook of American
         Indians north of Mexico.*

North America --- Refugees

11.53   Haines, David W., ed. *Refugees in America in the 1990s: a reference
         handbook.* Westport, Connecticut: Greenwood Press, 1996. 467 p.

HV640.4 .U54 R425 1996.

11.54   Haines, David W., ed. *Refugees in the United States: a reference handbook*. Westport, Connecticut: Greenwood Press, 1985. 243 p. E184.A1 R43 1985.

Part 1 summarizes the resettlement of refugees in the United States, programs of assistance, and processes on integration. Each chapter includes a list of recent journal articles and books. Part 2 consists of chapters on major refugee groups: Chinese from southeast Asia, Cubans, Haitians, Hmong, Khmer, Lao, Salvadorans and Guatemalans, Soviet Jews, and Vietnamese. Each chapter treats the social background of the refugees, reasons for migration, and aspects of adjustment.

Oceania
11.55   Osborne, Charles, ed. *Australia, New Zealand and the South Pacific: a handbook*. London: Blond, 1970. 580 p. 990 Os105.

Oceania --- Anthropology
11.56   Tindale, Norman B. *Aboriginal tribes of Australia: their terrain, environmental controls, distribution, limits, and proper names*. Berkeley: University of California Press, 1974. 404 p. GN665 .T56; 301.994 T492ab.

Contains summary of cumulative knowledge of distribution, size, composition, and dynamics of the Australian groups and the history of the Aborigines.

Oceania --- Linguistics
11.57   Dixon, R.M.W., and Barry J. Blake, eds. *Handbook of Australian languages*. Amsterdam: J. Benjamins, 1979-1991. 4 v. PL7001 .A3x 1979.

Includes short grammatical sketches of Australian languages.

12

Book Reviews and Yearbooks

Book Reviews

Book reviews are important sources of information. You may need to read the reviews of a published work to determine how authoritative an author is considered by his peers, for understanding a book that is confusing or difficult to comprehend, for deciding whether a book warrants being used in detailed study, and in staying informed of recent research and publication.

Book reviews provide a critical opinion about particular authors and their works. Not all books are reviewed, and some may have reviews that are difficult to find. For example, for inclusion in *Book review digest,* a volume must have been published or distributed in the United States, and must have been reviewed in at least two of the more than seventy periodicals this index covers. Some of the book reviewing indexes will include an abstract of each critique. A good book review should provide a critical analysis of the book; at times it may give a different viewpoint or question the accuracy of the material. It should not be a platform from which the reviewer expounds his own opinion; it should be objective.

For additional review literature, consult the library catalog under the appropriate subject with the subdivision *Book Reviews.* For example,

Anthropology --- Book Reviews
Latin America --- Book Reviews
Indians of North America --- Book Reviews

Anthropology

12.1 *Reviews in anthropology.* Westport, Connecticut. v. 1 - , 1974 - . 4/yr.
Publishes long detailed reviews of approximately 100 new books in anthropology each year.

Africa

12.2 Easterbrook, David L. *Africana book reviews, 1885-1945: an index to books reviewed in selected English-language publications.* Boston: G.K. Hall, 1979. 247 p. DT3 .E2x 1979.
An attempt to provide access to Africana reviewed in a select list of forty-four English-language journals from the late nineteenth-century through 1945.

12.3 Henige, David. *Works in African history: an index to reviews, 1960-1974.* Waltham, Massachusetts: African Studies Association, 1976. 54

p. DT20 .H46x 1976.
Lists book reviews and review articles dealing with Africa south of the Sahara; continued by: *Works in Africa history: an index to reviews, 1974-1978* (Waltham, Massachusetts: African Studies Association, 1978. 58 p.); *Works in African history: an index to reviews, 1978-1982* (Los Angeles: Crossroads Press, 1984. 127 p.).

Europe
12.4   *Etnologiske ekstrakter*. Kobenhavn. v. 1 - , 1970/72 - . 1/yr.
Issued by the Nordisk Etnologisk-Folkloristisk Arbetsgrupp.

General
12.5   *Book review digest*. New York: H.W. Wilson. v. 1 - , 1905 - . 10/yr. Z1219 .C96.
General, selective index to reviews published in 80 journals; contains excerpts from the reviews and indicates the length of reviews. In order to be listed in *Book review digest*, a non-fiction book must have had two or more reviews appear in the periodicals indexed; arranged by author with a subject and title index. Cumulative author-title indexing to *Book review digest* is provided by *Book review digest author-title index, 1905-1974* (New York: H.W. Wilson, 1976).

12.6   *Book review index*. Detroit: Gale. v. 1 - , 1965 - . 6/yr. Z1035 .A1 B6.
Covers book reviews published in approximately 250 English-language humanities and social sciences periodicals; cumulated quarterly and annually. The twenty-year cumulation, *Book review index: a master cumulation, 1965-1984* (Detroit: Gale, 1985. 10 v.) lists some 1,600,000 reviews of approximately 750,000 book titles.

Yearbooks
The purpose of a yearbook or annual review is to update and expand information found in a general encyclopedia. For additional yearbooks, consult the library catalog under the appropriate subject with the subdivision *Yearbooks*. For example,

> ***Anthropology --- Yearbooks***
> ***Latin America --- Yearbooks***
> ***Indians of North America --- Yearbooks***

12.7   *Annual review of anthropology*. Palo Alto, California: Annual Reviews. no. 1 - , 1972 - . 1/yr. GN1 .A623.
Annual review of current research, with bibliographies and articles by experts, often forecasts coming research trends; international in coverage. Provides continuous review of the progress of research and evaluates the most significant published work to help scientists keep abreast of developments; continues: *Biennial review of anthropology* (v. 1-13, 1959-1971. Stanford, California.)

12.8   *Boletín de antropología americana.* México: Instituto Panamericano
        de Geografía e Historia. v. 1 - , 1980 - . 2/yr. E51 .B59.
        General overview of anthropological developments in the
        Americas; includes book, reviews, contents of selected journals, and
        obituaries, in English, Portuguese, or Spanish; continues: *Boletín
        bibliográfico de antropología americana* (v. 1-41, 1937-1979.
        México).

12.9   *Yearbook of physical anthropology.* New York: Alan R. Liss. v. 1 - ,
        1945 - . 1/yr. GN60 .Y4.
        Reproduces articles from various scientific journals that are
        important but not easily available, publishes articles on new research
        problems or key research; creates a collection of articles on physical
        anthropology that will familiarize the student with the diversity of
        interests in the field; since 1980 issued as a supplement to the
        American journal of physical anthropology.

13

Indexes and Abstracts

Indexes to periodical literature are essential for obtaining current information available for a subject. Some of the most recent information in anthropology is published in periodical or journal articles. It often takes from one to three years from the beginning of a research project to the publication of results in an article, and from two to five years to be issued in book form. An index lists published articles in magazines, journals, and yearbooks from a subject and/or an author approach. Other items may include book and film reviews, and obituary notices. An abstract is a specific kind of index which provides summaries for the material in articles, reports, and journals. In many abstracts some of the entries are submitted by the authors of the works themselves. The material covered by an abstract may not depend entirely upon a set number of publication sources, and will usually have a wider coverage than an index.

Several of the indexes and abstracts listed have a custom research service in which material on a specific subject can be located. You may be charged for the computer timer needed to complete the search. Since the information in the index has been placed on computer tape, you must be careful to define your problem as accurately as possible so that a search can be made economically. Additional information regarding computer based literature searches is presented in Chapter 20.

This chapter lists a number of the more useful indexes and abstracts for anthropology. The indexes, in most cases, provide thorough bibliographic information for periodicals including author, title, journal name, volume, date, and pagination. For monographs, author, title, publisher, place of publication, and date are supplied. Most of the indexes and abstracts listed here are arranged in a topical arrangement, frequently with author and subject indexes. The subject approach is usually the most useful for locating material.

For additional abstracts and indexes, consult the library catalog under the appropriate subject with the subdivisions *Abstracts, Abstracting and Indexing, Indexes,* and *Periodicals --- Indexes.* For example,

Anthropology --- Abstracts
Archaeology --- Abstracting and Indexing
Latin America --- Abstracting and Indexing
Indians of North America --- Indexes
Indians of North America --- Periodicals --- Indexes

Indexes

Since indexes of periodical literature index published articles, the frequency with which the indexes themselves are issued is important. Indexes that are published quarterly (i.e., four times each year) will have more recent material than the indexes that are only issued on an annual basis. Indexes of periodical literature usually give only an abbreviated or incomplete bibliographic entry. Therefore, this information must be translated into an accepted form before the researcher can add the references to the working bibliography. For example, the two primary periodical indexes for anthropology give the following:

Anthropological index:
1037   Burkhart, L.M. Sahagún's Thauculcuicatl', a Náhuatl lament [with Náhuatl text]. *Estud Cul Náhuatl* 1986(18) 181-218.

Anthropological literature:
1345   Burkhart, Louise M. Sahagún's Thauculcuicatl', a Náhuatl lament [with Náhuatl text]. *Estudios de Cultura Náhuatl* 18:181-218 (1986), ill.
        [L.SOC.77.88.3.45]

Information provided in both indexes identifies Louise M. Burkhart as the author of an article, "Sahagún's Thauculcuicatl', a Náhuatl lament," published in 1986 by the journal *Estudios de Cultura Náhuatl,* volume 18, pages 181 through 218. *Anthropological index* also indicates that the article includes a text in the Náhuatl language, and *Anthropological literature* notes the article is accompanied by illustrative materials and includes the library number at Tozzer Library, Harvard University, where the journal is produced. The bibliographic entry, in the form preferred by the American Anthropological Association, would be as follows:

Burkhard, Louise M.
1986   Sahagún's Thauculcuicatl', a Náhuatl lament [with Náhuatl text]. *Estudios de Cultura Náhuatl* 18:181-218.

There are a number of both specialized and general indexes in other allied fields of interest to anthropology students. These are not listed here but may be identified in reference books, such as the following:

13.1   Brewer, Annie M., ed. *Indexes, abstracts, and digests: a classified bibliography reproduced from Library of Congress cards arranged according to the Library of Congress classification system.* Detroit: Gale Research, 1982. Z1002 .I58 1982.

A few indexes have published a thesaurus of descriptors or terms that have been used by the people doing the indexing. These references are cited with the particular index to which they refer. A number of the published catalogs of specialized libraries, identified in Chapter 5, include listings for periodicals articles. Only the catalogs which consist primarily of periodicals articles have been repeated in this section.

Anthropology

13.2   *Anthropological index.* London. v. 21 - , 1983 - . 4/yr. GN1 .R64x
        Issued by the library of the Museum of Mankind, London,
        maintains a regional, classified approach to the indexing of some 600
        current periodicals. Arranged by geographical area, with entries in
        each area listed by author under anthropological subdiscipline;
        international in scope, with an author index at the end of each volume;
        continues: *Anthropological index to current periodicals received in
        the Library of the Royal Anthropological Institute of Great Britain
        and Ireland* (London. v.1-5, 1963-1968); *Anthropological index to
        current periodicals in the Library of the Royal Anthropological
        Institute* (London. v. 6-14, 1968-1976); and *Anthropological index to
        current periodicals in the Museum of Mankind (incorporating the
        former Royal Anthropological Institute)*(London. v. 15-20, 1977-
        1982).
        Anthropological index online [computer file] is available on the
        Internet via the URL http://lucy.ukc.ac.uk/aio.html.

13.3   *Anthropological literature.* Cambridge, Massachusetts. v. 1 - , 1979 -
        . 4/yr. GN1 .A58x.
        An index to periodical articles and essays published in edited
        volumes, *festschriften,* and symposia received at Tozzer Library
        (formerly library of the Peabody Museum of Archaeology and
        Ethnology, Harvard University. Divided into five sections:
        Cultural/social anthropology; Archaeology; Biological/Physical
        Anthropology; Linguistics; and General/Method/Theory. Coverage
        includes research articles and reports, commentaries, review essays,

and obituaries published in approximately 800 journal titles and more than 150 monographic series titles. Entries are arranged alphabetically by author within each section and indexes are provided for authors, archaeological sites and cultures, ethnic and linguistic groups, and geographical area. Volumes 6-10, 1984-1988, are available only on microfiche format. This publication serves as a continuation of the published catalogs of the Peabody Museum of Archaeology and Ethnology.

Anthropological Literature [computer file]. The *Anthropological Literature* file contains records describing articles and essays in anthropology and archaeology of two or more pages, from works published in English and other European languages, from 1984 to the present. As of June, 1996, *Anthropological Literature* included more than 106,000 records. The data base in updated quarterly with approximately 2,000 records per update. *Anthropological Literature* is a commercially-prepared electronic index usually available either in the library or remotely. To access the data base remotely, login as instructed for your library, and then follow the path to indexes and *Anthropological Literature*. Then type in an account name and password when prompted (specific details should be available from your local subject librarian). Unless you specify otherwise, a keyword search of Anthropological Literature will look for words you choose as authors, titles, or subject names. You can begin a search by typing *Browse* (to scan lists of author, title, or subject headings) or *Find* (to do a broad word search using exact author names, titles, or subject headings). Then use one of the following indexes:

au	exact author name; exact personal or organizational names; last name first; e.g., au willey, gordon r; include commas and hyphens, and enough information to be distinctive; for organizations as authors, omit commas, hyphens, and initial articles
auw	words from names of personal or organizational authors
su	exact subject headings; su mesopotamia; invert personal names
suw	subject words
ti	exact title, without initial articles
tiw	title words

Copies of articles and essays indexed in *Anthropological Literature* can be obtained by contacting: Tozzer Library, Harvard University, 21 Divinity Avenue, Cambridge, Massachusetts 02138 (fax: 617-496-

2741). Costs as of April 1997 are: U.S. mail, up to 20 pages: $10.00; U.S. mail, over 20 pages: $10.00 plus $.20/page over 20; outside U.S. mail at cost (same cost as US and postage); U.S. fax: $10.00 plus $.50/page (20 page limit); and fax, outside U.S.: $10.00 plus $1.00/page (20 page limit).

Anthropological Literature on Disc 1996 [computer file]. New York: G.K. Hall, 1996. *Anthropological Literature on Disc* provides comprehensive access to the last ten years (1984-1995) and is updated annually. Each annual update includes all records from the previous disc.

13.4   *International bibliography of social and cultural anthropology; Bibliographie internationale d'anthropologie sociale et culturelle.* Paris: UNESCO. v.1 - , 1958-1979; New York: Tavistock, 1980-1986; London: Routledge, 1987-1989. 1/yr. GN1 .I55x.

Prepared by the International Committee for Social Sciences Documentation in co-operation with the International Congress of Anthropological and Ethnological Sciences, and published by UNESCO; indexes approximately 425 journals with citations arranged by broad topical outlines. Citations are given in the original language with an English translation for all but French titles. Worldwide in scope, includes author and subject indexes. With 1990, partially absorbed by the *London bibliography of the social sciences.* A listing of subject headings used is provided by *Thematic list of descriptors: anthropology; Liste thematique des descripteurs: anthropologie* (London: Routledge, 1989. 522 p. Z695.1 .A63 T74x 1989). Continued by *International current awareness services. Anthropology and related disciplines* (London: Routledge. v.1-5, 1990-1994. 12/yr. GN1 .I58x).

Archaeology

13.5   *Archaologische Bibliographie.* Berlin: W. de Gruyter. 1932-1993. 1/yr. CC27 .A73x.

Published by the Deutsches Archaologisches Institut; continues: *Bibliographie zum Jahrbuch des Deutschen Archaologischen Instituts* (1913-1931), and as supplements to the *Jahrbuch des Deutschen Archaologischen Instituts* (1932-1972).

13.6   *Current Swedish archaeology.* Stockholm: Swedish Archaeological Society. v. 1 - , 1993 - . 1/yr. DL621 .S84x.

Half of articles have direct reference to *Nordic archaeological abstracts.* Continues: *Swedish archaeological bibliography*

(Stockholm. 1939/48-1971/75. 6 v. DL621 .S84x) and *Swedish archaeology* (Stockholm. 1983-1987. 4 v. DL621 .S84x).

13.7   *Francis Bulletin signaletique 525: Prehistoire et protohistoire.* Paris, Nancy: Centre National de la Recherche Scientifique, Institut de l'Information Scientifique et Technique, Sciences Humaines et Sociales. v. 34-48, 1980-1994 .4/yr. GN740 .B84x.

Quarterly bibliography of periodical articles relating to prehistory and protohistory; supersedes partially *Bulletin signaletique 525: Prehistoire* (Paris. v. 24-33; 1970-1979) and *Bulletin signaletique 521: Sociologie, ethnologie, prehistoire et archeologie (*Paris. v. 23, 1969).

Francis [computer file]. Vanoeuvre-les-Nancy, France: France Institut de l'Information Scientifique et Technique (INIST). 1972 - . 12/yr. Contains more than 1.7 million citations, with abstracts, to the world's literature on humanities, social sciences, and economics. Includes 19 files, of which the following pertain to anthropology: *Amerique Latine:* contains more than 14,700 citations to social science literature relating to Latin America; *Archeology (Proche-Orient, Asie, Amerique)*: contains approximately 52,500 citations to literature dealing with the art and archaeology of the Near east, Asia, and prehispanic America; *Bibliographie geographique nternationale*: contains approximately 115,000 citations to literature on geography, including cartography, historical, human, physical, and theoretical geography; *Ethnologie*: contains approximately 71,500 citations to literature on ethnology and social anthropology, including social structures and relations, religion, magic and witchcraft, cognitive issues, arts and sciences, folk literature, and acculturation and social change; *Histoire et sciences des religions*: contains approximately 195,000 citations to literature on the history and philosophy of religions; *Prehistoire et protohistoire*: contains approximately 82,000 citations to literature on prehistoric and protohistoric archaeology, from the emergence of humankind until the appearance of writing; *Sciences du langage*: contains approximately 85,000 citations to literature on linguistics, incliuding biology and pathology of language, psycholinguistics, sociolinguistics, ethnolinguistics, historical linguistics, semiotics, and applied linguistics; and Sociologie: contains more than 100,000 citations to literature on sociology, including social psychology, social organization and structure, human ecology, demography, rural and urban sociology, sociology of knowledge, religion, art, communication, and organizations.

13.8   *Francis bulletin signaletique 526: Art et archeologie.* Paris: Centre
        National de la Recherche Scientifique, Institut de l'information
        Scientifique et Technique, Sciences Humaines et Sociales. v. 45-48,
        1991-1994. 4/yr. GN700 .B84x.
           Quarterly bibliography of periodical articles relating to the art and
        archaeology of the Near East, Asia, and the Americas; supersedes
        partially *Bulletin signaletique 526: Art et archeologie; Proche-Orient,
        Asie, Amerique* (Paris. v. 24-44, 1970-1990).

Biological/Physical Anthropology
13.9   *Current primate references.* Seattle: Primate Information Center,
        Regional Primate Research Center, University of Washington. 1966 - .
        12/yr.

Cultural/Social Anthropology
13.10   *Francis bulletin signaletique 529: Ethnologie.* Paris: Centre National
        de la Recherche Scientifique, Institut de l'information Scientifique et
        Technique, Sciences Humaines et Sociales. v. 45(1)-48(4), 1991-1994.
        4/yr. GN301 .B85.
           Quarterly bibliography of periodical articles relating to ethnology
        and sociology; continues: *Bulletin signaletique 521: Sociologie* (Paris.
        v. 40-44, 1986-1990; GN700 .B84x); *Bulletin signaletique 521:
        Sociologie-ethnologie* (Paris. v. 24-39; 1970-1985); *Bulletin
        signaletique 521: Sociologie, ethnologie, prehistoire et archeologie*
        (Paris. v. 23, 1969).

Africa
13.11   *Bibliographie ethnographique de l'Afrique sud-saharienne.* Tervuren,
        Belgique: Musee Royal de l'Afrique Centrale, 1960-1981. 1/yr.
        GN654.A1 B5x
           Published by the Musee Royal de l'Afrique Centrale; continues:
        Bibliographie ethnographique du Congo et des regions avoisinantes,
        and continued by *Bibliographie de l'Afrique sud-saharienne, sciences
        humaines et sociales.*

Europe
13.12   *Dyabola: Sachkataloge des Deutschen Archaologischen Instituts;
        Subject catalogues of the German Archaeological Institute (DAI) on
        CD-ROM* [computer file]. Ennepetal: Bierung und Brinkmann, 1995 -.
        CC27 .A72422.
           Contains several databases useful for locating publications on the
        history of art and the ancient world; includes the subject catalog of the
        German Archaeological Institute in Rome, the bibliography of Iberian

Archaeology from the German Archaeological Institute in Madrid, and the Archaeology of Roman Provinces from RGK in Frankfurt.

13.13   *Nordisk bibliografi for etnologi og folkloristi; Pohjoismainen folkloristiikan ja kansatieteen; Nordic bibliography of ethnology and folklore.* Helsinki Kobenhavn: NIF/NEFA Nordens dokumentationsudvalg. 1991 - . 1/yr. GN585 .S34 N67x.

Bibliography to periodical literature pertaining to Scandinavian ethnology and folklore published by the Nordic Institute of Folklore; headings and keyword lists are in Danish, English, and Finnish; continues *Nordisk bibliografi for folkelivsforskere* (Kobenhavn: NEFA's Forlag, 1969/70-1990. 1/yr),

13.14   *Novaia sovetskaia literatura po obshchestvennym naukam: istoriia, arkheologiia, etnografiia.* Moskva: Akademiia nauk SSSR, In-t nauch. informatsii po obshchestvennym naukam. 1976 - . 12/yr. D20 .N68x.

Periodical index for archaeology, ethnology, and history.

Latin America

13.15   *Hispanic American periodicals index (HAPI).* Los Angeles, UCLA Latin American Center Publications, University of California. 1970/74 - . F1401 .H5x.

Indexes approximately 200 journals published in Latin America and elsewhere. All major disciplines, including anthropology and related areas are covered. A listing of subject headings is provided by *HAPI thesaurus, 1970-1993* (B.G. Valk, comp. Los Angeles: UCLA Latin American Center Publications, University of California, Los Angeles, 1993. 126 p. F1408 .H5x 1993).

The *Hispanic American Periodicals Index* [computer file] contains citations to articles in more than 400 scholarly journals published in Latin America or treating Latin American and U.S. Hispanic topics. Coverage includes social sciences and humanities materials in English, French, German, Italian, Portuguese, and Spanish, from 1970 to the present. The data base is updated annually with approximately 9,000 records per update. As of June, 1996, the *Hispanic American Periodical Index* included more than 193,000 records. The journals are selected and indexed by an international panel of librarians and scholars.

Direct document requests to the HAPI office at Latin American Center, University of California at Los Angeles, 10349 Bunche Hall, Los Angeles, California, 90024; e-mail: rgutierr@ucla.edu; telephone: 310-825-1057; fax: 310.206.2634.The cost for documentary delivery is

$10.00 per article via U.S. mail, plus delivery cost; add $2.00 per page for fax delivery.

Middle East

13.16   *Index Islamicus.* East Grinstead, West Sussex, England: Bowker-Saur. no. 1 - , 1994 - . 4/yr. Z7835 .M6 L67x.

Continues: *Quarterly index Islamicus* (London: Mansell. v. 1-17, 1977-1993. 4/yr. DS36 .I5x; Z7835 .M6 L6x). Index, cumulated every five years, of current periodical and book literature dealing with Islam and Islamic civilizations of the Middle East and North Africa; supplements annual paperback compilations of *Index Islamicus: Supplement* (London: Mansell, 1956/60-1971/75) and J.D. Pearson, *Index Islamicus, 1906-1955: a catalogue of articles on Islamic subjects in periodicals and other collective publications* (Cambridge, England: W. Hefler, 1958. 897 p.; *Supplement 1: 1956-1960; Supplement 2: 1961-1965; Supplement 3: 1966-1970; Supplement 4: 1971-1975; Supplement 5: 1976-1980; Supplement 6: 1981-1985).*

13.17   *Libyca; anthropologie, prehistoirie, ethnographie.* Alger: Centre de Recherches Anthropologiques, Prehistoriques et Ethnographiques, 1953-1971. 19 v. DT281 .L5.

North America

13.18   *Index to literature on the American Indian.* San Francisco: Indian Historian Press. 1970-1973. E77 .I49x.

There are many other indexes to the periodical literature of the social sciences and humanities that are of interest to anthropologists. Some of these include:

Social Sciences

13.19   *Population index.* Princeton, New Jersey. v.1 - , 1935 - . 4/yr. HB848 .P6x.

Published by the Woodrow Wilson School of Public and International Affairs, Princeton University, and the Population Association of America, this index provides international coverage for books, articles, conference and other proceedings, and governmental publications on subjects such as population, mortality, fertility, and migration. Arranged by broad subject areas with geographical and author indexes which cumulate annually. Cumulated by: *Population index bibliography, cumulated 1969-1981, by authors and geographical areas* (Boston: G.K. Hall, 1984. 4 v. HA155 .P66x 1984).

13.20   *Social sciences citation index.* Philadelphia: Institute for Scientific
Information. 1972 - . 3/yr. AI3 .A63. H1 .A3 S62x

An international multidisciplinary index to the literature of the
social, behavioral, and related sciences published by the Institute for
Scientific Information, permits the reader to identify related writings
(periodical articles, reviews, etc.) by indicating sources in which a
known work by a given author has been cited. Covers approximately
2,000 journals, many of them selectively. Each issue has three parts:
Citation index (arranged alphabetically by cited author, with
references to articles in which a work is cited); *Source index* (arranged
alphabetically by author and giving full bibliographic citations plus the
author's address, if available); and *Permuterm subject index* (offering a
subject approach through a system of indexing which "involves the
permutation of all significant words within each sentence of the title
and subtitle of an article to form all possible pairs of terms"). For a
useful guide, see *An introduction to the Social sciences citation index*
(Philadelphia: Institute for Scientific Information, 1976. H1 .A3
S625x 1976). A kit including 47 slides and one sound cassette uses
citations from the 1973 edition of *Social sciences citation index* to
teach proper use.

Social sciences citation index compact disc edition [computer
file]. Philadelphia. 1989 - . 4/yr. Contains complete bibliographic data
plus citations to significant articles from the 1,400 most important
social sciences journals worldwide as well as social sciences articles
from 3,200 journals in the natural, physical, and biomedical sciences.

Social sciences citation index compact disc edition with abstracts
[computer file]. Philadelphia. 1986 - . 4/yr. Contains complete
bibliographic data plus citations and English-language author
abstracts to significant articles from the 1,400 most important social
sciences journals worldwide as well as social sciences articles from
3,200 journals in the natural, physical, and biomedical sciences.

Social SciSearch [computer file]. Philadelphia. 52/yr. Contains
complete bibliographic data plus citations and abstracts; covers 1,400
of the most significant social sciences journals worldwide.

13.21   *Social sciences index.* New York: H.W. Wilson. v.1 - , 1974/75 - .
4/yr. AI3 .S62.

Provides access by author and subject to articles in English-
language periodicals in the social sciences. Covers major journals in
anthropology, area studies, economics, environmental sciences,
geography, law and criminology, sociology, and related disciplines;
includes author and subject indexes; book reviews are cited under the
name of the author of the book being reviewed; continues: *Social*

sciences and humanities index (New York. v. 1-27, 1907/15-1973/74).
Social science index [computer file]. New York. 1983 - . 104/yr.
Contains approximately 395,000 citations to articles and book reviews
in some 400 English-language periodicals in the social sciences.

Humanities

13.22   *Arts and humanities citation index.* Philadelphia: Institute for
Scientific Information. 1976 - . 2/yr. AI3 .A63.

An international multidisciplinary index to the literature of the
humanities published by the Institute for Scientific Information,
permits the reader to identify related writings (periodical articles,
reviews, etc.) by indicating sources in which a known work by a given
author has been cited. Covers approximately 2,000 journals, many of
them selectively. Each issue has three parts: *Citation index* (arranged
alphabetically by cited author, with references to articles in which a
work is cited); *Source index* (arranged alphabetically by author and
giving full bibliographic citations plus the author's address, if
available); and *Permuterm subject index* (offering a subject approach
through a system of indexing which "involves the permutation of all
significant words within each sentence of the title and subtitle of an
article to form all possible pairs of terms").

Arts and humanities citation index compact disc edition
[computer file]. Philadelphia. 1990 - . every three years. Contains
bibliographic data on items from more than 1,100 arts and humanities
journals as well as selected items from 5,800 science and social
sciences journals.

Arts and humanities search [computer file]. Philadelphia. 1980 - .
52/yr. Contains complete bibliographic data from the 1,100 arts and
humanities journals as well as selected items from more than 5,800
science and social sciences journals.

13.23   *Film literature index.* Albany, New York: Filmdex. v.1 - , 1973 - .
4/yr. PN1993 .F5x.

This international publication provides author and subject
indexing of reviews and articles about specific films, film genres,
directors, cinematographers, and other aspects of the film industry.

13.24   *Humanities index.* New York: H.W. Wilson. v.1 - , 1974/75 - . 4/yr.
AI3 .H85.

Provides access by author to articles in English-language
periodicals in the humanities. Covers major journals in classics, art
and photography, literature, religion, archaeology, area studies,
folklore, linguistics, and related disciplines; includes author and

subject indexes; book reviews are cited under the name of the author of the book being reviewed; continues: *Social sciences and humanities index* (New York. v.1-27, 1907/15-1973/74).
Humanities index [computer file]. New York. 1984 - . 104/yr. Contains more than 300,000 citations to articles and book reviews in 400 general-interest periodicals.

Abstracts
Anthropology

13.25   *Abstracts in anthropology.* Westport, Connecticut: Greenwood Press. v.1 - , 1970 - . 8/yr. GN1 .A15.
Selectively provides abstracts of 50 to 100 words in length for articles in the major subdisciplines of anthropology: archaeology, physical anthropology, linguistics, and cultural anthropology; includes author and subject indexes.

13.26   *Abstracts in German anthropology.* Göttingen: Edition Herodot. no. 1 - , 1980 - . 2/yr. GN1 .A27x
Contains concise abstracts in English of anthropological publications appearing in German by German, Austrian and Swiss authors. Includes subject and author indexes.

13.27   *American Anthropological Association abstracts.* Washington, D.C. 1960 - . 1/yr.
Includes abstracts of papers and films since the 1960 annual meeting of the American Anthropological Association.

Archaeology

13.28   *Abstracts of New World archaeology.* Washington, D.C.: Society for American Archaeology. v. 1-2; 1959-1960. E51 .S73.

13.29   *Art and archaeology technical abstracts.* New York: Institute of Fine Arts, New York University. v.1 - , 1966 - . 2/yr. AM1 .A7.
Abstracts of articles, reports, news items, books and other publications dealing with the technical examination, investigation, analysis, restoration, preservation, and technical documentation of objects and monuments having historic or artistic significance. Global in scope, covers many journals not usually covered by other abstracting services. Especially good for preservation and restoration aspects of archaeology; continues: R.J. Gettens, and B.M. Usilton, comps., *Abstracts of technical studies in art and archaeology, 1943-1952*

(Freer Gallery of Art Occasional Papers, v. 2(2.1). Washington, D.C., 1955. 408 p. 016.7 G335).
Art and archaeology technical abstracts [computer file]. New York. 1955 - . 2/yr. Provides comprehensive abstracting and indexing of international literature on the conservation of movable and immovable cultural property and related disciplines.

13.30   *British archaeological abstracts.* London: Council for British Archaeology. v. 1-24, 1968-1991. DA90 .B82.
Published by the Council for British Archaeology. Emphasis is given to the archaeology of Great Britain, Ireland, and western Europe.

13.31   *Nordic archaeological abstracts.* Viborg, Denmark: Norhaven. v.1 - , 1974 - .1/yr. GN825 .N67x.
"Published with grants from the humanistic research councils of Denmark, Finland, Norway, and Sweden" with volumes published after 1975 including a list of archaeological papers from Estonia, Latvia, and Lithuania. Most of the original titles are in Scandinavian languages although abstracts are in English. Includes author, subject, and archaeological site indexes.

13.32   *Polish archaeological abstracts.* Wroclaw: Zaklad Narodowy Imienia Ossolinskich. v. 1 - , 1972 - . 1/yr. DK409 .P56.
Published by the Institute of the History of Material Culture of the Polish Academy of Sciences. Issues cover a three-year period and provide abstracts in English of Polish periodical articles, books, review articles, and excavation reports. Abstracts are arranged chronologically from the Palaeolithic period to the end of the fifteenth-century.

Linguistics
13.33   *Linguistics and language behavior abstracts: LLBA.* La Jolla, California: Sociological Abstracts. v.19 - , 1985 - . 4/yr. P1 .L2x
Covers more than 1,000 journals and abstracts the literature of linguistics and language-related research, book abstracts, book review listings, and enhanced bibliographic citations of relevant dissertations, including anthropological linguistics; continues: *Language and language behavior abstracts* (New York. v. 1-18, 1967-1984). A listing of subject headings used is provided by A. Colby, *Thesaurus of linguistic indexing terms* (San Diego: Sociological Abstracts, 1992. 97 p. P121 .C65x 1992).

LLBA disc [computer file]. Norwood, Massachusetts: SilverPlatter Information, 1993 - . 2/yr. P1 .L2x. Coverage includes *Language and language behavior abstracts* published between 1967-1984, and *Linguistics and language behavior abstracts* published since 1985.

Africa

13.34   *African abstracts; Bulletin analytique africaniste.* London: International African Institute. v. 1-23, 1950-1972. 4/yr. DT1 .I34x.

A quarterly review of ethnological, social, and linguistic studies appearing in periodicals. Articles and abstracts in English or French.

Asia

13.35   *Indian Council of Social Science Research (ICSSR) journal of abstracts and reviews. Sociology and social anthropology.* New Delhi: National. v.1 - , 1971 - . 2/yr. H35 .I52a.

Index of book reviews and abstracts of periodical articles.

Middle East

13.36   *The Middle East: abstracts and index.* Pittsburgh: Northumberland Press. v.1 - , 1978 - . 4/yr. DS41 .M44.

14

Journal Literature

There are many reasons for using journal articles in research papers. Journal are usually published regularly, either monthly, quarterly, or annually, and are more current than books in their coverage. They are shorter in length than books and frequently contain detailed information on subjects which may not warrant an entire book. Finally, they enable you to read the research results and arguments by several different scholars more quickly than could be done by reading books.

The most efficient way to locate information published in a journal. The terms *magazine, journal, and periodical* are used somewhat interchangeably. However, magazine usually refers to a popular publication, journal refers to more scholarly publications, and periodical refers to anything that is published at regular intervals. Individual articles published in magazines, journals, or other periodicals, and cited or referenced in library reference works known as *periodicals indexes*. Periodical indexes of interest to anthropology students are discussed in Chapter 13.

Once a list of the pertinent journal articles on a subject has been compiled, you will need to determine whether your library has each journal title and where they are located. *Ulrich's international periodicals directory* can indicate whether a specific journal has its own annual index. If not, *Ulrich's* will identify where it is indexes. It is also useful to determine which periodical indexing or abstracting service should be used to identify articles on similar and related subjects.

Electronic Journals

In recent years a number of anthropological journals have been available electronically. Academic Press, a major commercial publisher, is attempting to incorporate the capabilities of the Internet to expand and improve access to some 175 scientific journals. Anyone with Internet access can freely browse and search the journal tables of contents and abstracts on IDEAL (International Digital Electronic Access Library at http://www.idealibrary.com). Authorized users at sites within the licensed consortia, can view, search, print, and download complete articles in the Acrobat format without restriction for personal use or course packs. End users at your campus library only need an

Internet connection, a World Wide Web browser, and Adobe's free Acrobat Reader. The full text of journal articles is displayed in the Acrobat format, tables of contents, and abstracts in HTML. Journals of interest to anthropologists available through this program include:

International journal of nautical archaeology. London. v.25 - , 1995 - . 4/yr.
Journal of anthropological archaeology. New York. v.15 - , 1996 - . 4/yr.
Journal of archaeological science. London. v.23 - , 1996 - . 4/yr.
Journal of human evolution. London. v. 32 - , 1996 - . 6/yr.

Other electronic journals available on the Internet are identified in Chapter 21. For additional journals in anthropology and related fields, consult your library catalog under the appropriate subject with the subdivision *Periodicals.* For example,

Anthropology — Periodicals
Latin America -- Periodicals -- Bibliography
Indians of North America -- Periodicals – Indexes

Guides to Anthropology Journals

14.1   Library-Anthropology Resource Group. *Serial publications in anthropology.* 2 ed. South Salem, New York: Redgrave, 1982. 177 p. GN1 .S437x 1982.
    An alphabetical listing of current serial titles for anthropology with address of publisher and frequency of publication. Indexes are arranged by topical and geographic subjects.

14.2   Williams, John T. *Anthropology journals and serials: an analytical guide.* New York: Greenwood Press, 1986. 182 p. GN1 .W5 1986.
    Provides fully annotated entries for currently published English language serials, including indexing and abstracting services. Arrangement is by traditional subdiscipline (archaeology; cultural anthropology, including folklore; linguistics; physical anthropology).

14.3   *Ulrich's international periodicals directory: a classified guide to current periodicals, foreign and domestic.* New York: R.R. Bowker, 1965/66 - . 1/yr. AP1 .U47.
    This basic reference work has been published since 1932 and lists over 60,000 periodicals published more than once a year, and usually at regular intervals. A typical entry would be:

Anthropology 572CN   ISSN 0706-4845
*Canadian journal of anthropology/Revue canadienne
d'anthropologie.* 1980. s-m. Can $20. to individuals;
institutions Can $48. University of Alberta, Department of
Anthropology, Edmonton, Alta. T6G 2H4, Canada. Tel 403-
432-5903. bk. rev. cir. 450. (back issues avail.) Indexed: Biol.
Abstr.; Abstr. Anthropol.

Entries are arranged by subject (e.g., anthropology, archaeology) and
provide title of the journal; beginning date of publication; subscription
cost to individuals and institutions; publisher and place of publication;
book review notification; circulation size; and indexing information.

Important Anthropology Journals

Anthropology is an eclectic discipline and maintains various kinds of
relationships with the natural and social sciences, as well as the humanities. A
number of important journals for anthropology can be identified despite this
broad range of interests. Beyond these, it is almost impossible to assemble a
group of journals reflective of the interests of contemporary anthropologists.

14.4   *Aboriginal history.* Canberra. v.1-14 , 1977-1990. 1/yr.
        A journal devoted to Aboriginal issues, especially biography,
        ethnohistory, linguistics, and evaluation of political programs or
        activities of Aboriginal organizations.

14.5   *Africa: journal of the International African Institute.* Manchester,
        England. v.1 - , 1928 - . 4/yr.
        A scholarly international journal for research in African social
        sciences and humanities with contributions in English and French;
        includes an excellent book review section.

14.6   *African archaeological review.* Cambridge, England. v.1 - , 1983 - .
        1/yr.
        Publishes original articles on the archaeology and prehistory of
        Africa, with an emphasis on cultural continuities, interregional inter-
        action, biocultural evolution, cultural dynamics, cultural ecology, and
        the application of ethnohistorical, textual, and ethnoarchaeological
        data in archaeological interpretation.

14.7   *América indígena.* México. v.1 - , 1941 - . 4/yr.
        Published in Spanish by the Instituto Indigenista Interamericano
        with English summaries; provides information on contemporary

American Indians, and various programs and policies being developed on their behalf.

14.8   *American anthropologist.* Washington, D.C. v.1 - , 1888 - . 4/yr.
        This major American anthropological journal is published by the American Anthropological Association. There are five to seven major articles per issue, primarily from cultural/social anthropologists and physical anthropologists, but also occasionally from archaeologists. Contributions range from short essays to field reports, and theoretical reviews. The journal is particularly valuable because of its authoritative book, film, and recording reviews.

14.9   *American antiquity.* Washington, D.C. v.1 - , 1935 - . 4/yr.
        Published by the Society for American Archaeology, this journal is of primary importance for American archaeologists. Regional coverage includes the archaeology of the Americas and related areas of interest. Contents include several theoretical papers as well as shorter articles treating artifact analyses, dating, and excavation summaries. Detailed obituaries and a lengthy collection of critical book reviews appear in each issue.

14.10   *American ethnologist.* Washington, D.C. v.1 - , 1974 - . 4/yr.
        Another publication of the American Anthropological Association, this journal publishes theoretical and comparative studies in ethnology and emphasizes culture change and ethnicity in traditional and urban societies. North American anthropologists contribute most of the articles.

14.11   *American journal of archaeology.* New York. v.1 - , 1885 - . 4/yr.
        Published by the Archaeological Institute of America, this journal contains scholarly articles written by American and European archaeologists about the Near East, and Classical and Mediterranean areas. Short notes of progress of excavations and special studies are included. The journal is of special interest to students in the fields of archaeology, classics, history, and art.

14.12   *American journal of physical anthropology.* Philadelphia. v.1 - , 1919 - . 6/yr.
        Publishes original research on human evolution and variation, with an emphasis on human genetics and adaptation, growth, development and behavior, and primate studies. There are also brief reports, communications, and summaries of scholarly conferences.

14.13   *Ancient Mesoamerica.* New York. v.1 - , 1990 - . 2/yr.
Published essays, primarily in English, on the archaeology,
ethnohistory, and art history of Mexico and northern Central America.

14.14   *Anthropologica.* Ottawa. v.1 - , 1959 - . 2/yr.
The focus of this general anthropological journal is on native
peoples of the Americas, especially Canada. Most articles are
ethnographic or ethnohistoric papers, although there is a significant
number of theoretical studies on topics such as state formation, music,
and religion. The primary language is English, but some contributions
in French.

14.15   *Anthropological linguistics.* Bloomington. v.1 - , 1959 - . 9/yr.
Designed primarily for the publication of data oriented linguistics
papers, this journal includes papers on phonology, morphology,
syntax, and comparative grammar, particularly on non-written
languages. Theoretical and methodological papers in related subjects
appear occasionally.

14.16   *Anthropological quarterly.* Washington, D.C. v.1 - , 1928 - . 4/yr.
This journal is published by the Catholic University of America
and emphasizes urban anthropology and the ethnographic study of
Western Societies.

14.17   *L'Anthropologie.* Paris. v.1 - , 1890 - . 4/yr.
An important general anthropology journal published in France.

14.18   *Anthropology and archeology of Eurasia.* Armonk, New York: M.E.
Sharpe. v. 31 - , 1992 - . 4/yr.
Quarterly journal on the anthropology and archaeology of the
former Soviet Union.

14.19   *Anthropology and education.* Washington, D.C. v.1 - , 1970 - . 4/yr.
This journal concentrates on the application of anthropology to
research development in education. Articles emphasize the cultural
context of the American school, the education of ethnic minorities, the
role of the school in global cultural change, and the potential use of
anthropological data and theory in the training of educators.

14.20   *Anthropology and humanism quarterly.* Tallahassee. v.1 - , 1976 - .
4/yr.
Published by the Society for Humanistic Anthropology, this

journal considers anthropological accounts of human experience, essays, fiction, poems, and art.

14.21   *Anthropology newsletter.* Washington, D.C. v.1 - , 1959 - . 12/yr.
        Published by the American Anthropological Association, this important newsletter provides news of association affairs, people, grants and support, research reports, announcements, meeting and seminar calendars, annual reports, and annual meeting programs.

14.22   *Anthropology today.* London. v.1 - , 1974 - . 6/yr.
        This newsletter is published by the Royal Anthropological Institute of Great Britain and Ireland and provides research reports, news of Institute affairs, book and film reviews, and so forth.

14.23   *Anthropos: Zeitschrift für Völker- und Sprachenkunde; Revue International d'Ethnologie et de Linguistique.* Freibourg, Switzerland. v.1 - , 1906 - . 2/yr.
        Anthropos covers cultural; anthropology, linguistics, history of religions, and less frequently, archaeology and prehistory of Europe, Asia, Africa, the Americas, and Oceania. Authorship is international, and articles are published in English, French, or German. There are numerous book reviews and shorter notes.

14.24   *Antiquity: a quarterly review of archaeology.* Cambridge, England. v.1 - , 1927 - . 4/yr.
        A British journal concentrating primarily on the Neolithic through Iron Age periods of Western Europe although coverage has been expanded to include Asia, Africa, and the Americas. A regular *Notes and News* section includes information on chronology, mapping, and other techniques, as well as brief excavation and survey reports.

14.25   *Archaeology.* New York. v.1 - , 1948 - . 6/yr.
        A popular magazine, published by the Archaeological Institute of America, of short articles about Old and New World excavations, *Archaeology* also offers a news section with brief notes of activities in the field, current museum exhibitions, and new discoveries. This is the best popular archaeology magazine available.

14.26   *Archaeology in Oceania.* Sydney. v.1 - , 1966 - . 3/yr.
        Devoted to the study of the archaeology and physical anthropology of Australia, New Guinea, southeastern Asia, and the islands of the Pacific, this journal includes articles on prehistory, genetics, migration

history, microevolution, and related studies on the populations of the Pacific.

14.27   *Archaeometry.* Oxford, England. v.1 - , 1958 - . 2/yr.
An interdisciplinary journal with articles on the development and application of mathematical and scientific techniques used in the analysis of artifacts and other remains from archaeological sites.

14.28   *Arctic Anthropology.* Madison. v.1 - , 1965 - . 2/yr.
Arctic Anthropology is devoted to the ethnographic and archaeological study of circumpolar peoples. Contributions are international and articles are published in English by Russian, Japanese, Scandinavian, and American scholars.

14.29   *Bijdragen tot de Taal-, Land-, en Volkenkunde.* Dordrecht. v.1 - , 1853 - . 4/yr.
This publication from the Koninklijk Instituut voor Taal-, Land- en Volkenkunde emphasizes the anthropology of Indonesia and Malaysia.

14.30   *Chinese sociology and anthropology.* White Plains, New York: M.E. Sharpe. v.1 - , 1968 - . 4/yr.

14.31   *Cultural anthropology.* Washington, D.C. v.1 - , 1986 - . 4/yr.
Published by the Society for Cultural Anthropology, this journal includes articles, reviews, and interviews on the study of culture in anthropology.

14.32   *Cultural survival quarterly.* Cambridge, Massachusetts. v.1 - , 1976 - . 4/yr.
Addresses issues of immediate and long-term concern to indigenous peoples throughout the world.

14.33   *Culture and history.* Copenhagen. v.1 - , 1986 - . 2/yr.

14.34   *Culture, medicine, and psychiatry.* Dordrecht. v.1 - , 1977 - . 4/yr.
Emphasis on topics in psychological and medical anthropology, with cross-cultural studies ranging from depression to conflict resolution in the family; each issues contains book reviews.

14.35   *Current anthropology: a world journal of the sciences of man.* Chicago. v.1 - , 1960 - . 5/yr.
Current anthropology serves as a major clearinghouse for new

ideas and as an indicator of trends in anthropology. The journal builds a broad interdisciplinary knowledge base for the study of all aspects of humankind by selecting topics which are "broad in terms of time, available data and methodology." Most of the scholarly contributions are accompanied by two or more critical comments by other subject experts. There are five to seven articles per issue.

14.36   *Dialectical anthropology.* Amsterdam. v.1 - , 1975 - . 4/yr.
Publishes essays and studies dealing with Marxist critiques of anthropology.

14.37   *Eastern anthropologist.* Lucknow, India. v.1 - , 1947 - . 4/yr.
Eastern anthropologist publishes material on all aspects of Indian anthropology, usually including folklore, archaeology, linguistics, and social anthropology.

14.38   *Ethnic groups.* New York. v.1 - , 1976 - . 4/yr.
Continues: *Afro-American Studies.*

14.39   *Ethnohistory: devoted to original research in the documentary history of the culture and movements of primitive peoples and related Problems of broader scope.* Lubbock. v.1 - , 1954 - . 4/yr.
Most of the papers published in this journal deal with Native American groups, and are written by scholars trained in history and anthropology. Contributions usually emphasize the integration of archaeological, anthropological, and historical data sets.

14.40   *Ethnology: an international journal of cultural and social anthropology.* Pittsburgh. v.1 - , 1962 - . 4/yr.
Covers cultural anthropology on a global scale and encompasses related studies in cultural and social history. Most of the articles are written by American or European scholars and are generally based on original field research rather than theoretical or methodological analyses.

14.41   *Ethnomusicology.* Bloomington. v.1 - , 1966 - . 3/yr.
Published by the Society for Ethnomusicology, presents scholarly articles are reviews on folk and tribal music, jazz, and the psychosocial basis of music in world cultures.

14.42   *Ethnos.* Stockholm. v.1 - , 1936 - . 2/yr.
Ethnos is published by the Ethnographical Museum of Sweden and offers a combination of traditional ethnography and innovative

studies. Contributors are usually European, and all articles are in English, French, German, or Swedish.

14.43   *Ethos.* Berkeley. v.1 - , 1973 - . 4/yr.
Published by the Society for Psychological Anthropology, this journal bridges the work of anthropologists and psychiatrists. Contributions consider the relationship between individuals and their social/cultural context.

14.44   *Expedition.* Philadelphia. v.1 - , 1958 - . 3/yr.
This popular magazine is published by the University Museum of the University of Pennsylvania and reports on recent excavations, discoveries, and anthropological studies for the interested non-professional.

14.45   *Folklore.* London. v.1 - , 1878 - . 2/yr.
The major folklore journal from the United Kingdom includes articles ranging from the comparative study of oral traditions and cultures to those on material culture, folk song, dance, and folk tales.

14.46   *Geoarchaeology.* New York. v.1 - , 1986 - . 6/yr.

14.47   *Gradhiva.* Paris: Departement d'Archives de l'Ethnologie du Musée de l'Homme. v.1 - , 1986 - . 2/yr.

14.48   *Historical archaeology.* Bethlehem, Pennsylvania. v.1 - , 1967 - . 2/yr.
Published by the Society for Historical Archaeology, this journal provides one of the best sources for historic-site archaeological information.

14.49   *History of anthropology newsletter.* Chicago. v.1 - , 1973 - . 2/yr.
Includes research notes, bibliography, and source material for the history of anthropology.

14.50   *L'Homme: Revue Française d'Anthropologie.* Paris. v.1 - , 1961 - . 4/yr.
General anthropological journal published in France.

14.51   *Homo: Zeitschrift für die Vergleichende Forschung am Menschen.* Göttingen. v.1 - , 1948 - .
Homo is published by the Deutsche Gesellschaft für Anthropologie.

14.52   *Human biology.* Detroit. v.1 - , 1929 - . 4/yr.
The focus of this journal is research on "human biological variation and its underlying and environmental causes." The general approach is multidisciplinary, including genetics, population, biology, physical anthropology, physiology, and demography.

14.53   *Human ecology.* New York. v.1 - , 1972 - . 4/yr.
Human Ecology publishes technical articles dealing with the interaction between human behavior and the environment. Topics range from hunter-gathering subsistence strategies to the division of labor.

14.54   *Human evolution.* Florence. v.1 - , 1986 - . 6/yr.
A multidisciplinary journal involved in the study of human evolution reflecting the current interests in molecular evolution, genetics, and biological variation considered ion social, cultural, and physical contexts.

14.55   *Human organization.* Washington, D.C. v.1 - , 1941 - . 4/yr.
This journal is published by the Society for Applied Anthropology and promotes the use of anthropological theory and method in the study of urban and developing societies. Articles consider human behavior in its community context, and examine such issues as housing, health care, conflict, work, and government.

14.56   *International journal of American linguistics.* Chicago. v.1 - , 1917 - . 4/yr.
Published scholarly studies about all aspects of the indigenous languages of the Americas, including description, history, typology, and linguistic theory.

14.57   *International journal of nautical archaeology.* London. v.1 - , 1972 - . 4/yr.
Contains reports on research and excavations at nautical sites around the world.

14.58   *Israel exploration journal.* Jerusalem. v.1 - , 1950 - . 4/yr.
Israel exploration journal publishes scholarly works on the history and archaeology of Israel and the ancient Near East.

14.59   *Journal of American folklore.* Washington, D.C. v.1 - , 1888 - . 4/yr.
Published by the American Folklore Society, presents scholarly

articles on all aspects of folklore; includes sections of notes from the field, announcements, and book reviews.

14.60   *Journal of anthropological archaeology.* New York. v.1 - , 1982 - . 4/yr.
This journal is devoted to the development of theory and methodology for a rigorous, systematic understanding of the past.

14.61   *Journal of anthropological research.* Albuquerque. v.1 - , 1945 - . 4/yr.
Journal of anthropological research offers coverage of all branches of anthropology. papers deal primarily with cultural/social anthropology although some attention is given to archaeology and linguistics. There are a few book reviews and book notes. Formerly known as *Southwestern journal of anthropology.*

14.62   *Journal of archaeological method and theory.* New York . v.1 - , 1994 - . 4/yr.
Includes topical syntheses and original articles that critically assess and integrate research on a specific subject in archaeological method and theory.

14.63   *Journal of archaeological science.* London. v.1 - , 1974 - . 4/yr.
This journal publishes papers, reviews, and short notes combining archaeology and other branches of the sciences, including the physical sciences, biological sciences, earth science, and mathematics.

14.64   *Journal of California and Great Basin anthropology.* Banning, California. v.1 - , 1974 - . 2/yr.
Publishes papers and book reviews on the ethnography, ethnohistory, archaeology, and linguistics of the Native Americans of California, the Great Basin, and Baja California.

14.65   *Journal of ethnobiology.* Gainesville. v.1 - , 1981 - . 2/yr.
Publishes interdisciplinary research of interest to biologists and anthropologists.

14.66   *Journal of family history.* St. Paul, Minnesota. v.1 - , 1976 - . 4/yr.
A scholarly journal, published by the National Council on Family Relations, deals with the relationship of "family, kinship, and demography."

14.67 *Journal of field archaeology.* Boston. v.1 - , 1974 - . 4/yr.
This journal publishes articles on significant recent archaeological projects. Other features include an archaeometric clearinghouse, reports on legal and ethical questions, and news of illicit trade in antiquities.

14.68 *Journal of human evolution.* London. v.1 - , 1972 - . 8/yr.
A major journal for the publication of papers on human evolution, including primate studies, research on anatomy, physiology, and on the origins of language and social structure.

14.69 *Journal of Latin American lore.* Los Angeles. v.1 - , 1974 - . 2/yr.
Published by the Latin American Center at University of California at Los Angeles, this journal considers the lore of the peoples of Latin America from prehispanic to contemporary times.

14.70 *Journal of Near Eastern studies.* Chicago. v.1 - , 1984- . 4/yr.
Scholarly journal devoted to artifact interpretation and translation of inscriptions discovered in archaeological contexts in southwestern Asia and the Near East.

14.71 *Journal of peasant studies.* London. v.1 - , 1973 - . 4/yr.
An interdisciplinary journal covering peasants and their role in the history, economy, and socioeconomic structure of nonindustrial and undeveloped societies.

14.72 *Journal of quantitative anthropology.* Dordrecht. v.1 - , 1989 - . 4/yr.

14.73 *Journal of world prehistory.* New York. v.1 - , 1987 - . 4/yr.
Publishes syntheses of the prehistory of an area or a time-horizon within a larger region.

14.74 *Kiva.* Tucson. v.1 - , 1935 - . 4/yr.
Publishes original articles on the archaeology of the southwestern United States and adjacent Mexico.

14.75 *Language: journal of the Linguistic Society of America.* Baltimore. v.1 - , 1925 - . 4/yr.
Publishes scientific research about basic issues in general linguistics, sociolinguistics, descriptive linguistics, and theoretical linguistics.

14.76   *Latin American antiquity.* Washington, D.C. v.1 - , 1990 - . 4/yr.
        Publishes contributions on the archaeology, prehistory, and
        ethnohistory of Spanish-speaking Latin America, including
        Mesoamerica, Central America, and South America.

14.77   *Man: journal of the Royal Anthropological Institute.* London. v.1 - ,
        1966 - . 4/yr.
        Man is published by the Royal Anthropological Institute of Great
        Britain and Ireland and covers British social anthropology with an
        emphasis on such traditional interests as kinship, cognition,
        witchcraft, and so forth.

14.78   *Man in India.* Ranchi. v.1 - , 1921 - . 4/yr.
        An important general anthropology journal from India.

14.79   *Mankind.* Sydney. v.1 - , 1931 - . 2/yr.
        Mankind is published by the Anthropological Society of New
        South Wales for the Anthropological Societies of Australia and
        concentrates on the archaeology and ethnography of Australia and
        Oceania. Numerous critical book reviews and appended bibliographies
        enhance the value of the journal.

14.80   *Mankind quarterly.* Washington, D.C. v.1 - , 1960 - . 4/yr.
        This journal is published by the Institute for the Study of Man and
        considers physical and cultural anthropology, population, genetics,
        cultural history, and mythology.

14.81   *Meddelelser om Gronland; Man and society.* Copenhagen: Nyt
        Nordisk Forlag - Arnold Busck A/S. v. 1 - , 1980 - .
        Interesting journal on the anthropology of the Greenland Eskimos.

14.82   *Medical anthropology.* Salem, New York. v.1 - , 1977 - . 4/yr.
        Medical Anthropology publishes cross-cultural studies in health
        and illness of interest to anthropologists, physicians, and other health
        professionals.

14.83   *Medical anthropology quarterly.* Washington, D.C. v.1 - , 1968 - .
        4/yr.
        Published by the Society for Medical Anthropology, this journal
        disseminates news that promotes interest in medical anthropology,
        ethnomedicine, comparative medical systems, and human ecology.

14.84   *Midcontinental journal of archaeology.* Kent. v.1 - , 1976 - . 2/yr.
         Publishes site reports and research syntheses on the archaeology
         of the region between the Appalachian Mountains and the Great
         Plains.

14.85   *Ñawpa pacha.* Berkeley. v.1 - , 1963 - . 1/yr.
         Published by the Institute for Andean Studies and serves as an
         international outlet for Andean archaeology.

14.86   *North American archaeologist.* Farmingdale, New York. v.1 - , 1979 -
         . 2/yr.
         Publishes articles dealing with prehistoric and historical
         archaeology of the United States, Canada, and northern Mexico;
         includes book reviews.

14.87   *Northeast anthropology.* Albany, New York. v.1 - , 1971 - . 4/yr.
         Publishes articles on the prehistory and ethnohistory of the
         northeastern United States; formerly *Man in the Northeast.*

14.88   *Objets et mondes.* Paris. v.1 - , 1961 - . 4/yr.
         Journal of the Musee de l'Homme, publishes articles with French
         and English summaries dealing with ethnology and archaeology.

14.89   *Oceania: devoted to the study of the Native Peoples of Australia, New
         Guinea, and the islands of the Pacific Ocean.* Sydney. v.1 - , 1930 - .
         4/yr.
         Publishes articles on the social anthropology of Australia and the
         Pacific, ranging from kinship and religious ritual to trading and
         government. Most contributors are Australian.

14.90   *Plains anthropologist: a medium for the anthropological
         interpretation of the Plains area in the United States.* Lincoln,
         Nebraska. v. 1 - , 1954 - . 4/yr.
         This journal emphasizes studies of prehistoric and Native
         American peoples of the Plains states. Archaeology dominates but
         there are ethnographic and historical studies as well. Reviews,
         obituaries, and conference announcements are included.

14.91   *Polynesian Society. Journal.* Wellington, New Zealand. v.1 - , 1892 - .
         4/yr.
         Published articles on the anthropology of Polynesia.

14.92   *Practicing anthropology.* Washington, D.C. v.1 - , 1978 - . 6/yr.
A career oriented publication by the Society for Applied
Anthropology.

14.93   *Social analysis.* Adelaide. v.1 - , 1979 - . 2/yr.

14.94   *Social networks.* Amsterdam. v.1 - , 1979 - . 4/yr.
This scholarly journal is published by the International Network
fore Social Network Analysis (INSNA) and is intended for researchers
interested in the "structure of human relations and associations that
may be expressed in network form."

14.95   *Societe des Americanistes de Paris. Journal.* Paris. v.1 - , 1895/1896 -
. 2/yr.
Articles in English, French, German, Portuguese, and Spanish
dealing with the Americas.

14.96   *Steward Anthropological Society. Journal.* Urbana. v.1 - , 1969 - .
2/yr.
Created by graduate students at the University of Illinois, this
journal encourages the submission of student research.

14.97   *Studies in visual communication.* Philadelphia. v.1 - , 1974 - . 4/yr.
The official organ of the Society for the Anthropology of Visual
Communication and publishes the work of scholars studying human
behavior through visual means such as film or photography, or those
engaged in cross-cultural studies of art, aesthetics, or other non-verbal
communication.

14.98   *Urban anthropology and studies of cultural systems and world
economic development.* New York. v.1 - , 1972 - . 4/yr.
This international journal published papers by anthropologists and
sociologists on social structure and culture in an urban setting. Major
concerns include urbanization in non-Western cultures, rural
migration to urban areas, ethnicity, housing, and food distribution
systems.

14.99   *World archaeology.* London. v.1 - , 1969 - . 3/yr.
An international scholarly journal devoted to interpretive and
synthetic studies of central themes, such as hominid development,
subsistence strategies in prehistoric Europe, and nautical archaeology.

14.100   *Zeitschrift für Ethnologie.* Berlin. v.1 - , 1865 - . 2/yr.
Published in German by the Deutsche Gesellschaft für
Völkerkunde and Berliner Gesellschaft für Anthropologie, Ethnologie
und Urgeschichte, with scholarly ethnological contributions and book
reviews.

15

Biographical Information

It is often necessary to collect biographical information on anthropologists. Biographical information about noteworthy anthropologists may appear as separately published books, as articles in periodicals, or as entries in biographical dictionaries and directories. The amount of information needed, a book-length study or a brief summary, will determine the best approach to take.

For information about an anthropologist, or in the case that no complete book exists, a biographical dictionary or directory will often provide a summary of a person's life and work. Because there are so many dictionaries and directories devoted to biography, several indexes have recently been published and can lead you to specific biographical sources.

If a name cannot be found listed anywhere, the *Social sciences citation index* is a source as the institutional affiliation of authors is provided. For earlier generations of anthropologists the biographical supplement to the *International encyclopedia of the social sciences* is a very good source. The articles are thorough with extensive bibliographic information and all articles are signed.

Below are given some of the major general reference works which provide biographical information, as well as indexes which provide access to them and other biographical sources.

For additional biographical information, consult the library catalog under the appropriate subject with the subdivision *Biography* or *Bio-Bibliography*. For example:

> *Anthropologists -- Biography*
> *Anthropology -- Bio-Bibliography*
> *Mead, Margaret, 1901-1978*

Separately published biographies may be found by searching on the catalog under the name of the anthropologist (as subject) and other related headings. A number of general works provide differing amounts of information about prominent individuals in the arts, sciences, and public affairs. Other give data on professional and academic associations, councils, and organizations. Among the general references about important individuals and selected organizations the following are useful:

Anthropology

15.1   *Guide: American Anthropological Association.* Washington, D.C.: American Anthropological Association, 1962- . 1/yr. GN43 .A2 G84. Includes academic, museum, and research departments in the United States and Canada, and selected foreign countries; lists recent doctoral dissertations in anthropology and degree statistics; includes a name index.

15.2   Downing, Theodore E. and Robert Sayers. *Directory of rangelands scientists in the social sciences.* Washington, D.C.: Rangelands Directorate, Man and the Biosphere Program, UNESCO, 1978. 74 p. GN307.3 .D69. Includes scholars interested in the anthropology of rangeland peoples.

15.3   *Fifth international directory of anthropologists.* Chicago: University of Chicago Press, 1975. 496 p. GN20 .I5 1975. Offers brief biographical data on 4,373 anthropologists (name, date of birth, professional position and affiliation, sex, research interests, significant publications, languages); geographical. chronological, and subject/methodological indexes.

15.4   Gacs, Ute. *Women anthropologists: a biographical dictionary.* New York: Greenwood Press, 1988. 428 p. GN20 .W63 1988. Collection of biographies of 58 female anthropologists, mostly North American, born between 1835 and 1935. Most are cultural/social anthropologists, and entries are accompanied by selected lists of scholarly work, references, and sources concerning the anthropologist.

15.5   International Union of Anthropological and Ethnological Sciences. *Handbook, 1993-1998.* Bangor, Wales: International Union of Anthropological and Ethnological Sciences, 1993. 31 p.

15.6   Kinton, Jack F. *Leaders in anthropology: the men and women of the science of man.* Aurora, Ill.: Social Science and Sociological Resources, 1974. 113 p. GN20 .K5 1974.

15.7   Mann, Thomas L. *Biographical directory of anthropologists born before 1920.* Garland reference library of the humanities, 439. New

York: Garland, 1988. 245 p. GN20 .B56x 1988.

Biographical information on people from various professions and geographic areas, born before 1920, who have contributed to the development of anthropology. Each of the 3,488 entries contains such data as date of birth and death, place of birth, major publications, as well as published sources of bibliographical information.

15.8   Winters, Christopher, ed. *International dictionary of anthropologists.*
Garland reference library of social science, 638. New York: Garland, 1991. 823 p. GN20 .I5 1991.

Very useful biographical dictionary of 725 anthropologists compiled by the Library-Anthropology Resource Group (LARG). Entries include short biographical summaries of approximately 500 words followed by a listing of major works. Also included is a useful glossary of terms important to the discipline of anthropology.

Archaeology

15.9   Anati, Ariela F., Claude Lejus, and Azar Mohsenin, eds. *Who's who in rock art: directory of specialists, scholars and technicians working in the field of rock art, compiled as a service to research: a joint project by ICOMOS-CAR (International Committee on Rock Art) and CCSP (Centro camuno di studi preistorici).* Capo di Ponti, Italy: Centro Camuno di Studi Preistorici, 1985. 159 p. CC110 .W56.

15.10   Archaeological Institute of America. *AIA Directory of professionals in archaeology: a preliminary survey.* Boston: Archaeological Institute of America; New York: Kendall/Hunt, 1995. 140 p.

15.11   Dawson, Warren R., and Eric P. Uphill, eds. *Who was who in Egyptology.* 2 ed. London: Egypt Exploration Society, 1972. 315 p. PJ1063 .D3.

15.12   Desse-Berset, Nathalie. *Repertoire international de l'archeozoologie; International archaeozoological directory.* Paris: Editions du Centre National de la Recherche Scientifique, 1986. 2 v.

15.13   *Directory of archaeologists and archaeological resources in the University of California.* Los Angeles: Institute of Archaeology, 1982. 19 p.

15.14   Lees, W.B., and K.M. Kimery-Lees, eds. *Guide to contractors in cultural resource management.* Topeka, Kansas: ArchaeoPress, 1984- . 1/yr.

15.15   Oleson, John P. *Directory of Canadian Old World archaeologists and historians of ancient art and culture.* Victoria, British Columbia: J.P. Oleson, 1992.

15.16   Society for American Archaeology. *Archaeologists of the Americas: membership directory.* Washington, D.C.: Society for American Archaeology, 1994. 1/yr. CC21 .S486.

15.17   Society for Commercial Archeology. *SCA ... membership directory.* Washington, D.C.: Society for Commercial Archeology, 1989.

15.18   Society of Professional Archeologists. *Directory of certified professional archeologists.* Tampa, Florida: Society of Professional Archeologists. 1990. 1/yr.

Cultural/Social Anthropology
15.19   Wulff, Robert M. *Practicing anthropologists in the nation's capital.* Washington, D.C.: Washington Association of Professional Anthropologists, 1981. 61 p. GN20 .P7 1981.
Alphabetical listing of 100 applied anthropologists in the Washington, D.C. area; includes name, address, and research and geographical interests.

Demography
15.20   Nag, Moni., comp. *Population anthropology: an international directory of contributors and their works.* New York: Population Commission, International Union of Anthropological and Ethnological Sciences; Center for Policy Studies, The Population Council, 1978. 96 p. GN33.5 N33.

Linguistics
15.21   Sebeok, Thomas A., ed. *Portraits of linguists: a biographical source book for the history of western linguistics, 1746-1963.* Bloomington: Indiana University Press, 1966. 2 v. P83 .S4 1976.

Africa
15.22   *The ABA directory: members and other African American and African anthropologists.* Washington, D.C.: Association of Black Anthropologists, 1991- .

15.23   Duffy, James, Mitsue Frey, and Michael Sims, comps. *International directory of scholars and specialists in African studies.* Waltham, Massachusetts: Crossroads Press, 1978. 355 p. DT19.5 .D83.

Approximately 2,700 biographical sketches of Africanists throughout the world.

15.24   *Social scientists specializing in African studies; directory.* Paris: Ecole Pratique des Hautes Etudes, 1963. 375 p. DT19.5 U5.

Asia

15.25   Forth, Gregory. *Register of U.K. anthropologists specializing in South-East Asia.* Bangkok, Thailand: British Institute in South-East Asia, 1985. 16 p.

15.26   Ray, Shyamal K. *Bibliographies of eminent Indian anthropologists, with life-sketches.* Calcutta: Anthropological Survey of India, Government of India, 1974. 184 p. GN20 .R39.

15.27   Ray, Shyamal K, and Ajay K. Srivastav. *Directory of scientific personnel of the Anthropological Survey of India: with life-sketches.* Calcutta: Anthropological Survey of India, Ministry of Human Resource Development, Department of Culture, Government of India, 1988- . GN17.3 .I4 R39 1988.

15.28   *Who's who in American ethnic studies in Japan.* Tokyo, Japan: Ministry of Foreign Affairs, 1991. 44 p.

Europe

15.29   Association of Social Anthropologists of the Commonwealth. *Annals of the Association of Social Anthropologists of the Commonwealth and directory of members.* London: The Association, 1989. 136 p.

15.30   Husmann, Rolf, comp. *Studienfuhrer Ethnologie 1985; Directory of German cultural anthropologists and anthropological institutions.* Gottingen, Germany: Edition Herodot, 1985. 247 p. GN45 .G4 S78 1985.
         Includes institutions in Germany and German anthropologists worldwide; introduction in German and English.

15.31   Husmann, Rolf, and Gaby Husmann, eds. *The EASA register.* Göttingen: European Association of Social Anthropologists, 1990. 362 p. GN307.3 .E3 1990.
         Provides coverage for individuals (part 1) and institutions (part 2).

15.32 Meiner, Anke. *Verzeichnis zur deutschsprachigen Ethnologie; Guide to German-speaking anthropology.* Göttingen: Edition Re, 1993. 523 p.

15.33 *Repertoire de l'ethnologie de la France.* Paris: Ministere de la Culture, Direction du Patrimoine, Mission du Patrimoine Ethnologique, 1982.

15.34 Rey, Severine, ed. *Who's who: der Schweizer Ethnologie; de l'ethnologie suisse.* Ethnologica Helvetica, 19. Berne: Schweizerische Ethnologische Gesellschaft, 1995. 290 p.

15.35 Rogers, Susan C. *Directory of Europeanist anthropologists in North America.* Washington, D.C.: American Anthropological Association, 1987. 106 p. GN41.6 .R64 1987.
    "A publication of the Society for the Anthropology of Europe, a unit of the American Anthropological Association." Provides comprehensive listing of 340 individuals holding or working toward a graduate degree in anthropology, based in Canada or the United States, and having an active research interest in Europe. Listings include mailing address, title, institutional affiliation, and topical and geographical specialties. Also includes a selected bibliography of publications by each individual listed, a series of indexes grouping individuals by country, region, and topic; and a series of maps showing research sites of filed-workers. Replaces Susan T. Freeman, and Laura R. Walters, eds. *Europeanist social anthropologists in North America: a directory* (Washington, D.C.: American Anthropological Association, 1975. 34 p.).

15.36 *SAE directory: a publication of the Society for the Anthropology of Europe, a unit of the American Anthropological Association.* 2 ed. Arlington, Virginia: Society for the Anthropology of Europe, 1993.

Latin America

15.37 Harman, Inge M., ed. *National directory of Latin Americanists: biographies of 4,915 specialists.* 3 ed. Washington, D.C.: Library of Congress, 1985. 1,011 p. F1409.8 .A2 N37 1985.
    Biobibliographies of Latin Americanists, including anthropologists. Entries provide name, birthplace, date, major discipline, professional career, fellowships, honors, consultantships, officerships, editorships, membership in professional and honorary organizations, research specialties, publications, language knowledge, home or office address; continues *National directory of Latin*

234 / Introduction to Library Research in Anthropology

Americanists: biographies of 2,695 specialists in the social sciences and humanities (2 ed. Hispanic Foundation Bibliographical Series, 12. Washington, D.C.: United State Government Printing Office, 1972).

Latin America, Mexico and Central America

15.38   Díaz Polanco, Héctor. *Directorio de antropólogos latinoamericanos, México.* Pan American Institute of Geography and History, Publicación 410. México: Instituto Panamericano de Geografía e Historia, 1985. 191 p.

15.39   Méndez-Domínguez, Alfredo, ed. *Mesoamérica: directorio y bibliografía 1950-1980.* Guatemala: Universidad del Valle de Guatemala, 1982. 313 p. Z1209.2 .C45 M47.
          International directory and bibliography of approximately 5,000 entries for scholars in the fields of archaeology, cultural/social anthropology, folklore, linguistics, biological/physical anthropology, and demography.

Latin America, South America

15.40   *Antropólogos.* Sao Paulo: Associaçao Brasileira de Antropología; Departamento de Ciencias Sociais/FFLCH, Universidade de Sao Paulo, 1988. 94 p.

15.41   Friedemann, Nina S. de, and Jaime Arocha. *Bibliografía anotada y directorio de antropologos colombianos.* Bogotá: Sociedad Antropológica de Colombia, 1979. 441 p. GN25.X1 F75x 1979.
          Biographical summaries for 277 Colombian anthropologists.

Middle East

15.42   Rentz, Sophie B. *A Directory of social scientists in the Middle East; Dalil al-mushtaghilin bi-al-ulum al-ijtimaiyah.* Cairo: Organization for the Promotion of Social Sciences in the Middle East, 1977. 249 p. H57 .R4.

North America

15.43   Association for Anthropology and Gerontology. *Directory of anthropologists and anthropological research in aging.* 7 ed. Cincinnati: Association for Anthropology and Gerontology, 1983. 56 p.

15.44   Berry, John W. *Directory of cross-cultural research and researchers.* Bellingham, Washington: Center for Cross-Cultural Research,

Department of Psychology, Western Washington State College, 1973.
144 p.

15.45   Blakely, Thomas D., and Pamela A.R. Blakely, eds. *Directory of
visual anthropology.* Washington, D.C.: Society for Visual
Anthropology, 1989. 177 p. GN41.6 .D5x 1989.

15.46   Chatelain, Agnes B., and Louis F. Cimino. comps. *Directory of
practicing anthropologists.* Washington, D.C.: American
Anthropological Association. 1981.39 p. GN41.6 .C48x 1981.

15.47   *Directory of anthropologists and anthropological research in aging.*
11 ed. Washington, D.C.: Association for Anthropology and
Gerontology, 1992. (irregular). HQ1061 .D57x.

15.48   Johnson, Nancy, ed. *NAPA directory of practicing anthropologists.*
Washington, D.C.: National Association for the Practice of
Anthropology, 1991. 92 p. GN41.6 .N38x 1991.

15.49   *National directory of work anthropologists.* Stewartsville, New Jersey:
Society for the Anthropology of Work, 1988- .

15.50   *Washington Association of Professional Anthropologists. Directory of
members, 1984-1986.* Washington, D.C.: Washington Association of
Professional Anthropologists, 1986. 27 p.
        Updates: *Practicing anthropologists in the nation's capital*
(Washington, D.C.: Washington Association of Professional
Anthropologists, 1981).

15.51   Scrimshaw, Mary W. *Directory of anthropologists and sociologists
concerned with food and nutrition.* Cambridge, Massachusetts: UNU,
Cambridge Program Office, 1985. 337 p.

15.52   Southwestern Anthropological Association. *Member directory.*
Sacramento, California: Southwestern Anthropological Association,
1994/1995.

American Indians

15.53   Bataille, Gretchen M. *Native American women: a biographical
dictionary.* Garland reference library of the social sciences, 649. New
York: Garland, 1993. 333 p. E89.5 .B78 198.

15.54   *Biographical dictionary of Indians of the America.* Newport Beach,
California: American Indian Publishers, 1991. 2 v. E89 .B56 1991.
Biographical sketches of more than 1,000 prominent individuals.

15.55   Brumble, H. David. *American Indian autobiography.* Berkeley:
University of California Press, 1988. 278 p. E89.5 .B78 1988.
French translation: *Les Autobiographies d'indiens d'Amerique*
(Paris: Presses universitaires de France, 1993).

15.56   Brumble, H. David. *An Annotated bibliography of American Indian
and Eskimo autobiographies.* Lincoln: University of Nebraska Press,
1981. 177 p. E89 .B78 1981.

15.57   Juricek, Kay. *Contemporary Native American authors: a biographical
dictionary.* Golden, Colorado: North American Press, 1996.

Oceania

15.58   *Association for Social Anthropology in Oceania. Directory.* Honolulu:
Association for Social Anthropology in Oceania, 1993. 71 p.

15.59   Johnson, Vivien. *Aboriginal artists of the western desert: a
biographical dictionary.* Roseville East, N.S.W.: Craftsman House;
G+B Arts International, 1994. 237 p.

15.60   *Pacific anthropologists.* rev. ed. Honolulu, Pacific Scientific
Information Center, Bernice P. Bishop Museum. 1971. GN20 .P3.
Names arranged alphabetically, with addresses and fields of
interest; indexes by subject interest and residence.

Other

15.61   Duffy, James. *International directory of scholars and specialists in
Third World studies.* Los Angeles: Crossroads Press, 1981. 563 p.
HC59.7 .D783.

General Biographical Sources

There are many other biographical sources for locating established
historical figures in addition to the specialized biographical sources identified
in this chapter. For example, some of the include:

15.62   *Biographical dictionaries master index, 1975-1976.* Dennis La Beau
and Gary C. Tarbert, eds. Detroit: Gale Research, 1975. 3 v. with
supplements. CT213 .B56.

Perhaps the most comprehensive guide to biographical information ever published. Indexes the biographical information in 53 reference works including *Current biography yearbook* (New York: H. W. Wilson, 1940 - . 1/yr), and 28 *Who's who* books with entries for 725,000 persons, with an emphasis on living persons prominent in the United States. Continued coverage by: *Biography and genealogy master index: a consolidated index to more than 3,200,000 biographical sketches in over 350 current and retrospective biographical dictionaries* (Miranda C. Herbert and Barbara McNeil, eds. 2 ed. Detroit: Gale Research, 1980. 8 v.) and *Biography and genealogy master index* (Detroit: Gale Research, 1986 - . 1/yr. with cumulations every five years).

Biography and genealogy master index [computer file]. Detroit: Gale Research, 1993.

15.63   *Biography index: a cumulative index to biographical material in books and magazines.* New York: H.W. Wilson. v. 1 - , 1949 - . 4/yr. with annual cumulations. CT214 .B56.

Published every three years until 1974 when it changed to a quarterly with an annual cumulation; scans 2,200 periodicals and works of collective biography to include biography, critical material of biographical importance, autobiography, correspondence, obituaries, and bibliographies. Some categories are subdivided by nationality. Indexed by surnames and by profession.

15.64   *Historical biographical dictionaries master index: a consolidated index to biographical information concerning historical personages in over 35 of the principal retrospective biographical dictionaries.* Barbara McNeil and Miranda C. Herbert, eds. Detroit: Gale Research, 1980. 1,003 p. CT215 .H57.

Index of entries on historical persons in 42 biographical dictionaries.

15.65   *Directory of American scholars: a biographical directory.* 4 ed. New York; London: R. R. Bowker, 1982. 4 v. LA2311 .D57.

Includes over 35,000 profiles of United States and Canadian scholars active in teaching, research, and publishing. Entries contain primary discipline, vital statistics, education, honorary degrees, current professional position, honors and wards, etc.

15.66   *The National faculty directory.* Detroit: Gale Research. v. 1 - , 1970 - . 1/yr. GN405 .H34.

Information includes name, departmental affiliation, and

institutional addresses for teaching faculty at junior colleges, colleges, and universities in the United States and selected Canadian universities.

16

Directories of Organizations and Associations

The purpose of a directory is to provide accurate identification and addresses of people, organizations, places, and so forth. The directories listed in this chapter provide information on the addresses, personnel, and services of various institutions as well as information on prominent individuals in the arts, humanities, and social sciences. Directories with biographical information on anthropologists, educators, and museum personnel are identified in Chapter 16.

For additional directories of organizations and associations, consult the library catalog under the subject *Associations, Institutions, Etc.,* or the subdivision *Directories.* For example,

> *Anthropology --- Directories*
> *Associations, Institutions, Etc. --- Latin America*
> *Indians of North America --- Directories*

Anthropology

1.61   *Guide: American Anthropological Association.* Washington, D.C.: American Anthropological Association, 1995 - . 1/yr. GN43 .A2 G84.
        Premier information source for the academic study of anthropology in the United States and Canada. The *AAA Guide* 1995-1996 lists hundreds of U.S. and foreign anthropology departments in academic, museum, and research institutions and government. The *Guide* contains details about degrees offered in anthropology; degree requirements; number of students in residence and degrees granted; special sources and facilities; faculty/staff names, degrees, ranks, and fields of specialization; and graduate support available. Also included are statistical tables about degree information for individuals, locations of academic departments listed and highest degree offered in anthropology; levels of enrollment; and number of PhD degrees granted. Recent doctoral dissertations in anthropology are also listed.

16.2   Thomas, William L., and Anna M. Pikelis, eds. *International directory of anthropological institutions.* New York: Wenner-Gren Foundation for Anthropological Research, 1953. 468 p. 301.03 T368.
        Arranged by individual country or groups of countries under geographic division; each section includes a general outline of history

and scope of anthropological research, followed by detailed information on individual institutions; alphabetical indexes of institutions and cities.

Archaeology

16.3   *The Archaeologists' year book.* Park Ridge, New Jersey: Noyes Press. 1973-1977. CC15 .A724.

Directory of museums, universities, associations, and other institutions concerned with archaeology, ethnology, and folklore. Sections are divided as British and international; extensive coverage for societies and institutions in Great Britain.

Linguistics

16.4   *Directory of programs in linguistics in the United States and Canada.* Washington, D.C.: Linguistic Society of America. 1982 - . P57 .U7 D5x

Table of contents lists geographical guide to programs, institutional listing by region, linguistics societies and organizations, and an index of staff and languages taught.

Middle East

16.5   Ljunggren, Florence, ed. *An International directory of institutes and societies interested in the Middle East.* Amsterdam: Djambatan, 1962. 159 p. DS41 .L5.

Lists some 350 societies, institutes, and university departments concerned with research and instruction in the Middle East.

16.6   Tanlak, Acar. *International directory of Islamic cultural institutions.* rev. ed. Istanbul: Research Centre for Islamic History, Art, and Culture, 1989. 234 p. DS35.3 .T36 1989.

North America

16.7   Klein, Barry T., ed. *Reference encyclopedia of the American Indian.* 7 ed. West Nyack, New York: Todd Publications, 1995. 883 p. E76.2 .R43x 1995.

Primarily a directory of government agencies, associations, museums, reservations, etc.; biographical sketches of contemporary Native Americans is found in v. 2, "Who's who"; contains a selective list of magazines and periodicals by and about Native Americans.

16.8   La Potin, Armand S., ed. *Native American voluntary organizations.* New York: Greenwood Press, 1987. 193 p. E75 .N395 1987.

Descriptions of approximately 125 voluntary associations; intended for those who may want an understanding of major developments in Native American-White relations.

16.9   Marquis, Arnold. *A Guide to America's Indians; ceremonials, reservations, and museums.* Norman: University of Oklahoma Press, 1974. 267 p. E76.2 .M37.

Library Collections

16.10   Perry, Paula J., and Bonnie R. Nelson. *Directory of anthropological resources in New York City libraries.* New York: Wenner-Gren Foundation for Anthropological Research, 1979. 64 p.

16.11   Gabrovska, Svobodozarya, Manfred Biskup, and Anna Bossilkova, eds. *European guide to social science information and documentation services.* Oxford; New York: Pergamon Press, 1982. 234 p. H61.9 .G3 1982.
         Directory of 215 institutions and libraries providing social science information services (data or bibliographic) in 22 countries; services are grouped alphabetically under English name by country; subject index.

16.12   *Directory of special libraries and information centers: a guide to special libraries, research libraries, information centers, archives, and data centers maintained by government agencies, business, industry, newspapers, educational institutions, nonprofit organizations, and societies in the fields of science, technology, medicine, law, art, religion, history, social sciences, and humanistic studies.* Lois Lenroot-Ernt, and Brigitte T. Darnay, eds. 8 ed. Detroit: Gale Research Company, 1983. 3 v. Z675.A2 D6115 1983.
         Describes nearly 14,000 institutions in the United States and Canada; includes subject and geographic indexes; v. 1. Directory of special libraries and information centers in the United States and Canada; v. 2. Geographic and personnel indexes; v. 3. New special libraries (a periodic supplement to volume 1).

16.13   *Subject directory of special libraries and information centers.* Detroit: Gale Research, 1975 - . 1/yr. Z675 .A2 S9x.
         Includes address, telephone number, director's name, subject concentration, special services, and special collections for social science and humanities libraries in the United States and Canada; issued in 5 vols.: v. 1, Business and law libraries; v. 2, Education and information science libraries; v. 3, Health sciences libraries; v. 4, Social sciences and humanities libraries; v. 5, Science and technology libraries.

Museum Collections

16.14   Hunter, John E. *Inventory of ethnological collections in museums of the United States and Canada.* 2 ed. Milwaukee: Milwaukee Public Museum, 1967. 120 p.
         Describes collections and research facilities of 52 museums in the United States and Canada; alphabetical arrangement by museum and indexed by culture area; "Prepared ... for the Committee on Anthropological Research in Museums of the American Anthropological Association and the Wenner-Gren Foundation for Anthropological Research."

16.15   *Museums of the world; Museen der Welt.* E. Richter and K. Stimmel,
         eds. 5 ed. München; New York: K.G. Saur, 1995. 672 p. AM1 .M76
         1995.
               Arranged by country, city, and museum, entries include address,
         name of director, and type of museum.

In addition, there are numerous guides to museums and museum collections
throughout the world:

16.16   *Directory of museums in Africa; Repertoire des musees en Afrique.* S.
         Peters, ed. London; New York: Kegan Paul International, 1990. 211 p.
         AM80 .D57 1990.

16.17   Hudson, Kenneth, and Ann Nicholls. *The Cambridge guide to the
         museums of Britain and Ireland.* Cambridge; New York: Cambridge
         University Press, 1987. 435 p. AM41 .H79 1987.

16.18   Hudson, Kenneth, and Ann Nicholls. *The Cambridge guide to the
         museums of Europe.* Cambridge, England; New York: Cambridge
         University Press, 1991. 509 p. AM40 .H83 1991.

16.19   Hudson, Kenneth, and Ann Nicholls. *The Directory of museums.*
         London: Macmillan, 1975. 864 p. AM1 .H8 1975b.

16.20   Hudson, Kenneth, and Ann Nicholls. *The Directory of museums and
         living displays.* 3 ed. New York: Stockton Press, 1985. 1,047 p. AM1
         .H78 1985.

16.21   *Museums in Japan.* Tokyo: Maruzen, 1980. 279 p. AM77 .A2 M87.

16.22   Negri, Massimo, ed. *New museums in Europe, 1977-1993.* Milano:
         Mazzotta, 1994. 348 p. AM40 .H84 1994.

16.23   *The Official directory of Canadian museums and related
         institutions/Repertoire officiel des musees canadiens et institutions
         connexes.* Ottawa: Canadian Museums Association/Association des
         Musees Canadiens. 1984/85- . 1/yr. AM21 .A1 O37.

Grants and Other Funding Opportunities

16.24   *Directory of grants for study and research overseas.* Ocean Grove,
         New Jersey: Overseas Academic Opportunities, 1996 - . 1/yr.
               Provides current information about grant, contract, and fellowship
         support programs available for federal and state governments, private
         foundations, associations, and corporations for research and training.

16.25   *Directory of grants for study and research in the U.S.A.* Merrick, New
         York: Overseas Academic Opportunities, 1996 - . 1/yr.

16.26   *Directory of research grants, 1996.* 20 ed. Phoenix: Oryx Press, 1996.
1,174 p. LB2338 .D57.
Includes a guide to proposal writing by L.E. Miner.

16.27   *The Foundation directory.* 18 ed. M.M. Feczko and E.H. Rich, eds.
New York: Foundation Center, 1996. 2,068 p. AS911 .A2 F65.
Provides information for non-profit, non-governmental granting
foundations arranged geographically, with indexes by field of interest,
personal names, and corporate titles; see also: *User manual and
thesaurus for The Foundation directory and The Foundation grants
index: DIALOG files 26 and 27.* K.J. Neilsen, ed. rev. ed. New York:
Foundation Center, 1995. 158 p.

16.28   *The Foundation grants index 1996: a cumulative listing of foundation
grants reported in 1994.* L.G. Tobiasen, ed. 24 ed. New York:
Foundation Center, 1995. 2,266 p. AS911 .A2 F66.
Provides a cumulated record of grants of $5,000 or more as
reported by the donating foundation; includes four sections: Grants,
listed by state and donating foundation, recipient, amount awarded,
and description of the grant; Donating foundation; Index of recipients;
and Subject categories.

16.29   *Government research directory: a descriptive guide to more than
4,200 U.S. and Canadian government research and development
centers, institutes, laboratories, bureaus, test facilities, experiment
stations, data collection and analysis centers, and grants management
and research coordinating offices in agriculture, commerce,
education, energy, engineering, environment, the humanities,
medicine, military science, and basic and applied sciences.* 9 ed.
Detroit: Gale Research Company, 1996. 1,038 p. Q179.98 .G68.

16.30   *Grants database* [computer file]. Palo Alto: Dialog Information
Services, 1996- . 2/yr.
Covers grants offered by federal, state, and local governments;
commercial organizations; associations; and private foundations. Each
entry includes full description, qualifications, money available, and
renewability. Full name, address, and telephone number for each
sponsoring organization are included when available. Listing includes
current funding programs for research and development activities in
all academic disciplines, as well as social service and performance
programs.

16.31   *The International foundation directory.* H.V. Hodson, ed. 7 ed.
London: Europa, 1996. 817 p. HV7 .I57.
An international directory of foundations, trusts and similar
non-profit institutions, arranged by country with indexes by name of
foundation and activity.

16.32　*National Science Foundation directory of NSF-supported undergraduate faculty enhancement projects.* Washington, D.C.: Directorate for Science and Engineering Education, and Human Resources. 1995 - . 1/yr.

Grants and Other Funding Opportunities --- Anthropology

16.33　Cantrell, Karen, and Denise Wallen, eds. *Funding for anthropological research.* Phoenix, Arizona: Oryx Press, 1986. 308 p. GN42 .C36 1986.

Profiles 704 programs which support research in anthropology. Each profile includes a description of the program; eligibility, fiscal and application information; deadlines; and terms used for the program in the subject index. Includes also a subject index, a list of sponsors by type, an alphabetical list of sponsoring organizations, and a brief annotated bibliography of printed sources and online data useful in the search for funding.

Grants and Other Funding Opportunities --- Museums and Archives

16.34　Wallen, Denise, and Karen Cantrell, eds. *Funding for museums, archives, and special collections.* Phoenix: Oryx Press, 1988. 355 p. AM122 .F86 1988.

Grants and Other Funding Opportunities --- Asia

16.35　Wallen, Denise, and Karen Cantrell, eds. *Funding for research, study, and travel: The People's Republic of China.* Phoenix: Oryx Press, 1987. 230 p. E183.8 .C5 F4x 1987.

Grants and Other Funding Opportunities --- Latin America

16.36　Cantrell, Karen, and Denise Wallen, eds. *Funding for research, study, and travel: Latin America and the Caribbean.* Phoenix: Oryx Press, 1987. 301 p. F1409.95 .U6 C36 1987.

Profiles 393 sponsors, organizations, foundations, government agencies, institutes, cultural institutions, professional associations, and foreign sources; arranged alphabetically by sponsor. Information provided includes addresses, telephone numbers, project description, samples of previously funded projects, eligibility/limitations, fiscal and application information, and deadlines. Excellent starting point in search for funding.

Grants and Other Funding Opportunities in the Social Sciences

16.37　*Directory of European associations; Repertoire des associations europeennes; Handbuch der europaischen Verbande.* 3 ed. Beckenham, England: CBD Research Ltd., 1984. 331 p. F1409.95 .U6 C36 1984.

Provides information on national and regional associations in all fields of activity in all European countries; indexes in English, French, and German.

16.38   *Encyclopedia of associations: a guide to over 23,000 national and international organizations.* 31 ed. Detroit: Gale, 1996. 4,104 p. AS22 E56.
Originally comprised of national, non-profit membership organizations, the encyclopedia now lists some profit groups, non-membership organizations, local and regional groups, projects, political action committees and programs, inactive and defunct organizations, and some organizations which can no longer be located. Entries include title, address, telephone number, president, founding date, number of members, organizational; objectives, publications, conventions, etc.

16.39   *International directory of social science research councils and analogous bodies; Conference of Social Science Councils and analogous bodies.* New York: K. G. Saur, 1978/79 - . 1/yr. H62 .A1 C58a.
Compiled by the International Federation of Social Science Organizations, contains entries from 40 national and ten regional and international organizations, with information on history, structure, revenue and expenditures, grants, international cooperative programs, and publications.

16.40   *International organizations and ethnic conflict.* Milton J. Esman, Shibley Telhami, eds. Ithaca, New York: Cornell University Press, 1995. 343 p. JX4481 .I5545 1995.

16.41   *International organizations in the social sciences: a summary description of the structure and activities of non-governmental organizations in consultative relationship with Unesco and specialized in the social sciences.* J. Meynaud, ed. rev. ed. Westport, Connecticut: Greenwood Press, 1982. 145 p.
Inclusion limited to organizations with consultative relationships with the United Nations Educational, Social, and Cultural Organization (UNESCO).

16.42   *World directory of social science institutions: research, advanced training, professional bodies; Repertoire mondial des institutions de sciences sociales: recherche, formation superieure, organismes professionnels; Repertorio mundial de instituciones de ciencias sociales: investigacion, capacitacion superior, organismos profesionales.* 5 ed. Paris: UNESCO, 1990. 1,211 p. H62 .U4755x 1990.
Provides English, French, and Spanish descriptions for more than 2,000 international organizations; arranged by country; indexed by name and subject.

17

Government Documents

Most academic libraries will have a collection of local, state, national, and international documents, as well as indexes and guides for their use. Governments are among the most prolific publishers in the world and, in some nations, they comprise the major source of anthropological publishing. They issue not only books and reports, but also pamphlets, leaflets, guides, manuals, dictionaries, catalogs, maps, charts, translations, abstracts, monographs, bibliographies, and so forth. In all cases, you can expect from government publications data on social, economic, political, and demographic characteristics of the population, plus information on laws, judicial procedures, land use, health, education, and other topics.

Government publications offer a range of data, either 'raw' or analyzed. Such publications are usually widely available, at least within the major libraries of the nations issuing them. In the United States, for example, excellent collections of federal documents are found in depository libraries, those automatically receiving publications in selected categories. Some libraries have essentially complete holdings from the time they were designated as depositories, while others receive more limited materials. Libraries which need to publish governmental publications are likely to have smaller holdings. You should learn the extent to which the libraries used hold documents from international as well as various national, state or provincial, and local governments.

Government documents are generally more difficult to locate than other published material, not only because of their quality but also because of the ways in which they are classified by libraries. Many libraries do not use the Dewey Decimal or Library of Congress classification systems for government documents. Thus you will need to be familiar with the procedures used locally in classifying and storing such publications.

The Superintendent of Documents classification scheme has been in use since the late nineteenth century and is the system by which most United States government publications are organized. The Superintendent of Documents (SuDocs) number groups publications according to governmental agency, subordinate agency, and series, and not by subject. Thus, publications of the Department of the Interior begin with the letter I. The Bureau of Land Management within the Department of the Interior has the class I53, and the

Cultural Resources Series within the Bureau of Land Management has a SuDocs number beginning with I53.22. SuDocs numbers can usually be distinguished from Library of Congress or Dewey Decimal classification numbers by a colon which separates the class number from the book number.

International Governmental Organizations

The primary international organization today is the United Nations. United Nations publications are issued by its different organs, such as the Security Council, General Assembly, Economic and Social Council, the Trusteeship Council, and the Economic Commission for Africa, as well as more specialized agencies. Among the latter, the ones of greatest interest to anthropologists include the Food and Agricultural Organization (FAO), International Labor Organization (ILO), World Health Organization (WHO), International Bank for Reconstruction and Development, and the United Nations Educational, Social, and Cultural Organization (UNESCO). UNESCO, in particular, issues many publications dealing with race relations, women, conflict, fertility, migration, refugees, literacy, and other topics of interest to anthropologists.

There are numerous international bodies other than the United Nations which issue valuable information.. Most important of these for anthropologists are probably the Organization of American States (Pan American Union) and the South Pacific Commission, although such organizations as the International Committee for European Migration and the Organization for Economic Cooperation and Development may have relevant data. The classification schemes used both by these agencies and the receiving libraries are not standardized, and you may need the assistance of a reference librarian to locate material.

National and Other Governments

The multitude of publications by more than one hundred national governments provides a vast range of resources on many topics, not the least of which are anthropological. As with United Nations publications, special classification schemes are often used and, in many cases, assistance from librarians will be needed to start using these resources.

If you are working on research within other nations you should consult the appropriate governmental publication lists. You will often find that publications by or for overseas territories and possessions are entered in the library catalog under the name of the metropolitan or mother nation. In addition to the publications of national governments, others are issued by provincial, state, city, and smaller political units. Sometimes important anthropological data will be found in reports from commissions or administrative departments of cities, as in the case of Native affairs in Australia or South Africa, or social and political movements in India, Melanesia, and Mexico.

Many publications and proceedings of both houses of Congress, the United States Department of the Interior, the Smithsonian Institution, and so forth, are of potential interest to anthropologists and should not be overlooked. These publications may not be represented in the library catalog. Access to them is through the *Monthly catalog of United States government publications* and the *Congressional Information Service* (CIS).

The following books can be used to identify United States government agencies and their various activities.

17.1   *Federal regulatory directory.* Washington, D.C. 1979/80 - . 1/yr. KF5406 .A15.
A useful guide to regulatory agencies with a good subject index to agencies.

17.2   *Guide to U.S. government publications.* J.L. Andriot, ed. McClean, Virginia. 1973-1989. Z1223 .Z7 A574.
One of the most useful guides for identifying agencies and all of their major series, with cross references and historical notes. Entries are arranged according to SuDocs number. Indexes by agency name and series title provide quick access, and an Agency Class Chronology is useful for tracing changes in SuDocs numbers as agency organization has changed.

17.3   *United States government manual.* Washington, D.C. 1973/1974 - . 1/yr. JK421 .A3; AE2.108/2.
A basic guide to government agencies found in almost every library.

There are several excellent books that can be used as introductions and guides to publications issued by the government:

17.4   Morehead, Joe. *Introduction to U.S. public documents.* 3 ed. Littleton, Colorado: Libraries Unlimited, 1983. 309 p. Z1223 .Z7 M67 1983.
Introduction to the basic sources and structure of information contained in Federal government publications; includes sections on categories of documents and reports.

17.5   Robinson, Judith S. *Subject guide to U.S. government reference sources.* Littleton, Colorado: Libraries Unlimited, 1985. 333 p. J83 .R6 1985.
Sections deal with guides and general reference works, bibliographies of government publications, and biographical sources; includes also a subject guide to reference works.

17.6   Robinson, Judith S. *Tapping the government grapevine: the user-friendly guide to U.S. government information sources.* Phoenix: Oryx, 1988. 193 p. Z1223 .Z7 R633 1988.

17.7   Sears, Jean L., and Marilyn K. Moody. Using *government publications.* Phoenix: Oryx, 1985-1986. 2 v. Z1223 .Z7 S439 1985.

The first volume, *Searching by subjects and agencies,* gives an overview of a search strategy and of Federal documents in general; sources are listed for 20 subject areas and for agencies which implement various governmental regulations, programs, and grants. The second volume, *Finding statistics and using special techniques,* also includes a checklist of pertinent sources and a description of covered sources.

Indexes to Government Publications

17.8   United States Superintendent of Documents. *Monthly catalog of United States government publications.* Washington, D.C. 1895 - . 12/yr. J85 .GP3.
    The official list of government publications since 1895, gives the current publications issued by all branches of the federal government. Listed by issuing agency with full title, date of publication, pagination, and Superintendent of Documents classification number. Currently cumulative annual indexes include author, title, subject, title key-word, and series number.

Cumulative indexes to the *Monthly catalog of United States government publications* include the following:

17.9   *Cumulative subject index to the Monthly Catalog of United States Government Publications, 1900-1971.* W.W. Buchanan and E.M. Kanely, eds. Washington, D.C.: Carrollton Press, 1973-1975. 15 v. Z1223 .Z9 B83.
    Contains references to more than 800,000 publications through alphabetically arranged subject headings; the user is referred to the year and entry number (before 1947, the page number) in the *Monthly catalog of United States government publications;* continues: *Cumulative subject index to the Monthly Catalog of United States government publications, 1865-1899* (E.A. Kanely, ed. Washington, D.C.: Carrollton Press, 1977).

17.10   *Cumulative subject guide to U.S. government bibliographies, 1924-1973.* E.M. Kanely, ed. Arlington, Virginia: Carrollton Press, 1976-1977. 7 v. J83 .K36 1976.
    Bibliographies cited are both separate publications and those appended to other publications; arranged alphabetically by subject with subdivisions.

17.11   *Cumulative title index to United States public documents, 1789-1976.* D.W. Lester, S.K. Faull, and L.E. Lester, eds. Arlington, Virginia: United States Historical Documents Institute, 1979-1982. 16 v. Z1223 .Z7 L47.
    Useful index for finding documents for which the title is known.

Statistical Sources

17.12   United States Department of Commerce. Bureau of the Census. *Historical statistics of the United States: colonial times to 1970.* Washington, D.C.: Government Printing Office, 1975. 2 v. HA202 .B87 1975.
    Provides national statistics since colonial times; introductory paragraphs to individual tables provide explanations of terms.

17.13   United States Department of Commerce. Bureau of the Census. *Statistical abstract of the United States.* Washington, D.C.: Government Printing Office, 1878 - . 1/yr. HA202 .S73 1988.
    Published annually since 1878, this is the standard summary of statistics on the social, political, and economic organization of the United States. A subject index refers to numerous tables and pertinent additional sources of statistics.

Africa

17.14   Witherell, Julian W. *The United States and Africa: guide to U.S. official documents and government-sponsored publications on Africa, 1785-1975.* Washington, D.C.: Library of Congress, 1978. DT3 .W47 1978.
    Partially annotated bibliography of selected publications of the United States government pertaining to Africa.

17.15   Witherell, Julian W. *The United States and sub-Saharan Africa: guide to U.S. official documents and government-sponsored publications on Africa, 1976-1980.* Washington, D.C.: Library of Congress, 1984. DT3 .W57 1984.

North America

17.16   Bonnerjea, Biren. *Index to Bulletins 1-100, with index to contributions to North American ethnology, introductions, and miscellaneous publications.* United States Bureau of American Ethnology, Bulletin 178. Washington, D.C.: Government Printing Office, 1963. 726 p. E51 .U6 no. 178.

17.17   Bonnerjea, Biren. *General index to the annual reports of the Bureau of American Ethnology, v. 1-48 (1879-1931).* United States Bureau of American Ethnology, Annual Report 48. Washington, D.C.: Government Printing Office, 1933. 1,220 p.; Washington, D.C.: Carrollton Press, 1973. E51 .U552 B6.

17.18   Bonnerjea, Biren. *List of publications of the Bureau of American Ethnology, with index to authors and titles.* United States Bureau of American Ethnology, Bulletin 200. Washington, D.C.: Government Printing Office, 1971. 134 p. E77 .S55 1971.

17.19   Johnson, Steven L. *Guide to American Indian documents in the Congressional Serial Set, 1817-1899.* New York: Clearwater, 1977. 503 p. KF8201 .A1 J63.

Lists approximately 10,650 documents relating to Indian affairs; chronological section lists items sequentially, giving time and date, citation to the Serial Set, and brief description of the document; subject index, organized mainly by tribal headings.

17.20   Miller, Mamie R.T. *An author, title, and subject check-list of Smithsonian Institution publications to anthropology.* Albuquerque: University of New Mexico Press, 1946. 218 p. GN25 .M55 1946.

Useful guide to early anthropological publications from the Smithsonian Institution.

18

Atlases and Maps

Atlases are simply collections of maps. While it is generally recognized that atlases are essential for many of the social sciences, it is clear that atlases are valuable reference sources for anthropological research because of the descriptive material they contain. There are many sources of maps. Most general encyclopedias include maps either in a separate volume or as illustrative material within the text. Introductory textbooks, archaeological and ethnographic field reports, and other kinds of anthropological publishing contain detailed maps as well.

Atlases and maps are basic to anthropological research in that they depict locations and patterns of features on the surface of the earth. The recorded features may be physical, such as the distribution of land and water, types of landforms or climatic regions, isolines of temperature or precipitation, types of natural vegetation or soil, or combinations of natural resources. The features may be the result of human activity, as political or administrative boundaries, population, cities, roads, languages, religion, or ratios such as density of population.

Included in this chapter are sources of information for atlases and maps. The titles listed are those of current reference and research value to anthropology students, and no attempt is made to include comprehensively the many bibliographies for maps.

For additional atlases and cartographic materials, consult the library catalog under the appropriate subject with the subdivision *Maps*. For example,

Anthropology --- Maps
Latin America --- Maps
Indians of North America --- Maps

Thematic Atlases
Archaeology

18.1   Hawkes, Jacquetta H., ed. *Atlas of ancient archaeology*. New York: McGraw-Hill. 1977. 272 p. GN739 .H38 1977.
More than 170 archaeological sites are profiled with brief descriptions; arranged by area, text is accompanied by 350 maps, plans, and line drawings.

18.2   Hawkes, Jacquetta, and David Trump. 1976. *The Atlas of early man.*
        New York: St. Martin's Press, 1976. 255 p. CB311 .H35.
        Dated but useful guide to sites of evidence of early human beings;
        maps illustrate the locations of archaeological sites.

18.3   *Past worlds: The Times atlas of archaeology.* Maplewood, New Jersey:
        Hammond, 1988. 319 p. G1046 .E15 P3 1988.

18.4   Whitehouse, David, and Ruth Whitehouse. *Archaeological atlas of the
        world.* San Francisco: W. H. Freeman, 1975. 272 p. G1046 .E15 W5.
        Includes 103 maps that provide an excellent synthesis of
        archaeological knowledge for some 5,000 archaeological sites.

18.5   Wood, Michael. *The World atlas of archaeology.* Boston: G.K. Hall,
        1985. 423 p. G1046 .E15 W6 1985.
        Archaeological illustrations, photographs, and maps provides
        coverage for major regions and periods, summaries of archaeological
        syntheses, and a discussion of developments in dating and remote
        sensing techniques.

Biological/Physical Anthropology

18.6   Brace, C. Loring, Harry Nelson, and Noel Korn. *Atlas of human
        evolution.* 2 ed. New York: Holt, Rinehart and Winston, 1979. 178 p.
        GN282 .B7.

Cultural/Social Anthropology

18.7   *The Atlas of mankind.* Chicago: Rand McNally, 1982. 191, 15 p.
        GN378 .A84.
        World maps, diagrams, and photographs provide background for a
        range of topics, such as language, food production, kinship, etc. Each
        topic is cross-referenced to ethnographic groups described in "Peoples
        of the world" (pp. 56-91). Some ethnographic groups are described in
        summary essays.

18.8   Gaisford, John, ed. *Atlas of man.* London: M. Cavendish Editions,
        1978. 272 p. GN378 .A84 1978.
        First part briefly traces human cultural development from
        prehistoric times to the present. part 2, the atlas section, is divided into
        nine geographic regions and subdivided into countries and cultural
        groups. maps indicate languages, religions, land use, population, and
        colonial roots.

18.9   McEvedy, Colin, and Richard Jones. *Atlas of world population history.*
        Harmondsworth; New York: Penguin, 1978. 368 p.
        Estimates of population for continents, major regions, and
        individual countries at various time intervals from 400BC to 1975;
        projections to the year 2000.

18.10   Murdock, George P. *Atlas of world cultures.* Pittsburgh: University of Pittsburgh Press, 1981. 151 p. GN345.3 M86 1981.

18.11   Price, David H. *Atlas of world cultures: a geographical guide to ethnographic literature.* Newbury Park, California: Sage, 1989. 156 p. G1046 .E1 P7 1989.

18.12   Spencer, Robert F., and Elden Johnson. *Atlas for anthropology.* 2 ed. Dubuque, Iowa: W. C. Brown, 1968. 61 leaves. G1046 .E1 S7 1968.
         Includes maps of culture areas, language families, and tribal groups in North America, South America, Africa, Eurasia, and Oceania, maps of Old and New World archaeology and prehistory, and a map illustrating global racial distribution. Intended for beginning students.

Regional Atlases
Africa --- Archaeology
18.13   Clark, J. Desmond, comp. *Atlas of African prehistory.* Chicago: University of Chicago Press, 1967. 62 p. G2446 .E1 C5 1967.
         Maps on transparent overlays; scale of maps 1:20,000,000 and 1:38,000,000.

Africa --- Cultural/Social Anthropology
18.14   Ajayi, J.F. Ade, and Michael Crowder. *Historical atlas of Africa.* Cambridge; New York: Cambridge University Press, 1985. 165 p. G2446 .S1 H5 1985.
         Contains more than 300 multicolored maps in 72 sets, each accompanied by explanatory text on the facing page. Maps are of three types: event maps with information on historical places and events; process maps displaying historical processes, or quantitative maps.

18.15   Davies, Harold R. J. *Tropical Africa: an atlas for rural development.* Cardiff: University of Wales Press, 1973. 81 p. 912.6 D287.
         Includes some 40 maps covering physical background, traditional life, and modernization of Africa from the Sahara to the southern margin of the Zaire basin.

18.16   Fage, J. D. *An Atlas of African history.* 2 ed. New York: Africana Publishing Company, 1978. 84 p. G2446 .S1 F3 1978.
         The pioneering historical atlas of Africa now replaced by Ajayi and Crowder's *Historical atlas of Africa.*

18.17   Goldthorpe, J. E., and F. B. Wilson. *Tribal maps of East Africa and Zanzibar.* Kampala, Uganda: East African Institute of Social Research, 1960. 14 p. 912.676 G58.
         Includes eight ethnographic maps for East Africa.

18.18   Murray, Jocelyn, ed. *Cultural atlas of Africa.* New York: Facts on File, 1981. 240 p. DT14 M84.
Includes maps and overviews of topics such as languages, religion, urbanization, vernacular architecture, arts, music, etc.

Asia --- Cultural/Social Anthropology

18.19   *Asia today: an atlas of reproducible pages.* rev. ed. Wellesley, Massachusetts: World Eagle, 1991. 156 p. G2200 .W6 1991.

18.20   Davison, Julian, and Tan Lay Kee. *Mapping the continent of Asia.* Singapore: Antiques of the Orient, 1994. 88 p. GA1081 .A58x 1994.

Asia --- Cultural/Social Anthropology --- Central Asia

18.21   Zhdanko, T.A. *Materialy k istoriko-etnograficheskomu atlasu Srednei Azii i Kazakhstana.* Trudy Instituta etnografii im. N.N. Miklukho-Maklaia, Novaia seriia, 48. Moskva: Izd-vo Akademii nauk SSSR, 1961. 197 p. 301.06 Ak127.
Series of ethnographic maps for Central Asia and Kazakh S.S.R.

Asia --- Cultural/Social Anthropology --- East Asia

18.22   Blunden, Caroline, and Mark Elvin. *Cultural atlas of China.* New York: Facts on File, 1983. 237 p. DS721 .B56 1983.
Historical atlas of maps, photographs, and text treats Chinese cultural perspective from three perspectives: space, time, and symbols and society.

18.23   Collcutt, Martin, Marius Jansen, and Isao Kumakura. *Cultural atlas of Japan.* New York: Facts on File, 1988. 240 p. DS821 .C62 1988.

Asia --- Cultural/Social Anthropology --- Philippines

18.24   Conklin, Harold C. *Ethnographic atlas of Ifugao: a study of environment, culture, and society in Northern Luzon.* New Haven: Yale University Press, 1980. 116 p. 912.914 C761.
Includes a series of ethnological and agricultural maps of northern Luzon, Phillippines.

Asia --- Cultural/Social Anthropology --- South Asia

18.25   Breton, Roland J. L. *Atlas geographique des langues et des ethnies de l'Inde et du subcontinent: Bangladesh, Pakistan, Sri Lanka, Nepal, Bhoutan, Sikkim.* Quebec: Presses de l'Universite Laval, 1976. 648 p. PK1541 .A1 1976.

18.26   Mathur, U.B., comp. *Ethnographic atlas of Rajasthan; with reference to scheduled castes and scheduled tribes.* Delhi: Superintendent of

Census Operations, Rajasthan Statistical Service, 1969. 138 p. G2283 .R2 I15 1969.

18.27   Schwartzberg, Joseph E., ed. *A Historical atlas of South Asia*. 2 ed. New York; Oxford: Oxford University Press, 1992. 376 p. G2261 .S1 H5 1992.
         Provides comprehensive cartographic coverage for the history of South Asia (Afghanistan, Bangladesh, Bhutan, India, Nepal, Pakistan, Sri Lanka, and the Maldives) from the Palaeolithic period to the present.

18.28   Singh, K. Suresh. *An Anthropological atlas: ecology and cultural traits, languages and linguistic traits, demographic and biological traits*. Delhi: Anthropological Survey of India; New York: Oxford University Press, 1993. 156 p. GN635 .I4 S55x 1993.

Asia --- Linguistics
18.29   Wurm, S.A. *Language atlas of China*. Hong Kong: Longman Group, 1988. 1 case (33 unbound plates). PL1033 .L365x 1988.

Europe --- Archaeology
18.30   Finley, M.I., ed. *Atlas of Classical Archaeology*. New York: McGraw-Hill, 1977. 256 p. G1046.E15 A8 1977.

18.31   Wills, L. J., *A Palaeogeographical atlas of the British Isles and adjacent parts of Europe*. London, Blackie, 1951. 63 p. 554.2 W685.

18.32   *Europe today: an atlas of reproducible pages*. rev. ed. Wellesley, Massachusetts: World Eagle, 1990. 156 p. G1797.2 .W6 1990.

Europe --- Cultural/Social Anthropology
18.33   Ardagh, John, and Colin Jones. *Cultural atlas of France*. New York: Facts on File, 1991. 240 p. G1844.21 .E64 A7 1991.

18.34   Milner-Gulland, Robin R., and Nikolai J. Dejevsky. *Cultural atlas of Russia and the Soviet Union*. New York: Facts on File, 1989. 240 p. DK32 .M62 1989.

Latin America --- Archaeology
18.35   Coe, Michael D., Dean R. Snow, and Elizabeth Benson. *Atlas of Ancient America*. New York: Facts on File, 1986. 240 p. E61 .C66 1986.

Latin America --- Cultural/Social Anthropology
18.36   Lombardi, Cathryn L., and John V. Lombardi. *Latin American history, a teaching atlas.* Madison: Conference on Latin American History, University of Wisconsin Press, 1983. 104, 40 p. G1541 .S1 L6 1983.

18.37   Schneider, Ronald M. *An Atlas of Latin American affairs.* New York: Praeger, 1965; London, Methuen, 1966.. 136 p. G1540 .S3 1966.

Middle East --- Archaeology
18.38   Baines, John, and Jaromir Malek. *Atlas of ancient Egypt.* Oxford: Phaidon, 1980. 240 p. DT56.9 .B34..

18.39   Nebenzahl, Kenneth. *Maps of the Holy Lands: images of Terra Sancta through two millenia.* New York: Abbeville Press, 1986. 164 p. G2230 .N33 1986.

18.40   Roaf, Michael. *Cultural atlas of Mesopotamia and the ancient Near East.* New York: Facts on File, 1990. 238 p. DS69.5 .R63 1990.

Middle East --- Cultural/Social Anthropology
18.41   Al-Faruqi, Isma'il R., and Lois Lamya' al Faruqi. *Cultural atlas of Islam.* New York: Macmillan, 1986. 512 p. DS36.85 .A39 1986.

18.42   Brice, William C., ed. *An Historical atlas of Islam.* Leiden: Brill, 1981. 71 p. G1786 .S1 H1 1981.
General and regional maps provide a graphic view of the Islamic world from the rise of Islam to the beginning of World War I.

18.43   Dempsey, Michael W., and Norman Barrett. *Atlas of the Arab world.* New York: Facts on File, 1983. 62 leaves. DS36.7 .D45 1983.
Includes historical maps illustrating the rise and expansion of Islam as well as current factual statistical information, such as population distribution, literacy rates, etc.

18.44   *Hammond atlas of the Middle East.* Maplewood, New Jersey: Hammond, 1991. 48 p. G7420 .H35x 1991.

18.45   Robinson, Francis. *Atlas of the Islamic World since 1500.* New York: Facts On File, 1982. 238 p. DS35.6 .R6 1982.
Collection of maps outlining the development of Islam and essays on religion and culture.

North America --- Cultural/Social Anthropology
18.46   Clark, David S. *Index to maps of the French and Indian War in books and periodicals, illustrating the background of the conflict, British*

and French military operations in North America, the Cherokee War, the Havana Campaign and post-war boundaries. Fayetteville, North Carolina, 1974. 118 p. GA473.6 C53x 1974.

18.47   Ferguson, T. J., and E. Richard Hart. *A Zuni atlas.* Norman: University of Oklahoma Press, 1985. 154 p. G1496 .E1 F4 1985.
Includes 44 maps based on material; and data presented as evidence on behalf of the Zuni in a land claims case.

18.48   Fritsch, Albert J. *Ethnic atlas of the United States.* New York: Facts on File, 1989. 176 p.

18.49   Goodman, James M. *The Navajo atlas: environments, resources, people, and history of the Dine Bikeyah.* Norman: University of Oklahoma Press, 1982. 109 p. G1497 .N3 G6 1982.
Graphic representation of Navajo resources, demography, history, and political organization; each map is accompanied by informative background text.

18.50   Martin, James C., and Robert S. Martin. *Maps of Texas and the Southwest, 1513-1900.* Albuquerque: Amon Carter Museum; University of New Mexico Press, 1984. 174 p. G1370 .M3 1984.

18.51   Prucha, Francis P. *Atlas of American Indian affairs.* Lincoln: University of Nebraska Press, 1990. 191 p. G1201 .E1 P7 1990.

18.52   Spink, John, and D.W. Moodie. *Eskimo maps from the Canadian eastern Arctic.* Toronto: B. V. Gutsell, 1972. 98 p.

18.53   Tanner, Helen H. *Atlas of Great Lakes Indian history.* Norman: Newberry Library; University of Oklahoma Press, 1987. 224 p. E78 .G7 A87 1987.
Includes 33 maps accompanied by explanatory text covering the period 1640-1871.

18.54   Tanner, Helen H. *The Settling of North America: the atlas of the great migrations into North America from the Ice Age to the present.* New York: Macmillan, 1995. G1106 .E27 S4 1995.

18.55   Waldman, Carl. *Atlas of the North American Indian.* New York: Facts on File, 1985. 276 p. E77 .W195 1985.
Combines maps, illustrations, and extensive text top provide an excellent introduction to seven broad topics: Ancient Indians, Ancient Civilization, Indian lifeways, Indians and explorers, Indian wars, Indian land cessions, and Contemporary Indians; includes lists of

tribal groups, reservations, place names, museums, and archaeological sites.

18.56   Wexler, Alan. *Atlas of westward expansion.* New York: Facts On File, 1995. 240 p. G1201 .S1 W44 1995.

North America --- Linguistics

18.57   Voegelin, Charles F., and Erminie Wheeler-Voegelin. *Map of North American Indian languages.* Publications of the American Ethnological Society v. 20. New York: J. J.Augustin, 1944. 97x90 cm. 301.06 Am3p no.20.

Oceania --- Cultural/Social Anthropology

18.58   Perry, T. M. *The Discovery of Australia: the charts and maps of the navigators and explorers.* Melbourne, Australia: Nelson, 1982. 159 p. G2751.S12 P4 1982.

18.59   Clancy, Robert. *The Mapping of Terra Australis.* Macquarie Park, Australia: Universal Press, 1995. 192 p. GA1681 .C63 1995.

Oceania --- Linguistics

18.60   Wurm, S.A., and Shiro Hattorti, eds. *Language atlas of the Pacific area.* Canberra: Australian Academy of the Humanities; Japan Academy; Stuttgart, Germany: GeoCenter, 1981-1983. 1 atlas (73 leaves in case). G2861 .E3 L28.
Provides maps showing the distribution of languages, with explanatory notes and indexes; includes Part 1: New Guinea area, Oceania, Australia (maps 1-24) and Part 2: Japan area, Phillippines and Formosa, mainland and insular southeast Asia (maps 25-47).

Guides to Map Collections

18.61   American Geographical Society of New York. Map Department. *Index to maps in books and periodicals.* Boston, G. K. Hall, 1968. 10 v.; *First supplement,* 1971. 603 p.; *Second supplement,* 1976; *Third supplement,* 1987. 016.912 Am35.
An important bibliography of maps published in books and periodicals; entries are arranged chronologically by subject and regional divisions.

18.62   California. University. Bancroft Library. *Index to printed maps.* Boston: G. K. Hall, 1964. 521 p. 016.912 C128.
Continued by: *Catalog of manuscript and printed maps in the Bancroft Library: a supplement to Index to printed maps, University of California, Berkeley* (Boston: G.K. Hall, 1975. 581 p.).

18.63   Kelsay, Laura E., comp. *Cartographic records of the Bureau of Indian Affairs.* Washington, D.C.: National Archives and Records Service, General Services Administration, 1977. 187 p. GA195.W37 U6x 1977.

18.64   New York (City). Public Library. Map Division. *Dictionary catalog of the Map Division.* Boston, G. K. Hall, 1971. 10 v. 016.912 N42.
         Includes some 280,000 sheep maps and 6,000 atlases in the Map Division of the New York Public Library. "In addition [to entries for the Map Division] the catalog contains entries for manuscript maps in the Manuscript Division, early printed maps in the Rare Book Division, and the Phelps Stokes American Historical views in the Prints Division." Continued by: *Bibliographic guide to maps and atlases* (Boston: G. K. Hall, 1979 - . 1/yr.).

19

Theses and Dissertations

Doctoral dissertations and master's theses form a special class of library research material, and catalogs of dissertations and theses, both American and foreign, assume importance in university, reference, or special libraries. The value of a dissertation or thesis is considerable because they will usually consider some aspect of a subject not previously treated.

While some dissertations are issued by commercial publishers, and some may be privately printed, most are available only in typewritten form or on microfilm. Most dissertations are submitted in manuscript and are available, or interlibrary loan or for purchase, either on microfilm or in xerox. Many of these may be purchased from Xerox University Microfilms (300 North Zeeb Road, Ann Arbor, Michigan 48106-1346) but in some cases it is necessary to write directly to the university where the dissertation was written.

Doctoral dissertations in anthropology are listed annually in the *Guide to departments of anthropology,* published by the American Anthropological Association. For additional published catalogs of theses and dissertations, consult the library catalog under the appropriate subject with the subdivision *Bibliography.* For example,

> *Anthropology --- Bibliography*
> *Latin America --- Bibliography*
> *Indians of North America --- Bibliography*
> *Dissertations, Academic --- United States*

Guides to Thesis and Dissertation Writing

Style manuals are used to answer questions about grammar, usage, and correct form for footnotes and entries in reference lists. The manuals listed here contain formats which are often required by publications in anthropology and related fields. The form and style used in American anthropologist is sometimes required by anthropological publications and by professors in their courses. The style requirements for this publication may be found by examining recent issues.

19.1   Ernst, Mary O. *A Guide through the dissertation process.* New York: E. Mellen Press, 1981. 45 p. 808.02 Om15.

19.2   Slade, Carole, William G. Campbell, and Stephen V. Ballou. *Form and style: research papers, reports, theses.* 9 ed. Boston: Houghton Mifflin, 1994. 250 p. LB2369 .C3 1994.

19.3   Turabian, Kate L., John Grossman and Alice Bennett. *A Manual for writers of term papers, theses, and dissertations.* 6 ed. Chicago: University of Chicago Press, 1996. 308 p. LB2369 .T8 1996.
        The standard work for thesis and dissertation writing.

Guides to Theses and Dissertations

19.4   Reynolds, Michael M. *Guide to theses and dissertations: an international bibliography of bibliographies.* rev. ed. Phoenix: Oryx Press, 1985. 263 p. Z5053.A1 R49 1985.
        Lists bibliographies of these and dissertations produced through 1984; entries are arranged by broad subject area and indexed by name, title, and institution.

Theses

19.5   *Masters abstracts international.* Ann Arbor: University Microfilms International, 1986- , v.24 - . 6/yr. Z5055 .U49 M3.
        Lists theses accepted by participating institutions; arranged by broad subject subjects with author and subject indexes, cumulated annually. Full text copies of any thesis listed with an order number can be ordered from University Microfilms. Continues: *Masters abstracts* (Ann Arbor: University Microfilms International. v. 1-23; 1962-1985. 4/yr.).

19.6   *Master's theses directories: arts and social sciences.* Cedar Falls, Iowa: Master's Theses Directories, no. 15 - , 1991 - . 1/yr. LB2385 .M375x.
        An annual listing of theses in 36 subject categories in the arts and social sciences reported by United States and Canadian graduate schools. Continues: *Master's theses in the arts and social sciences* (Cedar Falls, Iowa: Research Publication. no. 1-14, 1976-1990).

Dissertations

19.7   *American doctoral dissertations.* Ann Arbor: University Microfilms. 1965 - . 1/yr. Z5055 .U49 A62.
        Annual listing of dissertations accepted by United States and Canadian institutions; lists both dissertations available from University Microfilms International and those which must be purchased or borrowed from the granting institution. Arranged by broad subject areas which are subdivided by institution.

19.8   *Comprehensive dissertation index, 1861-1972.* Ann Arbor: Xerox University Microfilms, 1973. 37 v. Z5053 .C6x.

Serves as a cumulated index for *Dissertation abstracts international*. It indexes more than 417,000 dissertations awarded by United States and other universities between 1861 and 1972. Includes: v. 1-4. Chemistry; v. 5. Mathematics and statistics; v. 6. Astronomy and physics, A-L; v. 7. Physics, M-Z; v. 8. Engineering: general and aeronautical; v. 9. Engineering: chemical, mechanical, and metallurgical; v. 10. Engineering: civil, electrical, and industrial; v. 11. Biological sciences: biology and zoology; v. 12. Biological sciences: anatomy, physiology, and genetics; v. 13. Biological sciences: botany, microbiology, and bacteriology; v. 14. Health and environmental sciences; v. 15. Agriculture; v. 16. Geography and geology; v. 17. Social sciences [including anthropology]; v. 18-19. Psychology; v. 20-24. Education; v. 25-26. Business and economics; v. 27. Law and political science; v. 28. History; v. 29-30. Language and literature; v. 31. Communications and the arts; v. 32. Philosophy and religion; v.33-37. Author index. Continued by: *Comprehensive dissertation index: five-year cumulation, 1973-1977* (Ann Arbor: University Microfilms International, 1979. 19 v.), *Comprehensive dissertation index. Five-year cumulation, 1973-1982* (Ann Arbor: University Microfilms International, 1984. 38 v.), *Comprehensive dissertation index. Five-year cumulation, 1983-1987* (Ann Arbor: University Microfilms International, 1989. 22 v.).

19.9   *Dissertation abstracts ondisc* [computer file]. Ann Arbor: University Microfilms International, 1986 - . 4/yr. CD-ROM Z5053 .D573x.
        Accompanied by archival laser optical disks (1861-June 1980, July 1980-Dec. 1984, Jan. 1985-Dec. 1988, Jan. 1989-Dec. 1990); irregularly issued computer magnetic disks (3 1/2 in. and 5 1/4in.) which contain the search software. Print counterpart: *Dissertation abstracts international*. Consists of bibliographic citations and abstracts as they appear in *Dissertation abstracts international*. Archival disk for 1861-June 1980 contains bibliographic citations only.

19.10   *Dissertation abstracts international*. Ann Arbor: University Microfilms International. v.30 - , 1969 - . 12/yr. Z5053 .D57ax.
        A monthly compilation of abstracts of doctoral dissertations submitted by more than 450 United States, Canadian, and European universities. Part A is devoted to the humanities and social sciences, including anthropology; Part B covers the sciences and engineering; and Part C contains abstracts of dissertations published worldwide. Each part is arranged by general subject categories with a keyword index derived from words in the title. There is also an author index. The *Comprehensive dissertation index* serves as a master index to *Dissertation abstracts international*. Continues: *Dissertation*

abstracts: A. Humanities and social sciences (Ann Arbor: University Microfilms. v.1-29, 1938-1968).

Anthropology

19.11   *Anthropology: a dissertation bibliography: supplement I.* Ann Arbor: University Microfilms International, 1980. 28 p. GN25 .U54x 1978 Suppl.1.

Lists 1,131 whose abstracts have appeared in *Dissertation abstracts* between 1977 and 1980. Continues: *Anthropology: a dissertation bibliography* (Ann Arbor: University Microfilms International, 1978. 65 p.), a list of some 3,400 United States doctoral dissertations written between 1911 and 1977. Broad subject classification is subdivided by topical and regional subfields.

19.12   McDonald, David R. *Masters' theses in anthropology: a bibliography of theses from United States colleges and universities.* New Haven: HRAF Press, 1977. 453 p. GN25 .M32x 1977.

Includes 3,835 theses submitted between 1898-1975 at 109 universities in the United States; arranged by broad subject classification (Social/cultural anthropology, Archaeology, Physical anthropology, and Linguistics), with subject, ethnic group, author, country, and institution indexes.

Cultural/Social Anthropology

19.13   Gilbert, Victor F., and D.S. Tatla. *Immigrants, minorities, and race relations: a bibliography of theses and dissertations presented at British and Irish universities, 1900-1981.* London, New York: Mansell, 1984. 153 p. JV6061 .G54 1984.

Includes 1,716 theses and dissertations relating to immigrant communities, ethnic minorities, and race relations; separate chapters cover Africa, Asia, Australia, Caribbean area, Latin America, Middle East, North America, Canada, and Europe.

19.14   Webber, Jonathan, ed. *Research in social anthropology, 1975-1980: register of theses accepted for higher degrees at British universities 1975-1980.* London: Royal Anthropological Institute, 1983. 425 p. GN316 .W42 1983.

Ethnomusicology

19.15   Gillis, Frank, comp. *Ethnomusicology and folk music: an international bibliography of dissertations and theses.* Middletown, Connecticut: Society for Ethnomusicology by the Wesleyan University Press, 1966. 148 p. 016.78 G416.

Linguistics

19.16   *Doctoral dissertations on linguistics.* Ann Arbor: University
Microfilms International, 1979. 39 p. 016.41 Un3.

Women

19.17   Gilbert, Victor F., and D.S. Tatla, comps. *Women's studies: a
bibliography of dissertations 1870-1982.* New York: B. Blackwell,
1985. 496 p. HQ1180 .G5 1985.

Africa

19.18   Bratton, Michael, and Anne Schneller, comp. *American doctoral
dissertations on Africa, 1886-1972.* Waltham, Massachusetts: African
Studies Association, 1973. 165 p. 016.96 B737.

19.19   Dinstel, Marion. *List of French doctoral dissertations on Africa,
1884-1961.* Boston: G. K. Hall, 1966. 336 p. DT3 .D56 1966.

19.20   Köhler, Jochen. *Deutsche Dissertationen über Afrika: ein Verzeichnis
für die Jahre 1918-1959.* Bonn: Kurt Schroeder, 1962. Z3501 .K6.
Classified listing of 800 dissertations on Africa submitted at
German universities.

19.21   Harris, Marjorie, comp. *Africa-related doctoral dissertations and
masters theses completed at the University of Wisconsin through 1986.*
3 ed. Madison: African Studies Program, University of Wisconsin,
Madison, 1986. 62 p. DT3 .U55x 1986.

19.22   Ng'ang'a, James M., ed. *Theses and dissertations on Kenya: an
international bibliography.* Nairobi, Kenya: Africa Book Services,
1983. 272 p. DT433.522 .N5 1983.

19.23   Sims, Michael, and Alfred Kagan, comps. *American and Canadian
doctoral dissertations and master's theses on Africa, 1886-1974.*
Waltham, Massachusetts: African Studies Association, Brandeis
University, 1976. 365 p. DT3 .S5 1976.
More than 6,000 titles arranged by country or region, and broad
subject field.

19.24   Lauer, J.J., G.V. Larkin, and A. Kagan, comps. *American and
Canadian doctoral dissertations and master's theses on Africa,
1974-1987.* Atlanta: Crossroads Press, Emory University, 1989. 377 p.

Africa --- South

19.25   Pollak, Oliver B., and Karen Pollak. *Theses and dissertations on* southern Africa: an international bibliography. Boston: G. K. Hall, 1976. 236 p. DT729.5 .P65 1976.

Lists 2,400 academic theses accepted between 1884 and 1974 by more than 200 institutions in 30 countries; includes 447 items under anthropology.

Asia

19.26   Stucki, Curtis W. *American doctoral dissertations on Asia, 1933 - June 1966.* Ithaca, New York: Southeast Asia Program, Cornell University, 1968. 304 p. DS5 .S78 1968.

Includes East Asia, Philippines, South Asia, and the Pacific islands.

Asia --- South

19.27   Bhatia, Kanta. *Doctoral dissertations on South Asia at the University of Pennsylvania, 1898-1981.* Philadelphia: South Asia Regional Studies, University of Pennsylvania, 1981. 249 p. DS335 .U53 1981.

List of 189 doctoral dissertations accepted at the University of Pennsylvania.

19.28   Grunendahl, Reinhold. *Hochschulschriften zu Sud- und Sudostasien: Deutschland, Osterreich, Schweiz (1959-1979).* Wiesbaden: Harrassowitz, 1981. 254 p. DS335 .G78 1981.

19.29   Singh, Indera P., ed. *Doctoral dissertations in anthropology, 1959-1978: summaries of theses awarded degree of doctor of philosophy.* Delhi: Department of Anthropology, University of Delhi, 1981. 103 p.

Asia --- Southeast

19.30   Chety, Sida. *Research on Thailand in the Philippines: an annotated bibliography of theses, dissertations, and investigation papers.* Ithaca, New York: Southeast Asia Program, Department of Asian Studies, Cornell University, 1977. 90 p. 016.9593 C426.

Bibliography of some 400 dissertations, theses, and research papers on Thailand written by Thais, Filipinos, and other nationals, and published in the Philippines.

19.31   *Southeast Asia: a dissertation bibliography.* Ann Arbor: University Microfilms International, 1981. 41 p. DS521 .S68x 1981.

Latin America

19.32   Deal, Carl W., ed. *Latin America and the Caribbean: a dissertation bibliography.* Ann Arbor: University Microfilms International, 1978. 164 p. F1408 .D388x 1978.

Listing of 7,200 dissertations, arranged by geographic and subject areas, and available through University Microfilms; The introduction provides a list of sources for locating other dissertations; author indexing. Continued by: M.C. Walters, ed., *Latin America and the Caribbean II: a dissertation bibliography* (Ann Arbor: University Microfilms International, 1980. 78 p.), a listing of 1,868 dissertations and 100 theses.

19.33   Olivera, Ruth R., comp. *A Bibliography of Latin American theses and dissertations, Tulane University, 1912-1978.* New Orleans: Center for Latin American Studies, Tulane University, 1979. 67 p.

Latin America --- Caribbean
19.34   Baa, Enid M., comp. *Theses on Caribbean topics, 1778-1968.* San Juan: Institute of Caribbean Studies, University of Puerto Rico, 1970. 146 p. F2161 .B33 1970.

19.35   Dossick, Jesse J. *Doctoral research on Puerto Rico and Puerto Ricasn.* New York: New York University, 1967. 34 p. 016.97295 D741.

Middle East
19.36   Selim, George D. *American doctoral dissertations on the Arab world: supplement, August 1981-December 1987.* Washington: Library of Congress, 1989. 265 p. DS36.77 .S44 1989.
        Continues: G.D. Selim, *American doctoral dissertations on the Arab world. Supplement, 1975-1981* (Washington: Library of Congress, 1983. 200 p.) and G.D. Selim, *American doctoral dissertations on the Arab world, 1883-1974* (Washington: Library of Congress. 1976. 173 p.).

19.37   Sluglett, Peter, comp. *Theses on Islam, the Middle East and North-West Africa, 1880-1978: accepted by universities in the United Kingdom and Ireland.* London: Mansell, 1983. 147 p. DS44 .S598 1983.
        Inventory of 3,051 doctoral dissertations and master's theses submitted to approximately 70 institutions in Great Britain and Ireland.

North America
19.38   *Black studies: a dissertation bibliography.* Ann Arbor: University Microfilms International, 1978. 65 p. E185 .U55x 1978.

19.39   Davis, Nathaniel, *et al.*, comps. *Graduate research in Afro-American studies: a bibliography of doctoral dissertations and master's theses completed at the University of California, Los Angeles, from 1942 to*

1980. Los Angeles: Center for Afro-American Studies, University of California, Los Angeles, 1980. 35 p. E185 .G73x 1980.

19.40   Dockstader, Frederick J., comp. *The American Indian in graduate studies: a bibliography of theses and dissertations.* New York: Museum of the American Indian, Heye Foundation, 1973-1974. 2 v. E77 .D63 1973.
        Lists 7,446 dissertations from 1890 to 1970 indexed for topics, tribal groups, archaeological sites, geographical names, etc.

19.41   Kerst, Catherine H. *Ethnic folklife dissertations from the United States and Canada, 1960-1980: a selected, annotated bibliography.* Washington: American Folklife Center, Library of Congress, 1986. 69 p. GR105 .K34x 1986.

19.42   Manson, Sperro M., *et al. Psychosocial research on American Indian and Alaska native youth: an indexed guide to recent dissertations.* Westport, Connecticut: Greenwood Press, 1984. 228 p. E98 .Y68 P79 1984.

19.43   Nickerson, Grifford S. *Native North Americans in doctoral dissertations, 1971-1975: classified and indexes research bibliography.* Monticello, Illinois: Council of Planning Librarians, 1977. 77 p. Z1209.2 .N67.

19.44   *North American Indians: a dissertation index.* Ann Arbor: University Microfilms International, 1977. 169 p. Z1209 .N67 N67.

Oceania

19.45   Coppell, W.G. *Austronesian and other languages of the Pacific and south-east Asia: an annotated catalogue of theses and dissertations.* Canberra: Department of Linguistics, Research School of Pacific Studies, Australian National University, 1981. 521, 15 p. GR105 .K34x 1986.

19.46   Coppell, W.G., and S. Stratigos. *A Bibliography of Pacific Island theses and dissertations.* Canberra: Research School of Pacific Studies, Australian National University in conjunction with the Institute for Polynesian Studies, Brigham Young University, Hawaii Campus; Honolulu, Hawaii: University of Hawaii Press, 1983. 520 p. DU17 .C66x 1983.

19.47   Dickson, Diane, and Carol Dossor, comps. *World catalogue of theses on the Pacific Islands.* Canberra, Australian National University Press, 1970. 123 p. DU17 .D53 1970.

Oceania --- Australia and New Zealand

19.48 Coppell, W.G. *World catalogue of theses and dissertations about the Australian Aborigines and Torres Strait Islanders.* Sydney: Sydney University Press, 1977. 113 p. GN665 .C67 1977.

Oceania --- Melanesia

19.49 Coppell, W.G. *World catalogue of theses and dissertations relating to Papua New Guinea.* IASER bibliography, 2. Boroko, Papua New Guinea: Institute of Applied Special and Economic Research, 1978. 124 p. DU740 .C66.
700 items arranged by author with subject index.

Oceania --- Polynesia

19.50 Coppell, W.G. *Catalogue of theses and dissertations relating to Fiji and Rotuma.* Suva, Fiji: University of the South Pacific Library, 1976. 29 p. DU600 .C66.
Author listing, with subject index, of undergraduate honors and master's theses, and doctoral dissertations.

19.51 Coppell, W.G. *Catalogue of theses and dissertations relating to the Samoan Islands.* Suva, Fiji: University of the South Pacific Library, 1978. 31 p. DU813 .X1 C67.

Other

19.52 Sims, Michael. *United States doctoral dissertations in third world studies, 1869-1978.* Atlanta: Crossroads Press, 1980. 436 p. HC59.7 .S466 1980.

20

Online Databases

Nancy K. Herther

The rise of the microcomputer in the early 1980s has had a significant impact on the discipline of anthropology. Statistical programs have made the gathering and analysis of information from the field and from published sources much easier for the researcher. Computer technology has effectively made the discipline more productive and effective for both the individual researcher in the field and for data analysis and report generation.

Online computer searching requires a computer which has a modem device for making telephone communication with the remote database, a telephone line, a communications software package, as well as a basic computer system (printer, monitor, etc.)

With a microcomputer or other computer terminal anyone can now have access to hundreds of commercial databases that may be useful to anthropologists. These databases cover a wide range of subjects from business to zoology, from atoms to agriculture. This chapter will offer an overview of some of the features and capabilities of some online information sources. It is strongly advised that you consult with a librarian before you begin any research project. In recent years, CD-ROM, locally-mounted databases and other types of computer databases have become available that may also be relevant for your research and available free or at a reduced cost.

Other Databases

The diversity and interdisciplinary nature of anthropology produces a variety of databases that may be appropriate for any research project. For example, research in cultural/social anthropology may draw theoretically or methodologically from other disciplines such as psychology, sociology, religion, history, art, and economics. Similarly research in biological/physical anthropology may involve such fields as architecture, nutrition, biomedicine, agriculture, or geology.

Questions to Ask About Online Databases

One should find out the answers to the following questions when considering whether to use a particular database. This information will make it possible to determine if a particular database would be most appropriate to your needs.

- What is the content of the database?
- Who created or owns the database?
- How extensive is the database? How far back doers the database go in time? Does it index everything on a topic or from some specific set off journals or does it give selective coverage?
- Are there printed equivalents to this database that can be examined?
- Are there other databases which give similar results?

Databases can be expensive so it is best to be as informed as possible when considering using an online database. Faculty and librarians should be able to provide advice and information.

Some Useful Databases for Anthropology

Most college and university libraries will have some type of directory of available online databases. Some of the standard directories include:

20.1 *Canadian machine-readable databases: a directory and guide.* H.F. Rogers, comp. Ottawa: National Library of Canada, 1987. 134, 140 p. Z699.22 .R64x 1987.

20.2 *Data base directory.* White Plains: American Society for Information Science, 1984/85 - . 2/yr. QA76.9 .D3 D295.

20.3 *Dial in ... : an annual guide to library online public access catalogs in North America.* Westport, Connecticut: Meckler, 1990/91 - . 1/yr. Z 699.35 .C38 D53x.

20.4 *Eusidic database guide.* Oxford, New Jersey: Learned Information, 1979 - . Z699.22 .E9x.

20.5 *Gale directory of databases.* Detroit: Gale Research, 1993 - .2/yr. Z699.22 .G34.
Provides descriptions of online, CD-ROM, diskette, magnetic tape, handheld, and batch access databases available throughout the world.

The following list is intended to give a general idea of some of the databases most useful to anthropologists. The database industry is constantly changing. Databases change their focus and content, and new databases appear as others are dropped.

Anthropology
Anthropological index see Entry 13.2.

Anthropological literature see Entry 13.3.

Art and archaeology technical abstracts see Entry 13.29.

Bibliography of Native North Americas on disc see Entry 9.393.

Dyabola see Entry 13.12.

Francis see Entry 13.7.

General
20.6   *Academic index.* Foster City, California. 1980 - .
         Includes journals and magazines, some full-text, on astronomy, religion, law, history, psychology, humanities, current events, sociology, communications and the general sciences.

Biography and genealogy master index see Entry 15.62.

20.7   *Current contents search.* Philadelphia. varies.
         Provides complete bibliographic coverage, with abstracts, to articles listed in the tables of contents of approximately 6,900 leading journals in the sciences, social sciences, and arts and humanities.

Dissertation abstracts on disc see Entry 19.9.

Grants database see Entry 16.30.

Handbook of Latin American studies see Entry 11.33.

Hispanic American periodicals index see Entry 13.15.

20.8   *OCLC/WorldCat.*
         Over 36 million records of any type of material cataloged by OCLC member libraries. Includes manuscripts written as early as the 11th century. Updated daily.

20.9   *RLIN bibliographic files.*
         The Bibliographic file (BIB) contains information about more than 22 million books, periodicals, recordings, scores, archival collections, and other kinds of material held in major research institutions.

20.10 *Russian Academy of Sciences, books and articles.* 1992 - .
The Russian Academy of Sciences Bibliographies file (RAS) covers material in the humanities and social sciences published in the Commonwealth of Independent States, in Eastern European countries, and elsewhere, including periodicals, books, and manuscripts.

Agriculture, Biology, and Ecology

20.11 *AGRICOLA.* 1970 - . 4/yr.
The *AGRICOLA* (Agricultural On Line Access) database contains citations to agricultural literature acquired by the National Agricultural Library cooperating institutions from 1970 to the present. Related subjects such as food and nutrition, agricultural economics, parasitology, etc. are also included. Many citations include abstracts.

20.12 *Biological and agricultural index.* 1983 - . 12/yr.
Nearly 250 English-language periodicals in life sciences and agricultural subjects, published in the U.S. and elsewhere. Includes book reviews.

20.13 *Geobase.* 1980 - . 12/yr.
More than 500,000 records covering the worldwide literature on geology, geography, and ecology.

20.14 *GEOREF: guide to materials in geology and other earth sciences.* 1785 - . 6/yr.
Nearly two million records about geology and earth sciences. Coverage from 1785 to the present for North America, and since 1933 for the entire world.

Arts and Humanities

20.15 *America: history and life.* Santa Barbara, California: ABC-CLIO. 4/yr. 1964 - .
Contains more than 325,000 citations, with abstracts, to social science and humanities literature on all aspects of United States and Canadian history and culture from prehistoric times to the present. Includes books, book reviews, dissertations, and articles from approximately 2,100 journals.

20.16 *Art abstracts.* 1984 - . 12/yr.
More than 250 key international, English-language arts publications. Includes periodicals, yearbooks, museum bulletins, competition and award notices, exhibition listings, interviews, film reviews, etc. Abstracts since 1994. Updated monthly.

20.17 *Art index.* New York. 1984 - . 4/yr.
Contains citations to articles and book reviews in approximately 400 periodicals, yearbooks, and museum bulletins published

worldwide. Covers archaeology, architecture, art history, film, folk art, and museology.

Arts and humanities citation index see Entry 13.22.

20.18   *Avery index to architectural periodicals.* 1977 - .
The *Avery index* file contains records describing articles in more than 1,000 periodicals in the field of architecture and related disciplines.

20.19   *Conservation Information Network.*
Prepared by the Canada Department of Canadian Heritage, Canadian Heritage Information Network (CHIN), contains information on the conservation of cultural property, both movable and immovable, including sites, architecture, and museum objects. Comprises the following three files: *Conservation bibliographic database*: contains more than 120,000 citations to the worldwide conservation and restoration literature. Corresponds in part to the Art and archaeology technical abstracts (AATA) and the holdings of the International Centre for the Study of the Preservation and the Restoration of Cultural Property (ICCROM) library; *Conservation materials database*: contains more than 1300 records on products relevant to conservation practice, including chemical, optical, physical, mechanical, and thermal properties as well as the safety of adhesives, consolidants, coatings, solvents, backing, support materials, and pesticides; *Conservation product/supplier directory*: contains names, addresses, and telephone numbers of more than 1,900 manufacturers, distributors, and retailers of conservation materials. Produced in cooperation with the Smithsonian Institution, Conservation Analytical Laboratory; the International Centre for the Study of the Preservation and the Restoration of Cultural Property (ICCROM); the International Council on Monuments and Sites (ICOMOS); the International Council of Museums (ICOM); and the Getty Conservation Institute (GCI).

20.20   *Humanities abstracts.* 1984 - . 12/yr.
Contains citations, with abstracts (from March 1994), to more than 400 English-language periodicals in such areas as archaeology, classical studies, art, performing arts, philosophy, history, music, linguistics, literature, and, religion.

Humanities index see Entry 13.24.

20.21   *ISOC database.* Madrid. 1975 - .
Prepared by the Consejo Superior de Investigaciones Cientificas de Espana (CSIC), contains comprises eight files, including *HISTORIA*: contains approximately 36,000 citations to literature on

history, archaeology, and the science of history; *ISOC-ARTE*: contains approximately 32,000 citations to literature on the fine arts; *LIN-LIT*: contains citations to literature on language, linguistics, and literature; and *URBISOC*: contains more than 17,100 citations to literature on geography, urban planning, architecture, environment, and municipal administration. Some 25,000 records are added annually.

Linguistics and language behavior abstracts see Entry 13.33.

20.22   *Mosaique Grecque.* Nanterre, France. varies.
        Prepared by the Centre National de la Recherche Scientifique (CNRS, contains descriptions of approximately 600 Greek mosaics created from the beginning of the ancient Greek culture to the end of the Hellenistic period. Covers the entire Greek empire (e.g., modern Afghanistan, Albania, Egypt, Greece, Italy, Malta, Rumania, Spain, Tunisia, Turkey, and the former USSR). Includes place of discovery, current location, date created, mosaic technique, placement within the building, decoration, subject, and iconography. Corresponding illustrations are available on the videodisc *Images de l'Archeologie.*

Physical Sciences
20.23   *Applied science and technology abstracts.* 1983 - . 12/yr.
        More than 350 international, English-language periodicals, covering engineering, mathematics, physics, and computer technology. Includes articles, interviews, meetings, conferences, exhibitions, new product reviews/announcements, etc.

20.24   *History of science and technology.* 1976 - .
        The *History of science and technology* file includes references from *Isis Current bibliography of the history of science,* 1976-present, and *Current bibliography in the history of technology,* 1987-present. Records describe journal articles, conference proceedings, books, book reviews, and dissertations.

Health Sciences
20.25   *DRUGINFO.* Minneapolis. 1960 - .
        DRUGINFO indexes and abstracts literature on alcohol, tobacco, and other drug use/abuse. It covers the educational, psychological, and sociological literature comprehensively, and the medical and biological literature selectively. It is restricted to English language print material. All indexed materials are part of the collection of Drug Information Services, located in the Bio-Medical Library, University of Minnesota, Minneapolis campus.

20.26   *EMBASE CD.* Amsterdam, Netherlands.
        Contains more than 3.5 million citations, with abstracts, to the

worldwide biomedical literature on human medicine and areas of biological; sciences related to human medicine, including drugs and toxicology, health affairs, environment and pollution, and alternative medicine.

Social Sciences

20.27   *Archaeological sites national database.* Hull, PQ, Canada: Canadian Department of Canadian Heritage, Canadian Heritage Information Network (CHIN). 52/yr.
Contains information on more than 80,000 archaeological sites in Canada, including information on site name, location, jurisdiction, researcher, site type and features, culture, dates, and references. Electronic access: service@calvin.chin.doc.ca (Internet).

20.28   *Bibliografía especializada sobre materias específicas Instituto de la Mujer.* Madrid. 1900 - . varies.
Consists of seven files of citations to Spanish periodicals, books, and conference proceedings,. Including the following of interest to anthropologists: *Bibliografía especializada sobre arqueologia*: contains some 6500 citations to literature on archaeology; *Bibliografía especializada sobre la mujer*: contains approximately 7000 citations to literature on women's issues; *Bibliografía especializada sobre museos*: contains approximately 637 citations to literature on museums.

20.29   *Chicano database.* 1967 -
The *Chicano database* file contains records for all types of material on Mexican-American topics and Chicanos. Since 1992, *Chicano database* describes material on the broader Latino experience, including Puerto Ricans, Cuban Americans, and Central American immigrants.

Cross-cultural CD see Entry 23.10.

Electronic HRAF see Entry 23.12.

20.30   *FRANTIQ.* Lyon, France. varies.
Contains more than 47,000 citations to works held by French university archaeological research institutes. Also includes an electronic bulletin board service.

20.31   *Holocaust and genocide bibliographic database.* Jerusalem, Israel.
Prepared by the Institute on the Holocaust and Genocide, contains approximately 9750 citations of books, chapters of books, book reviews, journal articles, and dissertations on the study of genocide, including the Holocaust, Armenian genocide, Cambodian genocide, Ukrainian famine, American Indians, antisemitism, art and literature

of genocide, psychological studies of survivors and second generation, denial of genocide, ethnic relations, genocide prevention and early warning systems, human rights, museums, memorials, and monuments; altruism; massacres; personal narratives of survivors, resistance to genocide, and state genocidal tendencies and policies.

20.32 *Multicultural Australia information system.* Canberra. 1988 - . 4/yr.
Bibliographic database containing more than 15,000 citations, with abstracts, pertaining to Australia literature on multicultural issues, including ethnicity, cultural heritage, racism, immigration, and language policy.

20.33 *PAIS decade.* current ten years. 12/yr.
More than 200,000 records representing articles, books, conference proceedings, government documents, book chapters, and statistical directories about public policy and international affairs. Covers the most recent 10 years. Updated monthly.

20.34 *PsycINFO.* 1967 - . 12/yr.
More than 1,300 journals on psychology and related fields.

20.35 *Pyrenees.* Toulouse, France. 1970 - . 3/yr.
Prepared by the Centre National de la Recherche Scientifique (CNRS), contains about 4000 citations, with abstracts, to literature and current research projects on the Pyrenees regions of France (Aquitaine, Midi-Pyrenees, Languedoc-Roussillon), Spain (Aragon, Navarre, Catalonia, and the Basque provinces), and Andorra. Subject coverage includes research projects in agriculture, ecology, history and prehistory, language and culture, and tourism.

Social sciences citation index see Entry 13.20.

20.36 *SocioAbs.* 1963 - . 6/yr.
More than 300,000 abstracts covering sociology, social work, and other social sciences.

20.37 *Social sciences abstracts.* 1983 - . 12/yr.
More than 400 international, English-language periodicals in sociology, anthropology, geography, economics, political science, and law. Abstracts are included since January, 1994.

Social Sciences Index see Entry 13.21.

20.38 *Yacimientos arqueológicos españoles.* Madrid. varies.
Prepared by the Dirección General de Bellas Artes y Archivos, Ministerio de Cultura de España, contains information on more than 13,000 archaeological sites in Spain. Includes site name, county and

province, location on national topographical map, culture and period of the site contents, a general description of the archaeological finds, and a relevant bibliography. Subject coverage includes Spanish archaeological sites, including physical descriptions of the artifacts, and culture and period information on the objects.

21

Internet Resources

The Internet is a linked series of worldwide electronic networks that provides an increasing wealth of information on every subject imaginable. In addition to providing access to a variety of information resources, the Internet serves as an important medium through which individuals may communicate with each other and exchange data. The Internet allows you to communicate electronically with anyone in the world also connected to the Internet.

A variety of electronic resources are available on the Internet. Some of these include: library catalogs; books, journals, and newsletters; dictionaries, thesauri, and encyclopedias; electronic mail; bulletin boards; discussion groups; software; and data sets.

The Internet permits both passive and active use. You may merely view the electronic resources available such as library catalogs or the text of books, journals, newsletters, etc. Or, you may send of receive electronic messages or files through e-mail, subscriptions to bulletin boards, newsgroups, etc.

Guides to Internet Resources

Although no single comprehensive directory to the Internet exists, there are many print and electronic directories and guides you can consult to discover more about the Internet and its resources. A selective list of these resources includes:

21.1 Battle, Stafford L., and Rey O. Harris. *The African American resource guide to the Internet.* Columbia, Maryland: On Demand Press, 1995. 85 p. TK5105.875 .I57 B38x 1995.

21.2 Campbell, David R., and Mary V. Campbell. *The Student's guide to doing research on the Internet.* Reading, Massachusetts: Addison-Wesley, 1995. 349 p. LB2369 .C28 1995.

21.3 Ebihara, Wataru, comp. *An Asian American Internet guide.* Los Angeles, California: APNet, 1995. 48 p. E184 .O6 E25x 1995.

21.4 Gilster, Paul. *Finding it on the Internet: the essential guide to Archie, Veronica, Gopher, WAIS, WWW (including Mosaic), and other search* and browsing tools. New York: Wiley, 1994. 302 p. TK5105.875 .I57 G53 1994.

21.5   Gilster, Paul. *Finding it on the Internet: the Internet navigator's guide to search tools and techniques.* 2 ed. New York: Wiley, 1996. 379 p. TK5105.875 .I57 G54 1996.

21.6   Gilster, Paul. *The New Internet Navigator.* New York: Wiley, 1995. 735 p. TK5105.875 .I57 G563 1995.

21.7   Glossbrenner, Alfred. *Internet 101: a college student's guide.* Windcrest/McGraw-Hill, 1994. TK5105.875 .I57 G563i 1994.

21.8   Harmon, Charles, ed. *Using the Internet, online services and CD-ROMS for writing research and term papers.* New York: Neal-Schuman Publishers, 1996. 167 p. LB1047.3 .U75 1996.

21.9   Holledge, Simon. *Archaeology on the net: an Internet resource list.* Cambridge, England: Wessex International Archaeology, 1994. 79 p.

21.10   *Internet World's on Internet.* Westport, Connecticut: Mecklermedia, 1994. TK5105.875 .I57 I585x.

21.11   Kehoe, Brendan P. *Zen and the art of the Internet: a beginner's guide.* 4 ed. Upper Saddle River, New Jersey: Prentice Hall PTR, 1996. 255 p. TK5105.875 .I57 K44.

21.12   Krol, Ed. *The Whole Internet user's guide and catalog.* Belmont, California: Integra Media Group; Sebastopol, California: O'Reilly, 1996. 609 p.
        Includes a brief, user-friendly glossary of Internet-related terminology.

21.13   Levine, John, and Carol Baroudi. *The Internet for dummies.* San Mateo, California: IDG Books, 1994. 427 p. TK5105.875 .I57 L655i 1994.

21.14   Marine, April, Susan Kirkpatrick, Vivian Neou, and Carol Ward. *Internet: getting started.* Englewood Cliffs, New Jersey: PTR Prentice Hall, 1993. 360 p. TK5105.875 .I57 I57x.

The Internet resources presented in this chapter does not pretend to be comprehensive and is based, in part, on the following: Anita Cohen-Williams, and Julia A. Hendon, Internet resources for anthropology (*College and research libraries news,* February, pp. 87-90, 113, 1995), Allen H. Lutins (alleycat@spectra.net), *Allen H. Lutins Anthropology resources on the Internet* (http://www.nitehawk.com/alleycat/welcome/html), and *Danny Yee's anthropology page* (http://www.anatomy.su.oz.au/danny/anthropology/). This compilation assumes a basic knowledge of Internet commands, such as gopher, telnet, and ftp.

Internet Discussion Groups and Listservs

These are topic oriented forums distributed by e-mail, dealing with a wide range of subjects, many of which pertain to anthropology. Once you have subscribed to a discussion list, messages from other subscribers are automatically sent to your electronic mailbox.

Anthropology
ACRA-L (American Cultural Resources Association); send message "subscribe acra-l" to majordomo@lists.nonprofit.net
ACTIV-L (Activists for peace, empowerment, human rights, justice, etc.); listserv@mizzou1.missouri.edu.
ANSS-L (Discussion forum for information specialists in anthropology, sociology and related fields); send message "subscribe anss-l first name-last name" to listserv@uci.edu.
ANTHRO-L (Anthropology); send message "subscribe anthro-l first name-last name" to listserv@ubvm.cc.buffalo.edu; general anthropology list with discussions ranging from hominid brain sizes to ethnographic fieldwork.
ANTHRO-LIB (Liberation anthropology; Liberation Anthropology Group); third- and fourth-world peoples and cultures); send message "subscribe anthro-lib first name-last name" to listproc@lists.colorado.edu.
WOMANTH-L (Women in anthropology); send message "subscribe coswa-l your-first-name your-last-name" to listserver@relay.doit.wisc.edu.
SBANTH-L (Anthropology and graduate students); send message "subscribe sbanth-l first name-last name" to listserv@ucsbvm.ucsb.edu.

Archaeology
ADS-ALL (Digital archiving of archaeological data); send message "join ads-all first name last name" to mailbase@mailbase.ac.uk; archives at http://www.mailbase.ac.uk/lists-a-e/ads-all/archive.html
AEGEANET (Pre-Classical Aegean world); send message "subscribe aegeanet" to majordomo@acpub.duke.edu.
AIA-L (Archaeology and technology; moderated); send message "subscribe aia-l first name-last name" to majordomo@brynmawr.edu.
ANCIEN-L (History of ancient Mediterranean); send message "subscribe ancien-l first name-last name" to listserv@ulkyvm.louisville.edu.
ANE (Ancient Near East); send message "subscribe ane" to majordomo@oi.uchicago.edu.
ANT-ARQ (Anthropology and archaeology in Spanish);send message "subscribe ant-arq your-first-name your-last-name" to majordomo@ccc.uba.ar.
ARCHAEOBOTANY; send message "subscribe archaeobotany your first name your last name to listproc@eng-h.gov.uk.

ARCH-ARCTIC (Arctic archaeology); contact maiser@natmus.min.dk.

ARCH-L (Archaeology; general archaeology list, international in scope, and covers all aspects of archaeology; has bibliographic files available); send message "subscribe arch-l first name-last name" to listserv@tamvm1.tamu.edu.

ARCH-METALS (Archaeology/history of metals); send message "join arch-metals first name-last name" to mailbase@mailbase.ac.uk.

ARCH-STUDENT (Students in archaeology); send message "subscribe arch-student first name-last name" to listproc@lists.colorado.edu.

ARCH-THEORY (Archaeological theory in Europe); send message "join arch-theory first name-last name" to mailbase@mailbase.ac.uk; a group from England that covers archaeological theory, material culture, cultural identity, and perspectives from anthropology and history. Send message "Join arch-theory your name" to mailbase@mailbase.ac.uk.

ARCHCOMP-L (Archaeological computing); send massage "sub ARCHCOMP-L first name last name" to listserv@listserv.acsu.buffalo.edu.

ARTIFACT (Material culture study/methods); send message "subscribe artifact first name-last name" to listserv@umdd.umd.edu.

ARQUEOANDINA (Moderated; for professionals interested in Andean archaeology); send message "subscribe arqueoandina" to listasrcp@rcp.net.pe.

AZTLAN (Mesoamerican studies); send message "subscribe aztlan first name-last name" to listserv@ulkyvm.louisville.edu.

C14-L (Carbon 14 dating issues; list for researchers involved in radiocarbon and other radioisotopes used in dating, and in scientific dating issues in general); send message "subscribe C14-l first name-last name" to listserv@listserv.arizona.edu.

CELTIC-L (Celtic culture list); listserv@irlearn.ucd.ie.

EAAN (East Asian archaeology network); send message "subscribe eaan" to listserv@ccat.sas.upenn.edu.

GAARCH-L (Georgia archaeology); send message "subscribe gaarch-l first name-last name" to listserv@sun.cc.westga.edu.

GISARCH (GIS and archaeology); send message to mailbase@mailbase.ac.uk with the following two lines: subscribe gisarch your-first-name your-last-name stop.

GREEKARCH (Archaeology of the ancient Greek world); send message "subscribe greekarch e-mail address" to majordomo@rome.classics.1sa.umich.edu.

HISTARCH (Historical archaeology); a list devoted to historical archaeology (European expansion and after); send message "subscribe histarch first name-last name" to listserv@asuvm.inre.asu.edu.

HTECH-L (History of technology discussion group); send request to listserv@sivm.si.edu.

IND-ARCH (Industrial archaeology); send message "join ind-arch your-first-name your-last-name" to mailbase@mailbase.ac.uk.

JWA (Journal of world archaeology); send message "subscribe jwa first name-last name" to listserv@ubvm.cc.buffalo.edu.

LITHICS-L (Analysis of archaeological lithics, natural and artificial); send message "sub lithics-l first name last name to listserv@acsu.buffalo.edu.

LT-ANTIQ (Late antiquity, AS 260-640; late Roman, early Byzantine, early medieval, and early Islamic periods; geographic coverage: western Europe to the Middle East and from the Sahara to Russia); apply to listserv@univscvm.csd.scarolina.edu.

NAGPRA-L (Native American Graves Protection and Repatriation Act); send message "subscribe nagpra-l" to majordomo@world.std.com.

NAUTARCH (Nautical/maritime archaeology); send request to nautarch-request@santafe.edu.

NUMISM-L (Ancient and medieval numismatics); apply to listserv@uniscvm.csd.scarolina.edu.

PACARC-L (Pacific rim archaeology); send message "subscribe pacarc-l first name-last name" to listserv@listproc.wsu.edu.

PAPY (Papyrology and history/epigraphy/archaeology of Greco-Roman Egypt); send request to papy@igl.ku.dk.

PRESERVATION-L (Architectural restoration and preservation); apply to listserv@netcom.com.

QUATERNARY (Research in the Quaternary sciences, particularly in Canada); apply to listserv@morgan.ucs.mun.ca.

ROCK-ART (Petroglyphs, pictographs, etc.); send message "subscribe rock-art first name-last name" to listserv@asuvm.inre.asu.edu.

ROMARCH (Art and archaeology of ancient Italy and the Roman provinces; covers material culture of ancient Italy, from ca. 1000 BC to AD 600, including Etruscans, Romans, Greeks, etc.; material culture of all Roman provinces, including Roman interaction with local populations and cultures); send message "subscribe romarch" to majordomo@rome.classics.lsa.umich.edu.

SAS-NET (Society for Archaeological Sciences); request to Jim Burton [jhburton@macc.wisc.edu].

SOPA (Society for Professional Archaeology); send message "subscribe sopa name e-mail address" to majordomo@mail.smu.edu.

SPANBORD (History and archaeology of the Spanish borderlands; covers the history and archaeology of the Spanish borderlands of North America (including northern Mexico), 1521-1900); send message "subscribe spanbord first name-last name" to listserv@asuvm.inre.asu.edu.

SUB-ARCH (Underwater archaeology; covers underwater archaeology from an academic/professional viewpoint; members are from all over the world, including Australia, England, and Canada);send message "subscribe sub-arch first name-last name" to listserv@asuvm.inre.asu.edu.

XYLHIST-L (History and archaeology of timber-framed construction); send message "subscribe xylhist-l first name-last name" to listserv@bloxwich.demon.co.uk

Biological/Physical Anthropology

CBR-L (Craniofacial biology research); send message "subscribe cbr-l" to majordomo@po.cwru.edu.

HUMBIO-L (Human evolution/physical anthropology); send message "subscribe humbio-l first name-last name" to listserv@acc.fau.edu.

HUMEVO (Human evolutionary research discussion group); apply to listserv@gwuvm.bitnet).

IBERPAL (Lista de discussion sobre paleontologia iberica e iberoamericana); send message "subscribe iberpal" to listserv@listserv.uv.es.

LPN-L (Laboratory primate newsletter); send message "subscribe lpn-l first name-last name" to listserv@brownvm.brown.edu.PAN-L (physical anthropology); send message "subscribe pan-l first name-last name" to listserv@psuorvm.cc.pdx.edu

PRIMATOLOGY (Human/nonhuman primates); send message "join primatology first name-last name" to mailbase@mailbase.ac.uk.

Cultural/Social Anthropology

AFROAM-L (Critical issues in African American life and culture); afroam-l@harvard.harvard.edu.

AISESnet (American Indian Science and Engineering Society (AISES) Network); provides communication and information for AISES chapters, students, and faculty associated with AISES, and for members of industry and government. List is divided into four groups: AISESnet General (AISES issues, position openings, scholarship announcements, conference information, pow-wow information, and chapter newsletters); AISESnet Discussion (discussion of Native American issues, engineering and science issues, public opinion, creative writing, etc.); Alcohol and Drug (deals only with drug- and alcohol-related issues; and AISESnet Drums (dedicated to drum groups, deals with issues concerning drum groups, pow-wow drum groups, drum building, pow-wow singers, etc.); aisesnet@selway.umt.edu.

ANTHAP (Open only to members of Society for Applied Anthropology or National Association of Practicing Anthropologists; applied anthropology news, announcements, jobs, etc.); send request to anthap-request@oakland.bitnet (not a server).

ANTHAP4 (Issues relating to refugees, internally displaced persons, forced and involuntary migration and resettlement); send request to geiger@pegasus.cc.ucf.edu.

AnthEurasia-L (Anthropology of the former Soviet Bloc); send message "subscribe AnthEurasia-L your first name your last name to majordomo@fas.harvard.edu.

ANTHTHEORY-L (Anthropology theory); send message "subscribe anththeory-l your-first-name your-last-name" to listserv@list.nih.gov.

ANTHROPOLOGY (Field-oriented list for experienced cultural anthropologists); send message "subscribe anthropology first name-last name" to majordomo@iinet.net.au.

ASAONET (Anthropology of Oceania); send message "subscribe asaonet first name-last name" to listserv@uicvm.uic.edu.

COLORCAT (Color categorization; explores how the color continuum is partitioned into categories by various human processes; apply to listerv@brownvm.brown.edu).

COSWA-L (Women in anthropology); send message "subscribe coswa-l first name-last name" to listserv@relay.doit.wisc.edu.

CRFA-L (Center for Research and Fieldwork in Anthropology, University of Texas at Arlington); send message "subscribe crfa-l" to listserv@utarlvm1.uta.edu.

CROSS-L (Cross-cultural research in information); contact Roberto Evaristo [evaristo@umnsom.bitnet].

DANCE-L (Folk and traditional dance); send message to listserv@hearn.nic.surfnet.nl.

DARWIN-L (Cultural evolution); apply to listserv@iris.uncg.edu.

DEVEL-L (Technology transfer in international development); send message "subscribe devel-l first name-last name" to listserv@american.edu.

EASIANTH (East Asian anthropology); send message "subscribe easianth first name-last name" to listserv@vm.temple. edu.

ETHMUS-L (Global ethnomusicology); send message "subscribe ethmus-l first name-last name" to listserv@umdd.umd.edu.

ETHNET-L (Irish and British ethnography); send message "subscribe ethnet-l first name-last name" to listserv@ysub.ysu.edu.

ETHNO (Ethnomethodology/conversion analysis); send message "subscribe ethno first name last name" to comserve@vm.ecs.rpi.edu.

ETHNO-BIO (Ethnobiology; use of plants and animals by native peoples worldwide); send message "subscribe ethno-bio to majordomo@sfu.edu.

ETHNOHIS (Ethnology and history); send message "subscribe ethnohis first name-last name" to listserv@hearn.nic.surfnet.nl.

FOLKLORE (Folklore); send message "subscribe folklore first name-last name" to listserv@tamvm1.tamu.edu

H-SAE (H-Net list for the anthropology of Europe); send message to listserv@msu.edu.

HERB (Medicinal and aromatic plants) covers cross-cultural and folk/herbal medicine); send message to listserv@trearnpc.ege.edu.tr.

IND-NET (American Indian discussion list); send message to listproc@listproc.wsu.edu.

INDIANnet (Census Information and Computer Network Center); National computer listserv to provide civic information useful to American Indian and Alaskan Natives; includes computer conferences and private electronic mail for Indian tribes, nonprofit organizations, and individuals; also a specialized collection of American Indian and Alaskan Native research reports extracted from the Educational Research Information Clearinghouse (ERIC); listserv@spruce.hsu.edu.

INDKNOW (Discussion of indigenous knowledge systems); listserv@uwavm.u.washington.edu.

INTERCUL (Intercultural communication); send message "subscribe intercul first name-last name" to comserve@rpiecs.bitnet.

LORE (Folklore); apply to listserv@ndsuvm1.bitnet.

MAPC (Materialist anthropology and the production of culture workshop); send message "subscribe mapc first name-last name" to listserv@vm.utcc.utoronto.ca.

NAHUAT-L (Covers Nahuatl and Nahua studies); apply to nahuat-l@acc.fau.edu.

NAT-EDU (Aboriginal education issues); listserv@indycms.iupui.edu.
NATFOOD-L (Native American foods); send message "subscribe natfood-l first
name-last name" to listproc@listproc.wsu.edu.
NATIVENET An overlapping set of electronic discussion lists, including:
NAT-1492 is a Columbus quincentenary mailing list dealing with the
500th anniversary of Columbus's voyage to the New World;
listserv@tamvm1.tamu.edu; NATCHAT provides a forum for general
discussion pertaining to indigenous people of the world;
listserv@tamvm1.tamu.edu; NATIVE-L (Indigenous Peoples Information)
provides a general forum for exchanging information and perspectives on
matters relating to the indigenous people of the world;
listserv@tamvm1.tamu.edu; NAT-HLTH (Health Issues of Native
Peoples); listserv@tamvm1.tamu.edu; NAT-LANG for exchange of
information concerning the languages of indigenous people;
listserv@tamvm1.tamu.edu; NAT-EDU deals with issues regarding the
provision of culturally sensitive educational programs for native people;
listserv@indycms.iupui.edu.
NATFOOD-L (Native American foods); send message to
listproc@listproc.wsu.edu
NATIVE-LIT-L (Native American literature by autochthonous people of the
North Americas (U.S., Canada, and Mexico) and neighboring islands).
Discussion of native literature as well as book reviews, articles about
poetry, fiction, and criticism; information about publications, talks, and
conferences. listserv@cornell.edu.
NAT-WORK (Native American work issues); send message to
listserv@akronvm.uakron.edu.
NIPC (National Indian Policy Research Institute Electronic Clearinghouse);
information clearinghouse on a wide range of policy issues to the 500
United States Native American tribes since 1900; access:
listserv@gwuvm.gwu.edu.
OHA-L (Oral history); apply listserv@ukcc.bitnet.
ORTRAD-L (Interdisciplinary forum for discussion on oral traditions); apply to
listserv@mizzou1.missouri.edu.
SEANET-L (Southeast Asian studies); apply to listserv@nusvm.bitnet.
SEASIA-L (Southeast Asia); apply to listserv@msu.edu.
XCULT-X (intercultural communication); send message "subscribe xcult-x first
name-last name" to listserv@umrvmb.bitnet.

Linguistics

CELTLING (Celtic linguistics); celtling@mitvma.mit.edu.
GERLINGL (Old Germanic languages to 1500); send request to
gerlingl@vmd.cso.uiuc.edu.
IROQUOIS (Iroquois language); send message "subscribe iroquois first name-
last name" to listserv@vm.utcc.utoronto.ca.
LATAMLIN (Latin American linguistics); apply to latamlin@mitvma.mit.edu.
LINGUIST (linguistics); send message "subscribe linguist first name-last
name" to listserv@tamvm1.tamu.edu.

NAT-LANG (Native American indigenous languages); send message "subscribe nat-lang first name-last name" to listserv@tamvm1.tamu.edu.

Museology
CONDIST (Conservation of cultural materials); send message to condist-request@lindy.stanford.edu.
CONSERVATION DISTLIST (Moderated list for professionals engaged in the conservation of cultural materials); to subscribe, send a note to consdist-request@lindy.stanford.edu.
H-LOCAL (State and local history, and museum studies); send message "subscribe h-local first name-last name" to listserv@msu.edu.
MUSEUM-L (Museum issues); send message "subscribe museum-l first name-last name" to listserv@unmvma.unm.edu.

Usenet Discussion Groups
The Usenet Discussion Groups are global bulletin boards in which people exchange public information on a range of topics. Unlike messages received through e-mail, the Usenet messages are not stored on your computer unless you specifically save each one.

Name	Topic
rec.food.historic	ancient foods
sci.anthropology	anthropology
sci.anthropology.paleo	evolution of humans and other primates
sci.archaeology	archaeology
sci.archaeology.mesoamerican	archaeology of Mesoamerica
sci.lang	linguistics
soc.misc	miscellaneous social issues
soc.culture.native	Native American issues
soc.culture.*	issues pertaining to culture area or country "*" [numerous]

Programs and Files via Anonymous FTP
FTP stands for File Transfer Protocol and is both a program and a method used to transfer files between computers on the Internet. Anonymous FTP is a type of FTP that permits you to transfer and of millions of files from several thousand computers on the Internet to your personal computer. By using FTP, the Internet becomes like an enormous disk drive attached to your computer.

Anthropology
Anthropology/archaeology information and software
    ftp.neosoft.com:/pub/users/claird/sci.anthropology.
Anthropology hypertext book (hypercard stack for Macintosh)
    sumex-aim.stanford.edu:/info-mac/info/nms.
Archives for the sci.anthropology.paleo newsgroup
    joyce.cs.su.oz.au:/danny/sci.anthropology.paleo.

Computing and humanities archive
  ucsbuxa.ucsb.edu:/hcf.
Library of Congress on-line museum exhibits
  seq1.loc.gov:/pub/vatican.exhibit and pub/deadsea.scrolls.exhibit.
Worldwide e-mail directory of anthropologists (can also be searched via gopher
  and World Wide Web)
  ubvm.cc.buffalo.edu.

Archaeology
Archaeology software and Society for Archaeological Sciences database; use
  "cd:.archaeometry:"
  grv.dsir.govt.nz:/Archaeometry and /sas.
Archaeology software; World Archaeological Council News
  ftp.tex.ac.uk:/pub/archaeology:?:
Bonn archaeological statistics package for DOS
  ftp.oak.oakland.edu:/pc/msdos/statistics/baspdos.zip.
Centre for Computer-Aided Egyptological Resources (CCER); also available
  via World Wide Web
  newton.newton.cam.ac.uk:/pub/ancient.
Geology software
  sparky2.esd.mun.ca:/pub.
GIS software (OzGIS)
  oak.oakland.edu:/pub/msdos/mapping.
Mayan Epigraphic Database Project (also available via gopher and WWW)
  jefferson.village.virginia.edu /pub/publications/med.
Radiocarbon calibration program for IBMs
  ftp.u.washington.edu:/public/calib.

Cultural/Social Anthropology
ANTHAP (Applied anthropology computer network) archives
  vela.acs.oakland.edu:/pub/anthap.
CSAC Ethnographic Gallery/Intermedia Library; also available via gopher,
  WAIS, WWW, etc.; use same address (e.g., http://lucy.ukc.ac.uk. for
  WWW)
  lucy.ukc.ac.uk.
Fourth World Documentation Project; information on indigenous peoples; also
  available gopher and World Wide Web
  ftp.halcyon.com:/pub/FWDP.
Native American information
  ftp.cit.cornell.edu:/pub/special/NativeProfs/usenet.
Shamanism-general overview - frequently asked questions (FAQ)
  ftp://rtfm.mit.edu/pub/usenet-by-group/sci.anthropology/Shamanism
  General_Overview-Frequent.

Linguistics
Linguistics archive
  csli.stanford.edu:/linguistics.

Linguistics archive; syllabi, handouts, fonts, lexica, software, papers, digests, etc.
ftp.uu.net:/pub/linguistics.

Other
Census information
info.umd.edu:/info/Government/US/Census-90.
State Department travel advisories
rascal.ics.utexas.edu:/misc/misc.
USGS maps
isdres.er.usgs.gov.
USGS maps, census data, etc.
spectrum.xerox.com:/pub/map.

Gopher Services

Gopher provides menu access to a variety of Internet resources. It is a client/server based tool that provides a user friendly front end to many types of Internet resources located all over the world. By using Gopher you are spared from having to learn many of the Internet and special computer commands. Gopher presents the Internet as if it were all part of a single directory system such as directories on a DOS machine or folders on a Mac.

Anthropology

Anthro-Gopher
server: toto.ycc.yale.edu or uniwa.uwa.edu.
Anthropology information
server: uniwa.uwa.edu.au/11/depgoph/artsarch/anthrop (University of Western Australia).
Anthropology information
server: uniwa.uwa.edu.au; select 'Departmental', then 'People with a common interest.'
Buffalo server:"Worldwide E-mail directory of anthropologists" and back issues of Journal of World Anthropology; both also available via ftp and World Wide Web
server: wings.buffalo.edu; select "Academic and Departmental Information," then "Academic Departments," then "Anthropology Department."
Worldwide E-mail directory of anthropologists
server: wings.buffalo.edu; select "Academic and Departmental Information," then "Academic Departments," then "Anthropology Department," and finally "WEDA" (also available as a single file via ftp).

Archaeology

Archaeology information/software
server: ftp.tex.ac.uk; select item 4 (Archaeology).
Archnet (prehistoric archaeology of the Northeast)
server: spirit.lib.uconn.edu: or use World Wide Web server.

Classics and archaeology
> server: rome.classics.lsa.umich.edu; also available via World Wide Web.

Council for British Archaeology
> server: britac3.britac.ac.uk:70/11/cba.

Exploratorium of Science and Art
> server: gopher.exploratorium.edu; also available via World Wide Web.

FAQ: careers in archaeology in the United States
> server: info.tamu.edu:8300/00/.data/anthr-dept/career.faq; also available via World Wide Web.

Internet resources for heritage conservation, historic preservation, and archaeology
> server: gopher.npctt.nps.gov/00/cultural_announce/directories/irg.txt; also available via World Wide Web.

Mayan epigraphic database project
> server: jefferson.village.virginia.edu; also available via ftp and World Wide Web.

World Heritage Gopher (Institute for Global Communications/International Council on Monuments and Sites)
> server: hpb.hwc.ca; or use World Wide Web server.

Biological/Physical Anthropology

Primate information
> server: saimiri.primate.wisc.edu.

Cultural/Social Anthropology

ANTHAP (Applied Anthropology Computer Network) archives
> server: gopher.acs.oakland.edu; select 'Applied Anthropology Computer Network.'

Bishop Museum Gopher: access to nearly every museum that is on the Internet
> server: bishop.bishop.hawaii.org

Center for World Indigenous Studies/Fourth World Documentation Project
> server: fir.cic.net; select Politics; Fourth.World; also available via World Wide Web

Disaster Research Center (University of Delaware)
> server://nisei.ce.berkeley.edu://70/1/1/dc

Flora Mesoamericana
> server: gopher2.nhm.ac.uk.70/11botany/.florames; also available via World Wide Web

Georgia Anthro (includes general southeastern anthropology, CRM, etc.)
> server: julian.dac.uga.edu

Historical documents
> server: scilibx.u7csc.edu; select item 7 (The library), then 3 (Electronic books and other texts), then 19 (Historical documents)

Hollis (access to Tozzer Library materials; premier anthropology resource)
> server: telnet: hollis.harvard.edu.

Marx and Engels (Marxist classics in ASCII text files)
> server://csf.colorado.edu:70/1/1/psn/Marx.

Native American issues and culture
    server: absolut.gmu.edu.
Native American net server
    server: alphal.csd.uwm.edu; select "UWM information."

Museology
Material culture resources
    server: info.umd.edu; select "Educational resources," "Colleges and schools
    at UMCP," "College of Arts and Humanities (ARHU," "Departments,
    programs and majors," "American studies," "Material culture resources."
Museum list
    server: ulkyvm.louisville.edu; select "some other ...," the "Museums."
National Center for Preservation Technology and Training
    server: gopher.ncptt.nps.gov.
Peabody Museum of Natural History (Yale University) collections data
    server: gopher.peabody.yale.edu.
Smithsonian Natural History Museum
    server: nmnh.si.edu.
UC-Berkeley Museum of Paleontology
    server: ucmpl.berkeley.edu.

Other
USGS data and reports
    Server: merlot.welch.jhu.edu; select the following menu choices from each
    succeeding menu: 13 (search/retrieve software), 8 (search retrieve
    graphics), 3 (search all), then 2 (graphics software).

World Wide Web Servers
    World Wide Web (WWW) is a hypertext front end program based on
client/server architecture that permits you to access information on the Internet
as if it were part of a seamless web. The goal of WWW is to make all online
knowledge part of one interconnected web of documents and services. You can
move around the WWW by browsing and selecting certain links to explore, by
using keyword search tools, or by issuing commands to go to a specific Internet
resource.

Anthropology
Allen H. Lutins' anthropology resources on the Internet; site includes web
    pages, discussion lists, newsgroups, gophers, and FTP sites.
    http://www.nitehawk.com/alleycat/anth-faq.html
ANTHAP (Applied Anthropology Computer Network) home page
    http://www.oakland.edu/~dow/anthap.htm
Anthronet at University of Virginia; facilitates access to anthropological
    sources on the Internet for the graduate students and faculty at the
    University and the world- wide community as a whole.
    http://darwin.clas.virginia.edu/~dew7e/anthronet/
Anthropological Index; published by the Royal Anthropological Institute;
    covers the periodical collection of the British Museum Department of

Ethnography (Museum of Mankind)
   http://lucy.ukc.ac.uk/rai/AnthIndex.html
Anthropological multimedia: a collaborative document; deals with
   anthropology and multimedia in the classroom.
   http://www.rsl.ox.ac.uk/isca/marcus.banks.02.html
Anthropology in the news
   http://www.tamu.edu/anthropology/news.html
Anthropology on the Internet; sections include cultural anthropology,
   archaeology, linguistics, physical and biological anthropology, electronic
   journals, institutes, labs, associations, societies, directories, museums, etc.
   http://dizzy.library.arizona,edu/users/jlcox/first.html
Center for Anthropology Communications home page; good site with links to
   other anthropology documents online.
   server: http://pegasus.acs.ttu.edu/~wurlr/anthro.html
Classics of out(land)ish anthropology; review of web sites that contain
   information that violate basic anthropological thinking.
   server: http://www.lawrence.edu/dept/anthropology/classics.html
CSAC ethnographics gallery/intermedia library [also available via gopher,
   WAIS, FTP, etc; use same address (e.g., lucy.ukc.ac.uk)]
   http://lucy.ukc.ac.uk
Culture tour (a multimedia introduction to anthropology)
   http://www.pic.net/~willep/culturetour.html
Cyber anthropology home page (anthropology of the Internet and related)
   http://www.clas.ufl.edu/anthro/cyberanthro/frontdoor.html
Demography and population studies WWW Virtual Library; provides over 140
   links to demographic resources.
   http://coombs.anu.edu/ResFacilities/Demography Page.html
Ethnoarchaeology bibliography {compiled by Dr. Nicholas David, Department
   of Archaeology at the University of Calgary}
   http://www.ucalgary.ca/UofC/faculties/SS/ARKY/nicintro.html
Ethnomusicology online
   http://umbc.edu/eol and http://www.wiu.edu/eol
H-SAE (Society for the Anthropology of Europe discussion group) web page
   http://h-net.msu.edu/~sae/
Internet resources for heritage conservation, historic preservation, and
   archaeology [also available via gopher]
   http://www.cr.nps.gov/ncptt/irg/
Kinship and social organization: an interactive tutorial
   server: http://www.manitoba.ca/anthropology/kintitle.html
   Site that deals with the fundamentals of marriage systems.
Theoretical anthropology (electronic Journal)
   http://www.univie.ac.at/voelkerkunde/theoretical-anthropology/
UCSB anthropology web site (inc. virtual tour of Great Kiva @ Chetro Ketl)
   http://www.sscf.ucsb.edu/anth/
World Heritage Centre {see World Heritage Gopher, above}
   www.icomos.org//world.heritage.htmlANTHRO-L home page/Archives
   http://www.anatomy.su.oz.au/danny/anthropology/anthro-l/index.html

Worldwide email directory of anthropologists (also available via FTP and gopher)
    http://wings.buffalo.edu/academic/department/anthropology/weda/

Archaeology
Ancient world web
    http://atlantic.evsc.virginia.edu/julia/Ancient World.html
Andean bioarchaeology
    http://www.missouri.edu/~c569310/Bioarch_Web_Page.html
Anglo-American Project at Pompeii
    http://atlantic.evsc.virginia.edu/julia/AncientWorld.html
Archaeological Data Archive Project
    http://csasws.brynmawr.edu:443/web1/adap.html
Archaeology Data Service (digital archive for archaeology in the UK)
    http://ads.ahds.ac.uk/ahds/welcome.html
Archaeological field work opportunities (Archaeological Institute of America)
    http://durendal.cit.cornell.edu/TestPit.html
Archaeological Predictive Modelling Project, Ontario Ministry of Natural Resources
    http://caa.lakeheadu.ca/apmp.homepage
Archaeological resource guide for Europe
    http://www.bham.ac.uk/BUFAU/Projects/EAW/index.html
Archaeologists using GIS
    http://www.ncl.ac.uk/~napm1/gis_archies.html
Archaeology and architecture (European and Mediterranean archaeology)
    http://www.xs4all.nl/~mkosian
Archaeology and history in the California State Park System
    http://www.indiana.edu/~maritime/caparks/
Archaeology and tourism in Sicily
    http://www.infcom.it/kalat/welcomeuk.html
Archaeology magazine (web page for the popular magazine published by the Archaeological Institute of America).
    http://www.he.net/~archaeol/index.html
Archaeometry Research Group (Heidelberg, Germany)
    http://goanna.mpi-hd.mpg.de/
ArchDATA (French archaeological resource guide; in French)
    http://www.pratique.fr/~archdata
Archéologie en Martinique (in French)
    http://web.culture.fr/culture/archeo/martiniq.htm
Archéologie sous les mers (in French)
    http://mistral.culture.fr/culture/archeosm/archeosm.htm
Archnet (prehistoric archaeology of the northeast) [also available via gopher]
    http://spirit.lib.uconn.edu/HTML/archnet.html
ARISITUM (History and archeology in France; in French)
    http://www.arisitum.org/adihaf/index.htm
Ashkelon excavations (ancient seaport in Israel)
    http://www.fas.harvard.edu/~peabody/ashkelon_dig.html

Bangladesh archaeological sites and monuments list
http://ee156.eee.kcl.ac.uk/shabbir/bdsarch.htm
Beirut archaeology
http://www.hiof.no/almashriq/
Biblical archaeology and historical geography of Israel
http://www.iorcom/~jmcmath/
BRASS/El Pilar Project (Mayan site on the Belize/Guatemala border)
http://alishaw.sscf.ucsb.edu/~ford/index.html
Cameron's archaeology photo gallery
http://www.aracnet.com/~icecap/archgall.htm
Canadian Association of Palynologists (study of palynology, paleozoic to
quaternary)
http://gpu.srv.ualberta.ca/~abeaudoi/cap/cap.html
Çatalhöyük (virtual dig in Turkey)
http://catal.arch.cam.ac.uk/catal/catal/html
Classical archaeology (list of web/gopher/ftp sites)
http://www.duke.edu/web/jyounger/kapatija.html
Classics and Mediterranean archaeology world wide web server
http://rome.classics.lsa.umich.edu/welcome.html:or use gopher server
Colchester-Stanway burials (England)
http://www.archaeology.co.uk/colchest.htm
Combined Caesarea excavations: underwater excavations of Sebastos, King
Herod's Harbor
http://www.carleton.ca/~ereinhar/CaesareaHome.html
Contract archaeology companies
http://www.acs.appstate.edu/~rq12560/acl_index.html
Costa Rican archaeology (one hundred years of anthropology in Costa Rica)
http://kuhub.cc.ukans.edu/~hoopes/biblio.html
Dig site (documents an archaeological dig in Wadi Natrun, Egypt)
http://www.scriptorium.org/TheDigSite/
Egyptology resources
http://www/gdb.org/hopkins.html
Ethnoarchaeology bibliography (compiled by Nicholas David, Department of
Archaeology at the University of Calgary)
http://www.ucalgary.ca/ca/UofC/faculties/SS/ARKY/nicintro.html
Exploring ancient world cultures
http://www,evansville.edu/~wcweb/wc101
FAQ:careers in archaeology in the United States
http://www.museum.state.il.us/ismdepts/anthro/dlcfaq.html
Glossary of archaeological terms
http://www.smu.edu/~anthrop/glossary.html
Greg Reeder's Egypt page
http://www.sirius.com/~reeder/egypt.html
Guide to resources for the study of the ancient Near East
http://www-oi.uchicago.edu/OI/DEPT/RA/ABZU/ABZU.HTML
Harappan archaeology
http://www.harappa.com/har/har1.html

Excavations at Kamianets-Podilsky, Ukraine
  http://sjfc.edu/~mandzy/KPF_excavations.html
Hawaiian archaeology
  http://www.aloha.net/~colvin
Index of online archaeological reports for sites in the Near East
  http://www-oi.uchicago.edu/OI/DEPT/RA/ABZU/ABZU_
  SUBINDX_ARCH_SITES.HTML
Internet resources for heritage conservation, historic preservation, and
  archaeology [also available via gopher]
  http://www.cr.nps.gov/ncptt/irg/
Kamal archaeology page (Malaysian Archaeology)
  http://www.alang.ukm.my/kamal/
L-Arch-ecologie sous les mers
  http://www.culture.fr/culture/archeosm.htm
Lithic procurement technology
  http://www.geology.bsu.edu/archeo/cjd.htm"
Mittle Salt Spring Archaeological Project (GIS/Digital imaging at a southwest
  Florida site)
  http://www.rsmas.miami.edu/groups/lssw.html
Manitoba archaeology
  http://www.umanitoba.ca/faculties/arts/anthropology/Manitoba
Maya astronomy page
  http:www.astro.uva.nl/michielb/maya/astro.html
Mayan Epigraphic Database Project (also available via FTP and gopher)
  http://jefferson.village.virginia.edu/med/medwww.html
Mayan hieroglyphic syllabary
  http://www.he.net?~nmcnelly
Mayan links (collected by Brian Ampolsk)
  http://www.netaxs.com/~bampolsk/maya.html
Mayanist resource page
  http://denton.computek.net/pub/wagers/ousia/Mayanist.Shtml
MayaQuest (Interactive Mesoamerican expedition)
  http://www.mecc.com/mayaquest.html
Mesoamerican archaeology
  http://copan.bioz.unibas.ch/meso.html
Mugello Valley Archaeological Project (SMU excavations in Turkey)
  http://www.oberli.edu/~scarrier/Poggio_Colla/Intro.html
National archaeological database (United States)
  http://www.cast.uark.edu/products/NABD/
National Park Service's links to the past
  http://www.cr.nps.org
Nemea Valley Archaeological Project
  http://classics.lsa.umich.edu/NVAP.html
Nordic underwater archaeology
  http://www.abc.se/~m10354/uwa
Notre Dame archaeology field school
  http://www.nd.edu/~mschurr

Ohio State University excavations at Isthmia
http://www.acs.ohio-state.edu/history/isthmia/isthmia/html
Oriental Institute
server: http://csmaclab-www.uchicago.edu/oI/default.html
Ontario Ministry of Natural Resources Archaeological Predictive Modelling Project
http://www.pictographics.com/apmp.homepage
Ousia: for the Egyptologist
http://denton.computek.net/pub/wagers/ousia/Egyptologist.Shtml
Ousia: for the Mayanist
http://denton.computek.net/pub/wagers/ousia/Mayanist.Shtml
Palynology/paleoecology
http://life.anu.edu.au/landscape-ecology/pollen.html
PAST(Protecting Archaeological Sites Today)
http://home.uleth.ca/geo/jasweb/jasweb.html
Perseus Project on Art and Archaeology (on-line library of Classical art objects, sites, and buildings)
http://www.perseus.tufts.edu/art&arch.html
Pompeii Forum Project
http://jefferson.village.virginia.edu/pompeii/page-1.html
Prehistory of Alaska (National Park Service)
http://www.nps.gov/akso
Regional archaeological survey resource
http://www.biddeford.com/~mkimball
ROMARCH archives (see Bitnet and Internet Discussion Groups section)
http://www.sys.uea.ac.uk/Research/ResGroups/JWMP/ostia/ROMARCH.html
http://www.vol.it/mirror/ROMARCH/ROMARCH.html
http://www.vol.it/mirror/ROMARCH/2rom.arch.html (for Netscapr 2.0)
Sierra Club policy regarding archaeological resources
http://www.sierraclub.org/policy/411.html
Southhampton University Archaeology Department
http://avebury.arch.soton.ac.uk/arch-top.html
Southwestern Archaeology (SWA) Interest Group
http://seamonkey.ed.asu.edu/swa/
For information and links to archaeology sites in the Southwestern United States and northern Mexico; also has an anti-archaeology section.
Southwestern Archaeology Special Interest Group (SASIG; current events)
A bulletin board, serves current events data
http://aspin.asu.edu/provider/swa/sasig.html
Stone Pages (megalithic sites of Europe)
http://joshua.micronet.it/utenti/dmeozzi/homeng.html
Syracuse University historical archaeology:
http://www.maxwell.syr.edu/anthro/anarcheo.html
Theoretical anthropology (electronic journal)
http://www.univie.ac.at/voelkerkunde/theoretical-anthropology/
UC-Berkeley Museum of Paleontology hypertext server
server: http://ucmp1.berkeley.edu:80/welcome.html

UCSB anthropology web site (incl. virtual tour of Great Kiva @ Chetro Ketl)
  http://www.sscf.ucsb.edu/anth/
UCSD summer session 1996, Nahal Tillah (regional archaeological project in Israel)
  http://weber.ucsd.edu/Depts/Anthro/classes/tlevy
UK archaeology on the Internet (maintained by the Trent and Peak Archaeological Unit at Nottingham University)
  http://www.cc.nottingham.ac.uk/~aczkdz/links.html
Underwater archaeology (ASSONET)
  http://www.mclink.it/n/assonet/inarcsub.html .(English)
  http://www.mclink.it/n/assonet/itarcsub.html (Italian).
University of Michigan Papyrology Collection
  http://www.lib.umich.edu/pap/HomePage.html
World Heritage Centre (see World Heritage Gopher, abobe)
  www.icomos.org//world.heritage.html
World Heritage materials
  http://hpb.hwc.ca.7002/world.heritage.html
  http://hpb.hwc.ca:7002/heritage.list.html

Biological/Physical Anthropology
African primates at home (with audio of primate vocalizations)
  http://www.indiana.edu/~primate/primates.html
Fossil hominids
  http://earth.ics.uci.edu:8080/faqs/fossil-hominids.html
Fossil hominids FAQ (creationism vs. evolutionism)
  http://rumba.ics.uci.edu:8080/faqs/fossil-hominids.html
Hominid paleo-ethology
  http://www.ub.es/SERP/EtoHom/index.html
Origins of humankind (resources concerning human evolution)
  http://www.dealsonline.com/origins.
Origins of mankind web site
  http://www.pro-am.com/origins/origins.html
Primate handedness and brain lateralization research site (with links to other primate sites)
    http://www.indiana.edu/~primate/index.html

Cultural/Social Anthropology
ANTHAP (Applied Anthropology Computer Network) home page; site with information from the Applied Anthropology Computer Network.
  http://www.acs.oakland.edu/~dow/anthap.html
Anthropologist in the field (Hypertext guide to field work, based on work in Papua New Guinea by Dr. Laura Zimmer Tamakoshi)
   http://www.truman.edu/academics/ss/faculty/tamakoshil/index.htmlCSAC
Center for World Indigenous Studies/Fourth World Documentation Project
  ftp://ftp.halcyon.com/pub/FWDP/WWW/fwdp.html; or use gopher server or anonymous ftp.

Cultural anthropology methods (CAM)
    http://www.lawrence.edu/~bradleyc/cam.html
Ethnographics galley/intermedia library [also available via gopher, WAIS,
    FTP, etc.; use same address (e.g., lucy.ukc.ac.uk)]
    http://lucy.ukc.ac.uk.
Ethnomusicology online
    http://umbc.edu/eol and http://www/wiu.edu/eol.
Kinship and social organization: interactive on-line tutorial
    http://www.umanitoba.ca/faculties/arts/anthropology/kintitle.html
The Nacirema
    http://www.nyu.edu/gsas/admin/beads/nacirema.
Reflections on fieldwork among the Sinai Bedouin women (with link to Live
    AOL chat on Sinai Bedouin Women);
    http://www.sherryart.com/women/bedouin.html
Society for the Study of Symbolic Interaction (SSSI) homepage
    http://sun.soci.niu.edu/~sssi.

Linguistics
Ethnologue (Languages of the world); a catalog of the world's languages
    including information on alternate names, number of speakers, location,
    dialects, linguistic affiliation, and other sociolinguistic and demographic
    information
    http://www.sil.org/ethnologue/ethnologue.html
Human languages page
    http://www.williamette.edu/~tjones/Language-Page.html
Language resource site I (fonts for indigenous languages and more)
    http://babel.uoregion.edu/yamada/guides.html
Language resource II
    http://www.pitt.edu/~grouprev/Language/index.html
LinguaWEB (linguistics links)
        http://www.umanitoba.ca/linguistics/main.html

Library Catalogs (Selective)
Arizona State University
    http://www.lib.asu.edu/.
Boston University
    http://web.bu.edu/#Tools.
Columbia University
    http://www.cc.columbia.edu/cu/libraries/indiv/.
Harvard University
    http://www.harvard.edu/home/library.html
Tulane University
    http://www.tulane.edu/~html/hp_tula.html
Tulane University, Latin American Library
    http://www.tulane.edu/~latinlib/lalhome.html
University of Arizona
    http://sabio.library.Arizona.EDU/screens/opacmenu.html
University of California, Berkeley

http://www.lib.berkeley.edu/Catalogs/.
University of Chicago
    http://www.lib.uchicago.edu/LibInfo/Catalogs/Chicago/.
University of Florida
    http://www.uflib.ufl.edu/luiscat.html
University of Michigan
    http://www.lib.umich.edu/libhome/mirlyn/mirlynpage.html
University of Pennsylvania
    http://www.library.upenn.edu/resources/catalogs/catalogst.html
Yale University
    http://www.library.yale.edu/.

Museums
Adan E. Treganza Anthropology Museum, San Francisco State University
    http://www.sfsu.edu/~anthro/treganza.html
Alexandria Archaeology Museum
    http://ci.alexandria.va.us/libraries_museums/aarch.html
Archaeological Museum of Cagliari, Italy
    http://www.crs4/it/HTML/RUGGIERO/MUSE/mus_ind.html
Archaeological Museum of Kibbutz Ein Dor (Israel)
    http://www.geocities.com/Athens/3603.
Archaeologisches Landesmuseum, Baden Wurttemburg (Germany)
    http://www.bawue.de/~wmwerner/alm.html
Ashmolean Museum of Art and Archaeology
    http://www.ashmol.ox.ac.uk/.
Bernice Pauahi Bishop Muiseum
    http://www.bishop.hawaii.org/.
Buffalo Museum of Science
    http://freenet.buffalo.edu/~bms/.
California Academy of Sciences, Anthropology Department
    http://www.calacademy.org/research/anthropology
Canadian Museum of Civilization
    http://www.cmcc.muse.digital.ca/
Carnegie Museum of Natural History
    http://www.clpgh.org/cmnh/
Cleveland Museum of Natural History
    http://www.clpgh.org/cmnh/
Conservation information network
    http://www.chin.gc.ca/CHIN/CHINPubs/English/cin_e.html
Conservation online (full-text database of conservation information)
    http://palimpsest.stanford.edu
Consortium for the computer exchange of museum information
    http://www.cimi.org/cimi
Corning Museum of Glass
    http://www.pennynet.org/glmuseum/corningm.htm
Cranbrook Institute of Science
    http://www.walrus.com/~sha/cranbrook.html

Deal Sea Scrolls exhibit
  http://www.sunsite.unc.edu/expo/deadsea.scrolls.exhibit/intro.html
Exploration of science and art
  http://www.exploration.edu/.
Field Museum of Natural History, Chicago
  http://rs6000.bvis.uic.edu:80/museum/.
Flints and stones: real life in prehistory (exhibition)
  http://www.ncl.ac.uk/~nantiq/menu.html
Florida Museum of Natural History
  http://www.flmnh.ufl.edu/.
Fowler Museum of Cultural History, Los Angeles
  http://www.fmch.ucla.edu/.
Franklin Institute Virtual Museum
  http://sln.fi.edu.
Glenbow Museum, Calgary, Alberta (Canada)
  http://www.glenbow.org/.
Gold, jade, forests: Costa Rica (an exhibition at the Spencer Museum of Art,
  University of Kansas)
  http://falcon.cc.ukans.edu/~hoopes/gold.html
Guide to museums and cultural resources on the web; the best place to begin
  looking at museum web pages; links are to both national and international
  museums
  http://www.lam.mus.ca.us/webmuseums
Heard Museum
  http://hanksville.phast.umass.edu/defs/independent/Heard/Heard.html
Hudson Museum of Anthropology, University of Maine
  http://www.ume.maine.edu/~hudsonm
Hungarian National Museum
  http://origo.hnm.hu/
Illinois State Museum
  http://www.museum.state.il.us/
Internatgional Council of Museums
  http://www.icom.org/ICOM
Irakliuon Archaeological Museum (Crete)
  http://www.dilos.com/region/crete/ir_mus.html
Iroquois Indian Museum
  http://www.cobleskill.edu/projects/archeo/museum.htm
Israel Museum
  http://www.macom.co.il/museum/index.html
Italian Ethnographic Museums (comprehensive list)
  http://www.delta.it/mucgt/
Keilschrifttexte des Dritten Jahrtausends V. Chr. im Vorderasiatischen
  Museum, Berlin (digitized images of cuneiform tablets)
  http://fub46.zedat.fu.berlin.de:8080/~uruk/VAM/
Kelsey Museum of Archaeology, University of Michigan
  http://classics.lsa.umich.edu/Kelsey/Outreach.html
Kibbutz Ein Dor Archaeological Museum (Israel)
  http://www.geocities.com/Athens/3603/

London Museum of Natural History
  http://www.nhm.ac.uk/
MASCA (Museum Applied Science Center for Archaeology at the University of
  Pennsylvania Museum)
  http://masca.museum.upenn.edu
Maxwell Museum of Anthropology, University of New Mexico
  http://www.unm.edu/~maxwell/Maxwell/MMhp.html
Michael C. Carlos Museum, Emory University
  http://www.emory.edu/CARLOS/
Milwaukee Public Museum
  http://www.mpm.edu/
Musée archéologique de Nice Cimiez (in French)
  http://www.culture.fr/culture/archeosm/nice-mus.htm
Musee Schwab (Bienne, Switzerland)
  http://www.museums.ch/museums/musch/
Museo Archeologico di Bologna
  http://www.comune.bologna.it/Cultura/Museicomun/Archeologico/
  ArcheoMuseumHomePage.html
Museo Arqueológico San Miguel de Azapa (Universidad de Tarapacá, Chile; in
  Spanish/en español)
  http://www.quipu.uta.cl/utahtml/museo.htm
Museu d'Arqueologia de Catalunya (Spain)
  http://www.arsweb.com/mac/m01g.htm
Museo Chileno de Arte Precolombino (Chilean Museum of PreColumbian Art)
  http://www.conicyt.cl/otros/museo/inicio.html
Museum computer network
  http://world.std.com/~mcn/MCN.html
Museum Documentation Association
  http:www.comlab.ox.ac.uk/archive/other/museums/mda
Museum Informatics Project, University of California, Berkeley
  http://www.mip.berkeley.edu
MuseumNet (Listings of all the major UK museums)
  http://www.museums.co.uk
Museum of Anthropology, Wake Forest University,
  http://www.wfu.edu/Academic-departments/Athropology/museum/
  general.htm
Museum of Antiquities, University of Newcastle Upon Tyne
  http://www.ncl.ac.uk/~nantiq/
Museum of Archaeology and Anthropology, University of Pennsylvania
  http://www.upenn.edu/museum
Museum of International Folk Art
  http://www.state.nm.us/MOIFAOnLine/MOIFAhome/MOIFAhome.html
Museums around the world (Natural History Museum of Los Angeles County)
  http://www.lam.mus.ca.us/webmuseums/
National Archaeological Museum (Spain)
  English: http://www.gti.ssr.upm.es/~man/index_eng.html
  Spanish: http://www.gti.ssr.upm.es/~man/

National Museum of the American Indian
   http://www.si.edu/nmai/nav.htm
Nova Scotia Museum
   http://www.ednet.ns.ca/educ/museum/arch/
Oriental Institute virtual museum
   http://www.www-oi.uchicago.edu/OI/MUS/QTVR96/QTVR96.html
Peabody Essex Museum
   http://www.pem.org/
Peabody Museum of Archaeology and Ethnology, Harvard University
   http://fas-www.harvard.edu/~peabody/
Phoebe Hearst Museum of Anthropology
   http://www.qal.berkeley.edu/~hearst/index.html
Prince of Wales Northern Heritage Centre
   http://tailpipe.learnnet.nt.ca/pwnhc/
Provincial Museum of Alberta
   http://www.pma.edmonton.ab.ca/
Robert S. Peabody Museum, Phillips Academy
   http://www.andover.edu/rspeabody/geninfo.html
Royal British Columbia Museum
   http://rbcm1.rbcm.gov.bc.ca/
Royal Ontario Museum, Toronto (Canada)
   http://www.rom.on.ca/
San Diego Museum of Man
   http://www.globalinfo.com/noncomm/man/Man.HTML
Santa Barbara Museum of Natural History
   http://www.rain.org/~inverts/
Science Museum of Minnesota
   http://www.sci.mus.mn.us/
Simon Fraser University, Museum of Archaeology and Ethnology
   http://www.sfu.ca/archaeology/museum/
Smithsonian Institution
   http://www.yahoo.com/Government/Agencies/Smithsonian_Institution/
Southern Utah University Museums and Galleries
   http://www.suu.edu/Museums_Galleries
Southwest Museum
   http://www.annex.com/southwest/museum.htm
Traditions of magic in late antiquity web site (based on a display in the
   University of Michigan Library's Special Collections)
   http://www.hti.umich.edu/exhibit/magic
Trips Museum
   http://seawifs.gsfc.nasa.gov/scripts/JASON.html
WebMuseum
   http://www.oir.ucf.edu/wm/
William Hammond Mathers Museum, Indiana University
   http://www.indiana.edu/~mathers/home.html
Yahoo-Museums and Galleries
      http://www.yahoo.com/Arts/Museums_and_Galleries

Academic Departments
Adelphi University: http://www.adelphi.edu:80/acad/artsciANTR.html
Appalachian State University, Department of Anthropology
http://www.anthro.appstate.edu/
Australia National University Department of Archaeology and Anthropology
http://online.anu.edu.au/AandA/
Baylor University, Department of Sociology, Social Work, Anthropology, and
Gerontology
http://www.baylor.edu/baylor/Departments/acad/sociology/undergraduate/
undergrad_faculty.html
Boston University, Department of Anthropology
http://web.bu.edu/ANTHROP/
Brown University, Department of Anthropology
http://www.brown/.edu/Departments/Anthropology/index.html
California Academy of Sciences
http://www.calacademy.org/research/anthropology/
California State University, Sacramento
http://www.csus.edu/anth/index.html
California State University, Stanislaus
http://www.csus.edu/anth/index.html
Central Connecticut State University, Department of Anthropology
http://wwwas.ccsu.ctstateu.edu/depts/anth/
Colby College, Department of Anthropology
http://www.colby.edu/anthropology/
Columbia University, Department of Anthropology
http://www.columbia.edu/cu/anthropology/
Cornell University, Department of Anthropology
http://falcon.arts.cornell.edu/~anthro/
Cornell University, Program of Archaeology
http://falcon.arts.cornell.edu/~arkeo/
University of Denver, Museum of Anthropology
http://www.du.edu/duma/duma.html
Emory University, Department of Anthropology
http://www.emory.edu/COLLEGE/ANTHROPOLOGY/
Flinders University, Archaeology home page (Australia)
http://cmetwww.cc.flinders,edu.au/Archaeology/Home_Page.html
Florida Atlantic University, Department of Anthropology
http://www.fau.edu/divdept/anthro/home/anthro.htm
Franklin and Marshall College, Department of Anthropology
http://server1.fandm.edu/Departments/Anthropology/anthropology.html
Florida State University, Department of Anthropology
http://www.fsu.edu/~anthro/
George Mason University, Anthropology Program, Department of Sociology
and Anthropology
http://mason.gmu.edu/~mhovis/anthro/
Hamline University, Department of Anthropology
http://www.hamline.edu/depts/anthropology/index.html

Harvard University, Department of Anthropology
http://www.wjh.harvard.edu/anthro/
Humboldt State University (California)
Department of Anthropology: http://sorrel.humboldt.edu/~anthro
Archaeology Laboratory: http://sorrel.humboldt.edu/~archlab
Hunter College [CCNY], Department of Anthropology
http://maxweber.hunter.cuny.edu/anthro
Indiana University, Department of Anthropology
http://www.indiana.edu/~anthro/home.html
James Cook University, Department of Anthropology and Archaeology
(Australia)
http://www.jcu.edu.au/dept/Anthropology_and_Archaeology
Kent State University, Department of Anthropology
http://www.kent.edu/anthropology/
Laval University (Canada), Department of Anthropology
http://www.fss.ulaval.ca/ant/ant.html
Lawrence University, Department of Anthropology
http://www.lawrence.edu/dept/anthropology
Loyola University, Chicago, Department of Sociology and Anthropology
http://www.luc.edu/depts/anthropology/
Lund University, Department of Social Anthropology
http://www.rhas.lu.se/anthro/
McGill University (Canada), Department of Anthropologty
http://www.arts.mcgill.ca/programs/anthro/
McMaster University, Department of Anthropology
http://socserv2.socsci.mcmaster.ca/~anthro/
Melbourne University, Department of Classics and Archaeology
http://classics.arts.unimelb.edu.au/
New York University, Department of Anthropology
http://www.nyu.edu/gsas/dept/anthro/
Notre Dame, Department of Anthropology
http://www.nd.edu/~anthro
Oregon State University, Department of Anthropology
http://www.orst.edu/Dept/anthropology/index.html
Pennsylvania State University, Department of Anthropology
http://sol.la.psu.edu/anthro/home.html
Portland State University, Department of Anthropology
http://www-adm.pdx.edu/user/anth/
Princeton University, Department of Anthropology
http://www.princeton.edu/~antwww/
Rice University, Department of Anthropology
http://www.ruf.rice.edu/~anth/
San Diego State University, Student Anthropology home-page
http://rohan.sdsu.edu/dept/aas/AAS.html
San Francisco State University, Department of Anthropology
http://www.sfsu.edu/~anthro/
Simon Fraser University, Department of Archaeology
http://www.sfu.ca/archaeology/

Sonoma State University, Anthropological Studies Center
http://www.sonoma.edu/projects/asc/
Sonoma State University, Department of Anthropology
http://www.sonoma.edu/Anthropology
Southampton University, Department of Archaeology
http://avebury.arch.soton.ac.uk/arch_top.html
Southern Illinois University, Department of Anthropology
http://www.siu.edu/~anthro
Southern Illinois University, Center for Archaeological Investigations
http://www.siu.edu/~cai
State University of New York College ar Oneonta, Department of Anthropology
http://www.oneonta.edu/~anthro/anth1.htm
Texas A&M University, Department of Anthropology
http://www.tamu.edu/anthropology/
Trinity University, Department of Sociology and Anthropology
http://WWW.Trinity.Edu/departments/soc_anthro/index.html
Tulane University, Department of Anthropology
http://www.Tulane.EDU/~anthro/
University College, Dublin Department of Greek and Roman Civilization
http://www.hermes.ucd.ie/~civilse/classics.html
University College, Institute of Archaeology (collected papers)
http://www.ucl.ac.uk/archaeology/pia/
University of Alabama, Department of Anthropology
http://www.as.ua.edu/ant/
University of Arkansas, Department of Anthropology
http://www.uark.edu/depts/anthinfo/
University of Calgary, Department of Archaeology
http://www.ucalgary.ca/UofC/faculties/SS/ARKY/ARKY.html
University of California, Berkeley, Center for Middle Eastern Studies home page
http://violet.berkeley.edu/~cmes/
University of California-Davis, Department of Anthropology
http://www.anthro.ucdavis.edu
University of California, Irvine, Department of Anthropology home page
http://www.socsci.uci.edu/anthro/anthro.html
University of California-Los Angeles, Department of Anthropology
http://www.sscnet.ucla.edu/anthro/
University of California-Santa Barbara, Department of Anthropology
http://www.sscf.ucsb.edu/anth/
University of California, Santa Cruz, Department of Anthropology
http://zzyx.ucsc.edu/Anthro/anthro.html
University of California, San Diego
http://dssadmin.ucsd.edu/anthro/
University of Chicago, Oriental Institute
http://www-oi.uchicago.edu/OI/default.html
University of Connecticut, Department of Anthropology
http://spirit.lib.uconn.edu/ArchNet/Depts/University/uconn/uconn.html

University of Durham, Department of Anthropology
　　http://www.dur.ac.uk/~dan0www/index.html
University of Maine. Department of Anthropology
　　http://www.ume.maine.edu/~anthrop/welcome.shtml
University of Manitoba, Anthropology Department
　　http://www.umanitoba.ca/faculties/arts/anthropology
University of Maryland, Department of Anthropology
　　http://www.bsos.umd.edu/anth/
University of Massachusetts, Amherst, Department of Anthropology
　　http://www.umass.edu/anthro/
University of Melbourne, Department of Classics and Archaeology
　　http://www.arts.unimelb.edu.au/Dept/ClassArch/
University of Memphis, Department of Anthropology
　　http://www.people.memphis.edu/~anthropology/
University of Nebraska - Lincoln, Anthropology Department
　　http://www.unl.edu/anthro/Homepage.html
University of Neuchatel (Switzerland)
　　http://www.unine.ch/ethno/welcome.html
University of Nevada, Las Vegas, Department of Anthropology
　　http://www.nscee.edu/unlv/Admissions/Broadsides/anthropology.html
University of New England, Department of Archaeology and
　　Palaeoanthropology (Australia)
　　http://www.une.edu.au/~Arch/ArchHome.html
University of Nijmegen (Netherlands), Centre for Pacific Studies (CPS)
　　http://www.kun.nl/cps/
University of Notre Dame, Department of Anthropology
　　http://www.nd.edu/~anthro/
University of Oklahoma, Department of Anthropology
　　http://www.uoknor.edu/anthropology/
University of Oxford, Institute of Social and Cultural Anthropology
　　http://www.rsl.ox.ac.uk/isca/
University of Pennsylvania, Department of Anthropology
　　http://www.ssc.upenn.edu/anthro/
University of Reading (England), Department of Archaeology
　　http://www.rdg.ac.uk/AcaDepts/la/Arch/index.html
University of Sydney, Archaeological Computing Lab
　　http://felix.antiquity.arts.su.edu.au/arch.html
University of South Dakota, Department of Anthropology
　　http://www.usd.edu/anth/USDanth.html
University of South Florida, Graduate Programs in Applied Anthropology
　　http://www.cas.usf.edu/anthropology/index.html
University of Southern California, Department of Anthropology home page
　　http://www.usc.edu/dept/elab/anth/deptdesc.html
University of Southern Mississippi, Department of Anthropology and Sociology
　　http://www.usm.edu/~antsoc/
University of Texas, Austin, Department of Anthropology
　　http://www.dla.utexas.edu/depts/anthro/main.html

University of Virginia, Department of Anthropology
    http://minerva.acc.Virginia.EDU/~anthro/
University of Washington, Anthropology Department
    http://weber.u.washington.edu/~anthro/anthrostart.html
University of Waterloo, Department of Anthropology
    http://arts.uwaterloo.ca/ANTHRO/rwpark/anthro.html
University of Western Australia, Department of Anthropology
    http://www.arts.uwa.edu.au/AnthropWWW/OVERVIEW.HTML
University of Western Ontario, Anthropology Department
    http://www.sscl.uwo.ca/anthropology/
University of York, Department of Archaeology
    http://www.york.ac.uk/depts/arch/welcome.html
University of Zurich, Department for Prehistory and Early History
    English: http://www.unizh.ch/prehist/indexe.html
    German: http://www.unizh.ch/prehist/index.html
Utah State University, Sociology, Social Work, and Anthropology
    http://www.usu.edu/~sswa/
Washington University (St. Louis), Department of Anthropology
    http://www.artsci.wustl.edu/~anthro
Western Connecticut State University, B.A./B.S. Degrees in Anthropology &
    Sociology
        http://www.wcsu.ctstateu.edu/socialsci/anthsoc.html

Other Institutions

American Anthropological Association, Council on Anthropology and
    Education
    http://www.ameranthassn.org/cae.htm
American Anthropological Association, Council for General Anthropology
    http://www.ameranthassn.org/cga.htm
American Anthropological Association, Council for Museum Anthropology
    http://www.ameranthassn.org/cma.htm
American Anthropological Association, Council on Nutritional Anthropology
    http://www.ameranthassn.org/cna.htm
American Anthropological Association, Culture and Agriculture
    http://www.ameranthassn.org/cag.htm
American Anthropological Association, Middle East Section
    http://www.ameranthassn.org/mes.htm
American Anthropological Association, National Association for the Practice of
    Anthropology
    http://www.ameranthassn.org/napa.htm
American Anthropological Association, National Association of Students
    Anthropologists
    http://www.ameranthassn.org/nasa.htm
American Anthropological Association, Society for Anthropology in
    Community Colleges
    http://www.ameranthassn.org/sacc.htm

American Anthropological Association, Society for the Anthropology of
  Consciousness
  http://www.ameranthassn.org/sac.htm
American Anthropological Association, Society for the Anthropology of Europe
  http://www.ameranthassn.org/sae.htm
American Anthropological Association, Society for the Anthropology of North
  America
  http://www.ameranthassn.org/sana.htm
American Anthropological Association, Society for the Anthropology of Work
  http://www.ameranthassn.org/saw.htm
American Anthropological Association, Society for Cultural Anthropology
  http://www.ameranthassn.org/sca.htm
American Anthropological Association, Society for Humanistic Anthropology
  http://www.ameranthassn.org/sha.htm
American Anthropological Association, Society for Latin American
  Anthropology
  http://www.ameranthassn.org/slaa.htm
American Anthropological Association, Society for Linguistic Anthropology
  http://www.ameranthassn.org/sla.htm
American Anthropological Association, Society for Medical Anthropology
  http://www.ameranthassn.org/sma.htm
American Anthropological Association, Society for Psychological
  Anthropology
  http://www.ameranthassn.org/spa.htm
American Anthropological Association, Society for Urban Anthropology
  http://www.ameranthassn.org/sua.htm
American Anthropological Association, Society for Visual Anthropology
  http://www.ameranthassn.org/sva.htm
American Cultural Resources Association
  http://www.mindspring.com/~wheaton/ACRA.html
American Ethnological Society
  http://www.ameranthassn.org/aes.htm
Anthropology and Environment Section
  http://www.ameranthassn.org/ae.htm
Anthropology communications on-line
  http://pegasus.acs.ttu.edu/~wurlr/anthro.html
Archaeological and Anthropological Society of Victoria {Australia}
  http://www.vicnet.net.au/~aasv/aasvhom.htm
Archaeological Institute of America
  http://csaws.brynmawr.edu:443/aia.html
Archaeological Society of Virginia
  http://www2.dgsys.com/~asv/
Archaeology Division, American Anthropological Association
  http://www.ameranthassn.org/ad.htm
Archaeometry Group, Universität Bonn
  http://merlin.iskp.uni-bonn.de/mommsen/top.html
ArcheoTek (Universitat Zurich, Institute fror Prehistoric Technology
  http://www.unizh.ch/prehist/exparch/archeotec.html

Arkansas Archaeological Suervy
  http://www.uark.edu/campus-resources/archinfo/)
Association for Africanist Anthropology
  http://www.ameranthassn.org/afaa.htm
Association of Black Anthropologists
  http://www.ameranthassn.org/aba.htm
Association for Feminist Anthropology
  http://www.ameranthassn.org/afa.htm
Association of Latina and Latino Anthropologists
  http://www.ameranthassn.org/alla.htm
Association for Political and Legal Anthropology
  http://www.ameranthassn.org/apla.htm
Association of Senior Anthropologists
  http://www.ameranthassn.org/asa.htm
Biological Anthropology Section, American Anthropological Association
  http://www.ameranthassn.org/bas.htm
Central States Anthropological Society
  http://www.ameranthassn.org/csas.htm
California Office of Historic Preservation
  http://agency.resource.ca.gov/parks/ohp/ohp.html
Canadian Archaeological Association
  http://caa.lakeheadu.ca/caa.homepage
Center for the Study of Architecture (archaeological and architectural)
  http://csaws.brynmawr.edu:443/web1/csa.html
Center for the Study of Eurasian Nomads
  http://garnet.berkeley.edu/~jkimball
Centre for Computer-aided Egyptological Resources (CCER) [also available via
  FTP]
  http://www.newton.cam.ac.uk/egypt
Centro Camuno di Studi Preistorici/Camunian Center of Prehistoric Studies
  (Capo-di-Ponte, Valcamonica, Brescia, Italy)
  http://www.digibank.it/ccsp/
Colorado Archaeological Society, Indian Peaks Chapter (IPCAS; in Boulder)
  http://www.netone.com/~mlandem/
Connecticut State Archaeologist and Connecticut Historical Commission
  http://spirit.lib.uconn.edu/ArchNet/Topical/CRM/crmshpo.html
Council for British Archaeology
  http://britac3.britac.ac.uk/cba/
Crow Canyon Archaeological Center
  http://www.crowcanyon.org/
Cultural Survival
  http://www.cs.org/
Dutch Commission on Archaeological Heritage
  http://www.archis.nl/
Florida Division of Historical Resources
  http:199.44.58.12:80/sos/divisions/historical_resources/hist.html
G.A.P. Pisa, Tuscany, Italy (Heritage Volunteers Association)
  http://marolaws.iet.unipi.it:31442/gap/gap.htm

Gruppo Archeologico Pisano
http://venere.iet.unipi.it/gap/gap.htm
Institute of Field Archaeologists, Wessex regional group
http://csweb.bournemouth.ac.uk/consci/text/wessex.htm
International Council on Monuments and Sites [also available via gopher]
http://www.icomos.org/
Israeli Foreign Ministry (includes information on archeological excavations in
Israel)
http://www.israel.org/israel-info/display.cgi/ark@950100.ark
Iowa Archeological Society; includes links to other archaeology and
anthropology resources
http://www.uiowa.edu/~osa/ias/iashome.htm
Iowa Office of the State Archaeologist
http://www.uiowa.edu/~osa
London and Middlesex Archaeological Society (LAMAS)
http://orca.unl.ac.uk/lamas
Massachusetts Historical Commission
http:spirit.lib.uconn.edu/ArchNet/Topical/CRM/crmshpo.html
Minnesota State Historic Preservation Office
http://www.umn.edu/nlhome/g075/mnshpo/index.html
MURR Archaeometry Lab</A> (Nuclear Archaeology and Geochemistry
Group)
http://www.missouri.edu/~murrwww/archlab.html
National Center for Preservation Technology and Training [also available via
gopher]
http://www.cr.nps.gov/ncptt/
Ohio Historical Society
http://winslo.ohio.gov/ohswww/ohshome.html
Royal Anthropological Institute of Great Britain and Ireland
http://lucy.ukc.ac.uk/rai/
Society for American Archaeology
http://www.saa.org
Society for California Archaeology
http://www.scanet.org
Society for Economic Anthropology
http://www.lawrence.edu/~peregrip/seahome.html
Society for Ethnomusicology
http://www.indiana.edu/~ethmusic/
Society for Historical Archaeology
http://www.azstarnet.com/~sha
Society for Medical Anthropology
http://www.dur.ac.uk/~dan0ejs/smahomepage.html
Society for the Preservation of Natural History Collections
http://iscssun.uni.edu/vidal/spnhc
Society for Professional Archeologists
http://www.smu.edu/~anthrop/sopa.html
South Carolina Office of the State Archaeologist
http://www.cla.sc.edu/sciaa/osa.html

Texas Historical Commission
http://www.io.com/~kjolly/thc.htm
UV Uppsala (a branch of the Central Board of National Antiquities in Sweden)
http://www.bahnhof.se/~uvuppsala
West Virginia Archaeological Research Library
http://www.wvlc.wvnet.edu/wvarl/archp.html
World Archaeological Congress (University of Southampton Department of
Archaeology)
http://wac.soton.ac.uk/wac/

Commercial Sites
Cogitas (computer/technology consulting services for archaeological projects
and museums)
http://pobox.com/~cogitas
Cultural Resource Analysts, Inc.
http://www.crai-ky.com
Documentary educational resources (anthropology/ethnography, sociology and
documentary films)
http://der.org/docued
Ecoscience, Inc. archaeology page
http://www.scranton.com/ecoscience/archpg.html
Heritage marketplace
http://www.canlink.com/nickadams/
Hunter research (NJ-based CRM firm)
http://www.canlink.com/nickadams/
W.G. Winter, Bookseller [Used, Rare & Out-of-Print Books; Anthropology &
Archaeology section]
http://www.mercury.net/~wgwinter/antarch2.htm

Electronic Journals and Archives
Aerial archaeology newsletter
http://nmia.com/~jaybird/AANewsletter/
African archaeology review
http://www.plenum.com
Andean past
http://kramer.ume.maine.edu/~anthrop/AndeanP.html
Anthropology news network (makes anthropological perspectives on news and
issues available to the public); contact Fred Skanes
[fskanes@kean.ucs.mun.ca] for more information.
Anthropology today
http://lucy.ukc.ac.uk/rai/
Antiquity
http://intarch.ac.uk/antiquity
Archaeoastronomy and ethnoastronomy news
http://www.wam.umd.edu/~tlaloc/archastro/
Archaeological dialogues journal (promotion of theoretical approaches in
archaeology published by the Archaeological Dialgues Foundation, Leiden)
http:archweb.LeidenUniv.nl/ad/home_ad.html

Archaeology magazine
   e-mail:archaeol@spacelab.net
   http://www.he.net/~archaeol/index.html
At the edge (expoloring new interpretations of past and place in archaeology,
   mythology, and folklore)
   http://www.gmtnet.co.uk/indigo/edge/atehome.htm
Berkeley archaeology
   http://www.qal.berkeley.edu/arf/
Bulletin of Information on Computing in Anthropology (Its primary purpose is
   to promote the use of technology in anthropological research. Topics range
   from discussions of the use of expert systems to elucidate marriage patterns
   and musical improvisations, to the general problems of using computers in
   the field)
   http://lucy.ukc.ac.uk/bicaindex.html
Bulletin of Italian ethnomusicology
   http://muspe1.cirfid.unibo.it/ictm/home.htm
Current anthropology
   http://www.artsci.wustl.edu/~anthro/ca
Combspapers data bank (electronic repository of social science and humanities
   research papers and documents; ftp to coombs.anu.edu.au and get file
   INDEX from directory 'coombspapers' (available also via Gopher).
Current archaeology
   http://www.compulink.co.uk/~archaeology
Electronic antiquity (University of Tasmania)
   gopher: info.utas.edu.au
   ftp:ftp.utas.edu.au/departments/classics/antiquity/
Ethno-CA news (newsletter for researchers in ethnomethodology and
   conversation analysis).
   http://www.comp.lancs.ac.uk/sociology/staff/soajeo.html
European sociologist (European Sociological Association's newsletter for
   developments on the sociology of Europe).
   http://www.qub.ac.uk/socsci/miller/submit.html
Human ecology forum (leading journal in human ecology);
   gopher://gopher.enews.com//11/magazines/alphabetic/all/human_ecology/
   Sub.
ICPSR Bulletin (Inter-University Consortium for Political and Social Research
   (University of Michigan) offers access to the world's largest repository of
   computer-readable social science data; quarterly ICPSR Bulletin announces
   data collections most recently released or updated, and ICPSR activities,
   programs, and services.
   htp://www.icpsr.umich.edu/ICPSR_homepage.html or
   gopher://gopher/icpsr.umich.edu.
Internet archaeology
   http://intarch.york.ac.uk
Journal of field archaeology (Boston University)
   http://jfa-www.bu.edu
Journal of material culture
   http://www.sagepub.co.uk/journals/details/mcu.html

Journal of political ecology (Bureau of Applied Research in Anthropology, University of Arizona)
http://dizzy.library.arizona.edu/ej/jpe/jpeweb.html
Journal of Roman archaeology
http://www-personal.umich.edu/~pfoss/jra/JRA_Home.html
Journal of world anthropology
http://wings.buffalo.edu/academic/department/anthropology/jwa/
Journal of world systems research (research journal sponsored by Johns Hopkins Program in Comparative International Development) LISTPROC@CSF.COLORADO.EDU, message: subscribe wsn firstname lastname.
KMT: A Modern Journal of Ancient Egypt
http://www.sirius.cfom/~reeder/kmt.html
Mid-Continental Journal of Archaeology
http://www.uiowa.edu/~osa/public/mcja/
New Community: Journal of the European Research Centre on Migration and Ethnic Relations (contents and abstracts of latest issuers are posted with ordering information for print and electronic formats);
http://www.ruu.nl/ercomer/index.html
Online Archaeology (University of Southampton)
http://avebury.arch.soton.ac.uk/Journal/journal.html
Papers from the Institute of Archaeology
http://ww.ucl.ac.uk/archaeology/pia
Postmodern Culture (includes analytical essays, reviews, and various literary forms to stimulate discussion of postmodern culture, encouraging reconsideration of traditional forms of academic writing and publishing); http://jefferson.village.virginia.educ/pmc/ contents.all.html or ftp.ncsu.edu, cd/pub/ncsu/pmc or LISTSERV@LISTSERV.NCSU.EDU, message: subscribe pmc-list firstname lastname.
Social Science Japan (English-language newsletter on economic, political science, law, and sociological research on Japan);
http://www.iss.u=tokyo.ac.jp/center/SSJ.html
Society for American Archaeology Bulletin; gopher: alishaw.ucsb.edu;
http://www.sscf.ucsb.edu/SAABulletin
TRACCE-on-line rock art bulletin
http://www.geocities.com/Athens/2996/
World Systems Archive; announcements, documents, data, biographical and publications information.
ftp to csf.colorado.edu and connect to directory 'wsystems'.

Other Sources of Anthropological Information/Software
Anita Cohen's list of anthropology web sites
http://dizzy.library.arizona.edu:80/users/jlcox/first.html
Hal Rager's archaeology links
http://www.nevada.edu/home/22/rager/pub/archae.html
Lorelei's comprehensive list of archaeological links
http://hal9000.net.au/~siegloff/arch.html

National archaeological database
  Telnet to cast.uark.edu; login as "nadb" (omit quotes; use lower-case only).
  http://www.wsu.edu:8000/~i9248809/anthrop.html
Western Connecticut State University List: anthropology Internet resources
  http://www.wcsu.ctstateu.edu/socialsci/antres.html
Yahoo anthropology/archaeology server
  http://www.yahoo.com/Social_Science/Anthropology_and_Archaeology.

22

Anthropological Films and Photography

Films and photographs are valuable sources of information for anthropologists. Scholars working in the subdiscipline of visual anthropology rely on photographs and films as the primary medium for analysis. Ethnographic films supplement written ethnographies as a means of communicating the findings of cultural/social anthropology. Details and patterns in complex events, such as public religious rituals, which are often difficult to observe and describe, can be recovered from films. Anthropologists conducting historical research make use of old photographs for the quotidian detail they reveal or for what their stereotypical poses reveal of intergroup or class attitudes.

The sources listed in this chapter will be especially helpful to film researchers. The chapter is subdivided into film resources, that is, encyclopedias and dictionaries that provide definitions and information concerning motion picture terminology, film styles, etc., and bibliographies of film literature. The latter books are especially important since indexing of many film periodicals is relatively new.

For additional information about anthropological films and photography, consult the library catalog under the appropriate subject with the subdivision *Bibliography*. For example,

> *Indians of North America -- Film Catalogs*
> *Indians of North America -- Video Catalogs*
> *Indians in Motion Pictures*

Anthropology

22.1 *Catalogue de films d'interes archeologique, ethnographique, ou historique*. Paris: UNESCO, 1970. 546 p. CC85 .U5 1970.

22.2 *Cinema et sciences humaines: anthropologie visuelle, scenographie, praxeologie*. Paris: Formation de Recherches Cinematographiques, U.E.R. des Sciences Sociales, Universite Paris X Nanterre, v. 1 - , 1983 - . GN347 .C56.

22.3   Emrich, Ulrike. *Forschungsstelle fur Humanethologie in der Max-Planck-Gesellschaft*. Berichte und Mitteilungen, 90(1). München: Max-Planck-Gesellschaft, 1990. 103 p.

22.4   *Ethnographic films*. Canberra: National Film Lending Collection (Australia), 1984. 30 p.
Catalog of ethnographic films at the National Film Lending Collection, Canberra, Australia.

22.5   *Films: the visualization of anthropology*. University Park: Audio-Visual Services, Pennsylvania State University, 1977 - . irregular. GN42.3 .Z9 F55.
Catalog of films in the collection at Pennsylvania State University; most recent edition: Maryann Curione, *Films: the visualization of anthropology* (University Park: Audio-Visual Services, Pennsylvania State University, 1984. 170 p.).

22.6   *Guide to the collections of the Human Studies Film Archives*. Washington, D.C.: Human Studies Film Archives, Smithsonian Institution, 1987. 55 p.

22.7   Heider, Karl G., and Carol Hermer. *Films for anthropological teaching*. 8 ed. Arlington, Virginia: American Anthropological Association, 1995. 324 p. GN42.3 .Z9 H44 1995.
Covers a wide range of films, from descriptive documentaries (e.g., Yanomamo series) to more interpretive films (e.g., *The Nuer*).Includes an alphabetical listing with production and distribution information, as well as indexes by subject and geographical area. If available, references to critical comments found in the *American anthropologist* are noted at the end of film descriptions.

22.8   Husmann, Rolf, *et al. A bibliography of ethnographic films*. Gottinger kulturwissenschaftliche Schriften, 1. Göttingen: Lit, 1992. 335 p. GN347 .B53x 1992.

22.9   Millette, C. *Films ethnographiques: production française; Ethnographic Films: French production*. Paris: Interaudiovisuel, 1980. 335 . GN316 .F54 1980.

22.10   Wintle, Pamela, and John L. Homiak. *Guide to the collections of the Human Studies Film Archives: 100th anniversary of motion pictures: commemorative ethnographic edition*. Washington, D.C.: National Museum of Natural History, Smithsonian Institution, 1995. 152 p. GN14 .W56x 1995.

22.11   Zimmerly, David W. *Museocinematography: ethnographic film programs of the National Museum of Man, 1913-1973.* Canadian Ethnology Service, Mercury Series, Paper, 11. Ottawa: National Museums of Canada, 1974. 103 p. 312.71 N213 no.11.

Archaeology

22.12   Downs, Mary. *Archaeology on film.* 2 ed. Dubuque, Iowa: Kendall/Hunt, 1995. 115 p. CC85 .Z9 A4 1995.
Catalog of archaeology films.

22.13   Howell, Carol L., and Warren Blanc. *A practical guide to archaeological photography.* Archaeological Research Tools, 6. Los Angeles: Institute of Archaeology, University of California, 1992. 136 p. CC79 .P46 H68 1992.

22.14   Kruckman, Laurence. *The techniques and application of aerial photography to anthropology: A Bibliography.* Council of Planning Librarians. Exchange bibliography, 339. Monticello, Illinois: Council of Planning Librarians, 1972. 25 p.

Africa

22.15   *Africana at the Media Center of the University of Illinois Library.* Urbana: University of Illinois at Urbana-Champaign, 1992. 18 p.
"Africa related films and slides at the Media Center of the University of Illinois Library."

22.16   Ballantyne, James, and Andrew Roberts. *Africa: a handbook of film and video resources.* London: British Universities Film and Video Council, 1986. 120 p. Z3501 B85 1992.

22.17   *Films and Video for African Studies.* University Park: Audio-Visual Services, Pennsylvania State University, 1992. 41 p.

22.18   Karlsson, Jenni. *Videocatalogue, Africa.* 2 ed. Durban, South Africa: Educational Resources Information Service, Media Resource Centre, Department of Education, University of Natal, 1992. 102 p.

22.19   *Library of African Cinema: A guide to video resources for colleges and public libraries.* San Francisco: Resolution/California Newsreel, 1990. 35 p.

22.20   Marek, Stephen, Stuart Baker, and Rose Antonecchia. *An annotated guide to the Africana Documentary Video Collection.* Evanston, Illinois: Marjorie Iglow Mitchell Media Center, 1993. 34 p.

22.21   RuBlack, Carol, Celine Pelletier, and Dominique Jutras. *Africa on film and videotape: a guide to audio-visual resources available in Canada.* Montreal: Editions du CIDIHCA, 1990. 139 p.

22.22   Schmidt, Nancy J. *Sub-Saharan African films and filmmakers, 1987-1992: an annotated bibliography.* London; New Providence, New Jersey: Hans Zell, 1994. 468 p. PN1993.5 .A357 S37x 1994.

22.23   Sligh, Thomasina. *National Museum of African Art, Smithsonian Institute, Washington, D.C., Education Department Video Collection.* Washington, D.C.: National Museum of African Art, 1994. 14 leaves.
        Catalog of film archives at the United States National Museum of African Art.

22.24   *University of California at Berkeley-Stanford University Joint Center for African Studies film and video resources guide.* Berkeley: University of California at Berkeley-Stanford University Joint Center for African Studies, 1989 - . 1/yr.
        Includes Africa film and video resources available from University of California at Berkeley Media Extension Center, Moffitt Library Media Resource Center, and Language Laboratory, from Stanford University Meyer Library, Audio-Visual Center, and Residential Education, and from California Newsreel.

Asia

22.25   *Films on Southeast Asia available at the University of Hawaii.* Honolulu: School of Hawaiian, Asian and Pacific Studies, Center for Southeast Asian Studies, 1991. 39 leaves.
        Revision of *Films on Asia and the Pacific Available in Hawaii: A Critical Guide* (Honolulu: Pacific and Asian Affairs Council and the Asian Studies Program at the University of Hawaii, 1975. 92 p.)

22.26   Hymes, Jo Ann. *Asia through film: an annotated guide to films on Asia in the University of Michigan Audio-Visual Education Center.* Ann Arbor: Center for Japanese Studies, University of Michigan, 1976. 64 p.

22.27   International Committee on Ethnographical and Sociological Films. *Catalogue de films sur les arts du spectacle dans les pays arabes et en Asie.* Paris: Presses de l'UNESCO, 1975. 172 p.

22.28   Shaw, Sylvie. *Visions of Asia: a filmography of Asian films and films about Asia.* Carlton South, Victoria: Asialink, 1990. 78 p.

Europe

22.29   Balassa, Ivan, and Maria Regdonne Bagi. *Ketszaz neprajzi eloadas vazlata: irodalom es filmjegyzek.* Budapest: Tudomanyos Ismeretterjeszto Tarsulat, 1981. 232 p.
Catalog of Hungarian ethnographic films.

22.30   *Catalogue of French ethnographical films, analysed.* Reports and Papers on Mass Communication, 15. Paris: UNESCO, 1955.

22.31   Dall'Agnolo, Daniel, Barbara Etterich, Marc-Oliver Gonseth, eds. *Ethnofilm: Katalog, Beitrage, Interviews.* Ethnologica Helvetica, 15. Berne: Societe Suisse d'Ethnologie, 1991. 283 p. PN1993.5 .A357 S37x 1994.
Includes a bibliography (pp. 8-129) of Swiss ethnographic films in the Schweizerische Ethnologische Gesellschaft; text in German and French.

22.32   *Per un archivio filmografico del costume laziale: catalogo di documenti video-filmici conservati in archivi pubblici e privati di Roma.* Roma: Nuova Editrice Romana, 1992. 104 p.
Film and video catalog of the ethnographic of the Lazio region of Italy.

22.33   Raabe, Eva C., and Herbert Wagner. *Kulturen im Bild: Bestande und Projekte des Bildarchivs, Museum für Volkerkunde Frankfurt am Main.* Frankfurt am Main: Museum für Volkerkunde, 1994. 280 p. GN340 .M98x 1994.

22.34   Schlumpf, Hans-Ulrich, and Silvia Conzett. *Filmkatalog der Schweizerischen Gesellschaft für Volkskunde.* Basel: Verlag der Gesellschaft, 1993. 252 p.
Film catalog of the Swiss Folklore Society.

22.35   Vallisaari, Hilkka. *Kansatieteellisen elokuvan alkuvaiheet Suomessa; Early Ethnographic Films in Finland.* Helsingin yliopiston kansatieteen laitoksen tutkimuksia, 11 Helsinki: Helsingin yliopiston kansatieteen laitos, 1984. 131 p.
Catalog of ethnographic films in Finland, with summary in English.

Latin America

22.36   *A catalogue of feature-length films on videotape.* New Orleans, Louisiana: Latin American Curriculum Resource Center, Tulane University, 1994. 23 p.
"The Latin American Curriculum Resource Center ... provides specialized services to schools and colleges across the nation."

22.37   Coppens, Walter, Roberto Lizarralde, and Luis Jeremías. *Inventario de
         películas realizadas en las zonas indígenas de Venezuela hasta 1980.*
         Caracas: Instituto Autónomo Biblioteca Nacional y de Servicios de
         Bibliotecas, 1983. 44 p.
            Catalog of motion pictures pertaining to the indigenous
         populations of Venezuela.

22.38   Higgins, Susan J. *A Latin American filmography.* Austin: Institute of
         Latin American Studies, University of Texas at Austin, 1978. 132 p.
         791.438 H535.
            "Part of a series developed by the Latin American Culture Studies
         Project for Junior and Community Colleges."

Middle East

22.39   Albright, Charlotte F, and Ellen-Fairbanks Diggs Bodman. *A Middle
         East film sampler: resources at ten national centers.* Seattle: Middle
         East Resource Center, University of Washington, 1983. 105 p.

22.40   Bodman, Ellen-Fairbanks D., and Ronald L. Bartholomew. *Middle
         East and Islamic world filmography, 1992.* Chapel Hill: Nonprint
         Materials Collection, R.B. House Undergraduate Library, University of
         North Carolina, 1992. 53 p.

22.41   McClintock, Marsha H. *The Middle East and North Africa on film: an
         annotated filmography.* Garland Reference Library of the Humanities,
         159. New York: Garland, 1982. 542 p. DS44 .M43 1982.
            Lists films produced between 1903 and 1980 originally in English
         or with English-language subtitles.

22.42   Pouwels, Randall L. *A guide to films on Islam and the Middle East
         available in Australia.* Melbourne: La Trobe University, 1982. 10 p.

North America

22.43   Bataille, Gretchen M., and Charles L.P. Silet. *Images of American
         Indians on film: an annotated bibliography.* Garland Reference
         Library of Social Science, 307. New York: Garland, 1985. 216 p.
         PN1995.9 .I48 B3x 1985.
            Lists 364 entries of Native Americans in film between 1910 and
         1983.

22.44   Brathovde, Jennifer, comp. *American Indians on film and video:
         documentaries in the Library of Congress.* Washington, D.C.: Library
         of Congress. Motion Picture, Broadcasting, and Recorded Sound
         Division, 1992. 28 leaves. E77 .L455x 1992.
            "This is a selected, annotated list of American Indian related
         documentaries which are held in the collections of the Motion Picture,

Broadcasting, and Recorded Sound Division of the Library of Congress, as of May 1992."

22.45   Butler, Janet L., Gerald R. Belton, and Clarence Smith. *A guide to African, Hispanic, and Native American films.* Buffalo, New York: Regional Development Media Service, 1978. 100 p.

22.46   Hilger, Michael. *The American Indian in film.* Metuchen, New Jersey: Scarecrow Press, 1986. 196 p. PN1995.9 .I48 H54 1986.

22.47   Lund, Karen C., ed. *American Indians in silent film: motion pictures in the Library of Congress.* Washington, D.C.: Library of Congress. Motion Picture, Broadcasting, and Recorded Sound Division, 1992. 57 p. E77 .L4545x 1992.
         "This is an annotated list of silent fiction and non-fiction films with substantial American Indian content that are in the collections of the Motion Picture, Broadcasting and Recorded Sound Division of the Library of Congress."

22.48   Rothwell, Stephen J., and Alex Redcrow, eds. *Films on Indians and Inuit of North America, 1965-1978/Films sur les Indiens et les Inuit de l'Amerique du Nord, 1965-1978.* Ottawa: Indian and Inuit Affairs Program, Public Communications and Parliamentary Relations Branch, 1978. 255 p. E77 .R67 1978.

22.49   *Vers une perception plus juste des Amerindiens et des Inuit: guide a l'intention des enseignants et des enseignantes du primaire et du secondaire: filmographie selective commentee.* Quebec: Gouvernement du Quebec, Ministere de l'Education, 1992. 190 p.

22.50   Weatherford, Elizabeth, and Emelia Seubert. *Native Americans on film and video.* New York: Museum of the American Indian/Heye Foundation, 1981. 151 p. PN1995.9 .I48 N37 1981.
         Annotated listing of 400 films and videos about Native Americans.

Oceania

22.51   Douglas, Norman, and Diane Aoki. *Moving images of the Pacific Islands: a guide to films and videos.* Occasional Paper, 38. Honolulu: Center for Pacific Islands Studies, School of Hawaiian, Asian, and Pacific Studies, University of Hawaii at Manoa, 1994. 347 p.

22.52   *Pacific Islands film and video catalog.* Honolulu: Wong Audiovisual Center, University of Hawaii at Manoa, 1990. 53 p.

22.53   *Premier catalogue selectif international de films ethnographiques sur la region du Pacifique.* Paris: UNESCO, 1970. 342 p. GN342 .I5.
Lists 342 films, arranged geographically, some with detailed critical analysis.

Photography

22.54   *The Northwest Coast Collection of American Indian Art.* Boston: G.K. Hall, 1987. 35 microfiche.
Microform catalog of Northwest Coast Indians at the Museum of Mankind.

22.55   *The Peabody Museum: a visual record of artifacts.* Hillel Burger, and Barbara Isaac, comp. Boston: G.K. Hall, 1990. 8 microfiches.
High quality microfiche of 600 important objects curated at the Peabody Museum of Archaeology and Ethnology, Harvard University. The set is accompanied by, *The Peabody Museum: a visual record of artifacts: guide to the microfiche collection* (Boston: G.K. Hall, 1990. 54 p.), a printed catalog providing information on title, culture, acquisition date, measurements, medium, and the Peabody Museum transparency number for each image. Accompanied by printed guide. Coverage reflects the Museum's concentrations of Native American anthropology; contents include: Fiche 1. North America: Arctic, Subarctic, Northwest Coast; Fiche 2. North America: Northwest Coast, California, Southwest; Fiche 3. North America: Southwest, Great Basin; Fiche 4. North America: Plateau, Plains and Prairie, Great Lakes and Northeast; Fiche 5. Great Lakes and Northeast, Southeast, Daguerreotypes; Fiche 6. Mesoamerica; Fiche 7. Mesoamerica and South America; Fiche 8. Europe, Africa, Asia and Oceania.
See also: Melissa Banta and Curtis M. Hinsley, *From site to sight: anthropology, photography, and the power of imagery: a photographic exhibition from the collections of the Peabody Museum of Archaeology and Ethnology and the Department of Anthropology, Harvard University* (Cambridge, Massachusetts: Peabody Museum Press; Harvard University Press, 1986. 136 p.).

22.56   Ramsay, E.G. *Aboriginal artefacts in the Donald Thomson Collection: a microfiche catalogue.* Melbourne: University of Melbourne and the Museum of Victoria, 1987. 10 microfiche with a printed guide.
Microfiche catalog to the Donald Thomson collection of Australian Aborigine antiquities at the Museum of Victoria, University of Melbourne.

23

Human Relations Area Files

The Human Relations Area Files, Inc. (HRAF), centered at Yale University, is an incorporated, not for profit, international research organization sponsored by more than twenty major universities and museums. Since 1949, the Human Relations Area Files has devoted its resources to developing programs and services to encourage and facilitate the worldwide comparative study of culture, society, and human behavior. It has approximately 250 participating member institutions in some two dozen countries. The collection presently contains 3,500,000 pages of information organized into files on over 350 different cultural groups provided on over 21,500 microfiche. The Human Relations Area Files has been described variously as a "vast ethnographic encyclopedia," a "social science information retrieval system," a "laboratory without walls," and a "highly indexed ethnographic laboratory."

The purpose of the Human Relations Area Files is to provide a systematically organized body of information on various regions and culture areas for scientific, historical, and other research, and to provide, through the inclusion of information on a valid sample of all world cultures, a tool for testing hypotheses and generalizations about human behavior especially on a cross-cultural basis. The Human Relations Area Files contains minutely analyzed published and unpublished works on a significant number of the world's cultures and societies. The material is typically descriptive rather than theoretical, and the majority of the sources are primary documents which have resulted from field observation.

Factual information on a particular population, area, or subject may be rapidly located, cross-cultural comparisons, area studies, and interdisciplinary research projects facilitated, and the testing of many psychological, sociological, and anthropological hypotheses made feasible. Any problem in the human sciences requiring analysis of the literature on a number of different societies can usually be studied with the use of the files in a fraction of the time needed to accomplish the same work through ordinary techniques of library research to the extent that the relevant literature exists in the files.

Nature of the HRAF Files

The Human Relations Area Files constitute both a major cultural data archive and a rapid and efficient data retrieval system. In more specific terms, it is a continually expanding collection of mostly primary sources materials on a large sample of cultures or societies representing all areas of the world. The materials may include many rare sources not generally available and many exclusive translations of non-English-language texts.

Organization of the HRAF Files

The Human Relations Area Files are particularly valuable to you for the following reasons:

- Reduces research time,
- Enables you to focus on analyzing data rather than searching for relevant materials,
- Affords simultaneous access to the same source by several researchers through a multiple filing system,
- Provides a system for rapid and accurate retrieval of information on a particular culture, on a particular subject, or from comparative research, and
- Includes exclusive English-language translations of texts from fifteen languages.

The Human Relations Area Files are organized into culture files, with each file containing information on a particular cultural group such as the Zuni of the American Southwest or the Yoruba of Nigeria. The full collection contains files on more than 350 cultural groups (*Outline of world cultures*). The collection is further organized by subject, according to more than 700 subject categories (*Outline of cultural materials*).

The files are composed physically of 5 x 8 inch plastic sheets, each of which is a duplicate of an original page from a source document. Sheets containing information on a particular culture or society are filed together and arranged by subject content according to a topical outline developed for the HRAF project. For example, 20 sources on the Dogon people of West Africa (*Outline of world cultures* category FA 16) have been analyzed and processed for the Files. Every page in these sources that considers kinship (*Outline of cultural materials* categories 601-609) has been duplicated and placed with other pages treating the same subject in the file on the Dogon. A more complete description of the Human Relations Area Files can be found in the brochure, *HRAF: a world of research*, and the prefaces to the two Outline volumes listed below.

For additional information about the Human Relations Area Files, consult the library catalog under the appropriate subject headings. For example,

Human Relations Area Files
Ethnology -- Methodology
Cross-Cultural Studies

Guides

23.1   Lagacé, Robert O. *Nature and use of the HRAF files: a research and teaching guide*. New Haven: Human Relations Area Files, 1974. 49 p.
An introductory guide to the use and scope of the Human Relations Area Files system; see also: Carol R. Ember and Melvin Ember, *Guide to cross-cultural research using the HRAF archive* (New Haven: Human Relations Area Files, 1988. 24 p.) and *Toward explaining human culture: a critical review of the findings of worldwide cross-cultural research* (David Levinson and Martin J. Malone, eds. New Haven: HRAF Press, 1980. 397 p.).

23.2   *HRAF source bibliography, cumulative*. Joan Steffens and Timothy J. O'Leary, comp. New Haven: Human Relations Area Files, 1976. 1 v. (loose-leaf). GN301 .H86 1976.
Lists all books, articles, and manuscripts used as sources for material appearing in HRAF; arranged by culture group code; annual updates list material added to the file.

23.3   *Sixty cultures: a guide to the HRAF probability sample files*. Robert O. Lagacé, ed. New Haven: Human Relations Area Files, 1977 - . GN307 .S59.
Provides a guide to the 60 data retrieval files that constitute the HRAF Probability Sample Files. These files contain descriptive information on sixty cultural units representing all major areas of the world, and range from small hunter/gatherer groups to complex nations. Includes a cultural summary of each cultural unit, generally covering identification, location, language, population, settlement patterns, economy, social organization, religious system, and cultural change; a review of the literature, including subject coverage and information about the author, fieldwork dates and location, etc.; evaluative comments on this literature and/or each file as a whole, the quality of the sources, adequacy of the subject coverage. and the usefulness of each file for cross-cultural or other types of research; complete bibliographic citations of all sources in each file and of other references consulted for cultural summaries; a Sample Unit Concordance matching these sixty cultural units with the

corresponding units in the *Ethnographic atlas* and in Murdock and White's *Standard cross-cultural sample*; and a major subject index.

23.4   *A guide to social theory: worldwide cross-cultural tests.* David Levinson, ed. New Haven: Human Relations Area Files, 1977. 5 v. GN345.7 .G84.

An analytical propositional inventory of theories of human behavior that have been developed or tested by means of worldwide cross-cultural studies; contents include: v.1. Introduction; v.2. Indexes; v.3. Proposition profiles 1-482; v.4. Proposition profiles 483-971; v. 5. Proposition profiles 972-1379.

23.5   Murdock, George P. *Outline of cultural materials.* 5 ed. New Haven: Human Relations Area Files, Inc., 1982. 247 p. GN345.3 .O95 1982.

The *Outline of cultural materials* (OCM) includes a classification of subject categories used in the Files and divides these into very detailed subdivisions to permit cross-cultural studies of many aspects of culture; a numerical code is obtained from an extensive subject index on topics to be studied within cultural groups. Appendix C· summarizes the basic categories used in the *Outline of cultural materials*.

23.6   Murdock, George Peter. *Outline of world cultures.* 6 ed. New Haven: Human Relations Area Files, 1983. 259 p. GN345.3 .M87 1983.

The *Outline of world cultures* (OWC) inventories and classifies all known human cultures of the world and assigns each an alphabetical and numerical code reference to the Human Relations Area Files. Appendix D summarizes the basic categories used in the *Outline of world cultures*.

23.7   Naroll, Raoul, and Donald Morrison. *Index to the Human Relations Area Files.* Prepared under the auspices of the Council for Intersocietal Studies. Northwestern University. New Haven: Human Relations Area Files, Inc., 1972. 8 v. GN307.5 .H8.

"Most of the works included in the files before September 1967 are covered here." The *Index* is a complete subject index to more than 4,500 selected sources, covering over 300 cultures and nations based on the *Outline of cultural materials*, making it possible for the user to go directly to conventional library resources in situations in which the HRAF files are unavailable. The *Index* can be used to check coverage on any given subject without consulting the files themselves, serve as an inventory list for the files, and to be used to determine the quality of description available on various subjects; continued by: *Index to the*

Human Relations Area Files [microform] (New Haven: Human Relations Area Files, 1988. 31 microfiche). "This Index is a complete page-by-page subject index to the sources (books, articles, manuscripts, etc.) processed into the Human Relations Area Files cultural data archive through December 1986. As such, it updates and replaces the original Index (Naroll and Morrison 1972) and Index Supplement (Steffens 1979) and the microfiche edition through 1983." "This new edition was prepared for the Human Relations Area Files by the National Museum of Ethnology in Osaka, Japan."

23.8   Naroll, Raoul, Gary L. Michik, and Frada Naroll. *Worldwide theory testing.* New Haven: Human Relations Area Files, 1976. 131 p. GN345.7 .N37.

A manual describing how to conduct a cross-cultural study using the HRAF Probability Sample; discusses the theoretical background and methodological limitations of cross-cultural research; includes a basic list of useful sources.

23.9   Textor, Robert B., comp. *A cross-cultural summary.* New Haven: HRAF Press, 1967. 1 v. (various pagings). GN307 .T4.

The bulk consists of carefully selected and edited computer printout. A 400-culture sample derived from Murdock's *Ethnographic Atlas* has been analyzed according to 526 characteristics; designed to demonstrate that for a given cultural characteristic, a series of other characteristics may be expected to occur with a specified degree of probability.

Data Bases

23.10   *Cross-Cultural CD* [computer file]. Boston: SilverPlatter, 1989 -- . 2/yr.

Contains the complete full text files of more than 1,000 anthropological, selected aspects of sociological, and psychological books and articles dealing with life in 60 different societies worldwide during the nineteenth and twentieth centuries. Containing between 6,000 and 12,000 pages of text, each of five CD-ROM volumes centers on a specific topic, including:

1. *Human sexuality*, contains citations, with extracts, to monographs and journal articles on human sexuality. Covers sexuality, sexual stimulation, sexual relations, sexual practices, premarital sex, extramarital sex, sex restrictions, homosexuality, and celibacy. *Marriage*, contains citations, with extracts, to monographs and journal articles on marriage, including reasons for marriage, types of marriage, economic transactions and marriage, arranged marriages,

ceremonies, divorce, remarriage, and irregular marriages.

2. *Family*, contains citations, with extracts, to monographs and journal articles on the family. Covers postmarital residence, family authority, family relationships, adoption, nuclear family, polygynous family, and extended family. *Crime and social problems*, contains citations, with extracts, to monographs and journal articles on crime and social problems. Covers sanctions, homicide, rape, assault, sex crimes, property offenses, offenses against the state, alcohol and drug abuse, disasters, invalidism, poverty, and delinquency.

3. *Old age*, contains citations, with extracts, to monographs and journal articles on old age. Covers variable definitions of old age, longevity, rejuvenation, activities of the aged, and treatment of the aged. *Death and dying*, contains citations, with extracts, to monographs and journal articles on death and dying. Covers life force, causes of death, suicide, funeral practices, funeral specialists, mourning, adjustments to death, and cult of the dead.

4. *Childhood and adolescence*, contains citations, with extracts, to monographs and journal articles on childhood and adolescence. Covers naming, monographs and journal articles on childhood and adolescence. Covers naming, ceremonies, infant care, child care, development and maturation, childhood activities, puberty, adolescent activities, and age of majority. *Socialization and education*, contains citations, with extracts, to monographs and journal articles on socialization and education. Covers techniques of inculcation, weaning and food training, cleanliness training, sex training, aggression training, independence training, transmission of norms, skills and beliefs, educational system, and teachers.

5. *Religious beliefs*, contains citations, with extracts, to monographs and journal articles on religious beliefs. Covers types of religion, role of religion, cosmology, mythology, animism, the soul, spirits, gods, luck and chance, sacred objects and places, and theological systems. *Religious practices*, contains citations, with extracts, to monographs and journal articles on religious practices. Covers religious experiences, rituals, propitiation, purification, atonement, avoidance, taboo, asceticism, orgies, revelation, and divination.

23.11   *Human Relations Area Files* [microform]. Ann Arbor: University Microfilms International, 1968-1993.

Microfiche edition of the HRAF Paper Files (1949 -); complete microfiche format initiated in 1968. The organization of the HRAF files corresponds to the classification in *Outline of world cultures*. Within each culture, the subarrangement is topical, according to the

categories in *Outline of cultural materials*. Bibliographies in each
Cultural File include Categories 111 (Sources Processed), 112
(Sources Consulted), 113 (Additional References), 114 (Comments).
Microfiche format ceased with installment 42 (1993) and publication
in CD-ROM format began with installment 43 (1994).

23.12   *Electronic HRAF* [computer file]. New Haven: Human Relations Area
Files, 1995 - .
"The *Electronic HRAF* is a full-text database that provides
primarily descriptive information on the cultures of the world. The
first installment was issued on CD-ROM in December, 1994.
Subsequent installments are issued on an annual basis. These
installments will begin to replace and update the information currently
available in the microfiche version of the HRAF database and will
eventually replace it entirely." Annual installments will contain 50,000
or more pages of text on fifteen or more cultures. In addition to the
text, indexed by *Outline of cultural materials*, the *Electronic HRAF*
will also contain bibliography for each culture and a cultural summary.
Each installment will cover both North American ethnic groups and a
sample of cultures from around the world. About 20,000 pages each
year will be new material not already in the database. The additional
30,000 pages will be material already in the microfiche version that
has been converted. Some new material will be included for all
cultures in the *Electronic HRAF*. This means that from now on all
cultures will have more current information and each installment will
contain 2.5 times more text than an annual microfiche installment.
Installment 43, issued in December 1994, covers the following
cultures: Africa: Lozi, Mbuti, Shluh; Asia: Andamans, Iban, Taiwan
Hokkien; Europe: Highland Scot; North America: Cajuns, Chinese
Canadians, Chinese Americans, Tzeltal; Oceania: Tikiopia,
Trobriands; South America: Aymar, Yanoama. Installment 44, issued
in December 1995, covers the following: Africa: Maasai , Twi; Asia:
Chukchee, Khasi; Europe: Saami (Lapps); Middle East: Kurds; North
America: Copper Inuit, Irish Americans, Iroquois, Jewish Americans;
Oceania: Aranda (Australia), Lau Fijians; South America: Boror, Ona.

23.13   *HRAF research series in quantitative cross-cultural data* [computer
file]. D. Levinson, ed. New Haven: Human Relations Area Files, 1986
- . GN345.7 .H23 1986.
Contains ethnographic data on approximately 100 variables for
some 60 cultures in the *Probability Sample Files*, a bibliographical
controlled cross-cultural sample of distinct cultures representing major
cultures worldwide. Includes: v. 1: General cultural and religious data

(D. Levinson and R.A. Wagner, eds.), and *Death and dying in the life cycle* (A.P. Glascock and R.A. Wagner, eds.).

Appendix A: Library of Congress Classification Scheme for Anthropology and Related Subjects

GN	**ANTHROPOLOGY**
1	Periodicals, serials
2	Societies
3	Congresses
4-6	Collected works
11	Dictionaries, encyclopedias
12	Terminology, abbreviations
13	Information sources
17	History
20-21	Biography
23-25	General works, treatises, and textbooks
29	Addresses, essays, lectures
30-31	Popular works
32	Pictorial works
33	Philosophy, relation to other topics, methodology; see also BD450 Philosophical anthropology
35	Museums, exhibitions
36	By region or country
41	Private collections
41.6	Anthropologists
41.8	Anthropology as a profession
42	Study and teaching, research
42.3	Audio-visual aids
43	By region or country
GN	**PHYSICAL ANTHROPOLOGY; SOMATOLOGY;** see also QM Human anatomy; QP34 Human physiology
49	Periodicals, societies, serials
50	Congresses
50.2	Collected works
50.3	Dictionaries, encyclopedias
50.4	History
50.5	Biography

289   Population genetics; see also GN247 Hereditary functions; HB848+
        Population (economic theory); QH455 Genetics (general)
296   Medical anthropology; see also GN477 Primitive medicine

GN   ETHNOLOGY; SOCIAL CULTURAL ANTHROPOLOGY; see
        also CB History of civilization; GF Human ecology; GT Manners and
        customs (general); HM+ Sociology
301   Periodicals, societies, serials
302   Congresses
303   Collected works
307   Dictionaries, encyclopedias
308   History
310   General works, treatises, and textbooks
325   Addresses, essays, lectures
303   Popular works
345   Philosophy, relation to other topics, methodology
345.2   Relation to history
345.3   Classification
345.5   Cultural relativism
        Special methods
345.7   Cross cultural studies
346   Fieldwork
347   Photography
357   Culture and cultural processes
358   Culture change, social change
360   Cultural evolution, evolutionism
362   Structuralism, structural anthropology
363   Functionalism
365   Culture diffusion
365.6   Kulturkreis theory
366   Acculturation
367   Assimilation
370   Migrations of peoples
378   Collected ethnographies
        Ethnographies of special categories of peoples
380   Threatened societies
386   Oceanic peoples, maritime anthropology
387   Nomadic peoples
388   Hunting and gathering peoples
389   Fishing peoples
395   City dwellers, urban anthropology

397	Applied anthropology
	Cultural traits, customs, and institutions
406	Technology, material culture
407	Food and food production, subsistence
407.3	Hunting and gathering
407.4	Agriculture
407.8	Irrigation
409	Cannibalism
413	Shelter, habitation
414	Dwellings
415	Furniture
416	Fire, light and heat
418	Clothing and adornment
429	Arts and crafts, industries
	Special crafts
431	Basketmaking
432	Weaving and spinning, textile fabrics
433	Pottery making
	Special materials
434	Stone
434.3	Plant materials
435	Animal materials
435.3	Bone, tooth, horn
435.5	Leather, skin dressing
435.7	Shell
435.9	Feathers
436	Metals, metallurgy
436.2	Copper, bronze
436.3	Gold
436.4	Iron
437	Tools, implements
438	Transportation
439	Routes of communication
441	Vehicles, wheels
442	Snowshoes, skis
448	Economic organization, economic anthropology
448.3	Allocation of natural resources
448.5	Division of labor, organization of work
448.8	Cooperation, competition
449	Property, private ownership
449.3	Land tenure
449.6	Distribution of goods and services
450	Commerce and trade

450.2	Markets
450.4	Barter
451	Intellectual life
452	Communication
452.5	Symbolism, signs and symbols
454	Recreation, sports
468	Philosophy, world view
469	Religion and ritual, belief systems
470.5	Origin of religion
471	Animism
471.4	Mana, taboo
472	Fetishism
472.5	Supernatural beings
472.7	Nativistic movements
472.75	Cargo cults
472.8	Ancestor worship
473	Rites and ceremonies
473.4	Head hunting
474	Religious specialists, priests, etc.
475	Magic, witchcraft
475.3	Magic
475.5	Witchcraft, black magic, sorcery
475.7	Divination
476	Science and knowledge
476.73	Ethnobotany
476.76	Ethnozoology
478	Social organization
479.5	Matriarchy
479.6	Patriarchy
479.65	Social roles
480	Domestic groups, family, forms of marriage
480.3	Endogamy and exogamy
480.33	Polygamy
480.35	Polygny
480.36	Polyandry
480.4	Cross-cousin marriage
480.43	Levirate
480.5	Nuclear families
480.55	Extended families
	Residence rules
480.63	Matrilocal, uxorilocal
480.65	Patrilocal, virilocal

482	Life cycle
	Children
482.1	Birth
482.5	Infanticide
483	Adolescence
483.3	Initiations, puberty rites
484	Adulthood
484.3	Sexual behavior, sex customs
484.4	Marriage
484.7	Divorce
485.5	Death
487	Kinship systems, regulation of descent
487.3	Unilineal descent
487.5	Matrilineal
487.5	Patrilineal
487.6	Double descent
488	Cognatic descent, nonunilineal descent
488.2	Ambilineal descent
488.4	Bilateral, kindreds
489	Totemism
490	Associations
490.2	Institutionalized friendships, blood brothers
490.5	Age groups
490.7	Sex-based groups
490.8	Secret societies
491	Social stratification
491.4	Castes
491.45	Classes
491.7	Territorial groups
492	Political organization
492.25	Leadership, authority
	Types of political organization
492.4	Bands
492.44	Segmentary systems
492.5	Tribes
492.55	Chieftainships
492.6	States
492.7	Kingships, kings
493	Social control
493.3	Social norms
493.5	Deviance
494.5	Disputes
495	Retaliation, vendetta

495.4	Societal groups, ethnic groups
495.6	Ethnicity
496	Intergroup relations
497	Warfare
502	Psychological anthropology
504	Culture and personality
510	Socialization, enculturation
512	Self-concept, self identity
514	Psychology and social change
517	Culture shock
537	Ethnic groups and races
550	North America
560	Central and South America
564	Europe
625	Asia
643	Africa
662	Australia and Pacific Islands
673	Arctic regions

GN	**PREHISTORIC A+RCHAEOLOGY**
700	Periodicals, societies, serials
701	Congresses
705	Collected works
710	Dictionaries, encyclopedias
720	History
733	General works, treatises, and textbooks
743	Popular works
761	Study and teaching, research
766	Addresses, essays, lectures
	By time period
768	Stone Age
769	Archeolithic, Eolithic
771	Paleolithic
773	Mesolithic
775	Neolithic
777	Copper and Bronze Ages
779	Iron Age
	By special topic
783	Caves and cave dwellers
785	Lake dwelling and lake dwellers
787	Kitchen middens
789	Fortifications, earthworks
790	Megalithic monuments

795	Mounds, tumuli, etc.
799	Other special topics
799.A4	Agriculture
799.A5	Amber
799.F5	Fishing
799.M4	Metallurgy
799.P4	Petroglyphs
799.W3	Weapons
800	Museums
802	Private works
803	Europe
851	Asia
861	Africa
871	Australia and Pacific Islands

Other Classifications of Interest to Anthropologists

AM	Museology and museums
BL300-980	Mythology
CB	History of civilization and culture
CC	Archaeology
CN	Epigraphy
D	History (general), Europe (general)
DS	Asia
DT	Africa
DU	Oceania
E	History, America
E51-74	Precolumbian America
E77-79	Indians of North America
E81-93	Indian wars
E99	Indian tribes, A-Z
E101-139	Discovery of America and early explorations
E103-111	Precolumbian period
E141-143	Description and accounts of America to 1810
F	History
F1-999	United States, local history
F1001-1140	British America
F1170	French America, Spanish America
F1210-1392	Mexico
F1401-1999	Latin America
G	Anthropogeography, voyages and travel, oceanography
ML3547	Ethnomusicology
N5310-5400	Primitive art
N5410-5899	Classical

NA260-340	Museums of art
NK	Arts and crafts
P	Philology, linguistics
P24	Museums, exhibitions, collections
P41	Sociolinguistics
P106	Science of language
P901	Extinct Asiatic and European languages
PL-PM	Index to languages and dialects
PM3101	Baja California languages (Indian)
Q	Sciences
QE701-996	Paleontology, paleozoology, paleobotany
QH361-367	Evolution
QH431	Heredity
QL605-739	Vertebrate
QM	Human anatomy
TT	Handicrafts
Z	Bibliography
Z1208	Precolumbian America
Z1209	Indians
Z1210	Individual tribes, A-Z
Z1411	Mexico
Z5052	Museums
Z5053	Dissertations, theses
Z5111-5119	Anthropology and ethnology
Z5131-5134	Archaeology
Z5322 .E9	Evolution
Z5322 .G4	Genetics
Z5322 .H4	Heredity
Z5322 .E1	Ecology
Z5579	Civilization
Z5981-5985	Folklore
Z6011	Geography: voyages and travels
Z6026	Maps and cartography
Z6031-6035	Geology: mineralogy, paleontology
Z6663	Medicine: anatomy and physiology
Z6668	Dentistry
Z7001-7004	Philology and linguistics
Z7116-7119	American Indian
Z7120-7122	Mexico and Central America, Latin America
Z7161-7166	Comparative religion
Z7751	Theology and religion, religions (non-Christian)
Z7833	Primitive religions
Z7836	Mythology

Appendix B: Major Anthropology Collections in United States and Canadian Libraries

Many students, especially those in urban areas, have access to a variety of libraries. In your research project you should determine not only the range of resources available at your campus library, but also what other public and private collections exist in the general area. These may prove extremely valuable depending on the nature of your research project.

Some libraries of potential interest include those in institutions of higher education, such as other universities and colleges, as well as specialized schools of technology, law, medicine, theology, art, and music.

Others include public or governmental libraries operated by municipal, county, state, provincial, or national governments and their regional offices. Capital cities are especially favored with libraries since national legislative bodies, ministries, and departments tend top have very rich collections of official papers. This is most true with respect to various reports which may not be widely distributed.

Although various libraries throughout the United States are designated as depositories for selected governmental publications, few have the resources found in the Washington, D.C. area: the Library of Congress, the National Library of Medicine, and the libraries of the Departments of Interior, Agriculture, State, and other departments and agencies. A similar variety may be found in each state capital in the United States.

A third class covers a great variety of private libraries, including those of local, state, and regional historical societies. In the United States, great research collections in anthropology can be found in the Newberry Library in Chicago, the library of the American Philosophical Society in Philadelphia, the American Oriental Society Library in New Haven, the National Geographical Society Library in Washington, D.C., and in New York, the Missionary Research Library, and the libraries of the American Museum of Natural History, Museum of the American Indian/Heye Foundation, and the Wenner Gren Foundation.

Of special importance are the libraries of public and private museums, such as those of Tozzer Library in the Peabody Museum of Archaeology and Ethnology, Harvard University, in Cambridge, Massachusetts, and the Library of the University Museum at the University of Pennsylvania in Philadelphia. Other important library collections for anthropological research are identified in Chapter 6.

Finally, there are the archives of many nations, their administrative subdivisions, and private collections. Sometimes manuscripts and correspondence are housed in libraries and museums, but they may be stored elsewhere in separate buildings. Archives are important, of course, not only as a source of manuscripts, but also for valuable reports of expeditions, exploration, maps, and correspondence of governmental officials and scholars. Guides and catalogs of selected archival collections important for anthropological research are identified in Chapter 7.

This appendix identifies some of the major academic and research libraries in the United States and Canada with important collections for anthropology. Information is based on Lee Ash and William G. Miller, *Subject collections: a guide to special book collections and subject emphases as reported by university, college, public, and special libraries and museums in the United States and Canada* (6 ed. New York: R.R. Bowker, 1985. 2 v.).

Washington, D.C.

Center for Applied Linguistics, ERIC Clearinghouse on Language and Linguistics, 3520 Prospect St. NW, Washington, D.C., 20007
Comprehensive linguistics collection.

Georgetown University, Library, Special Collections Division, 37 and O St. NW, Washington, D.C., 20057
Important American Indian languages collection.

Library of Congress, American Folklore Center, Archive of Folk Culture, Washington, D.C., 20650
Laura Boulton Collection of recordings of traditional vocal and instrumental music of Canada, Africa, southeast Asia, American Indians, and Eskimos, collected from the 1930s through the 1960s.

Library of Congress, African and Middle Eastern Division, Washington, D.C., 20540
Important linguistics collection.

Library of Congress, Geography and Map Division, Washington, D.C., 20540
Includes papers of Ephraim George Squier and early maps of Central America.

Library of Congress, Manuscript Division, Washington, D.C., 20540
Partial collection (370,000 items) of the personal papers of anthropologist Margaret Mead, including general correspondence files, items dealing with teaching and lecturing activities, an extensive subject file, in addition to drafts, galley proofs, research materials, notes, memoranda, and correspondence

representing her publication of books and articles. Other parts of Mead's papers are at Amherst College (Massachusetts), and the Departments of Anthropology at the American Museum of Natural History (New York) and Columbia University (New York).

National Geographic Society, Library, 1146 16th St. NW, Washington, D.C., 20036
Approximately 63,000 volumes pertaining to land, sea, and space exploration, including anthropology.

Smithsonian Institution Libraries, Anthropology Branch, Washington, D.C., 20560
Includes 54,000 volumes on archaeology, ethnology, linguistics, and physical anthropology of American Indians.

Alabama

University
University of Alabama, Amelia Gayle Gorgas Library, PO Box S, University, Alabama, 35486
Collection includes 119 microfilm reels pertaining to the anthropology and history of the Yucatan peninsula of southern Mexico.

Alaska

Ketchikan
Tongass Historical Society, 629 Dock St., Ketchikan, Alaska, 99001
Collection on Northwest Coast Indian history and art.

Arizona

Dragoon
Amerind Foundation Research Library, Dragoon, Arizona, 85609
Collection on the archaeology of the Greater American Southwest and Mesoamerica.

Fulton-Hayden Memorial Library, Dragoon, Arizona, 85609
A specialized collection of some 17,000 books on the archaeology and ethnography of Mexico and the American Southwest.

Flagstaff
Northern Arizona University, Special Collection Library, CU Box 6022, Arizona, Flagstaff, 86011
Includes the David P. Seaman Collection of manuscripts on the Hopi language.

Fort Huachuca
Fort Huachuca Historical Association, Fort Huachuca, Arizona, 85705
Collection of documents pertaining to Fort Huachuca.

Parker
Colorado River Indian Tribes Museum, Library, Rt. 1, Box 23B, Parker,
Arizona, 85344
Library deals with the four tribes of the Colorado River Indian Reservation:
Mojave, Chemehuevi, Navajo, and Hopi; emphasis also given to the prehistoric
cultures of the area, Patayan and Hohokam.

Phoenix
Heard Museum, Library, 22 East Monte Vista Rd., Phoenix, Arizona, 85004
Includes 40,000 volumes on anthropology and ethnographic art.

Tempe
Cook Christian Training School, Mary M. McCarthy Library, 708 South
Lindon Lane, Tempe, Arizona, 85281
An interdenominational school for the preparation of Native American
adults for positions of church leadership.

Tsaile
Navajo Community College, Naaltsoos Ba'Hoogan, Library, Tsaile, Arizona,
86556
Includes the Moses/Donner Collection pertaining to the Navajo and other
groups of the American Southwest; also, all aspects of the geology, geography,
archaeology, ethnography, etc., of the Four Corners region.

Tucson
Arizona State Museum, Library, University of Arizona, Tucson, Arizona,
85721
Some 35,000 volumes on anthropology emphasizing the American
Southwest.

Window Rock
Navajo Tribal Museum, Navajo Historical Library, Window Rock, Arizona,
86515
Excellent collection on Navajo anthropology.

California
Berkeley
Pacific School of Religion, Bade Institute of Biblical Archaeology, 1798 Scenic
Ave., Berkeley, California, 94709

Collection dealing with Syro-Palestinian archaeology.

University of California, Berkeley, Bancroft Library, Berkeley, California, 94720
  Historical collection on California and other Pacific states, Alaska, and the Canadian province of British Columbia.

University of California, Berkeley, Humanities-Social Sciences Libraries, Anthropology Library, Berkeley, California, 94720
  Includes 60,000 volumes comprising general research collection covering all aspects of cultural/social and biological/physical anthropology, anthropological linguistics, and archaeology.

Claremont
Rancho Santa Ana Botanic Garden Library, 1500 North College Ave., Claremont, California, 91711
  Important collection on California flora and ethnobotany.

Eureka
Eureka-Humboldt Library, 636 F St., Eureka, California, 95503
  Collection on the Indians of northwestern California.

Hemet
Hemet Public Library, 510 East Florida Ave., Hemet, California, 92343
  Special emphasis on the Indians of southern California and the American Southwest.

Lakeport
Lakeport County Library, 200 Park St., Lakeport, California, 95453
  Excellent collection dealing with the Pomo Indians of California.

Los Angeles
Los Angeles Public Library, History Department, 639 West Fifth St., Los Angeles, California, 90071

University of California, Los Angeles, Library, 405 Hilgard Ave., Los Angeles, California, 90024
  Includes the Lorraine Miller Sherer Collection of the ethnohistory of the Mohave Indians.

University of California, Los Angeles, Music Department, Ethnomusicology Archive, 405 Hilgard Ave., Los Angeles, California, 90024

Tapes and recordings dealing with the ethnomusicology of non-Western cultures.

University of California, Los Angeles, Research Library, Indo/Pacific Collection, 405 Hilgard Ave., Los Angeles, California, 90024
South Asian Collection focuses on cultural, economic, political, and social history of India from approximately 1859 to 1947; especially important for linguistic and literary studies, particularly Sanskrit and Pali, and the history of Portuguese South Asia.

University of Southern California, School of Medicine, Norris Medical Library, 2025 Zonal Ave., Los Angeles, California, 90033
Includes the American Indian Ethnopharmacology collection.

San Diego
San Diego Museum of Man, Scientific Library, 1350 El Prado, Balboa Park, San Diego, California, 92101
General anthropology collection.

University of California, San Diego, Central University Library, Mandeville Collection of Special Collections, La Jolla, California, 92093
Includes Hill Collection, an important collection comprising over 2,000 accounts of and commentaries on important voyages to all parts of the Pacific Ocean from the sixteenth to mid-nineteenth centuries.

Santa Cruz
University of California, Santa Cruz, University Library, Special Collections, Santa Cruz, California, 95064
Includes approximately 10,000 monographs, rare books, serials, documents, and atlases pertaining to the Pacific areas of Australia, Melanesia, Micronesia, New Zealand, and Polynesia, but excluding western New Guinea (Irian Jaya), the Philippines and Southeast Asia.

Colorado
Boulder
Native American Rights Fund, National Indian Law Library, 1506 Broadway, Boulder, Colorado, 80302
National Library of Indian Law emphasizes information about treaties and rulings in cases involving land and water rights.

University of Colorado Libraries, Art and Architecture Library, Boulder, Colorado, 80309

Collection on Islamic architecture, Indian art, and South America Indian art.

Colorado Springs
Colorado Springs Fine Arts Center Library, 30 West Dale St., Colorado Springs,Colorado, 80903
Specializes in fine arts and the anthropology of the American Southwest.

Connecticut
Hartford
Trinity College Library, Watkinson Library, 300 Summit Ave., Hartford, Connecticut, 06106
Important American Indian languages collection.

New Haven
Yale University, Anthropology Library, Peabody Museum of Natural History, C-8 KBT, New Haven, Connecticut, 06511
Good general anthropology collection.

Yale University Libraries, New Haven, Connecticut, 06520
Includes personal and research papers of anthropologist Bronislaw Malinowski.

Yale University Libraries, Yale Collection of Western Americana, New Haven, Connecticut, 06520
Historical American Indian collection.

Sharoni
Philippine-American Research Center, Library, PO Box 507, Sharoni, Connecticut, 06069
Collection on Philippine history and culture from precolonial times to the present, as well as under Spanish, Japanese, and United States regimes, and post-independence.

Florida
Miami
Historical Association of Southern Florida, Charlton W. Tebeau Library of Florida History, 101 West Flagler St., Miami, Florida, 33130
Emphasis on the history of Florida and the Caribbean area. The Florida materials include anthropology, archaeology, and the ethnography of the Indians of Florida, especially the Seminole.

Idaho

Pocatello
Idaho Museum of Natural History, Research Library, Campus Box 8096
Pocatello, Idaho, 83209

Idaho State University, Library, Pocatello, Idaho, 83209
  Collection of papers on the Lemhi Indian Reservation.

Illinois

Chicago
Field Museum of Natural History, Library, Roosevelt Road and Lake Shore Dr.,
Chicago, Illinois, 60605
  Extensive collection on anthropology, especially the archaeology and
ethnography of the Americas, Africa, East Asia, and Oceania.

DeKalb
Northern Illinois University, Founders Memorial Library, Southeast Asia
Collection, Normal Road, DeKalb, Illinois, 60115
  Some 35,000 books and maps from or about southeast Asia (Brunei,
Burma, Indonesia, Laos, Malaysia, Philippines, Singapore, and Thailand); a
large collection of several thousand volumes in Thai.

Galesburg
Knox College, Henry M. Seymour Library, Galesburg, Illinois, 61401
  Special emphasis on the early European contacts in the Upper Mississippi
region of North America.

Rock Island
Augustana College, Library, Rock Island, Illinois, 61201
  Collection dealing with the Sauk and Fox tribes.

Urbana
University of Illinois, Urbana/Champaign, Library, University Archives, 1408
West Gregory Dr., Urbana, Illinois, 61801
  Original manuscripts and over 90 tapes of interviews by Oscar Lewis
concerning his studies of the culture of poverty.

Indiana

Bloomington
Indiana University, Lilly Library, Seventh St., Bloomington, Indiana, 47401
  Collection on the discovery and exploration of Latin America, the
Inquisition, and the religious orders and history of the Church in the region.

Kansas

Kansas City
Kansas City Public Library, 625 Minnesota Ave., Kansas City, Kansas, 66101
Collection on Wyandot (Huron) Indians.

Lawrence
University of Kansas, Kenneth Spencer Research Library, Kansas Collection,
Lawrence, Kansas, 66044
Several photographic collections devoted to American Indian subjects,
collections of personal papers, American Indian periodicals, nineteenth century
tracts and treatises, and reservation life in Kansas, Oklahoma, and Nebraska;
strong holdings on Potawatomi, Sauk, Fox, and Osage.

Louisiana

Baton Rouge
Louisiana State University, Troy H. Middleton Library, Louisiana Room, Baton
Rouge, Louisiana, 70803
Louisiana Collection includes anthropology and history.

New Orleans
Amistad Research Center, 2601 Gentilly Blvd., New Orleans, Louisiana, 70122
Historical research library devoted to the collection and use of primary
source materials on the history of minorities in the United States, with special
emphasis on African-Americans, Native Americans, and immigrant groups.

Maryland

Baltimore
Johns Hopkins University, Milton S. Eisenhower Library, Charles and 34 St.,
Baltimore, Maryland, 21218
Important archaeology collection.

Massachusetts

Amherst
Amherst College, Special Collections, Library, Amherst, Massachusetts, 01002
Includes personal working library of Margaret Mead, donated by Mary
Catherine Bateson; other collections of MeadÕs papers, books, manuscripts,
etc., are at the Library of Congress and the American Museum of Natural
History.

University of Massachusetts, Amherst, Library, Amherst, Massachusetts, 01003
Good collection on Aegean archaeology.

Boston
Pan American Society of New England, Shattuck Library, 75a Newbury St., Boston, Massachusetts, 02116
    Comprehensive collection on Latin American society and culture.

Cambridge
Harvard University Library, Botanical Museum Library, Cambridge, Massachusetts, 02138
    Includes the Tina and Gordon Wasson Ethnomycological Collection dealing with hallucinogenic mushrooms in art, religion, and folklore from the fifteenth to the twentieth century.

Salem
Peabody Museum of Salem, Phillips Collection, East India Square, Salem, Massachusetts, 01970
    Ethnology of Non-European Peoples Collection pertaining to the Pacific islands, China, Japan, and the American Indian.

Worcester
College of the Holy Cross, Dinand Library, College St., Worcester, Massachusetts, 01610
    Includes the Joseph J. Williams, S.J., Collection of manuscripts and correspondence concerning religious practices of tribal groups in Africa, and material on the Passamaquoddy Indians of Maine.

Michigan

Ann Arbor
University of Michigan, Museum Library, Ann Arbor, Michigan, 48109
    General anthropology collection, especially strong in the anthropology of the indigenous Americas.

East Lansing
Michigan State University, International Library, Africana Collection, East Lansing, Michigan, 48824
    Includes some 82,700 books, manuscripts, maps, and photographs relating to Africa.

Michigan State University, International Library, South and Southeast Asia Collection, East Lansing, Michigan, 48824
    Strengths include the anthropology and rural development of India, Nepal, Sri Lanka, and Pakistan.

Kalamazoo
Western Michigan University, Dwight B. Waldo Library, Kalamazoo, Michigan, 49008
Ann Kercher Memorial Collection of Africa covers sub-Saharan Africa and emphasizes anthropology, travel literature, and languages.

Sault Ste. Marie
Lake Superior State College, Library, Sault Ste. Marie, Michigan, 49780
Collection on Michigan history, including Chippewa (Ojibwa) Indians

Minnesota
St. Paul
College of St. Catherine, 2004 Randolph Ave., St. Paul, Minnesota, 55105
Good collection on the historical and cultural aspects of the Chippewa and Lakota Indians.

Missouri
Columbia
University of Missouri, Columbia, Museum of Anthropology Archives, 104 Swallow Hall, Columbia, Missouri, 65201
Copies of Latin American and colonial manuscripts from Mexico and northern Central America.

Point Lookout
School of the Ozarks, Lois Brownel Research Library, Ralph Foster Museum, Point Lookout, Missouri, 65726
Some 1,500 books and manuscripts dealing with North American archaeology.

St. Louis
Washington University, Art and Architecture Library, St. Louis, Missouri, 63130
Collection on the art and archaeology of East Asia.

Washington University, John M. Olin Library, Rare Books and Special Collections, 6600 Milbrook Blvd., St. Louis, Missouri, 63130
Collection of early travel literature of the Americas and accounts of exploration in the Mississippi Valley and Trans-Mississippi West.

Montana
Bozeman
Montana State University, Library, Bozeman, Montana, 59717
Leggat-Donahoe Collection of exploration and the fur trade.

Nebraska

Crawford
Nebraska State Historical Society, Fort Robinson Museum, Box 304, Crawford, Nebraska, 69339
Materials related to the history of Fort Robinson, including Indian Wars.

Lincoln
Nebraska State Historical Society, Library, 1500 R St., Box 82554, Lincoln, Nebraska, 68501
Good collection on the archaeology of Nebraska and the Great Plains.

New Hampshire

Portsmouth
Strawberry Banke, Thayer Cummings Historical Reference Library, Portsmouth, New Hampshire, 03801
Small, specialized library dealing with American art, architecture, and decorative arts; important for the literature of Anglo-American historical archaeology.

New Jersey

Newark
Newark Museum Library, 49 Washington St., PO Box 540, Newark, New Jersey, 07101
Outstanding collection of Tibetan religious books and over 1,000 photographs of Tibet and Tibetans.

Princeton
Princeton University, Marquand Library, McCormick Hall, Princeton, New Jersey, 08544
Collection on classical and medieval archaeology.

South Orange
Seton Hall University Museum, Archaeological Research Center, South Orange Ave., South Orange, New Jersey, 07079
Collection on the archaeology of New Jersey and the northeastern United States.

New Mexico

Albuquerque
Albuquerque Public Library, 423 Central Ave., Albuquerque, New Mexico, 87101
Collection on the Indians of New Mexico and Arizona, including Navajo, Hopi, and Pueblos.

Aztec
Aztec Ruins National Monument, Library, PO Box U, Aztec, New Mexico, 87410
> Some 500 volumes on the archaeology of Anasazi ruins.

Santa Fe
Museum of New Mexico, Laboratory of Anthropology Library, PO Box 2087, Santa Fe, New Mexico, 87503
> Includes 16,000 books, manuscripts and maps relating to the anthropology of the American Southwest and Mesoamerica; also the 2,000 volume personal library of the Maya scholar, Sylvanus G. Morley.

Museum of New Mexico, Photographic Archives, PO Box 2087, Santa Fe, New Mexico, 87503
> Extensive photographic collections of American Indians, especially Hopi and Blackfoot, as well as Australia, New Zealand, China, and the Near East.

New York

Albany
New York State Library, Albany, New York, 12224
> Excellent collection of American Indians, especially Iroquois and other Indians of New York State; includes material on Indian captives, treaties, biographies, laws, and various materials in indigenous languages.

Buffalo
Buffalo Museum of Science, Buffalo Society of Natural Sciences, Buffalo, New York, 14211
> General anthropology collection.

Corning
Corning Museum of Glass Library, Corning, New York, 14831
> Comprehensive coverage of the art, archaeology, history, and early manufacture of glass.

Hempstead
Hofstra University, Library, 1000 Fulton Ave., Hempstead, New York, 11550
> Includes the personal library of anthropologist Paul Radin.

New York City
American Museum of Natural History, Library Services Department, Central Park West and 79 St., New York City, New York, 10024
> Excellent general anthropology collection.

American Society for Psychical Research Library, 5 West 73 St., New York City, New York, 10023
Includes approximately 10,000 volumes on spiritualism, as well as general works in anthropology and other disciplines which may relate to parapsychology.

Australian Consulate-General, Australian Information Service, Reference Library, 636 Fifth Ave., New York City, New York, 10011
More than 10,000 volumes on Australian history, geography, social conditions, and Australian Aborigines.

Columbia University Libraries, Lehman Library, Slavic and East Central European Collection, 420 West 118 St., New York City, New York, 10027
The Soviet Nationalities Collection consists of more than 14,000 volumes in the Indo-European, Uralic, Altaic, Transcaucasian, and Paleo-Siberian languages of the former Soviet Union.

New York Public Library, Research Libraries, General Research Division, Fifth Ave. and 42 St., New York City, New York, 10018
Excellent library collection for African Americans, American Indians, Gypsies, Australian Aborigines, and the various peoples of the Pacific.

New York Public Library, Mid-Manhattan Library, History and Social Sciences Department, 455 Fifth Ave., New York City, New York, 10016
Excellent general anthropology collection; broad coverage for the study of over 100 languages and dialects.

New York Public Library, Oriental Division, Fifth Ave. and 42 St., New York City, New York, 10018
Includes works in approximately 100 Eastern languages and works in Western languages on Oriental subjects; its Arabic and Indic holdings, and those on ancient Egypt and the ancient Near East are among the largest in the United States.

Research Institute for the Study of Man, Library, 162 East 78 St., New York City, New York, 10021
Includes over 15,000 books, manuscripts, and maps, with special strengths on the non-Hispanic Caribbean.

Oneonta
Hartwick College, Library, Oneonta, New York, 13820
Good collection on Indians of the Eastern Woodlands.

Rochester
University of Rochester, Rush Rhees Library, Rochester, New York, 14627
Special strengths include East (China, Japan) and South Asia (India); extensive holdings in Hindi, Marathi, and Sanskrit.

Sands Point
Nassau County Museum, Sands Point Preserve, Middleneck Rd., Sands Point, New York, 11050
Comprehensive collection on the archaeology and ethnography of Long Island and coastal New York.

North Carolina
Chapel Hill
Carolina Population Center, Library, University Square East, Chapel Hill, North Carolina, 27514
Extensive area collections on Africa, Iran, Korea, Thailand, and Latin America.

Charlotte
Geo-Tech International, Paleontological Research Laboratory, 3616 Garden Club Lane, Charlotte, North Carolina, 28210
Interesting collection with special emphasis on paleontology, including paleoanthropology and human evolution.

Gastonia
Schiele Museum of Natural History, Library, 1500 East Garrison Blvd., Gastonia, North Carolina, 28502
General anthropology collection.

Wake Forest
Southeastern Baptist Theological Seminary Library, PO Box 752, Wake Forest, North Carolina, 27587
Collection on Near Eastern archaeology related to Biblical studies.

North Dakota
Grand Forks
University of North Dakota, Chester Fritz Library, Grand Forks, North Dakota, 58202
Various collections on the history of North Dakota and northern Great Plains.

Ohio

Cleveland
Cleveland Public Library, Fine Arts and Special Collections Department, 325 Superior Ave., Cleveland, Ohio, 44114
Contains many grammars, dictionaries, and other linguistic works in African, Asian, and Western Languages and dialects.

Columbus
Ohio Historical Society, Archives Library Division, 1982 Velma Ave., Columbus, Ohio, 43211
Collection pertaining with the exploration into the Northwest Territories, and the archaeology of Ohio.

Oklahoma

Lawton
Museum of the Great Plains, Research Center, 601 Ferris, PO Box 68, Lawton, Oklahoma, 73502
Includes archaeology and ethnology of the Trans-Mississippi West, especially the Great Plains.

Muskogee
Five Civilized Tribes Museum, Agency Hill, Honor Heights Dr., Muskogee, Oklahoma, 74401
Collection pertains to the history, culture, and traditions of the Five Civilized Tribes.

Oklahoma City
Oklahoma Historical Society, Library, Historical Building, Oklahoma City, Oklahoma, 73105
Contains the Indian Archives Collection dealing with the Five Civilized Tribes.

Tahlequah
Cherokee National Historical Society, Archives and Library, PO Box 515, TSA-LA-GI, Tahlequah, Oklahoma, 74464
Collection related to Cherokee culture and history.

Tulsa
Thomas Gilcrease Institute of American History and Art, Library, R.R. 6, Tulsa, Oklahoma, 74127
Collection on Trans-Mississippi West, and American Indian history in general.

Pennsylvania

Philadelphia

American Philosophical Society, Library, 105 South Fifth St., Philadelphia, Pennsylvania, 19106

Includes the papers of anthropologists Franz Boas, Sylvanus G. Morley, Ely S. Parker, Elsie Clews Parsons, Paul Radin, Frank G. Speck, and others, as well as a large collection of field notes and reports, linguistic texts, and other manuscripts.

University of Pennsylvania, Annenberg School of Communications Library, 3620 Walnut St., Philadelphia, Pennsylvania, 19104

Includes more than 20,000 volumes on theory and research in communication, including visual communication, anthropology, and other social sciences.

University of Pennsylvania, University Museum Library, 33 and Spruce St., Philadelphia, Pennsylvania, 19104

Extensive collection on anthropology, second only to Tozzer Library at Harvard University; special emphasis non North and Central America, Egypt, ancient Sumer, and the Classical world; the Brinton Collection includes manuscripts relating to American Indian linguistics and ethnohistory.

Pittsburgh

University of Pittsburgh, Hillman Library, Pittsburgh, Pennsylvania, 15260

General anthropology collection, especially strong in prehispanic archaeology and the indigenous cultures of Latin America.

Rhode Island

Kingston

University of Rhode Island, International Center for Marine Resource Development, Library, Main Library Building, Kingston, Rhode Island, 02881

More than 20,000 volumes relating to the development of marine resources in Third World countries, including the anthropology of fishing peoples.

Providence

Brown University, John Carter Brown Library, Providence, Rhode Island, 02912

Excellent historical collection pertaining to the colonial period in the Americas.

Brown University, John Hay Library, 20 Prospect St., Providence, Rhode Island, 02912

Collection pertaining to Central and South American anthropology and voyages of exploration and dictionaries of South American Indian languages.

South Carolina

Charleston
Charleston Museum Library, 360 Meeting St., Charleston, South Carolina, 29403
General anthropology collection.

Columbia
University of South Carolina, Institute of Archaeology and Anthropology, Robert L. Stephenson Research Library, Macy College, Columbia, South Carolina, 29208
More than 7,000 volumes on anthropology, with emphasis on North American archaeology; includes the personal library of Robert L. Stephenson, director of the Institute and State Archaeologist of South Carolina.

South Dakota

Pierre
South Dakota Historical Resource Center, Library, Soldiers Memorial Building, Pierre, South Dakota, 57501
Important collection on the Lakota Indians.

Rapid City
South Dakota School of Mines and Technology, Devereaux Library, Rapid City, South Dakota, 57701
Collection on the Indians of North America, with an emphasis on the Lakota.

Sioux Falls
Siouxland Heritage Museum, Pettigrew Museum Library, 131 North Duluth Ave., Sioux Falls, South Dakota, 57104
Collection on the anthropology and history of the Plains Indians.

Tennessee

Knoxville
University of Tennessee, Library, Knoxville, Tennessee, 37916
Collection on the Indians of southeastern United States.

Memphis
Chucalissa Museum, 1987 Indian Village Dr., Memphis, Tennessee, 38109
Collection emphasis is on the archaeology and ethnography on the mid-southern United States.

Texas
Dallas
Southern Methodist University, DeGolyer Library, Box 396, SMU, Dallas, Texas, 75275
General anthropology collection.

El Paso
El Paso Public Library, 501 North Oregon, El Paso, Texas, 79901
Good collection on Southwestern Indian arts and crafts.

Utah
Salt Lake City
University of Utah, Marriott Library, Special Collections, Salt Lake City, Utah, 84112
Collection on Utah and the American West.

Washington
Olympia
Washington State Library, Washington/Northwest Room, State Library Building, Olympia, Washington, 98504
Collection on the Indians of North America and Mexico, especially Indians of Washington State.

Pullman
Washington State University, Manuscripts, Archives, and Special Collections, Pullman, Washington, 99164
Includes papers covering Fr. Pierre-Jean de SmetÕs early travels and founding of the Rocky Mountain missions (1821-1873).

Seattle
University of Washington Libraries, Suzzallo Library, Manuscripts Section, FM-25, Seattle, Washington, 98195
Large collection of personal papers and organizational records pertaining to the Pacific Northwest.

Wisconsin
Beloit
Beloit College Libraries, Beloit, Wisconsin, 53511
Good general anthropology collection.

Milwaukee
Milwaukee Public Museum, Reference Library, 800 West Wells St., Milwaukee, Wisconsin, 53233

Good general anthropology collection.

Shawano
Shawano City-County Library, 128 South Sawyer St., Shawano, Wisconsin, 54116
Specialized collection on the Menominee Indians.

Canada
Alberta
Calgary
Glenbow-Alberta Institute, Historical Library and Archives, 122 Second St. SW, Calgary, T2R 0W5
Important collection on the indigenous peoples of northern and western Canada, and the fur trade in the United States Northwest.

British Columbia
Terrace
Terrace Public Library, 4610 Park Ave., Terrace, V8G 1V6
Collection relating to the Terrace, Skeena, and Nass River District, including the Niska and Tsimshian Indians.

Vancouver
Vancouver Public Library, Sociology Division, 750 Burrard St., Vancouver, V6Z 1X5
Good general anthropology collection.

Manitoba
Churchill
Eskimo Museum, Library, Box 10, Churchill, R0B 0E0
Collection of books on the North, mainly northern Canada, including journals of exploration, Eskimo ethnography and archaeology.

Winnipeg
University of Manitoba, Elizabeth Dafoe Library, Archives and Special Collections Department, Winnipeg, R3T 2N2
Includes collection on Arctic and Sub-Arctic cultural anthropology, as well as anthropological blood group studies of Eskimo, Indian, and Canadian-Japanese communities.

Northwest Territories
Hay River
Northwest Territories Public Library, Box 1100, Hay River, XOE 0R0
Important collection on the history of the Northwest Territories

Ontario

Chatham

Chatham Public Library, 120 Queen St., Chatham, N7M 2G8
Collection on the Potawatomi and Chippewa of Walpole Island Reserve, and the Delaware Indians brought to Canada by Moravian missionaries in the eighteenth century.

Ottawa

National Library of Canada, 395 Wellington St., Ottawa, K1A ON4
General anthropology collection

National Museums of Canada, Library Services Directorate, Ottawa, K1A 0M8
Collection of 70,000 volumes, manuscripts, and maps includes anthropology, archaeology, ethnology, folklore, Indians of North America, Inuit, American Indian linguistics, and material history

Toronto

Toronto

Canadian Association in Support of the Native Peoples Library, 277 Victoria St., Toronto, M5V 1W2
Collection of 40,000 volumes, manuscripts, and maps dealing with the native peoples of North America, especially Canada.

Metropolitan Toronto Library, Social Sciences Department, 789 Yonge St., Toronto, M4W 2G8
Collection on folklore, religion, and anthropology; also includes Bibles in Canadian indigenous languages.

Metropolitan Toronto Library, Languages Centre, 789 Yonge St., Toronto, M4W 2G8
Holdings on North American Indian and Eskimo languages.

Royal Ontario Museum, main Library and Archives, 100 QueenÕs Park, Toronto, M5S 2C6
General anthropology collection.

University of Toronto, Thomas Fisher Rare Book Library, 120 St. George St., Toronto, M5S 1A5
Includes Sheldon Collection of Australiana, especially rich in nineteenth-century accounts of the exploration of the South Pacific and the interior of the Australian continent; includes works on Aboriginal studies.

Saskatchewan

Regina

University of Regina, Library, Regina, S4S 0A2
  Collection on native peoples of North America, especially Canada.

Appendix C: Arrangement of the *Outline of Cultural Materials*

This appendix identifies the primary categories used in the *Outline of cultural materials* (OCM). For example, *Outline of cultural materials* code 16 refers to Demography, a category with eight subdivisions.

00 Material not categorized
10 Orientation (101-106)
11 Bibliography (111-118)
12 Methodology (121-128)
13 Geography (131-137)
14 Human biology (141-147)
15 Human processes and personality (151-159)
16 Demography (161-168)
17 History and culture change (171-179)
18 Total culture (181-186)
19 Language (191-198)
20 Communication (201-209)
21 Records (211-218)
22 Food quest (221-228)
23 Animal husbandry (231-237)
24 Agriculture (241-249)
25 Food processing (251-258)
26 Food consumption (261-266)
27 Drink, drugs and indulgence (271-278)
28 Leather, textiles, and fabrics (281-289)
29 Clothing (291-296)
30 Adornment (301-306)
31 Exploitative activities (311-318)
32 Processing of basic materials (321-328)
33 Building and construction (331-339)
34 Structures (341-349)
35 Equipment and maintenance of buildings (351-358)
36 Settlements (361-369)
37 Energy and power (371-379)
38 Chemical industries (381-389)
39 Capital goods industries (391-399)
40 Machines (401-407)
41 Tools and appliances (411-417)
42 Property (421-429)
43 Exchange (431-439)
44 Marketing (441-447)
45 Finance (451-458)
46 Labor (461-468)
47 Business and industrial organization (471-477)
48 Travel and transportation (481-489)
49 Land transport (491-499)
50 Water and air transport (501-509)
51 Living standards and routines (511-517)
52 Recreation (521-529)
53 Fine arts (531-539)
54 Entertainment (541-548)
55 Individuation and mobility (551-558)
56 Social stratification (561-567)
57 Interpersonal relations (571-579)
58 Marriage (581-589)
59 Family (591-597)
60 Kinship (601-609)

61 Kin groups (611-619)
62 Community (621-628)
63 Territorial organization (631-636)
64 State (641-648)
65 Government organization (651-659)
66 Political behavior (661-669)
67 Law (671-676)
68 Offenses and sanctions (681-689)
69 Justice (691-698)
70 Armed forces (701-708)
71 Military technology (711-719)
72 War (721-729)
73 Social problems (731-738)
74 Health and welfare (741-748)
75 Sickness (751-759)
76 Death (761-769)
77 Religious beliefs (771-779)
78 Religious practices (781-789)
79 Ecclesiastical organization (791-798)
80 Numbers and measures (801-805)
81 Exact knowledge (811-816)
82 Ideas about nature and man (821-829)
83 Sex (831-839)
84 Reproduction (841-848)
85 Infancy and childhood (851-858)
86 Socialization (861-869)
87 Education (871-877)
88 Adolescence, adulthood, and old age (881-888)

Appendix D:
Arrangement of the
Outline of World Cultures

This appendix identifies the primary categories used in the *Outline of world cultures* (OWC). For example, *Outline of world cultures* code AW60 refers to the Todas of the Nilgiri Hills region of India. The existing file for the Todas comprises 1,553 pages of text from 13 sources.

ASIA

A	Asia
AA	Korea
AA1	Korea (58; 6,148)
AB	Japan
AB6	Ainu (11; 1,573)
AB43	Okayama (30; 3,532)
AC	Ryunkuyus
AC7	Okinawa (3, 817)
AD	Formosa
AD1	Formosa (40; 1,836)
AD5	Taiwan (71; 8,665)
AE	Greater China
AE3	Sino-Tibetan border (7; 529)
AE4	Lolo (5; 564)
AE5	Miao (12; 1,182)
AE9	Monguor (8; 1,221)
AF	China
AF1	China (80; 19,442)
AF12	North (8; 2,595)
AF13	Northwest (3; 1,299)
AF14	Central (2; 1,130)
AF15	East (3; 1,384)
AF16	Southwest (7; 2,800)
AF17	South (8; 1,846)
AG	Manchuria
AG1	Manchuria (7; 1,820)

AH	Mongolia
AH1	Mongolia (9;1,358)
AH6	Inner (13; 1,840)
AH7	Outer (4; 2,821)
AI	Sinkiang
AI1	Sinkiang (3; 860)
AJ	Tibet
AJ1	Tibet (26; 6,313)
AJ4	West Tibetans (22; 1,905)
AK	Himalayan states
AK5	Lepcha (11; 1,038)
AL	Southeast Asia
AL1	Southeast Asia (22; 3,851)
AM	Indochina
AM1	Indochina (153; 19,663)
AN	Malaya
AN1	Malaya (193; 10,142)
AN7	Semang (3; 786)
AO	Thailand
AO1	Thailand (40; 6,114)
AO7	Central Thai (54; 11,086)
AP	Burma
AP1	Burma (31; 4,680)
AR	Assam
AR5	Garo (9; 1,169)

AR7	Khasi (21; 998)	EE	Bulgaria
AU	Afghanistan	EE1	Bulgaria (7; 988)
AU1	Afghanistan (74; 6,234)	EF	Yugoslavia
AU4	Pashtun (8; 1,926)	EF1	Yugoslavia (13; 2,765)
AV	Jammu and Kasmir	EG	Albania
AV3	Dard (4; 711)	EG1	Albania (9; 1,975)
AV4	Kashmiri (5; 893)	EH	Greece
AV7	Burusho (8; 2,157)	EH1	Greece (10; 1,153)
AW	India	EH14	Sarakatsani (3; 942)
AW1	India (41; 14,980)	EI	Italy
AW2	Bihar (1; 619)	EI9	Imperial Romans (18;
AW5	Coorg (4; 802)		5,739)
AW6	East Punjab (3; 1,106)	EK	Austria
AW7	Gujarti (4; 627)	EK1	Austria (6; 1334)
AW11	Kerala (13; 989)	EO	Finland
AW16	Tamil (41; 8,974)	EO1	Finland (1; 42)
AW17	Telugu (1; 265)	EP	Norway
AW19	Uttar Pradesh (4; 255)	EP4	Lapps (16; 3,284)
AW25	Bhil (7; 1,069)	ER	Ireland
AW32	Gond (4; 1,552)	ER6	Rural Irish (17; 1,673)
AW37	Kol (1; 347)	ES	Great Britain
AW42	Santal (5; 1,318)	ES3	Georgian Britain (15;
AW60	Toda (13; 1,553)		7,090)
AW66	Calcutta (64; 5,811)	ES10	Highland Scots (24;
AX	Ceylon		4,071)
AX4	Sinhalese (8; 1,984)	ES13	Stuart Britain (24;
AX5	Vedda (5; 776)		5,839)
AZ	Asiatic Islands	ES14	Tudor Britain (10;
AZ22	Andamans (11; 1,229)		3,459)
		EZ	European Islands
	EUROPE	EZ6	Malta (9; 1,069)
E	Europe		
E1	Europe (9; 1,599)		**AFRICA**
EA	Poland	F	Africa
EA1	Poland (31; 3,940)	FA	West Africa
EB	Czechoslovakia	FA8	Bambara (4; 1,127)
EB1	Czechoslovakia (75;	FA16	Dogon (20; 4,456)
	6,491)	FA28	Mossi (12; 942)
EC	Hungary	FC	Sierra Leone and the
EC1	Hungary (16; 1,401)		Gambia Mende
ED	Rumania	FC7	Mende (8; 605)
ED1	Rumania (9; 1,245)	FD	Liberia

FD6	Kpelle (30; 3,700)		FT17	Yao (11; 555)
FE	Ghana		FX	South Africa and Namibia
FE11	Talensi (10; 954)		FX10	Bushmen (16; 1,259)
FE12	Twi (27; 3,523)		FX13	Hottentot (14; 1,359)
FF	Nigeria		FX14	Lovedu (5; 455)
FF26	Igbo (36; 8,488)		FX20	Zulu (45; 8,067)
FF38	Katab (4; 252)		FY	Madagascar
FF52	Nupe (9; 858)		FY8	Tanala (1; 334)
FF57	Tiv (30; 2,891)			
FF62	Yoruba (45; 1,637)		**MIDDLE EAST**	
FH	Cameroon		M	Middle East
FH9	Fang (8; 1,117)		M1	Middle East (72;
FJ	Nilotic Sudan			13,908)
FJ22	Nuer (16; 1,541)		MA	Iran
FJ23	Shilluk (29; 1,073)		MA1	Iran (72; 7,000)
FK	Uganda		MA11	Kurd (11; 1,1018)
FK7	Ganda (16; 2,261)		MB	Turkey
FL	Kenya		MB1	Turkey (14; 1,493)
FL6	Dorobo (14; 354)		MD	Syria
FL10	Kikuyu (9; 1,950)		MD1	Syria (11; 1,395)
FL11	Luo (21; 463)		MD4	Rwala (2; 1,042)
FL12	Masai (19; 2,095)		ME	Lebanon
FL19	Nairobi (46; 4,115)		E1	Lebanon (11; 657)
FN	Tangayika		MG	Jordan
FN4	Chagga (6; 1,986)		MG1	Jordan (22; 3,358)
FN17	Ngonde (14; 1,474)		MH	Iraq
FO	Zaire		MH1	Iraq (8; 1,1825)
FO4	Pygmies (4; 1,285)		MJ	Saudia Arabia
FO7	Azande (68; 3,264)		MJ1	Saudi Arabia (30;
FO32	Mongo (9; 773)			3,371)
FO42	Rundi (10; 1,314)		MK	Oman
FP	Angola		MK2	Maritime Arabs (4;
FP13	Moundu (6; 847)			103)
FQ	Zambia		MK4	Trucial Oman (3; 256)
FQ5	Bemba (10; 830)		ML	Yemen
FQ6	Ila (6; 998)		ML1	Yemen (14; 446)
FQ9	Lozi (10; 1,635)		MM	Aden
FQ12	Tonga (11; 1,616)		MM1	Aden (8; 683)
FR	Malawi		MO	Somaliland
FR5	Ngoni (14; 1,123)		MO4	Somali (31; 2,194)
FT	Mozambique		MP	Ethiopia
FT6	Thonga (3; 1,231)		MP5	Amhara (12; 1,664)

MR	Egypt
MR13	Fellahin (9; 1,262)
MR14	Siwans (7; 518)
MS	Sahara and Sudan
MS12	Hausa
MS14	Kanuri
MS22	Teda
MS25	Tuareg
MS30	Wolof
MS37	Senegal
MT	Libya
MT9	Libyan Bedouin
MW	Morocco
MW11	Ahluh
MX	Spanish Morocco
MX3	Rif (7; 1,076)
MZ	Middle East Islands
MZ2	Bahrain (8; 428)

NORTH AMERICA

N	North America
N7	Chicano (34; 7,371)
NA	Alaska
NA6	Aleut (70; 2,253)
NA10	South Alaska Eskimo (28; 2,312)
NA12	Tlingit (19; 1,778)
ND	Northern Canada
ND8	Copper Eskimo (29; 2,277)
ND9	Hare (17; 2,024)
ND12	Nahane (19; 1,547)
NE	British Colombia
NE6	Bellacoola (8; 1,561)
NE11	Nootka (19; 1,547)
NF	Prairie Provinces
NF6	Blackfoot (58; 7,520)
NG	Ontario
NG6	Ojibwa (26; 4,354)
NH	Quebec
NH6	Montagnais (35; 2,388)
NJ	Maritime Provinces

NJ5	Micmac (8; 1,016)
NK	United States
NK4	Blacks (37; 10,057)
NM	Middle Atlantic States
NM6	Amish (11; 2,727)
NM7	Delaware (19; 1,733)
NM9	Iroquois (41; 3,115)
NN	Southeastern States
NN5	Mountain Whites (28; 6,852)
NN8	Cherokee (22; 4,007)
NN11	Creek (3; 757)
NO	South Central States
NO6	Comanche (36; 5,000)
NP	East Central States
NP5	Fox (89; 5,000)
NP12	Winnebago (10; 915)
NQ	West Central States
NQ6	Arapaho (29; 2,639)
NQ10	Crow (24; 1,479)
NQ12	Dhegiha (33; 1,968)
NQ13	Gros Ventre (8; 1,085)
NQ17	Mandan (10; 1,297)
NQ18	Pawnee (14; 1,703)
NR	Northwestern States
NR4	Plateau Indians (4; 303)
NR10	Klamath (9; 1,617)
NR13	North Paiute (15; 910)
NR19	Southern Salish (7; 945)
NS	California
NS18	Pomo (22; 1,220)
NS22	Tubatulabal (4; 180)
NS29	Yokuts (16; 975)
NS31	Yurok (13; 1,101)
NT	Southwestern States
NT8	Eastern Apache (4; 589)
NT9	Hopi (11; 2,325)
NT13	Navaho (232; 22,058)
NT14	Plateau Yumans (14; 927)

NT15	River Yumans (6; 561)	OE5	Javanese (36; 6,815)
NT16	Southern Paiute (58; 4,291)	OF	Lesser Sundas
		OF5	Alor (3; 726)
NT17	Taos (66; 2,685)	OF7	Bali (9; 1,297)
NT18	Tewa (15; 1,274)	OG	Celebes
NT19	Ute (47; 5,454)	OG6	Makassar (1; 379)
NT20	Washo (9; 521)	OI	Australia
NT21	Western Apache (53; 6,114)	OJ	New Guinea
		OJ13	Kwoma (2; 501)
NT22	Western Shoshone (26; 1,884)	OJ23	Orokaiva (27; 2,263)
		OJ27	Wogeo (15; 678)
NT23	Zuni (16; 2,842)	OJ29	Kapauju (5; 869)
NT24	Mormons (69; 9,776)	OL	Massim
NT25	Mescalero (45; 3,089)	OL6	Trobriands (24; 2,991)
NT26	Jicarilla (50; 4,091)	OM	Bismarck Archipelago
NT28	Mohave (63; 3,544)	OM6	Manus (7; 1,639)
NU	Mexico	OM10	New Ireland (5; 457)
NU7	Aztec (35; 6,067)	ON	Solomon Islands
NU28	Papago (19; 2,183)	ON6	Buka (5; 721)
NU31	Seri (12; 616)	ON13	Santa Cruz (6; 420)
NU33	Tarahumara (13; 2,055)	OO	New Hebrides
NU34	Tarasco (11; 655)	OO12	Malekua (3; 883)
NU37	Tepoztlan (5; 859)	OQ	Fiji
NU44	Zapotec (29; 5,098)	OQ6	Lau (10; 997)
NU54	Mexico, DF (23; 5,423)	OR	Micronesia
NV	Yucatan	OR11	Marshalls (21; 2,199)
NV9	Tzeltal (9; 1,127)	OR19	Truk (25; 3,131)
NV10	Yucatec Maya (11; 1,870)	OR21	Woleai (41; 2,665)
		OR22	Yap (21; 1,951)
NW	Guatemala	OT	Polynesian Outliers
NW8	Mam	OT11	Tikopia (26; 2,727)
		OU	Western Polynesia
	OCEANIA	OU8	Samoa (19; 3,008
O	Oceania	OU9	Tonga (105; 8,364)
OA	Philippines	OX	French Polynesia
OA1	Philippines (58; 7,451)	OX6	Marquesas (13; 1.163)
OA19	Ifugao (29; 2,973)	OY	Easter Island
OB	Indonesia	OY2	Easter Islanders (15; 960)
OB1	Indonesia (18; 4,367)		
OC	Borneo	OZ	New Zealand
OC6	Iban (18; 1,655)	OZ4	Maori (10; 3,257)
OE	Java	OZ11	Pukapuka (12; 860)

RUSSIA	
R	Russia
R1	Soviet Union (81; 1,987)
RB	Baltic countries
RB1	Baltic countries (3; 211)
RB5	Lithuanians (11; 990)
RC	Belorussia
RC1	Belorussia (5; 191)
RD	Ukraine
RD1	Ukraine (20; 2,219)
RF	Great Russia
RF1	Great Russia (4; 386)
RG	Finno-Ugrians
RG4	Estonians (5; 615)
RH	Caucasia
RH1	Caucasia (4; 1,500)
RI	Georgia
RI1	Georgia (5; 759)
RI3	Abkhaz (4; 207)
RL	Russian Central Asia
RL1	Turkestan (4; 707)
RL4	Turkic peoples (1; 235)
RQ	Kazakhstan
RQ2	Kazak (6; 919)
RR	Siberia
RR1	Siberia (4; 609)
RU	Northern Siberia
RU4	Samoyed (35; 2,073)
RV	Yakutia
RV2	Yakut (32; 933)
RX	Southeast Siberia
RX2	Gilyak (13; 2,281)
RY	Northeast Siberia
RY2	Chukchee (21; 2,191)
RY3	Kamchadal (11; 840)
RY4	Koryak (5; 810)

SOUTH AMERICA	
S	South America
SA	Central America
SA15	Mosquito (3; 263)

SA19	Talamanca (6; 479)
SB	Panama
SB5	Cuna (34; 3,932)
SC	Colombia
SC7	Cagaba (7; 1,134)
SC13	Goajiro (10; 724)
SC15	Paez (8; 700)
SD	Ecuador
SD6	Cayapa (4; 747)
SD9	Jivaro (34; 1,426)
SD13	Ecuadorian Quechua (32; 5,240)
SE	Peru
SE13	Inca (13; 2,646)
SF	Bolivia
SF5	Aymara (14; 1,772)
SF10	Chiriguano (7; 1,570)
SF21	Siriono (5; 692)
SF24	Uru (9; 434)
SG	Chile
SG4	Aracanians (12; 1,397)
SH	Patagonia
SH4	Ona (4; 2,198)
SH5	Tehuelche (6; 611)
SH6	Yahgan (3; 1,700)
SI	Argentina
SI4	Abipon (2; 452)
SI7	Mataco (8; 595)
SK	Paraguay
SK6	Choroti (2; 523)
SK7	Guana (6; 407)
SM	South Brazil
SM3	Caingang (Aweikoma)(4; 308)
SM4	Guarani (6; 484)
SO	Northeast Brazil
SO8	Timbira (2; 379)
SO9	Tupinamba (26; 1,637)
SO11	Bahia (5; 1,333)
SP	Mato Grosso
SP7	Bacairi (6; 1,085)
SP8	Bororo (9; 1,041)

SP9	Caraja (9; 687)
SP17	Nambicuara (8; 436)
SP22	Tapirape (13; 369)
SP23	Trumai (1; 120)
SQ	Amazonia
SQ13	Mundurucu (14; 649)
SQ18	Yanoama (11; 1,096)
SQ19	Tucano (7; 1,310)
SQ20	Tucana (5; 259)
SR	Guiana
SR8	Bush Negroes (6; 1,411)
SR9	Carib (2; 532)
SS	Venezuela
SS16	Pemon (4; 602)
SS18	Warao (32; 3,236)
SS19	Yaruro (7; 284)
ST	Lesser Antilles
ST13	Callinago (13; 524)
SU	Puerto Rico
SU1	Puerto Rico (3; 1,750)
SV	Hispaniola
SV3	Haiti (3; 1,052)
SY	Jamaica
SY1	Jamaica (19; 4,504)

Index

Indexes are provided for name of author, ethnic or cultural group, and geographic place. The author index lists the name of authors and co-authors given in the guide. The ethnic group index identifies individual cultural groups. Cultural groups which correspond to political entities will be found in the geographic index. For example, material pertaining to the Japanese will be found under Asia, Japan. The geographic index is arranged according to major region of the world (i.e., Africa, Asia, Europe, Latin America, Middle East, North America, and Oceania). These regions are further subdivided by region (e.g., Asia, South, and Asia, Southeast) and specific countries (e.g., Sri Lanka and Vietnam). A reader needing a bibliography for Paraguay may check the geographic index under Paraguay and locate entry 9.219. The numeral 9 refers to Chapter 9, and 219 refers to entry 219 within the chapter.

Ethnic/Linguistic Index

Geographic Index